HUMAN RESOURCE DEVELOPMENT

THEORY & PRACTICE

(Revised Edition)

Tapomoy Deb

Ane Books Pvt. Ltd.
New Delhi ♦ Chennai

Human Resource Development: Theory & Practice

Tapomoy Deb

Published by

Ane Books Pvt. Ltd.
4821, Parwana Bhawan, 1st Floor, 24 Ansari Road,
Darya Ganj, **New Delhi** - 110 002, India
Tel.: +91(011) 23276843-44, Fax: +91(011) 23276863
e-mail: kapoor@anebooks.com, Website: www.anebooks.com

Branch Office:

- Avantika Niwas, 1st Floor, 19 Doraiswamy Road, T. Nagar, **Chennai** - 600 017, Tel.: +91(044) 28141554, 28141209
  e-mail: rathinam@anebooks.com

ISBN : 978-81-8052-094-5

Printed at : R.K. Offset Process, New Delhi.

HUMAN RESOURCE DEVELOPMENT

THEORY & PRACTICE

(Revised Edition)

Dedicated in
loving memory of
my beloved Grand Parents

Shri Shrish Chandra Deb
Shrimati Hem Nalini Deb

"Human Resource Development (HRD) is a series of organised activities, conducted within a specified time and designed to produce behavioural change"

Leonard Nadler
(Concept Coiner)

Preface

With increasing globalisation of economy, marketplace has become increasingly complex, highly uncertain, competitive and transformational. Today, doing business is like a war. What makes the ultimate difference is whether an organisation is able to develop and establish competitive differentiator or not. Everything, including capital, technology, product design, and service deliverability can be copied by the competitors, except the talented people. Nobody can emulate a highly competent, charged/ motivated and committed workforce. Such talented people can provide an organization a sustained competitive advantage. However, managing people by any means is not easy. It requires organisations to adopt proactive development programmes towards the attainment of corporate objectives by nurturing a development-oriented culture. Contemporary organisations have to create and sustain shared values and then it should be carefully interwoven with the business strategy of organisations. This simply implies the crucial role of human resource development plays in an organisation. In global business scenario, it is not enough to say that people are the strategic assets of an organisation, but to believe that people are the greatest assets of customers of the organisation. People are not just knowledge workers, but free agents, capable of bringing enormous value to an organisation. And they know it. Human resources are the lifeblood of an innovative enterprise. Thus, human resource development is vital to achieving organisational excellence i.e. excellence in people, process and performance.

The paradigm of employee management has undergone rapid transformation in the last decade, from comparative advantage to a state of continuous innovation, strategic intent and intelligence framework for competitive advantage. Today's employees, unlike their predecessors, are more demanding and have high aspirations. They demand early development of their skills and competencies. This implies that to be successful, organisations have to develop and/or seriously re-look at appropriate HRD strategies to tap the human potential within the organisation and align it with their corporate strategic mission and objectives.

Against this backdrop, a humble attempt has been made to present the entire contemporary conceptual framework of human resource development in a refreshingly new style so as to facilitate devising of appropriate strategies for the organisation which will result in the delivery of a culmination of organisational goals and HR goals for creating and delivering better value to the various stakeholders of an organisation – including shareholders, customers and employees.

I take this opportunity to thank my wife Mrs. Swagata Deb for bearing with the inconveniences caused during the writing of this book.

I also take this opportunity to express my gratitude to my publisher for taking out the text in a nice, neat and well-conceived manner.

I hope that this text makes an enlightened reading for students, teachers and HRD practitioners as well.

Suggestions for the improvement of the book shall be gratefully accepted.

Tapomoy Deb

Contents at a Glance

Detailed Contents

List of Figures

CHAPTER

1 Introduction

Chapter Synopsis

Human Resource Development is a process involving training, learning and development of employees of an organisation for attaining the mission and objectives of an organisation. In today's knowledge based economy, the rules of doing business has dramatically and drastically changed, paving the way for people to occupy the center stage of the organisation. Their knowledge, creativity, innovation and commitment are the key differentiator between success and failure.

This chapter explains these concepts and strategies for achieving corporate growth and success in a marketplace of Olympian competition.

This Chapter contains:

Changing paradigms of growth, Business risks and challenges facing today's organisations, Theoretical foundations of HRD, Systems model of organisation, Nature and concept of HRD, Definitions of HRD, Scope of HRD, Objectives for HRD, Goals of HRD, Importance/Benefits of HRD, Principles of HRD, Functions of HRD, Approaches to HRD, Improving performance through HRD, Essentials of a good HRD system, Competencies of HRD Manager, Role and responsibilities of HRD Manager, Current leading ideas in HRD, Organisation of HRD function, Ethical dimension and issues in HRD, Emerging dimension in HRD, Recent scenario of HRD in India, Framework of HRD, HRM and HRD, Code of ethics for HRD professionals, Challenges of HRD, Review & discussion questions, Case situation and Case study.

Introduction

Changing Paradigms of Growth

Earth is probably 4.5 billion years old and the oldest life forms began some 3.5 billion years ago. The evolution of mankind can be traced back to some 2.5 million years ago. According to Christian creationism, a God created the world including all life about 6,000 years ago in six literal days. The variation of mitochondrian DNA suggests that the origins of mankind were between 140,000 to 290,000 years ago and it is believed that mankind began in Africa 150,000 years ago and moved to Australasia some 60,000 years ago, Europe and Asia some 40,000 years ago, The America some 30,000 years ago and the Oceania some 15,000 years ago. Ever since the evolution of mankind their population has been growing fast. In the 200 years from 1800 to 2000, world population has increased from one to six billion. Population is projected to reach about 9 billion by 2050.

Mankind in the prehistoric period lived in small groups and hunted animals, initially without tools and later in Stone Age they developed some stone made crude weapons for hunting animals for ensuring survival. At that time they had only animal instincts. But later on, mankind started learning about agriculture and gradually it became their prime source of making a living, which incidentally continued for a long time. Even today, we are all dependent upon agricultural produce for food although it in now no more a principal occupation. With agriculture, mankind learned and started with various basic systems and procedure. This period was characterized by use of natural resources and the critical factor for production of wealth was land.

Alvin Toffler (1981) describes how civilizations are shaped by 'waves'. The agriculture revolution was the first wave that transformed the human history. Industrial revolution, the second wave, transformed the society. It was characterized by standardization, specialization, synchronization, concentration, maximization and centralization. The technological and social changes that began in the mid-1950s, known as information revolution, is the third wave that is transforming organisationss, societies, and economies. It was characterized by de-standardisation, de-specialisation, spontaneity, segmentation, and decentralization. A detailed description of these waves is discussed below.

A quantum change came in the civilization of mankind when industrial revolution began in the 19th century in the Great Britain. This resulted in organized way of working called factory. Machine took precedence over man and the concept of mass production started taking a firm shape. This industrialization spread across the globe in a gradual fashion. This period is known as industrial revolution era, which saw many eminent thinkers coming up with various ideas of managing factory kind of set up, prominent being F.W. Taylor whose scientific management theory resulted in the evolution of management as a separate discipline. This period is known as period of scientific management/organisationalal efficiency and it lasted for a quite a long time. Taylorism led to bureaucratization of production and the employee and employer relationship was based, with few exceptions, on distrust. However, during this period, many great scholars started questioning the scientific management theory and its relevance and they started working on different paradigms which saw evolution of new research based concepts of human relations (era) and human resources (era), prominent being the work of Elton Mayo and his associates of Harvard Business School. The emergence of human relations theory, etc. represented a significant shift in organisational theory thus superceeding Taylorism in favour of a more democratic and humanistic approach to management of employees/labour within organisations. Man became equally important as machine as it was found that without taking into consideration the socio-psychological factors, management of people is difficult. With this, economic and social complexity started growing. Life remained no more simple and use of technology was growing in scope and significance. This period, known as period of organisational effectiveness, was characterized by increasing shift towards capital and after Second World War an enormous capital accumulation began.

However, with passage of time, people saw globalisation in the 20th century and subsequent integration of world economies. With capital easily available, the critical production factor changed to people. Focus shifted from control system to commitment and knowledge work. Globalisation was witnessed by increasing complexity, competitiveness and uncertainty in economic, social and technological and political arena. Today, boundaries between nations have political relevance only. In this period, service sector of the industrial activity started increasing as compared to manufacturing sector. Today, service industry accounts for around 50% of the GDP of a country and it is going to increase further in future. This service is not limited to a nation only; it is borderless proposition now. For example, customers of a Mobile Phone Company in US are serviced as per global quality standards by Indians in call centers located in India through various technology based customer interactive processes and tools. Service has assumed utmost importance and the success of an organisation now a day is measured not just by quality and product design but also more by its ability and responsiveness in delivering service to its customers at global level. With this, the role of people in organisational context assumed increasingly more relevance and occupied the center stage. This is because of the fact that competitiveness of an organisation lies in the knowledge and creativity of its people, which cannot be imitated by any competitor/s. This increasing emphasis on knowledge and creativity requires use of 'brainpower' of people. This led to development of various theories, approaches and concepts pertaining to people management in organisations. Thus, it not simply labour, but knowledge which has displaced capital as the scarce production factor – the key to corporate success. Knowledge is needed about products, services, business processes, markets, customers, competitors, laws, cultures, ethics, environment and society. Positive customer experiences can only happen when processes and people (with passion) work in harmony. This kind of harmony is essential in global marketplace to create '**Service Excelleration**' (*Chris Daffy: 2004*) i.e. using customer service as a focus to accelerate organisational excellence. Management orientation has changed with time, from efficiency of 1885-1930 periods to periods of 1930-1980s of effectiveness to mid 1980s emphasis on excellence. *Thomas J. Peters, Robert H. Waterman Jr., and Nancy Austin* are the pioneers of the excellence movement in management. Organisational excellence simply means doing superior things through simple means. Therefore, organisational excellence is the capability of an organisation to produce results better than those of its competitions over a long period of time. There are eight principles of organisational excellence:

- Result orientation;
- Customer focus;
- Leadership and constancy of purpose;
- Management by processes and facts;
- People development and involvement;
- Continuous learning, performance improvement and innovation;
- Strategic partnership development;
- Social responsibility.

Passion for excellence is the need of the hour, if organisations are to prosper. By integrating leadership with people, policy and strategy and partnerships and resources, excellent results in business processes which in turn results in excellence in people results, customer results and resources which ultimately results in excellence in organisational performance. Organisations follow the following process to create service excelleration as depicted in figure 1.1.

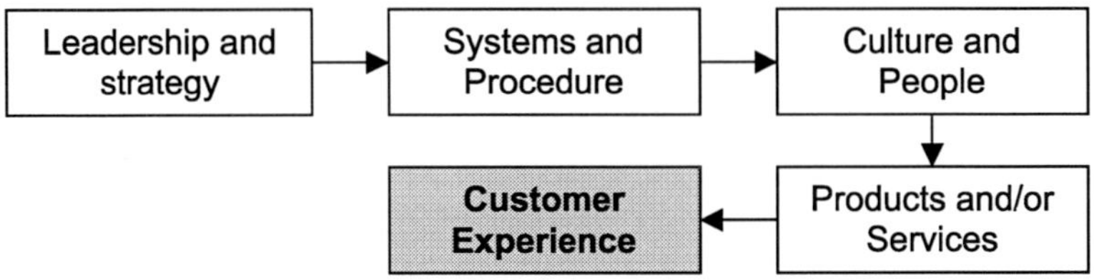

Fig. 1.1 : Creating Service Excelleration

To summarize, with the passage of time, growth in social and economic complexity has been of paramount proportions as depicted in figure 1.2.

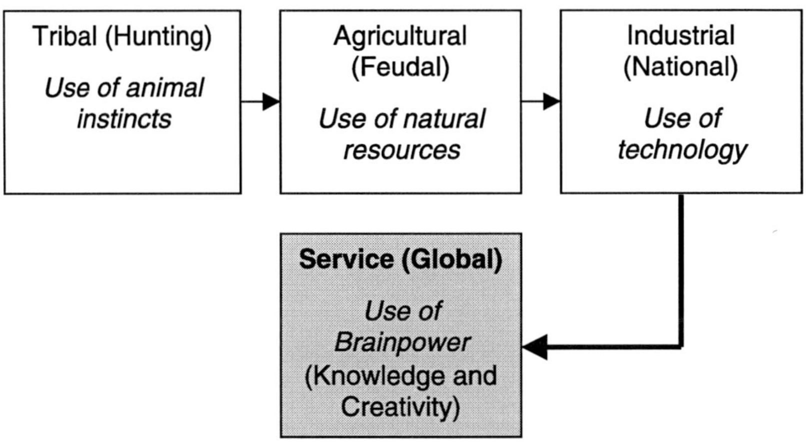

Fig. 1.2 : Changing Paradigm of Growth

Service industry is growing very fast and is likely to continue to do so in future. According to a recent definition by *Zeithaml and Bitner* (2001), Service can be defined as 'deeds, processes and performances'. Services are inherently and essentially intangible, heterogeneous, perishable and inseparable in nature and are evaluated on the basis of outcome as well as the cues and processes involved therein. This distinctive nature of service make the critical role of people (called as human resources in the organisational context) amply clear and brings to the forefront the increasing relevance of development of people in the organisational context.

With these evolutionary changes, there have been increasing changes in business environment as depicted in figure 1.3.

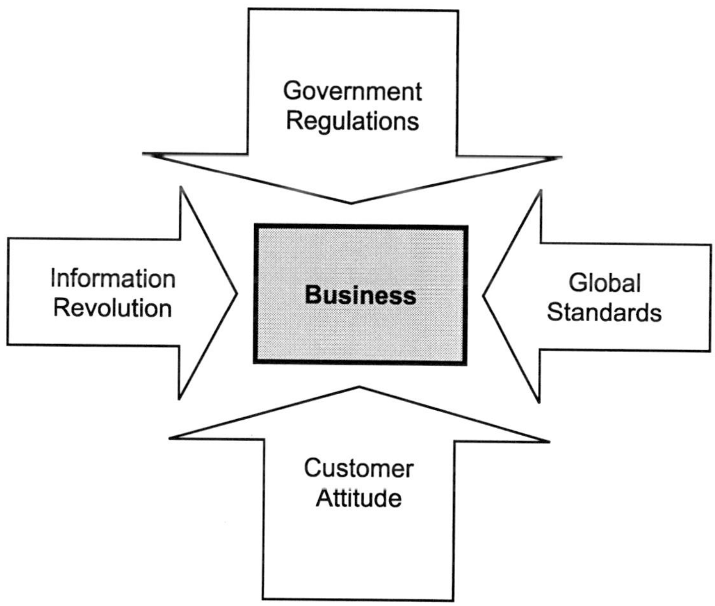

Fig. 1.3 : Changes in Business Environment

Together with this, the following changes are affecting the human civilization:

- Widening gap between rich and poor;
- Many of the 2 billion young people entering the workforce over the next 20 years won't be able to find jobs;
- Psychological impacts are evident even in prosperous regions; and
- Growing sense of emptiness and dissatisfaction with life.

Hence, people (human resources) are the most important and perhaps the only limitless resource, which has the ability to either make or break the fortune of any organisation.

Business Risks and Challenges Facing Today's Organisations

The business environment in the 21st century is global, customer centric, talent dependent, information based, fast paced, continually changing, technology driven, new partnerships and alliances, increasing organisational vulnerability/espionage, unstoppable capital flow, continuous learning and open to everyone. Against this backdrop, business organisations has to grapple with acquisition, support, development and retention of human resources, increase productivity, quality and service and built appropriate culture, leadership, innovation, accountability, commitment and readiness of human resources. Thus, organisations face various risks and challenges. Few management decisions are made under conditions of perfect certainty. Infact most of the decisions are made under conditions of uncertainty. The business climate is ever changing. Organisations operate under various internal and external constraints. Internal factors/constraints can be controlled but external constraints are not directly under the control of the organisation and thus its impact can be minimized but not totally negated/eliminated as depicted in figure 1.4.

Because of these factors, risk analysis should be given due consideration. Risk may be defined as the measure of the probability and severity of adverse effects (*William Lowrance: 1976*). Risks are the potential for realization of unwanted negative consequences of events, which may result in loss, injury, harm, disadvantage or destruction of something valued. These risks may be classified as political risks, competitive risks, operational risks and economic risks. The risks associated with an organisation are as depicted below:

Fig. 1.4 : Business Risks of an Organisation

Political Risk means the possibility of an unexpected politically motivated event affecting the outcome of an organisation. Any changes in political environment may adversely affect the value of the organisation's business activities such as loss of property, loss of income, etc. Lobbying and financial influence of politicians by organisations may result in favouratism and nepotism in licences, permits and government tenders. Such changes may be:

Public: changes in labour laws, consumer protection, nationalization, currency, inflation, taxation issues, investment restrictions, etc.

Private: terrorism, extortion, violence, cyber-terrorism, etc.

Other: confiscation, expropriation, domestication, operating restrictions, etc. in respect of foreign firms.

Competitive Risks means risks attributable to competition. Competitive risks arises due to imitation by competitors, changes in technology, loss of competitive advantages on account of cost or differentiation, market becoming structurally unattractive, disappearance of demand, new competitors, unethical competitive intelligence (Competitive Intelligence can be defined as a systematic and ethical programme for gathering, analyzing, and managing external information that can affect an organisation's plans, decisions, and operations), etc. These factors affect the competitive position of an organisation.

Operational Risks means unexpected events responsible for interruption or cessation or loss of ongoing activities of an organisation. Further, use of operations to add value for customers, winning in the marketplace on the dominions of cost, quality, timeliness and flexibility and the comparative advantages of the operational design of the organisation affects its bottom-line.

Economic Risks means those risks that can potentially impact the business. These risks could result in failure or loss of business. Economic risks include things such as changes in price of inputs and outputs, inflation, recession, depression or anything that generally affects organisation's profitability. Economic risks may be:

Exchange controls: a multitude of exchange rates to products.

Import restrictions: restricting import of raw materials and spare parts.

Tax controls: taxes can be raised without warning.

Price controls: putting products under price control order of the government.

Labour problems: layoffs, profit sharing, fringe benefits, amount and cost etc.

Assessing risks by organisation is critical to its survival. A systematic approach to optimize risk to support best mission outcomes is therefore essential. Increasing mission success, while reducing the risk to organisation's personnel, resources and the environment, is the essence of risk assessment and management.

Managing change is perhaps the single most important issue facing organisations. Contemporary business environment is a paradox. Organisations face various kinds of business challenges such as increasing complexity of business processes, increasing pressure to reduce costs, attracting and retaining talent and technology changes. The extent to which an organisation is able to attain its objectives depends on its ability to understand the opportunities presented to it and the constraints imposed by its environment. The six major business challenges are depicted in figure 1.5.

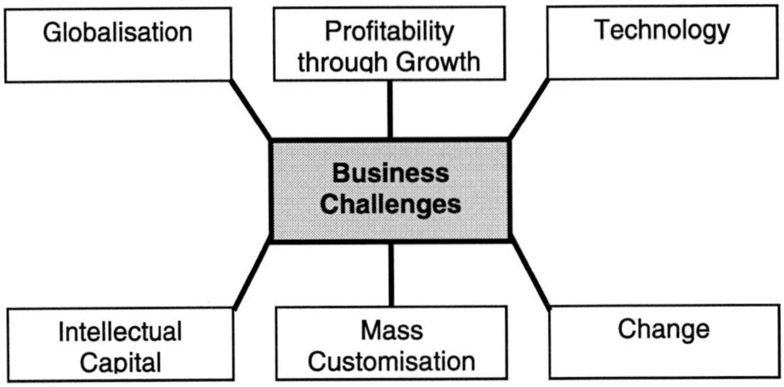

Fig. 1.5 : Business Challenges of an Organisation

1. Globalisation:

Globalisation refers to the worldwide interdependence of resource flows, product markets and business competition. It is about human interconnections that have assumed global proportions and transformed themselves. Globalisation as a human dynamic has always been with us even if we have been unaware of its embrace until recently. Since the 1980s, governments in many countries (especially in developing countries like India) have undergone a dramatic change in their development strategies, abandoning statist philosophies in favour of market-based approaches. By the late 1990s, most countries of the world had integrated into the global economy. Economies are now becoming at the same time more global and more local. This means that organisations need to move people, ideas, products, and information around the world to meet local needs. Globalisation is surely one of the most powerful and has pervasive influences on nations, businesses, workplaces, communities, and life.

Organisations face the following challenges on account of globalisation:

- Organisation's are still poorly adjusted to globalisation;
- Development of global manager is still at an infancy stages;
- Crippling shortage of global leadership;
- Driving transfer of management methods to global setting;
- The environmental challenge of addressing issues of sustainability globally; and
- Human diversity now globally presents to all societies that once defined themselves exclusively as homogeneous nations.

The prime effects of globalisation have been:

- More customers

This means that there is more eagerness of organisations to please its customers, which results in increased customer focus.

- More competitors

This means that organisations need to increase their competitiveness in order to gain or sustain a competitive advantage.

Globalisation is a dynamic component of human experience. It is not and has never been a single event, let alone a single process of change. Far from being a technological or capitalist juggernaut, globalisation reflects the material consequences of mankind's desires for security and well-being.

2. Profitability through Growth:

In this era of highly competitive, complex and dynamic business environment of global proportions, organisations are increasingly finding it difficult to make decent profit and even sustain their profitability and yet continue to grow. Earlier organisations had carried on re-engineering exercise, as part of TQM strategy, to improve performance and thereby boost profitability. Re-engineering means the rethinking and radically redesigning business processes to stimulate innovation and change and improve performance. But, in a highly dynamic and complex business environment, cost saving through re-engineering is insufficient. Organisations need to acquire new customers and develop innovative products and responsive services using an integrated array of skills, capabilities and cultures.

Organisations face the following challenges on account of profitability with growth:

- Re-engineering being done, cost gains have already been realized and therefore gains must come through growth; and
- This will influence corporate strategy, which will in turn influence HRD strategy.

3. Technology:

Technology means the systematic knowledge and action that deals with the industrial arts and sciences; utilization of such knowledge; the knowledge and means used to produce the material necessities of a society.

Technology is fast changing to meet customer's demands. Every minute somewhere in the world something new is being discovered or innovated. Faster technological progress has considerably changed the face of business and influenced the rules of competition. New generation customers demands the very best and latest in terms of technology. Therefore, organisations have to continuously upgrade its capabilities in order to make and deliver just in time the right technology to its customers. Technology is not how much to modernize, but how much to make obsolete. Therefore, technology means nothing without business ideas to power it.

Organisations face the following challenges on account of technology:

- Organisations must find which technology adds value and will make largecontinuing effect in future;
- Technological changes business processes (e.g. production process), which has profound effects on all areas of HRD; and
- Technology is also changing the way in which human resources are managedand developed and many clerical functions are fast disappearing.

4. Intellectual Capital:

In 1969, *J.K. Galbraith* used the term 'Intellectual Capital' for the first time. *Stewart* (1991) defines Intellectual Capital as 'the combinations of patents, processes, management skills, technologies, information about customers and suppliers and experience'. Conceptually, intellectual capital consists of human capital and structural capital. Human capital is a function of the competence, intellectual agility, and attitudes of the employees and structural capital refers to the learning and knowledge that is enacted in processes (process capital), knowledge that is codified as documents, objects, and intellectual property (intellectual capital) and the reputation and relationships the organisation has developed over time with customers and partners (relationship capital). Intellectual Capital is those intangible assets that do not show up on the organisation's financial statements, and specifically those, which can be codified and valued and managed by an organisation.

The journey from the industrial era to the knowledge era has seen a change in the mindset of the workforce. In the former era, machines made the difference, as mass production was order of the day. But, in the new era, people as knowledge resource are in the forefront. People, knowledge and technology are the determining factors for an organisation's success because knowledge is more powerful and valuable than natural resources. In an economy based on knowledge, intellectual capital – the untapped, unmapped knowledge of organisations has become an organisation's greatest competitive weapon. It is found in the talent of the people who work there, the loyalty of the customers it serves and learns from, the value of its brands (including employer brand) and intellectual properties, the collective knowledge embodied in its cultures, systems, management techniques, and history. Thus, intellectual capital is the only differentiator between organisations.

The components of Intellectual capital are as depicted in figure 1.6.

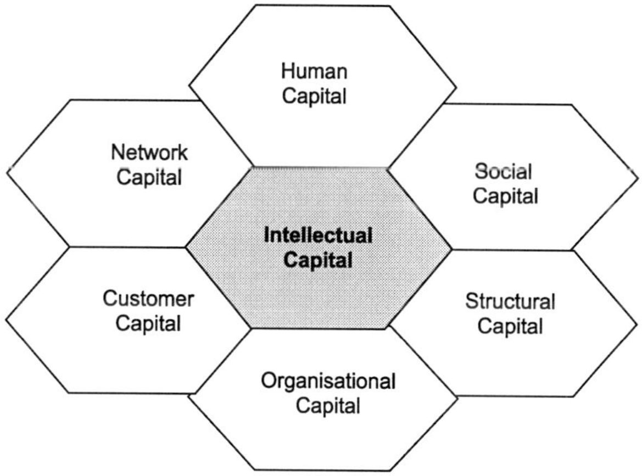

Fig. 1.6 : Components of Intellectual Capital

Organisations face the following challenges on account of intellectual capital:

- Knowledge is increasingly important, as a source of competitive advantage. Knowledge creation leads to continuous innovation, which in turn results in competitive advantage;
- Management of knowledge employees is much different from management of production employees; and
- Fundamental shits are occurring in the nature of work and in individual attitudes towards employment.

5. Change:

Change is the continuous process by which future invades our lives (*Alvin Toffler:* 1981). Change is inevitable and fast. Change is part of life, almost a defining characteristic of life. Change may be predictable (self-determined) or sudden (imposed) and it also has its costs. Change is a glorious and life enhancing feature of human existence. Change is the link between the past and the future. Various kinds of changes take place both in external environments as well within the organisation as response to external changes or as a result of internal requirements for change. The rules of the business are continuously shifting creating new challenges for all organisations in the global economy. Today staying competitive means embracing change, building relationships, optimizing human resources and talent, and transforming organisations into interactive, customer and HR driven organisations. As organisations are social sub-systems, therefore changes in the environment of the organisation such as competitive environment, economy, customer attitudes, competitors, and etc. all affect an organisation. Organisations have to adapt to accelerating non-stop changes with impunity. For this, lot of focus must be placed on business intelligence. Business intelligence has been defined by *Rouibah and Ould-al (2002)* as ' a strategic approach for systematically targeting, tracking, communicating and transforming relevant weak signs into actionable information on which strategic decision making is based'. Business intelligence can be an excellent tool for organisations to reduce operating costs through more effective financial analysis, risk management, and fraud management.

Organisations face the following challenges on account of change:

- Environmental change occurs more rapidly than in the past, thereby compelling organisations to become more adaptive;
- Changing human resources are the toughest challenge; and
- Job design is changing in order to allow faster adaptation.

6. Mass Customization:

Organisations intending to stay competitive have to increase efficiency, enhance responsiveness, reduce cost and quickly sense and capture customer's needs, maximize customer's satisfaction and address diversity of customer's needs. This requires change from mass production system to mass customization system, wherein business process is programmed to choose ingredients to produce custom designed products and/or services. Mass Customization is the technologies and systems to deliver goods and/ or services that best meet individual customer's needs with near mass production efficiency (*Tseng and Jiao: 1998*). It is depicted in figure 1.7.

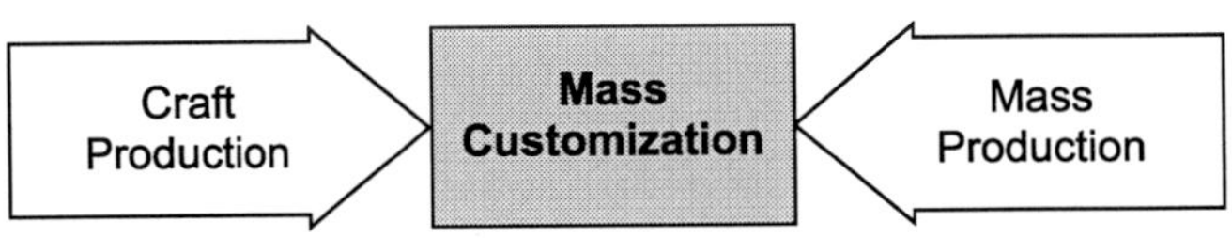

Fig. 1.7 : Mass Customization

Mass customization requires using technology and imagination to rapidly mass-produce products and/or services that cater to sundry unique customer desires. Under this, there are three process models – repetitive focus (flexible equipment), product focused (low variety, high volume) and process focused (high variety, low volume).

Organisations face the following challenges on account of mass customization:

- Problem of standardization;

- Problem of product uniformity;
- Reduce cost escalation to keep customer loyalty especially profitable customers; and
- Effective and efficient negotiation, given the enormous uncertainty and complexity associated with multi-attribute negotiation in mass customization.

Also, given the globalisation of economy, organisations arc facing the various emerging trends that are posing challenges such as:

1. Competition for expert employees (people whose minds rather than physical capabilities create value for the organisation);
2. Locus of control has shifted to some where between organisations and individuals;
3. Marketability of knowledge;
4. Future age; and
5. Technology explosion.

Today, tremendous amount of information is flowing within and outside organisations. Personal computers and networking capabilities has dramatically impacted on organisational practices of acquiring, deploying and delivering technology and the way organisations faces global competition. These factors have resulted in changing work roles, paving the way for new sets of competencies to meet these roles in order to build and sustain competitive advantages through developing new product and services capabilities, creating revolutionary changes, improving core capabilities and enhancing collaborative capabilities. Accordingly organisations are becoming improvement focused as depicted in figure 1.8.

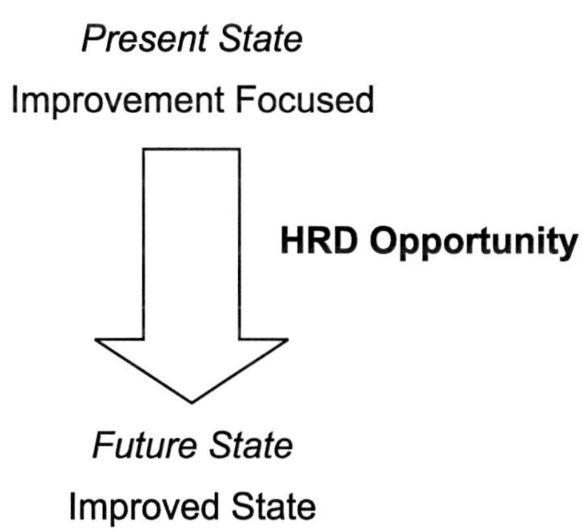

Fig. 1.8 : Improvement Focus of Organisation

There is increased need to deal with the ambiguity of global competition i.e. co-operation and competition simultaneously. For many countries such as Japan, human resources are their primary resource. Human resources are critical for national, local and organisational stability because if the cycle of welfare, poverty, violence, unemployment, illiteracy and socially undesirable employment are to be broken, then an integrated and coordinated mechanism for people to develop has to be evolved. Unlike other resources, human resources can be developed and improved to an unlimited extent. It must be understood that beyond economics, human resource development has the potential to improve individual's quality of work life.

Increased productivity is always a major goal for all organisations to increase its competitiveness (competitiveness may be defined as the degree to which an organisation can, under demanding and rapidly changing market conditions, produce products and services that meet the test of international markets while simultaneously maintaining or expanding the real incomes of the organisation). Dynamic changes in technology keep pressure on the upgrading of all human resources in a planned and continuous way. Given these factors, workforce commitment and employee satisfaction have received much attention in recent years. Facilitating personal growth, employee involvement, communication and supervision can enhance employee commitment. In order to survive, businesses must be more strategy focused, with keen accountability for results. Essentially strategy formulation involves four phases as depicted in figure 1.9.

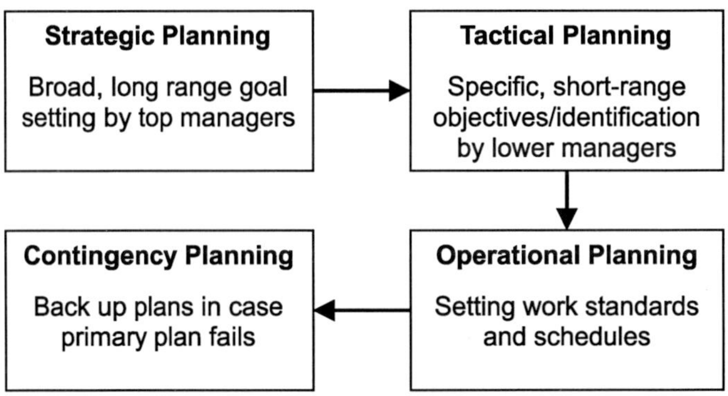

Fig. 1.9 : Phases of Strategy Formulation

In a global, highly competitive and dynamic economic environment, organisations have to focus on improving its competitive position within the specific industry or market segment that it serves in conjunction with the above four phases of strategy formulation. Organisations must find a strategic fit between external opportunities and internal strengths while working around external threats and internal weaknesses through an integrated and coordinated set of commitments and actions in order to gain and sustain competitive advantage by exploring core competencies in specified markets. Organisations can then make more strategic decisions about how to serve customers better and intiate improvement programmes.

In economics, the prime resources of an organisation are – land, labour and capital. As we have seen in the previous section, that today 'service' is key to business success and sustainability and service essentially indicates the role of people constituting an organisation. Organisations are striving to build themselves as high performance organisations to meet the emerging challenges. High performance organisations are the organisations, which are characterized by members who are driven by achievement, self-actualisation, humanistic values and affiliative behaviour. American Strategic Management Institute (ASMI) views five pillars of high performance organisations as performance management, financial management, Information technology, strategic management of human capital (Human Capital refers to the economic value of people with job relevant abilities, knowledge, ideas, energies and commitments) and Competitive sourcing. Technology is no more the prime source of getting and maintaining competitive advantage, simply because like capital, technology can be duplicated by the competitors. Thus, people are the only resource which can be relied upon for gaining competitive advantage because the talents lying in the people working in an organisation have knowledge, skill, commitment, motivation, devotion, etc. which is innovative, creative and transferable can not be imitated by any organisation. Hence, people in an organisation are the source of competitive advantage of the organisation. These people working in the organisation in order to achieve the goals and objectives of the organisation are the 'human resources' of the organisation. Organisations need to provide a rationale, framework, and vision for co-operation in order to generate economic growth and stability. Organisations also have to institute improved monitoring and information sharing mechanisms for effective collaboration, co-ordination and resource optimization and utilization.

But why has the evolution of human resource development been necessary? Quite simply the world of people and the environments in which they work has changed. A decade ago, *Peter Drucker* anticipated this change when he said in 'The Age of Discontinuity': "Businessmen will have to learn to build and manage innovative organisations." Thus, can human resource development stand firm in a world of chaos or will is need to develop further new strategies to protect its value to a given organisation? The world is changing and as long as the interpretation and subsequent management of the change is influenced by human organisations the human resource development function.

Human resource development has emerged as a distinct area of concern in organisations for effectively coping with business risks, challenges and changes in the environmental context, the need for adjustments to rapid changes in technology and to meet the changing expectations of the employees. Today, there are high expectations from human resource development as it represents worldview that takes a positive view of people and their potential. It also attempts to foster a climate conducive to growth and development.

In present global and complex economic scenario, there has been a move away from organisational directed learning, as it sees the individual start to take more control of their own development needs. Due to the differences in organisational needs, cultural context, organisational structure and resources available, the concept of the individual taking more responsibility for their development is a significant shift away from earlier ideas.

Additionally, there has been a shift in the last decade from organisations training to meet competence voids, towards a more learning environment that relies on experiential learning and self-direction. It is argued, such an approach, does not limit itself to training, but stretches to facilitating and supporting learning processes within the organisation, with the aim to contribute to meaningful organisational learning programmes.

This clearly has an impact on the concept of human resource development and any approach it may take within an organisation. A key role of human resource development is to create and/or maintain a learning organisational environment as the foundation to any training and learning within an organisation.

However, there are views that human resource development should be subject to tight quantitative justification and it needs to demonstrate that its activities add value to the organisation. However, value lies in developing a learning organisation through a human resource development function. Yet there remains a broad body of support that does lean towards this view. Human resource development in an organisational context has no meaning unless the connection is made to performance because an employer doesn't teach for the sake of learning ... what are the rewards? There needs to be a systematic method of linking business goals with the learning process. However, there remains a danger that the human resource development function, however defined, becomes over indulgent, becoming the end rather than the means to add some value to the organisation. Maybe it is this fear, which when added to high-level managerial naivety of modern human resource development approaches, which has seen many a human resource development organisation become the first casualty of any downsizing.

Theoretical Foundations of Human Resource Development

The field of Human resource Development in the organisational context has been borrowed from other disciplines such as economic theory, psychological theory and systems theory. The central argument is that human resource development must continue to mature as a discipline and that the recognition and integration of economic, psychological and systems theories serve as the unique theoretical foundation of human resource development. The relevance of these theories lies in improving practice of HRD.

The three foundations of human resource development have been discussed below:

1. Economic Foundation of Human Resource Development:

Since economics as a theoretical foundation of human resource development has considerable influence on research and practice of HRD, therefore this part has been described elaborately.

Business is a necessary and inevitable economic activity. Business has always existed since the dawn of human civilization in one or other form. In order do business, some formalized form as a means of carrying out business is made. In the earlier period, it was carried out on individual basis, but gradually with time it took more formal and organized structure and it then came to be known as 'Organisation'. Organisation is an organic entity in which people could co-operate, aimed at realizing objectives both individual and collective. Business through organisation is carried out primarily for achieving economic objectives of the organisation. The economic justification of having HRD in the organisational context is depicted in figure 1.10.

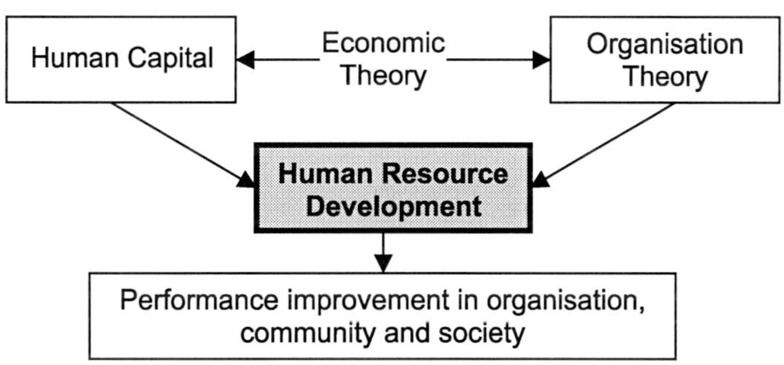

Fig. 1.10 : Economic Foundation of HRD

Economics is the backbone of any organisation. As can be seen from the figure 1.10, economic theory holds centre stage of evolution of human resource development concept in organisational context.

A theory is a general statement or set of related statements about cause and effect, action and reaction. Theories involve models, and models involve variables.

Economics is the study of how individuals and societies choose to use the scarce resources that nature and previous generations have provided.

Economics involves the study of societal and global affairs concerning resource allocation.

It studies how economic agents choose to use their scarce resources because scarcity necessitates choice. Economic theory involves building models of behavior. Economic theory should be able to predict what a utility or profit maximizing economic agent will do.

Economic theory contains concepts of efficiency, which can help establish criteria for ensuring maximum societal well-being. The development and growth of people at work is, and always be, a necessary and vital part of successful economic and productive activity.

Thus, economics is the study of Human Behavior. Human dimension relates to human capital of the organisation on one hand and can be explained by the Human Capital Theory whereas Behaviour dimension on the other hand pertains to Organisation Behaviour, which can be explained by Organisation Theory. Human Capital theory is an economic theory that addresses the macroeconomics of production and economic success of any organisation.

Every organisation wants to increased market size, increased product market competition, access to foreign ideas and capital (knowledge spillovers and technology transfer) and elimination of duplication in innovation. This has resulted in the evolution of new growth theory. Although many economists worked on theoretical models of growth, it wasn't until *Paul Romer* published his model in 1986 that there was a resurgence of interest in growth. The new growth theory attempts to explain the sources of organisational progress. Three important sources of such progress are:

- Ideas
- International Openness
- Human Capital Formation. Labour is used to produce new ideas and to produce output.

Human resources are developed and employed by the organisation in order to achieve its mission and objectives. In the 1950s, the main factor of production consisted of the four traditional factors viz-physical capital, labour and management. In the early 1960s, economic growth accounting studies were conducted in the United States in terms of the traditional factors of production. However, the income growth accounting equations never balanced. There existed a gap. This gap was referred to as the residual factor by *Theodore W. Shultz (1961)* as Human Capital, which was later popularized by *Becker (1964, 1993)*. He defined human capital theory as "the knowledge and skills that people acquire through education and training as being a form of capital, and that this capital is a product of deliberate investment that yields returns". Thus, human capital theory views human capabilities – their knowledge, skills, talents and efforts as integral parts of the capital of an organisation along with financial and physical resources. The fundamental principle of human capital theory is the belief that people's learning capacities are comparable to other resources involved in the production of goods and services and when the resource is effectively utilized, the results are profitable both for the individual and the society at large. The point is clear from *P.M. Romer's* (1990) observation that the economy with larger total stock of human capital would experience a faster rate of growth. Human Capital refers to the knowledge, skills, abilities that can be applied to create value within an organisation. A recent broad based definition of Human Capital has been given by *Jack Fitz Enz (*2000*)* who defines human capital as "the traits one brings to the job: intelligence, fulfilling work energy, a generally positive attitude, reliability, and commitment. One's ability to learn: aptitude, imagination, creativity, and what is often called 'street smarts' savvy and one's motivation to share information and knowledge: team spirit and goal orientation".

Human capital is embodied in employees and is an amalgam of factors such as education, training, experience, intelligence, energy, work habits, trustworthiness, and initiative that affect the value of an employee's marginal product. It is presented schematically in figure 1.11.

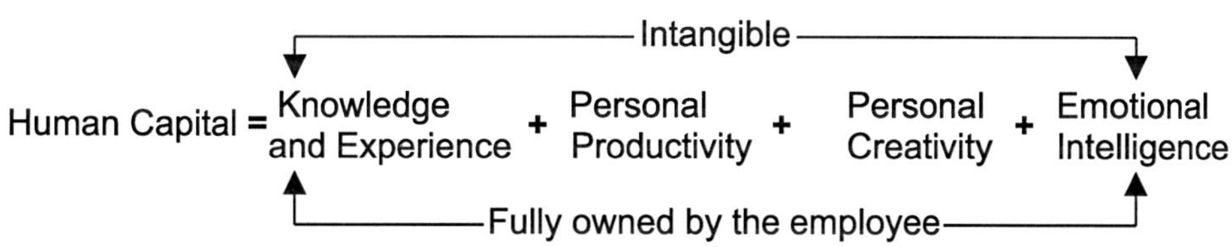

Fig. 1.11 : Human Capital

The time when it was possible for organisations to procure skilled employees from the local human resources market easily has not completely disappeared but it is increasingly difficult and expensive to procure such people today. Therefore, to deal with this, there are many investments that individuals and organisations make that represent investments in human capital. These include education and training. The theory of human capital states that education and training equips employees with competencies i.e. knowledge, skills, attitude and behaviours that can make them more productive. It equips employees with competent and durable traits and makes them good performers in the organisations, communities and in society at large. Human Capital Theory is also a theory of pay determination that says an employee's wage will be proportional to his or her stock of human capital. Individuals are concerned with maximizing lifetime earning and it is assumed that each level of education and training is uniquely related to an earning stream. This relationship reflects a causal relationship from education to skills and between skills and marginal productivity. Thus, Human capital theory is concerned with analysis of importance of education and training. Training can be viewed as an investment in human capital. Training can be used to increase productivity, improve quality, strengthen interpersonal skills or strengthen organisation's culture. Also, human capital includes contribution of ideas for economic growth and development of an organisation.

In a fast changing environment, organisations must develop new strategies and new ways of organizing to deal with exceedingly complicated landscape and this requires use of latest technology, continuously develop new technology, participate in global markets, structure themselves to gain advantage in the market, develop strategic flexibility, build vision that allows balance between short term and long term organisational needs. Therefore, the only way to improve individual performance is to increase their productivity through education and training on continuous basis. It is human resource's intelligence, their fulfilling work energy, positive attitude, reliability, and commitment, their ability to learn, aptitude, imagination, creativity, and motivation to share information and knowledge that makes a difference that leads to innovation and process capital which have become very important to the economic growth process of organisations. The rational investor in human capital will invest up to that level of education and training where marginal benefits just exceed marginal costs.

However, Human Capital Theory is being criticized for:

- Treating humans as resources to be used or manipulated to achieve purely economic organisational strategies (disregards human potential);
- Theory ignores qualifications as screening device;
- The impact of occupational monopolies;
- Relationship of self-typing and perceptions of skill;
- The effects of market shortages of skills;
- Treating or equating people as 'Capital' *i.e.* economic resource; and

- Skill is not just a matter of time served – it is the variations in abilities within any given time and/or personnel that have also to be considered.

However, the theory of human capital is still widely acceptable to the scholars and practitioners as it is the one theory that better explains the gains of education and training as a form of investment in human resources.

Organisation Theory is the discipline that studies the structure and design of organisations. Organisation is a group of people working together towards a common goal in such a way that even if the individuals of the organisation change, the behavioural models remain stable and predictable. Organisations can be viewed as an open system wherein which lies an input-output relationship between variables. Organisations obtain resource inputs from the environment, transform these resource inputs and then return transformed inputs to the environment as outputs in the form of products and services. The environment of the organisation consists of immediate environment, which is internal to the organisation, such as distributors, unions, competitors, customers, suppliers and government and external environment consists of social and cultural forces, technological forces, political forces and economic forces. These profoundly impact the overall efficiency and effectiveness of the organisation.

It is a macro perspective concerned with behaviour of organisations and human resource development at micro level as depicted in figure 1.12 for clarity:

Macro Perspective	Organisation Theory	Organisational Development
Micro Perspective	Organisational Behaviour	Human Resource Development

Fig. 1.12 : Economic Justification of HRD - Organisation Theory

Behaviour is a function of the person and the environment. The purpose of organisation theory is to apply such knowledge as to behaviour of individuals and groups related to jobs, work, absenteeism, employment turnover, productivity, human performance, perception, motivation, learning and management toward improving an organisation's effectiveness and ushering in excellence.

Human resource development, beyond its effect on individuals and organisations, also carries with it the potential for economic growth.

2. Psychological Foundation of Human Resource Development:

In organisational context, psychology is concerned with individual behavior in work situations. Creation of work environments compatible with human skills, talents, and limitations is essential for organisational efficiency and effectiveness in a complex, competitive and global business scenario. The application of psychological tools to solve problems of people working in organisations facilitates their integration and results in improved performance. Psychology essentially entails:

- Leadership;
- Motivation;
- Job Satisfaction;
- Conflict management; and
- Group processes.

Psychological theory operates at the individual, group and organisational level. It describes and explains as to how the behaviours and mental processes of humans affect technologies, processes, internal subsystems and organisational mission and objectives. It provides useful and relevant knowledge and methods for understanding and influencing human behaviour and mental processes in order to achieve the organisation's mission, objectives and relationship with the external environment.

Organisations in order to stay competitive and profitable have to continuously emphasize:

i) Organisational renewal;

ii) Initiate and manage culture change;

iii) Ensure health and well being of employees;

iv) Facilitate learning and development of employees;

v) Improve problem-solving skills;

vi) Increase effectiveness;

vii) Support adaptation of employees to change.

Understanding of psychological perspective is critical to the performance of an organisation because it brings key skills and perspectives that effectively facilitate change in culture and shifts in strategy to address the complex challenges and risks facing organisations. To foster organisation's effectiveness requires balancing the needs and objectives of individuals with those of the organisation. Human considerations such as coping with change, and value attached to organisational decisions based on potential individual outcomes and perceived equity has immense impact on individual and ultimately organisational effectiveness.

3. Systems Foundation of Human Resource Development:

Systems Theory is the trans-disciplinary study of the abstract organisation of phenomena, independent of their substance, type, or spatial or temporal scale of existence. Systems theory (or general systems theory or systemic) is an interdisciplinary field, which studies systems as a whole. Systems theory was founded by Ludwig von Bertalanffy, William Ross Ashby and others between the 1940s and the 1970s on principles from physics, biology and engineering and later grew into numerous fields including philosophy, sociology, organisational theory, management, and economics among others. It sees the world in terms of 'systems', where each system is a 'whole' that is more than the sum of its parts, but also itself a 'part' of larger system.

Systems theory emphasizes that real systems are open to, and interact with, their environments, and they can acquire qualitatively new properties through emergence, resulting in continual evolution. Systems concepts include: system-environment boundary, input, output, process, state, hierarchy, goal-directedness, and information.

Organisations are open systems as they interact with their environment to maintain a state of fit between internal arrangement and the environment. Organisations are therefore a product of their surroundings. Systems theory assumes that individuals and their organisations cannot operate in a vacuum; therefore, systems should be considered as situational and contingency oriented. Human resource development is a sub-system in the organisational context and a system of its own because human resources are the prime movers of all other physical input resources and with the help of technology and other physical resources transform input resources into valuable output resources in the form of products and/or services. This transformational process involves a host of human resource development processes. This is because of the fact that such processes involve implementing systematic change in behaviours of human resources for the purpose of improving performance of the organisation. Organisation includes not only a geographic domain, but also the culture and social factors of the people living or visiting the area, the demographic features of the people living or visiting the area, the level of technological advances of that area such as technological superiority, R & D efforts, technology transfer, adoption, adaptation and absorption issues, technology-human interface, etc., the economic situation of the area such as economic climate, institutional framework, financial market depth, national as well as global, GDP trend, inflationary conditions, sectoral health, balance of payment positions, export-import trends, etc., and the political situations pertaining to that place such as political system, political institutions, the political ideologies of different political parties, the political culture and maturity, etc., and natural setting of the area. These diverse factors are called environmental factors. Organisations interact with internal sub-systems of the organisation such as distributors, trade unions, competitors, customers, suppliers, government, etc. in order to develop and unleash human expertise for the purpose of effectively dealing with environment such as social and cultural forces/changes, technological forces/changes, economic forces/changes, and political forces/changes.

The systems model of an organisation is depicted in figure 1.13.

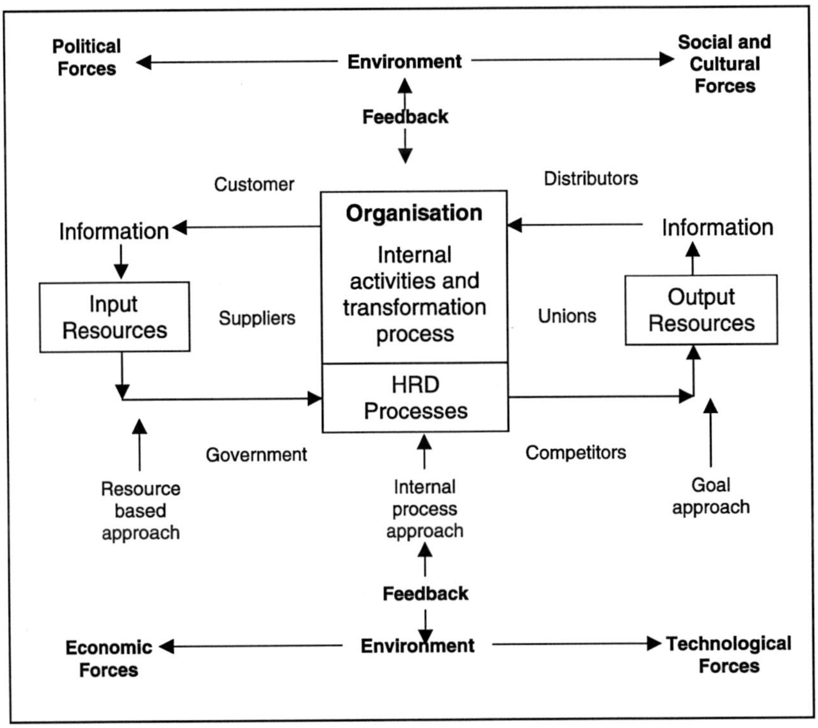

Fig. 1.13 : System Model of Organization

As can be seen from the figure 1.13, organisations are a collectivity and this collectivity exists on a relatively continuous basis in an environment and engages in activities that are usually related to a goal.

Resource refers to an asset, competency, process skills or knowledge controlled by the organisation. Resource based approach argues that the reasons for differences in organisation's profitability within the same industry is due to the capabilities that are internal to the organisation. Resource based approach suggests that competitive advantage is derived through a combination of unique organisational resources in obtaining virtual monopoly positions in their respective markets.

Internal process approach is concerned with various activities that that are undertaken to facilitate the transformation of input resources into valuable outputs in most efficient and effective manner.

Goal approach pertains to operation of the organisation's all resources in a co-coordinated and cohesive manner so as to attain the goals and objectives of the organisation.

However, The systems model isn't very helpful when it comes to management development.

Only recently has **ethics** been given equal footing with economics, psychology and general systems theory as a theoretical foundation for human resource development. Ethics of practice and self-regulation are necessary pre-requisite for achieving status and credibility as a profession, institution, organisation, business, or practice. This aspect has been dealt with separately in this chapter.

Nature and Concept of Human Resource Development

The greatest resources of the world are the humans, without whom nothing could ever be a resource! Of what value, for instance, would gold or silver or other natural endowments be if there were no men? The *Homo sapiens* is, indeed, the resource of all resources.

Resources may be wasted by neglect, depleted by consumption, destroyed by misuse or enhanced by developmental interventions. Obviously no one will ever advocate neglect, depletion or misuse of this greatest of resources. And yet, humans have for long wallowed in these very predicaments - for reasons of either ignorance or failure of the chosen few to recognize and appreciate the potential of their fellow humans. The times are changing, now. The human potential and the need for conscious attempts to develop it are more readily acknowledged today than ever before in many parts of the world. Efforts are afoot today to devise and implement methods of developing human resources.

In 1970, *Leonard Nadler* published his now-classic book "Developing Human Resources", in which he coined the term 'Human Resource Development', in short HRD. The term human resource development provided a conceptual umbrella under which the field began to unify, using the three-fold notion of training, education, and development. Human resource development provided purpose and direction for the continued growth of the field; organized learning to provide the possibility of performance change. It further identified a core discipline from which a field of study could develop: adult learning in the workplace.

In 1989, there were signs of an emerging concern for economic impact. The field began to move from focusing to what is performed to what is produced. One of the forces in 1989 was an increased use of systems approaches in human resource development. Another shift in the field that took place was that the focus on individual learning was shifting to organisational learning as the primary activity and goal of the field. The scope of human resource development has broadened beyond training and organisation development. The move was toward human resource development responsiveness and relevance.

But why has the evolution of human resource development been necessary? Quite simply the world of people and the environments in which they work has changed. A decade ago, *Peter F. Drucker* anticipated this change when he said in "The Age of Discontinuity", 'Businessmen will have to learn to build and manage innovative organisations'. Organisations reducing its reliance on structure, as structure will become a dynamic enabler of both change and unchange, the ultimate model of 'organized chaos'. The world is changing and as long as the interpretation and subsequent management of the change is influenced by human organisations, the human resource development function will continue to occupy center stage.

The word Human resource Development can be broken up as under:

Human Resource Development = 'Human Resource' + 'Development'

'*Human Resource*' refers to the talents and energies of people who are available to an organisation as potential contributors to the creation and realization of the organisation's mission, vision, values and goals.

'*Development*' refers to a process of active learning from experience, leading to systematic and purposeful development of the whole person: body, mind and spirit. Development combines the concepts of development (change and growth) and training (learning specific skills).

Thus, Human Resource Development is the integrated use of training, organisational development, and career development efforts to improve individual, team and organisational effectiveness.

Each one of the various activities that constitute human resource development could be carried out in different ways; some ways of doing them would make human resource development efforts more effective than some other ways of doing the same activities.

For making human resource development effective, besides choosing the right activities, one must pay adequate attention to their process, too. Process refers to the specific style, method or the way in which a particular activity is implemented. The process can make or mar any activity. The style, method or process of carrying out a human resource development activity is to be guided by the anticipated impact and ultimate concern for human dignity. Thus, human resource development is a set of inter-related activities, by which human potentialities are assessed, selectively upgraded and appropriately deployed for achievement of envisioned goals, which foster human dignity. The term used to describe an integrated and holistic approach to changing work-related behaviour, using a range of learning techniques and strategies.

Various organisations are engaged in developing human resources. The human resource development practices represent attempts to meet the in-house human resource development needs of various organisations. There are also organisations whose attempts are to provide human resources to other organisations.

Organisations have an integrated human resource development role: development of its internal human resources for its own effectiveness in conjunction with its customers. People who join the organisation, however, bring their personal values with them. The organisation's ideology would be consequential only to the degree the individuals in the organisation identify with the ideology, reflect it or share it. Congruence can be brought about by the organisation through appropriate methods, including screening a candidate who matches the organisations ideology or rope in those who hold out a clear promise of being "scripted" through adequate and well-planned induction and socialization programmes. A combination of these strategies may also be practical: A part of the candidates is screened in for congruence and the rest be made congruent by in-house socialization or indoctrination.

Who should do HRD?

Responsibility for HRD programmer & practices is shown in figure 1.14. Human resource development Managers and Line Managers have shared accountability for

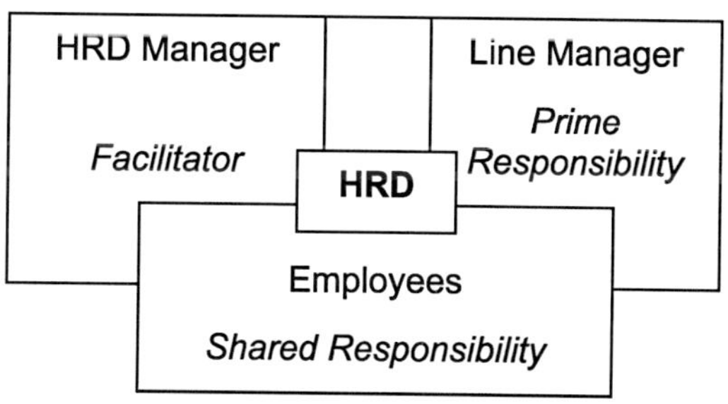

Fig. 1.14 : Responsibility for HRD

developing people for better business results. Implementation of human resource development will certainly call for constructive participation of all. Therefore, human resource development, to be effective in the long run, must be spearheaded by those who espouse a developmental ideology that is humanistic; those who have faith in the human beings; those who believe in the intrinsic worth of humans; those who are urged by an inner fire to help and guide others to grow; those who derive happiness from seeing others scale the ladder of the latter's potentialities. Others should keep their hands off human resource development and content themselves with training and management of human resources. Everybody can and must be the "target" of human resource development. Human resource development people appear to be on the verge of extinction in these days of speeding materialism and individualism. Nevertheless, few and vanishing as they are, these are the people who should be entrusted with the responsibility of human resource development, irrespective of their functional status or affiliation (line manager or HRD manager).

Definitions:

A few noteworthy definitions of Human Resource Development (HRD) are as under:

1. "Human Resource Development is a process or processes of organized capability and competency based learning experiences undertaken by employees within a specified period of time to bring about individual and organisational performance improvement, and to enhance national economic, cultural, and social growth".

(Lynham and Cunningham: 2004)

2. "Human Resource Development is a process for developing and unleashing human expertise through organisation development and personnel training and development for the purpose of improving performance".

(Swanson and Holton: 2001)

3. "Human Resource Development is any process or activity that, either initially or over the long term, has the potential to develop work based knowledge, expertise, productivity and satisfaction, whether for personal or group/team gain, or for the benefit of an organisation, community, nation, or ultimately, the whole of humanity".

(McLean and McLean: 2001)

4. "Human Resource Development is a holistic concept, incorporating intrinsically social, cultural, and spiritual dimensions to build capacity and empower people".

(Rogers: 2001)

5. "Human Resource Development is equipping people with relevant skills to have a healthy and satisfying life".

(The South Pacific Commission: 2001)

6. "Human Resource Development is the process of increasing the capacity of the human resource through development. It is thus a process of adding value to individuals, teams or an organisation as a human system".

(The American Society for Training and Development)

7. "Human Resource Development is organized learning experiences provided by employers within a specified time to bring about the possibility of performance or personal growth".

(Giley and Eggland: 1989)

8. "Human Resource Development is fostering long term; work related learning capacity at individual, group and organisational level"

(Watkins: 1989)

9. "Human Resource Development is a process in which the employees of an organisation are continuously helped in a planned way to: (1) acquire or sharpen their capabilities required to perform various tasks and functions associated with their present and future expected roles; (2) develop their general enabling capabilities as individuals so that they are able to discover and exploit their own inner potential for their own and/or organisational development purposes and develop an organisational culture where superior-subordinate relationships, teamwork and collaboration among different subunits are strong, and contribute to the organisational health, dynamism and pride of employees".

(Dr. T.V. Rao: 1985)

However, in this era of globalisation (Globalisation refers to the processes whereby social relations acquire relatively distanceless and borderless qualities, so that human lives are increasingly played cut in the world as a single place), the definitions of human resource development can not be distinct and disjointed any more as more and more organisations are going global and the whole world is emerging as one single economic market. G.N. McLean and L.D. McLean after having studied the various definitions of human resource development of different countries, proposed the definition of human resource development as mentioned at serial number 3.

Thus, from analytical study of all the above definitions, we may conclude that Human

Resource Development is an organized learning experience, conducted in a definite time period, to increase the possibility of improving job performance and growth. Human resource development can be now be modeled as shown in figure 1.15.

Human Resource Development is concerned with *Building* of
Competence
Commitment and Motivation
Culture

Fig. 1.15 : Model of HRD

Differences in national culture are reflected in the definitions, including the influence of the economy and of government and legislation, and of professional organisations. Definitions of human resource development from the following European countries have been analysed:

France: the term of 'development social' is often used as a synonym of human resource development.

Germany: a training industry, consultants and personnel specialists mark the field corresponding to human resource development.

Netherlands: human resource development is related to all training and development interventions that are made to create and further develop human expertise within the context of an organisation.

Russia: human resource development is associated with personnel staffing, selection and training, the focus being on managing the employee pool rather than helping individual employees to develop.

UK: key elements of human resource development include activities and processes having an impact on organisational and individual learning.

Furthermore, there appears to be a difference in both the perception and practice of human resource development in local organisations compared with multinational organisations, with the latter being much more likely to be influenced by their home countries.

Developed, educated, motivated people are an unlimited resource for any organisation.

Thus, the definitions of HRD can be summarized as shown in figure 1.16.

National HRD Definition (India)

Human Resource Develoment is a process in which the employees of an organisation are continuously helped in a planned way to:
(1) acquire or sharpen their capabilities required to perform various tasks and functions associated with their present and future expected roles;
(2) develop their general enabling capabilities as individuals so that they are able to discover and exploit their own inner potential for their own and/or organisational development purposes and develop an organisational culture where superior-subordinate relationships, teamwork and collaboration among different subunits are strong, and contribute to the organisational health, dynamism and pride of employees.
(Dr. T.V. Rao: 1995)

Western HRD Definition

Human Resource Development is a process for developing and unleashing human expertise through organisation development and personnel training and development for the purpose of improving performance."

(Swanson and Holton: 2001)

Global HRD Definition

Human Resource Development is any process or activity that, either initially or over the long term, has the potential to develop work based knowledge, expertise, productivity and satisfaction, whether for personal or group /team gain, or for the benefit of an organisation, community, nation, or ultimately, the whole of humanity.

(McLean and McLean:2001)

New HRD Definition

Human Resource Development is a process or processes of organized capability and competency based learning experiences undertaken by employees within a specified period of time to bring about individual and organizational performance improvement, and to enhance national economic, cultural, and social growth.

(Lynham and Cunningham: 2004)

Fig. 1.16 : Development of Concept of HRD over time

The essence of Human Resource Development is that employees are valued assets and that their value should be increased by a systematic and coherent approach to investing in their training and development, which is made possible by instituting trust in people as depicted in figure 1.17.

People	T	Policy
	R	
Training	U	Procedure
	S	
Performance	T	Systems

Fig. 1.17 : Essence of HRD

The model that predominated early, back in the 1960s, was *Leonard Nadler's* model. Its a model that is not talked about too much today although it is emerging in subtle ways as conversation goes on about human resource development. *Nadler's* model started with training and he differentiated training from education and development. Training was seen as preparation immediately for the job, education was seen as preparation for a job some time in the future, and development had more of an individual focus whereby the individual is developing himself, which may or may not have implications for the organisation. This is a model that has migrated around the world. Because *Nadler* spent considerable time in Thailand, for example, it is a model that is still widely used there.

Clearly the predominant model in human resource development in the US is accepted around the world, in spite of all the criticisms about it. There are eleven different components of human resources. These include three areas that have the word development in them and, therefore, are regarded as human resource development: training and development, organisation development, and career development. Four areas are seen as exclusively human resource management, and four areas are considered as the overlap between human resource development and human resource management. Its a model that probably has been most significant in influencing the development of academic programmes in the US. So it is very common to find a human resource development programme that has course work in each of the three areas, much less common to find course work in the overlap areas, and uncommon to find anything in the areas that are identified only as human resource management.

Today, human resource development must be the strategic partner with the business in all of the eleven areas of the people management in order to sustain organisations competitieness.

There is a debate around what the supporting theories for human resource development are and the foundations of human resource development. Human resource development is supported by three disciplines: systems theory, economics and psychology, all resting on a rug of ethics. However, limiting to three disciplines is extremely simplistic with the complexity of the work that people are called on to do. It may be suggest that anthropology is absolutely the core of work and other discipline such as philosophy; sociology and communications should be included.

Altogether, there is a lot of discomfort with the models that exist today. There is a lot of interest in developing the field to recreate a new model that is more inventive, dynamic, and theoretically sound.

In India, from the early days of human resource development interventions introduced in Larsen & Tubro in 1975, we have traversed a period of 34 years and during these period, in Indian organisations the importance of human resource development has been comprehensively felt and various processes and instruments of human resource development are being applied in different organisations in the manufacturing, financial and service sectors. Whether it is a case of SBI, LICI, GIC or Canara Bank, Indian Bank or it is a case of HMT, TISCO, TELCO, NDDB, Thermax, Hindustan Motors, the importance of human resource development in managing people for results and bringing effectiveness in the field of 'management' have been widely appreciated.

Critical issues, which are identified by the Top Management team in different organisations, share the same concern and deal with identical problems. It is found on a survey of the Indian Organisations that in the following fields human resource development has to be strengthened:

1. Recruitment and Promotion Policies of different organisations are to be reviewed on a recurrent and continuous basis. Merit and competence should be given greater emphasis in promotions;
2. Performance Appraisal systems in the organisations are to be modified so that the right persons are rewarded in the right manner and placed in the right jobs;
3. Greater emphasis is to be laid on human resource development and training;
4. Communication system is to be improved;
5. Motivation, morale, commitments and sense of belongingness and involvement of employees at all levels should be enhanced;
6. Greater attention is to be paid regarding development of first line supervisors, second and third line executives; and
7. Policies, Rules and Procedures of organisations are to be consolidated and reviewed on a consistent and recurrent basis.

After discussion of concept and perspectives on human resource development, the various dimensions of an organisation in the context of human resource development can be depicted as in figure 1.18.

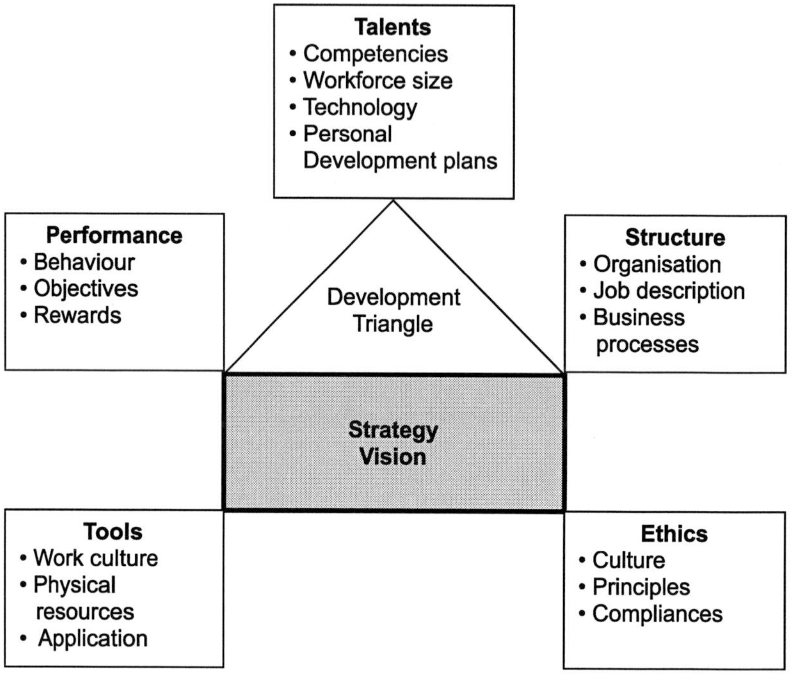

Fig. 1.18 : Dimension of Organisation in HRD Context

Trends in Human Resource Development

According to phillips (1996), the trends are :

- As the budget for HRD increases, more questions will be asked about its ability to enhance organisational effectiveness;
- HRD has become a powerful change management tool to assist organisations to successfully meet the challenges of the future;
- HRD is one of the many functions responding to the pressures in order to show their contribution in measurable terms; and
- Top management requires the HRD function to measure training results.

Bibliography

Phillips, J.J., "Measuring the results of Training" In R.L. Craig (ed.), The ASTD Training and Development Handbook, 1996, 4th edition, McGraw-Hill, New York, Pp. 313-314.

Scope of HRD

Human resource development being a systematic process for bring desired behavioural changes in employees, involves some focus areas which are as follows:

FOUNDATIONS	DELIVERY	ADVISING / COACHING	DESIGNING	MANAGING / LEADING	CONSULTING
SYSTEMS & STRUCTURES • General systems • Psych-social systems • Management systems • HRD systems • Systems, allied fields MODELS & PARADIGMS HRD GENERAL & FIELD • Assumptions • Theories • Definitions • Ideologies HRD TRAITS, SKILLS & CERTIFICATION HRM/HRD DISTINCTIONS NEW TECHNOLOGY • Automation • Software GLOBALIZATION PRODUCTIVITY; QUALITY WORK/SOCIETY	PLANNING; ORGANIZING "STAND-UP STRATEGIES" • Learning styles and modes • Methods, techniques & settings • Learner involvement & internalization BRAIN/MIND STRATEGIES • Accelerated learning • Imaging, metaphor • Cognitive process LEARNING MANAGEMENT SYSTEMS • Learning systems • Automated processes EVALUATION STRATEGIES APPLICATIONS, FOLLOW-UP VARIETIES OF TRAINING • Sales • Customer service • Technical • Supervisory • Management • Etc.	EMPLOYEE DEVELOPMENT • Career access & development • Mentoring • Mobility • Asset-based manpower planning and use • Outplacement WORKPLACE ISSUES • Political, social, economic climate • Interpersonal effectiveness • Ethnic, gender diversity • Equity • Autonomy; power • Literacy • Parental leave • Child care • Health care & fitness • Access to T&D • Access to EAP • Layoff, termination • Misconduct • Work rules	PERFORMANCE APPRAISAL • ISD; other models • Front-end analysis • Template-making for analysis, design, implementation, evaluation of all varieties of training and development MEDIATED TEACHING/LEARNING STRATEGIES, TOOLS • Hypermedia • Hypertext • AII • Other computer • Other media SOCIOTECHNICAL SYSTEMS • Productivity & quality systems • Communication & reporting systems • Accountability systems • Employee involvement and participation	GENERAL MODELS & PHILOSOPHIES MANAGEMENT CAREER PATHS • Reporting relations • Central/decentralizing • Admin. Systems • T & D systems • Strategic vision • Planning; proposals • Executive presentation; other communication • Marketing • Staffing, supervision • Performance monitoring • Contracting, brokering services HRD FINANCE • Budget • Cost/benefit analysis • Profitability • Corporate accounting • Financial reports • Forecasting HRD IMAGE • Internal • External	ORGANISATION DEVELOPMENT: CHANGE ORIENTATIONS & PHILOSOPHIES • OD • T & D • MBO • Corporate culture • Ergonomics EMPOWERMENT STRATEGIES & STRUCTIONS • Participative mgt. • Reticular work groups • Flat & hierarchical • Sociotechnical strategies & accommodations • Other power shifts TRANSFER OF CHANGE AGENTRY SKILLS TO ORGANISATION RESEARCH & WRITING PROFESSIONAL ASSOCIATIONS

Objectives of HRD

The prime objective of human resource development is to facilitate an organisational environment wherein people come first and everything else comes next. The major objectives of HRD are as follows (see figure 1.19) :

1. Equity:

Recognising human being as strategic asset, organisations have to create environment of respect, trust and sense of belongingness. HRD seeks to develop all employees

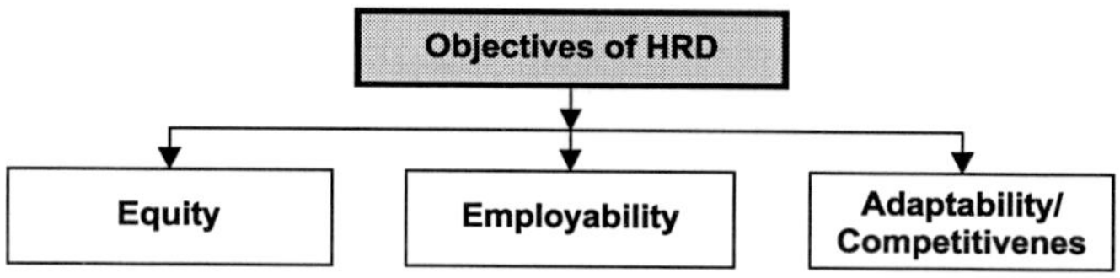

Fig. 1.19 : HRD Objectives

irrespective of caste, colour, creed, religion, language, race, culture, etc. Actions should also be devoted to the disadvantaged categories of employee such as handicapped; socially excluded, immigrated, unemployed, etc. Besides according free development opportunities to employees, HRD must ensure that the organisation creates achievement oriented organisational culture and provides equal opportunities to all employees in matters of career planning and development, career management, promotion, reward, training and development, quality of work life, etc. to enhance their professional abilities. This will require both relational communications through open, supportive and interactive system.

2. Employability:

In today's highly competitive business scenario, employment has lost its true significance given high retrenchment, layoffs, voluntary retirement schemes, etc. and paved the way for employability as flexible employment is increasing. Employability means the ability, skills and competencies of an individual employee to seek gainful employment anywhere. Therefore, HRD needs to continuously upgrade the skills and competencies of the employees to keep them motivated, engaged and retained but also make them employable. HRD should also accord appropriate opportunity of training for young people in search of first occupation and unemployed people.

3. Adaptability/Competitiveness:

HRD facilitates the adaptability of employees to organisational change, which takes place on continuous basis. Therefore, continuous training devoted to development of the professional skills of employees and the re-adaptation of the professional skills of the employees assumes crucial importance for HRD. This will result in both increased employee satisfaction and improved organisational decision-making.

Goals of Human Resource Development

There are specific goals for HRD to achieve in an organisation. All leaders within an organisation should become visibly involved in human resource development programmes affecting organisational culture change and evaluating and articulating policies that govern diversity. To do so, display of leadership that eradicates oppression of all forms is vital. The result is enhanced productivity, profitability, and market responsiveness by achieving a dynamic organisation and work force. This is the first goal of human resource development, to train the leadership.

The main goals of HRD are as follows (see figure 1.20):

1. Facilitating Organisational Effectiveness:

To ensure that adequate number of persons with ability, and experience both in generalist and specialist domains are available at different operative, supervisory and managerial levels in order to facilitate organisational effectiveness.

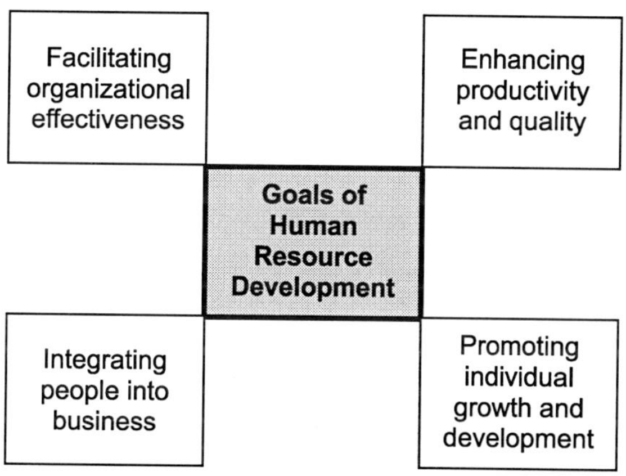

Fig. 1.20 : HRD Goals

Inspiring diversity in the work force helps in promoting an environment conducive to human resource development. Employees want to belong to an organisation that believes in them, no matter what kind of background or culture they come from. They, like their leadership, want to be productive, share in the profits, and be a totally dynamic. Almost no one sets out to do wrong. If human resource development trains the leadership, this goal will be relatively easy to achieve. It is much easier to train people when they have role models to base their behaviours upon.

2. Enhancing Quality and Productivity:

To evolve the human resource development system so that the employees are provided equitable opportunities to move up in the organisation on the basis of their performance and ability so as to enhance quality and productivity. Organisations should ensure that responsibility for results is provided right from the lower level so that employees can develop a sense of independence and self-confidence.

3. Promoting Individual Growth and Development:

The employees' confidence in the HRD policies and practices must be reposed The policy should not only be fair and just but also to be perceived as fair and just so as to promote individual growth and development.

4. Integrating People into Business:

Jobs should be enlarged and enriched so that they are performed in a manner that nurtures team work providing opportunity for learning new and varied skills thus, making the work more satisfying and meaningful. This will ensure integration of human resources into business strategy.

Those employees who show special aptitude for different skills are carefully provided appropriate training and learning experiences so as to generate a larger pool of talents supported and nurtured by HRD interventions.

Thus, in nutshell the goals of human resource development are:

1. To achieve a 'learning organisation';
2. Equipping employees with new skills;
3. Becoming an ongoing process; and
4. Characterised by:
   –Coaching and mentoring culture.
   –Self –directed systems.
   –Learner led.

Importance/Benefits of Human Resource Development

Human potential interest in every employee is vast; it can be further enhanced by various interventions like training, job-rotation, counseling, organisation action, etc.

The importance/benefits of human resource development are (see figure 1.21).

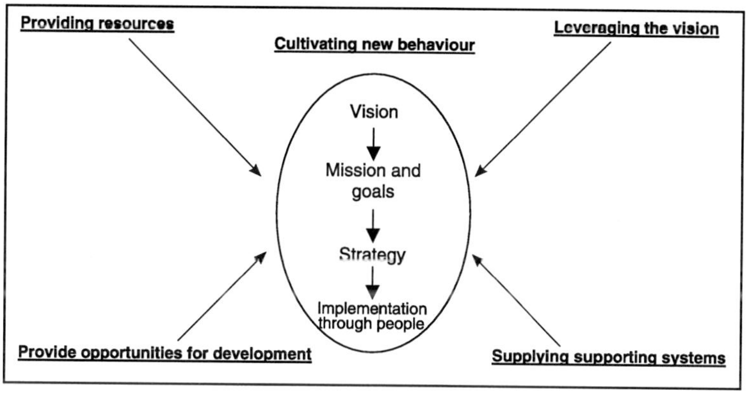

Fig. 1.21 : Importance of HRD

1. Human resource development emphasizes that people are major assets and that an organisation can make full utilization of individual potential by providing a developmental environment and opportunities by encouraging and rewarding innovation and creativity;
2. People who are unable to contribute to the organisation fully due to reasons beyond their control can also give their best if they are taken care of and proper environment and conditions are provided;
3. Competency can be developed in people at any point of time and organisations must encourage competency enhancement;
4. Human resource development provides higher quality of work-life through opportunities of a meaningful career, job satisfaction and professional development;
5. Human resource development philosophy emphasizes human well-being and organisational growth;
6. Human resource development policies are relationship centered and the extent of relationship under human resource development is life long and not merely for 8 hours a day;
7. If an employee perceives a nurturing environment, automatically there would be a positive response to match individual aspirations with organisation's needs;
8. Human resource development processes have to be planned and continuous in order to be effective;
9. A signal to the employees that management believes they are important and should motivate them to acquire new skills and consequent rewards;
10. Human resource development fosters commitment through the communication of values;

11. Human resource development facilitates identification with organisational goals through better employee understanding;
12. Human resource development provides for two-way, open and interactive communication between management and employees;
13. Human resource development focuses on needs satisfaction through achievement and recognition;
14. Human resource development provides job enrichment through training and the acquisition of new skills;
15. Human resource development increased awareness of the importance of change management and consequent adaptability of employees;

Principles of Human Resource Development

The major principles of human resource development are:

1. Principle of Development of Organisational Capability:

Human resource development systems should help the organisation to increase enabling capabilities. The capabilities include: development of human resources in all aspects, organisational health, improvements in problem solving capabilities, diagnostic skills, capabilities to support all the other systems in the organisation, etc.

2. Principle of Potential Maximisation:

Human resource development systems should help individuals to recognize their potential and help them to contribute their best towards the various organisational roles they are expected to perform and excel in it.

3. Principle of Autonomy Maximisation:

Human resource development systems should help maximize individual autonomy through increased responsibility.

4. Principle of Maximum Delegation:

Human resource development systems should facilitate decentralization through delegation and sharing of responsibility.

5. Principle of Participative Decision-making:

Human resource development systems should facilitate participative decision-making.

6. Principle of Change Management:

Human resource development system should attempt to balance the current organisational culture with changing culture;

7. Principle of Periodic Review:

There should be a continuous review and renewal of the human resource development function.

Functions of Human Resource Development

Human resource development seeks to achieve the goals and objectives of an organisation in an effective manner through developing the employees of the organisation. Therefore, HRD performs a number of functions in an organisation as (see figure 1.22) :

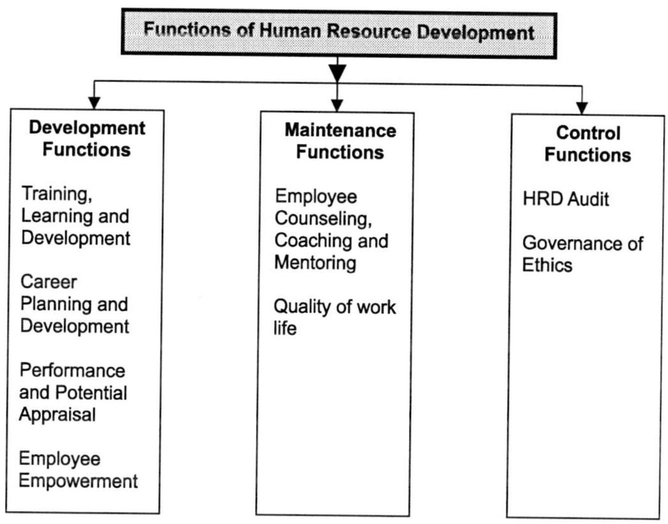

Fig. 1.22 : HRD Functions

1. Development Functions:

These functions relate to the development of the employees and their competencies for effective job performance. Given highly competitive nature of business today it is crucial for organisations to develop the skills and competencies of employees at all levels for achieving the goals and objectives of the organisation effectively. Appropriate programmes such as training of workers/operatives, and supervisors on job specific skills for improved job performance, management development programmes for managers for providing them with opportunities to learn, grow, and change, in hopes of producing over the long term a cadre of managers with the skills necessary to function effectively in the organisation and fostering a learning environment wherein all the employees of the organisation are learners, paving the way for permanent change of behaviour necessary to adopt to a highly dynamic business scenario.

Human resource development programmes like career planning and development of employees is necessary to systematically match career goals and individual capabilities with opportunities for their fulfillment so as to attract, engage and retain best professionals necessary to achieve organisational excellence, and performance and potential appraisal helps to improve job performance on going basis and identify, develop and groom best talents. However, unless employees are empowered to perform their jobs, customer centric business orientation is difficult to practice.

2. Maintenance Functions:

These functions relate to the maintenance of the employee's satisfaction levels by removing grievances, difficulties, and problems, both at professional and personal level. This is necessary to maintain current performance levels of employees. Maintenance programmes such as counseling and coaching provides opportunities to employees to discuss their emotional problems with an objective of reducing it amicably. Other programme of mentoring helps employees to be supported by a more experienced employee to help learn, adapt and become skillful and articulate in one's job.

Human resource development function plays a vital role in fostering an human resource development oriented work culture, which is conducive to professional and personal well-being through which all members of the organisation, through appropriate channels of communication, have some say about the design of their jobs in particular and work environment in general. This implies the importance of quality of work life which is a process by which all members of the organisation, through appropriate channels of communication, have some say about the design of their jobs in particular and work environment in general.

3. Control Functions:

These functions relate to the control mechanisms within the organisation, established to keep synergy between various human resource development programmes, sub-sets and organisation's mission and objectives. Human resource development helps senior leadership of an organisation to keep tab on the current state of human resource development endeavour in attaining competitive advantage through people processes. If any gap is found then immediate corrective action can be taken to rectify. Failure to do so may result in drifting away of human resource development processes and organisational strategy, which will ultimately result in business failure. In order to do so, human resource development audit is undertaken. Human resource development Audit is a comprehensive evaluation of human resource development encompassing strategies, systems, practices, structures, competencies, styles and culture and their appropriateness to achieve the short and long term business goals of the organisation.

Being the conscience keeper for the organisation, human resource development function plays a pivotal role in upholding and adhering employees to ethical behaviour in business through training, motivation and education.

Approaches to Human Resource Development

Integrated systems approach to human resource development has the following elements: (i) A separate and differentiated human resource development department with full time HRD staff. (ii) Four human resource development subsystems and OD, (iii) Interlinkages between the various subsystems, (iv) designed with sound principles in mind, and (v) linked to other subsystems of human resource management function.

As human resource development came to prominence, other frameworks and models came into existence. Some of these are briefly reviewed here.

1. The Strategic HR Framework Approach:

This framework formulated by *Ulrich and Lake* (1990) aims to leverage and/or align human resource development practices to build critical organisational capabilities that enable an organisation to achieve its goals. This framework offers specific tools and paths to identify how an organisation can leverage its human resource development practices. Business strategy, organisational capabilities and human resource development practices are the three important elements in this framework.

2. The Integrative Framework:

The integrative framework offered by *Yeung and Berman* (1997) identifies three paths through which human resource development practices can contribute to business performance: (i) by building organisational capabilities; (ii) by improving employee satisfaction; and (iii) by shaping customer and share holder satisfaction. There must be dynamic changes in human resource development measures to refocus the priorities and resources of the human resource development function. They argued that human resource development measures should be business driven rather than human resource development driven; impact driven rather than activity driven; forward looking and innovative rather than backward looking; and instead of focusing on individual human resource development practices should focus on the entire human resource development system, taking into account synergies existing among all human resource development practices.

3. Human Capital Appraisal Approach:

This approach outlined by *Friedman et al* (1998) of Arthur Anderson consulting Company is based on the belief that there are five stages in the management of human capital: clarification stage, assessment stage, design stage, implementation stage and monitoring stage. There are five areas of human capital management: Recruitment, retention and retirement; rewards and performance management; career development, succession planning and training; organisational structure, and human capital enablers. A 5 X 5 matrix using these five stages and five areas could be used to evaluate and manage the human capital well. For example, in the clarification stage the managers examine their human capital programmes to fit into their strategy and overall culture. They may also examine each of the areas to fit into the strategy, etc.

4. PCMM Approach:

Curtis and team (1995) developed this approach for software organisations. The People Capability Maturity Model (PCMM) aims at providing guidance on how to improve the ability of software organisations to attract, develop, motivate, organize and retain the talent needed to steadily improve their software development capability. A fundamental premise of the maturity framework is that a practice cannot be improved if it cannot be repeated. In an organisation's least mature state, systematic and repeated performance of practices is sporadic. The PCMM describes an evolutionary improvement path from an ad hoc one. Inconsistently performed practices, to a continuously mature, disciplined, and continuously improving development of the knowledge, skills, and motivation of the work force. The PCMM includes practices such as work environment, communication, staffing, managing performance, training, compensation, competency development, career development, team building, and culture development. The PCMM is based on the assumptions that organisations establish and improve their people management practices progress through the following five stages of maturity: initial, repeatable, defined, managed, and optimizing. Each of the maturity levels comprises of several Key Process Areas (KPAs) that identify clusters of related workforce practices. When performed collectively, the practices of a key process area achieve a set of goals considered important for enhancing work force capability.

5. Integrated Systems Approach:

The integrated systems approach envisaged a separate human resource development department for effective designing and implementation of human resource development systems. It envisaged strategy as a starting point and therefore focused on all the systems to achieve business goals and employee satisfaction. It aimed at synergy (like in the integrated approach), proposed the phased evolution of HRD function (like

PCMM approach) and included most of the elements of the Human Capital approach. While each of the latter models have brought to focus one or the other most neglected dimensions that could be good pointers for not getting the best out of HR, the essence is very similar to integrated approach. If the locally developed frameworks are not implemented well for reasons not associated with the framework but those associated with lack of understanding and seriousness, it may be presumed that advanced frameworks are even more difficult to adopt and get results. It is with this view that an attempt is made to assess the current status of human resource development structures and practices in Indian Industry.

6. HRD Score Card Approach:

A recent approach formulated by *Dr. T.V. Rao* (1999) envisages that human resource development interventions in order to make the right business impact should be mature in terms of the human resource development systems, competencies, culture (including styles), and business linkages. The maturity level and the appropriateness of each of the subsystems of human resource development, the appropriateness of the human resource development structures and the level of competencies of HRD staff, line managers, top management, etc.: the human resource development culture (defined in terms of Openness, Collaboration, Trust, Autonomy, Pro-action, Authenticity, Confrontation and Experimentation) and the congruence of the top management and HRD staff styles with human resource development culture, and the extent to which all the systems and practices result in employee satisfaction and customer satisfaction, etc. are assessed through a well formulated HRD audit.

Improving Performance through Human Resource Development

Organisations find themselves dealing with strong competitive markets and/or fast changing technologies. In response, their strategies focus on improving organisational flexibility. Human resources are regarded as a key to competitiveness. Employee learning and related strategies, such as knowledge management/ knowledge sharing and creating a learning culture, are key issues for these organisations.

The role of human resource development professionals is changing from trainer to consultant. Their strategic role is to link human resource development closely to business; their practical role is to provide learning opportunities for employees. The execution of human resource development activities is a shared responsibility of human resource development professionals, managers and employees.

Off-the-job training is still an important strategy, but it must be complemented by strategies to support self-directed and informal learning and to link training with organisational strategy.

People need fair compensation, but money alone does not improve performance. Studies indicate that the positive effects of a salary increase usually last for between six to seven weeks. Meaningful work that is integral to the goals of the organisation, has the respect of fellow employees, and provides opportunities to develop individual skills results in a more sustained level of employee performance. A human resource development system that integrates performance management with organisational goals will ensure that the employees understand how their work relates to and contribute to the success of their organisation. A carefully planned and implemented human resource development system addresses the kinds of employee concerns that can affect performance. Human resource development can improve performance if the following components are an integral part of such system as elaborated below:

1. HRD Responsibility for Fairness in the Workplace:

One important managerial responsibility is making sure that all managers and employees apply human resource development policies on a day-to-day basis and distributes tasks and responsibilities fairly and equitably among employees. When developing an integrated human resource development system, organisation's job classifications and related salary scales should be reviewed to ensure that salaries are appropriate to the level of responsibility and are competitive when compared with local economic conditions. In some cases it may be difficult to correct salary imbalances, but every effort should be made to take corrective action internally to ensure that all employees are receiving fair and equitable compensation.

Organisation's human resource development policies should be reviewed, updated as needed, and make the updated information available to all employees. In addition, it must be ensured that all supervisors and managers are informed about the new human resource development policy and that they apply the rules fairly and equitably to all employees.

2. HRD Responsibility for Setting Work Priorities:

One of the steps to take in strengthening a human resource development system is to make sure that all employees have a current and up-to-date job description that provides them with information about their general duties and responsibilities. The description should clearly describe all job responsibilities and the supervisory relationship. The job description provides the supervisor with a starting point for developing a work plan with the employee.

Because the job description is general, it does not describe the specific responsibilities or performance objectives for which a supervisor may hold an employee accountable in a certain time period. Most employees do not perform all of the duties listed in their job description all the time, even if the job description is up to date, as work and organisational priorities change, a supervisor and employee should conduct work planning and performance review meetings on a periodic basis (e.g. quarterly, semi-annual basis, etc.). This allows them to jointly and systematically plan the specific performance objectives for which the employee will be responsible in a given period. This joint work planning process also helps the supervisor to identify in a timely way the skills and resources that the employee will need to successfully perform the tasks required to meet his work objectives.

3. HRD Responsibility for Encouraging Good Performance:

An important element of a work planning and performance review system is holding joint work planning and performance review meetings on a regular basis. The supervisor and employee should agree on specific performance objectives during these meetings. These agreed-upon objectives become the basis of the next performance review. This system allows both the supervisor and the employee to evaluate performance and to plan ahead for training or other career development activities, if needed. A work planning and performance review system can improve individual employee performance and increase employee motivation. Such a system becomes the basis for creating employee development plan, which will also help to align employee development efforts more closely with the organisation's goals. Ongoing supervision between the periodic work planning and performance review meetings is also the key.

4. HRD Responsibility for Providing Meaningful Work:

Communicating to employees that their work matters is an important element in a human resource development strategy. Engaging in systematic planning and taking steps to make sure that people's day-to-day work directly supports the priorities of the organisation is critical to meeting the organisation's objectives. These objectives represent the strategic areas in which the organisation has decided to focus in a given year, as identified during the organisation's annual planning process. These objectives may vary on an annual basis, depending on changing organisational priorities.

The work planning and performance review process can be linked to the organisation's annual work planning cycle by using the priorities of the organisation, department, or unit as the basis of the joint work planning between each supervisor and his employees. This will help to ensure that the work of each person does matter, and that each person understands how his work is important to the organisation.

5. HRD Staff Development Responsibility:

Making employee development a priority is an important component of a comprehensive human resource development system. Posting job opportunities within the organisation and supporting internal candidates will send a signal that the current experience of employees is valued. A well-managed programme of training and employee development can broaden the skills and competencies of employees and reap many pay-offs. Formal, organized training is only one vehicle for employee development. Other empolyee development strategies include:

-On-the-job learning through mentoring relationships;
-Cross-functional assignments;
-Membership in task forces and committees;
-Additional job assignments; and
-Technical presentations and discussions at staff meetings.

These can all provide the challenge and opportunity needed for personal and professional growth as well as increase the knowledge that people have in common and expose them to new ways of thinking and doing.

Essentials of A Good Human Resource Development System

Good HRD system posses the following qualities:

1. Top management philosophy and understanding of human resource development.
2. Competent HRD staff;
3. Attitude of line managers;
4. Support of union and employees;
5. Use of appropriate human resource development systems;
6. Periodic renewal exercises; and
7. Business relevance of human resource development systems and practices.

Hence, human resource development is about unleashing human capabilities for enhanced organisational performance and impact. This requires such competencies as training and development, performance and potential appraial, career panning and development and employee empowerment (see figure 1.23).

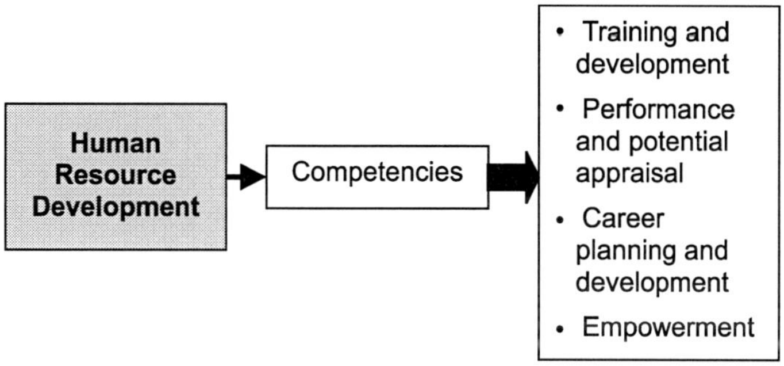

Fig. 1.23 : Competencies for HRD

Competencies of HRD Manager

HRD Managers are becoming increasingly more skilled and have a range of techniques and systems to offer to the line managers. They can contribute in solving complex organisational problems and also administer some of the more complex solutions. The critical competencies of a HRD Manager are as follows (see figure 1.24):

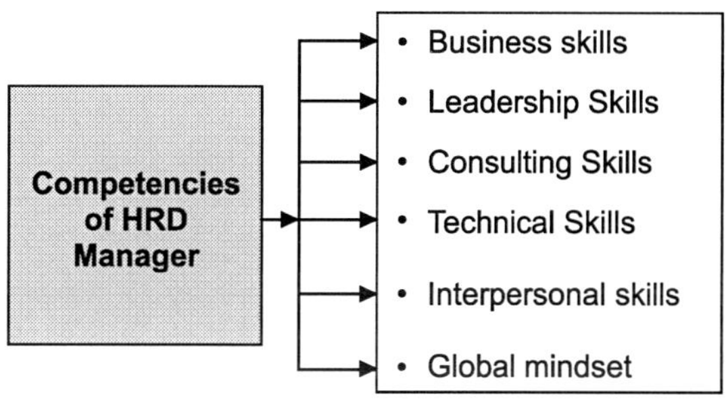

Fig. 1.24 : Competencies of HRD Manager

1. Business skills:

HRD Manager must understand the business of the organisation. Understanding of business processes, technologies and customer expectations helps him to develop appropriate human resource development strategies and systems with an object of developing employee competencies for meeting the business strategy of the organisation.

2. Leadership skills:

HRD Manager must posses' strategic leadership skills to align employee's personal growth and development need with that of the organisation so as to usher in organisational excellence. He must be an employee champion with high degree of personal and professional credibility.

3. Consulting skills:

Human resource development is primarily the responsibility of line managers. HRD Manager has a shared responsibility in this regard. Therefore, HRD Manager has advisory role to play in matters of human resource development programmes in the organisation. He must have good knowledge about latest tools and techniques and must market human resource development programmes to the top management in an articulate manner. He must help line managers in solving various human resource development problems by offering his professional expertise.

4. Technical skills:

HRD Manager must posses' in-depth and up to date knowledge and happenings in the field of human resource development. This is necessary not only to perform his duties and responsibilities well in the organisation, but also to do justice to his consulting role. Good job knowledge is a pre-requisite to his professional credibility.

5. Interpersonal skills:

HRD Manager must be articulate in dealing with people issues. He must thoroughly understand the background of each issue before attempting to offer solution. Since he lacks line authority, therefore lot of persuasive and negotiation skills are required to function effectively. Good interpersonal skills help to achieve the various goals and objectives of human resource development programmes.

6. Global mindset:

HRD Manager must broaden his mindset, and think beyond a particular organisation, industry and nation. Due to globalisation, diversity in workforce is increasing. Organisations now recruit best professionals from the global HR market. Since people come from different backgrounds, embodying divergent views, values and belief, therefore, he must respect these diversities but also must be able to cope well with cultural differences so that 'unity in diversity' can be achieved.

Sofo (1999) argued that senior management's expectations of HRD professionals are that : "they must understand the internal and external factors that impel the need for organisational transformation... assist in the setting the overall strategic direction in relation to HRD... establish appropriate and support structures that communicate, reinforce and institutionalize the new behaviours, values and attitues, and ensure the success and sustainability of the change effort".

Bibliographical reference:

Sofo, F., *Human Resource Development, 1999, Business and Professional Publishing, Warriewood.*

The competencies to be possessed by HRD Managers in a global scenario is summarized in the box as follows.

HRD Manager's Competencies Matrix Toolbox

Behavioural	Technical and Professional
• Approachable and co-operative	• Technology savvy
• Dedicated, determined, enthusiastic Frank and calm	• Continuously upgrading knowledge and skills
• Honest and open-minded	• Excellent analytical ability
• Kind, motivated, patient and prompt	• Systematic in documentation
• Reliable, self confident and spiritual	• Creative, innovative and excellent problem solving aptitude
• Sincere, trustworthy and mature	• Willingness to learn and excel
• Humble, optimistic and cheerful	• Accept new challenges
• Energetic, dynamic, responsible and Ambitious	• Effective communication skills
• Ready to accept mistakes	• Good leadership qualities
• Good time management	• Knowledge sharing attitude

Role and Responsibilities of HRD Manager

HRD Manager has to function under various constraints – internal and external. He has to perform a very challenging and demanding job. The main roles and responsibilities are as follows (see figure 1.25).

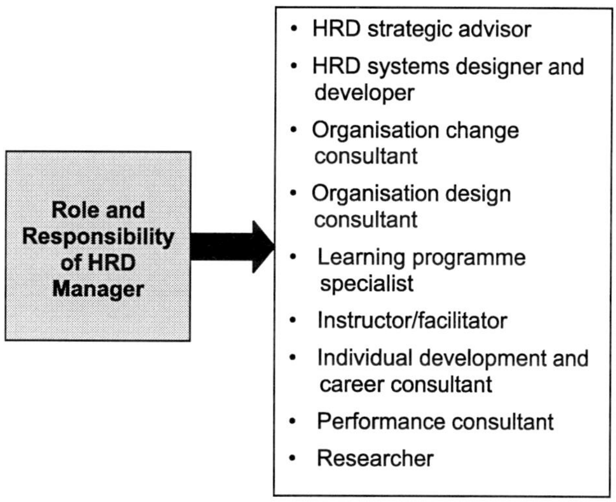

Fig. 1.25 : Roles & Responsibilites of HRD Manager

1. HRD strategic advisor:

In this role, the issues and trends concerning an organisation's external and internal people are brought to the attention of the strategic decision makers.

2. HRD systems designer and developer:

This role involves designing and preparing HRD systems for implementation so that human resource development systems and actions are mutually reinforcing and have maximum impact on organisational performance, development and endurance.

3. Organisation change consultant:

This role entails facilitating the development and implementation of strategies for transforming organisations.

4. Organisation design consultant:

This role involves identifying the work required to fulfill organisational strategies. It also involves organizing the work so that it makes efficient and effective use of resources.

5. Learning programme specialist:

In this role, learning needs are identified to design and develop structured learning programmes and materials in a variety of media formats for self-study and workshop or electronic delivery.

6. Instructor/facilitator:

This is an increasingly difficult role. In it information is presented, structural learning experiences are lead and group discussions and group processes facilitated.

7. Individual development and career consultant:

This role involves helping people assess their competencies, values and goals so they can identify, plan, and implement development actions.

8. Performance consultant:

This role means assisting a group or individuals to add value in the workplace. It's a coaching and consulting role in which HRD people perform both analytical and systems-design work.

9. Researcher:

This role involves assessing HRD practices and programs and their impact empirically. It also means communicating results so that the organisation and its people accelerate their change and development.

Current Leading Ideas in Human Resource Development

Given the dynamic changes in the field of human resource development, various ideas have come up for due consideration and action by organisations and individuals as discussed below:

1. Linking development to organisational strategy:

The capabilities of employees of an organisation largely determine its competitiveness. Thus, development of people can influence strategy of the organisation. Linking to strategy brings relevance to training, learning and development process by attending to the needs for learning that emerge from considering the strategic direction and goals of the organisation. The strategic linkage facilitates for prioritizing learning areas that can contribute directly to the organisation's goals and objectives.

2. Organisational learning:

Employees are in close touch with customers and suppliers and therefore have better understanding of external environment and therefore can provide better insight into various business issues. Organisations should accord opportunities to employees to further sharpen their skills and competencies in dealing with external environment and transform mistakes into opportunities for learning. "Five disciplines" key to achieving an effective learning organisation are:

- Personal mastery
- Mental models
- Shared vision
- Team learning
- Systems thinking

Organisational learning entails:

- An organisational philosophy that exists in many forms;
- No clear consensus as to the definition;
- Shared characteristics;
- Providing continuous learning opportunities;
- Using learning to reach individual and organisational goals;
- Linking individual performance with organisational performance;
- Fostering inquiry and dialog by making it safe for people to share openly and take risks;
- Embracing creative tension as a source of energy and organisational renewal; and
- Being continuously aware of and interactive with their environments;

3. Improved organisational communication:

Sharing issues, information and concerns within an organisation amongst employees helps to develop feeling of ownership. Employees are encouraged to contribute their best to the organisation for better and fruitful shared future. Therefore, improvement in communication builds commitment and motivation in the employee's minds and hearts.

4. Linking learning to work:

Linking learning to work helps employees to think deeply about their work needs and aspiration so that what they need to master, improve or change is set forth. Such attitude empowers employees to bring training and development results to their workstations more effectively for improved business results.

5. Knowledge management:

Knowledge Management is a process through which organisations generate value from their intellectual and knowledge-based assets. It is a way of managing an organisation, given that organisations are based on knowledge. Managing knowledge entails managing learning systems and their efficiency.

Knowledge is a fluid mix of contextual information, values, experiences and expertise. For an organisation this resides within employees and represents a source of creativity, innovation and adaptability to change. Knowledge management is an explicit system implemented to use this capital. In a global economy, knowledge may be an organisation's greatest competitive advantage. A knowledge advantage is a sustainable advantage. In near future, learning will be integrated into global performance support system.

6. Focus on training and development for gaining competitive advantage:

The purpose of any business includes achieve a competitive advantage, maintain a competitive advantage, earn above average returns and operate ethically and legally. Effective training and development programmes helps to Improve employee efficiency and effectiveness, which can build brand loyalty, to overcome competition.

7. Empowering employees:

Most of the employees who are in touch with the customers and suppliers are lower level employees who hardly have any decision making power. Empowering such employees helps employees to solve customers and supplier's problems, which bring customer satisfaction and help in building better image of the organisation. An organisation with better image ropes in increased customer loyalty.

8. Employee responsible for self-learning and development:

Organisations must encourage and facilitate individuals to take time alone to consider their own learning and development issues and the ways of doing it. Individuals must take full control of their own learning and development, rather than solely relying on their organisations and superiors, but also explore various other sources of learning such as peers, internet, self-study of books, journals, etc.

9. Talent management and leadership development:

One of the changes brought about by the new economy places organisations in a previously unknown scenario: the struggle to attract, engage and retain best professionals. There has been a shift from labour supply market to a labour demand market in which the search for best professionals is at a premium. This is something, which only a few years ago would have been impossible to believe. The individual is now in a privileged position and it is the organisation, which has to prove its worth in order to gain their professional services. This is essentially talent management, which may be defined as an integrated process that proactively plans and forecasts future talent needs, accelerates new hire's time to contribution, helps to retain key players, keeps the entire workforce engaged and facilitates the most effective deployment of talent within the organisation.

Talent management enhances an organisation's agility, responsiveness and capability to compete and gain business success in a global economy.

The scarcest resource in the world today is the leadership, which is capable of continuously transforming organisation to win in tomorrow's world. Given the speed of change facing business today, the need for effective leadership who can formulate and execute business strategies to produce desired results is critical to the competitiveness and very survival of an organisation.

10. E-Learning and integration of Information Technology and Human Resource Development:

Given globalisation of economy and business and revolutions in information technology, enormous data, information and transactions takes place in flash of the time. Human resource development can take advantage of this information technology revolution by developing IT friendly human resource development processes, programmes and systems to increase reach to employees in the shortest possible and thereby making human resource development processes, programmes and systems more responsive, dependable, employee friendly and cost saving. Human resource development programmes of learning, training, career information, performance appraisal, etc. can be more effectively used by using IT.

New Trends in Human Resource Development

- Building and maintaining trust by means of openness, transparency, and accountability
- Surmount the challenges posed by increasing complex conditions of the modern global economy
- Face successfully inescapable technological and scientific change from Internet as a marketing tool to the organisational impact of information technology
- Changing role from teaching skills and knowledge to business needs based knowledge creation and knowledge sharing

Organisation of Human Resource Development Function

Human resource development being a process for developing competitiveness of the organisation follows a specific model of organising. The generic model of organisation of HRD function in large organisation is depicted in figure 1.26.

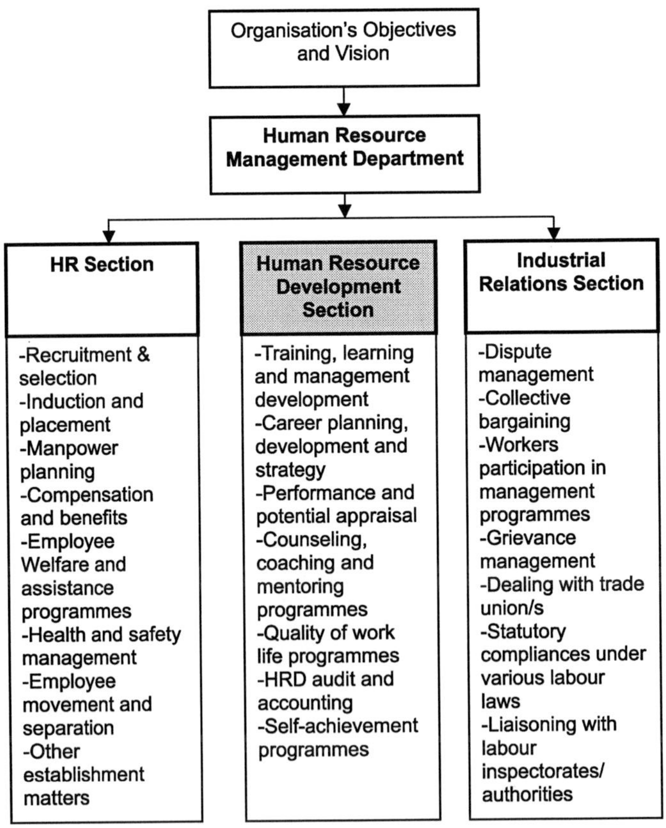

Fig. 1.26 : Organization of HRD function

Human Resource Development Barriers

Human resource development faces under various constraints in the organisational context. There are number of factors and reasons for this. One of the major factors is that the concept of HRD is still in an evolutionary phase. There are lot of difference amongst scholars and practitioners regarding its content and methodology.

Some of the major reasons of HRD barriers are as under:

1. Lack of management reinforcement:

In many organisations, either HRD function does not exist or is not upto the mark. This is because the top management does not propagate the HRD philosophy and does not view it as value adding function in the context of business strategy. They believe that is a soft function, which is sufficed by some training programmes being conducted over a period of time. Also, they consider HRD to be expenditure, which is drain on the valuable resources of the organisation. Such organisations focus on technology and better financial management as a strategic recourse. Human resources are not considered as a strategic asset.

2. Non-supportive organisation culture:

Sometimes organisational culture inhibits development of HRD in the organisation. One main reason is the misconception that training and HRD are one and the same. However, it is not so. Employees feel that HRD facilitates some training programme which does not either enhance their employability prospects or there are no tangible benefits attached to such programmes. It is felt that only marginal (poor) performers need training/HRD. Such mindsets of people hinder development of HRD in an organisation.

3. Interference from work environment:

Although HRD is essentially a line function, but many line managers considers this a waste of time and resources. They feel that HRD professionals do not understand business and their difficulties. Instead they thrust on them a number of HRD programmes, for which they hardly have time. Therefore, they do not educate their employees on the benefits HRD can bring to them and the organisation, lest they would loose power and authority on their subordinates. Besides that there are numerous line-staff conflicts, which add to the misery of the human resource development function.

4. Lack of business value addition:

Often senior leadership considers HRD their last priority as it is believed that organisation have other important businesses to do. This is because of the lack of professional competence of HRD professionals to align HRD programmes with the business strategies of the organisation. Many HRD managers feel – 'we know HRD, they (line managers) know business'. Today, the need of the hour is that HRD functionaries must understand business of the organisation in order to contribute effectively to its bottom line. This results in effective barrier to HRD.

Ethical Dimension and Issues in Human Resource Development

Human Resource Development is the processes of ensuring that the skills, knowledge, abilities and performance of the workforce meet current and future organisational and individual needs through developing, implementing and evaluating activities and programmes addressing employee training and development, change and performance management and the unique needs of particular employee groups.

Before assessing the ethical issues and dimensions in HRD, it is worth considering as to whether HRD is a mature discipline or not? We believe it is for the reasons shown below:

HRD: A mature discipline?

- Scientific/philosophical rigour
- Critical evaluation
- Complex synthesis
- Analytical explanation
- Technical application
- Contextual understanding
- Descriptive knowledge and categorisation

Ethics is a code of moral principles and values that governs the behaviours of a person or group with respect to what is right or wrong (*Daft: 2004*). Simply putting, ethics means 'accepted behaviour'. Organisations need to evolve programmes, practices and systems designed to motivate, measure and monitor an organisation's ethical performance. Prime Drivers for this imperative are a) Employees, through their interest in having fulfilling careers and their need for confidence in the ethical conduct of their organisations and b) Customers, through their increasing demands for services. Human resources are at the center stage of every organisation and are the main source of wealth creation. Human resources are the repositories of knowledge – explicit and implicit and are the generators of value; they are also the transmitters of value.

Ethics suffer when business is bad. Risks upon reputation could arise from:

- Management de-layering;
- Performance pressures;
- Expansion & growth;
- Globalization of operations; and
- Increasing media exposure.

Businesses are expected to contribute to global and human resource development. Ethics in the context of human resource development is the amalgamation of various linkages to employees, organisation's own norms, external stakeholders and society at large. Ethical concerns in HRD have four dimensions as depicted in figure 1.27.

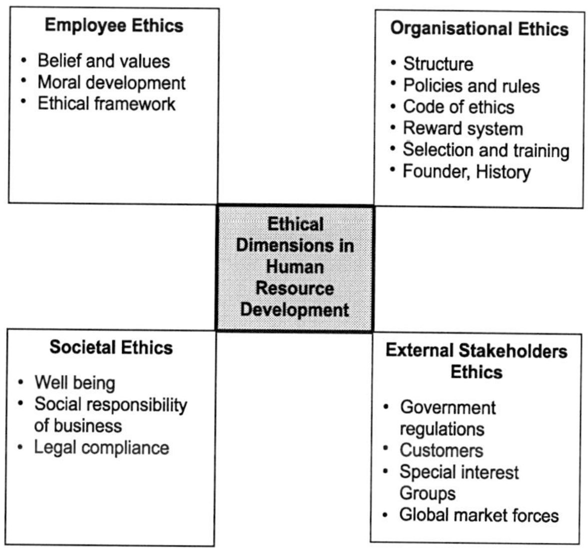

Fig. 1.27 : Ethical Dimension of HRD

The task of building values has to begin with the individual employee himself. It also depends on organisation, external stakeholders such as customers and government and society. Ethics can be transmitted because the human mind and behaviour is always open to learn, de-learn and re-learn continuously.

The values and ethics emerge from the people individually and collectively and get operationalised by the human resource. The role of HRD Manager in this process takes several objectives: create the environment for understanding and assimilation, codify core values, design an ethical charter, develop and transmit awareness, institutionalize value and ethics and revisit codes and systems.

Ethical conduct is more easily transmitted within an organisation by designing strategies and action programmes, which are ethical. The training function is essential to create awareness about values and ethics. Designing mission and vision statements, creating motivations, which are wholesome and positive, identifying strategies, which are positive, transmit values and ethical practices and through decision-making processes, transmitting the message that values and ethical dispensation are as essential as the bottom line.

External stakeholders such as government formulate various codes of ethical conduct for the organisations through legislative measures. In India, good governance norms are being stipulated by SEBI (Securities and Exchange Board of India) through various directives, circulars, provision of the Companies Act, 1965 and various statutory monitoring mechanisms. Customers, being the king, is lately been putting increasing pressures on the organisations in one hand and the government on the other hand, for increased ethical behaviour. Judiciary has also intervened in corporate social responsibility issues being brought to its notice by general public and/or NGOs.

Society norms on values and ethics also influence the conduct of individual employees and organisation. Individual employees in the process of socialization have been taught and imbibed social values through different agencies such as family and educational institutions. Organisations being part of the social system reflects predominant values and moral of the society.

Ethical Issues and Concerns in Human Resource Development

- Employee corruption potential and propensity
- Fair and equitable assessment of performance of employees
- Misuse of power and authority by Management
- Misuse of assets of the organisation by employees and management
- Conflict of interest
- Sexual harassment
- Senior Management Role
- Values Based Leadership
- Assessment of employees' potential for growth and development in the organisation
- Change management programmes and activities
- Techniques to assess HRD programme effectiveness (for example, satisfaction, learning and job performance of programme participants and organisational outcomes such as turnover and productivity)
- Opportunities for employees to raise their integrity questions and concerns
- Level of commitment and adherence of employees, managers and management to ethical aspects of business.

Emerging Dimensions in Human Resource Development

The workplace dynamics is undergoing sea change and human resource will be required to set need standards of increased productivity, improved performance and manage self-learning process in new and innovative ways because the rules determining successful organisation shall be entirely different in future than those of now. As HRD practitioners create rather than just respond, they will seek leverage and ways to help managers, teams, and individuals take charge of their own human resource practices. According to *Mc Lagan* "HRD may be the only function, which is in a clear position to represent human ethics and morality". It is in the following roles that the present HRD professionals are challenged to create new ways to address the human resource issues.

Accordingly, in the new century various emerging dimensions in human resource development are expected to be as, briefly capitulated below:

1. Plans and programmes around corporate social responsibility (a business approach that creates stakeholder value by embracing opportunities and managing risks deriving from economic, environmental and social developments) are bound to increase with the gradual distancing of the state from community activities. The corporate sector will be expected to play the role of the state wherever possible. The ability to form and sustain profitable partnership will become a key managerial competence.
2. Understanding oneself and following a partnering process are the keys to developing superior relationships.
3. Corporate sector would be expected to play more proactive role in dealing with non-traditional social issues. The organisation, in turn, would require more managers who are capable of participating in public policy debates.
4. Due to increased competition, the budget and funds meant for various developmental functions such as training, corporate social responsibility, etc. will be under great pressure. Efficacy in expenditure will be of paramount importance.
5. Competition will focus on customer service. Ability to provide good customer service will be included in the performance contract of every employee for better customer orientation.
6. Visibility, reputation and image will play increasingly important role in corporate decision-making and developmental issues around conflicts resolution, effective negotiation, leadership style, management skills, etc. will gain critical importance.

7. In future organisation shall be primarily concerned with:
    - Exploring the way tasks can be done;
    - Evolving new ways of working;
    - Leading improvisation;
    - Responding to a changing environment;
    - Be concerned with tacit knowledge;
    - Realising knowledge is web-like;
    - Helping bottom up generation of learning; and
    - Responding to invention;
8. Rather than being about imparting knowledge, capabilities and behaviours to employees, organisations in future shall be learning from employees, and then sharing that learning with all.
9. HRD shall not remain the sole prerogative of trainers or managers. It shall be about capturing and mapping knowledge gained from peoples' experience at work.
10. There will be increasing shift from e-learning to e-HRD which will encompass knowledge management, competency management, corporate social responsibility and community of practice. HRD needs to maintain a balance between accommodating the unique needs of a structured and creative workforce and enforcing necessary policies and procedures.

Top 5 Business and HRD Challenges of the Future	
Business Challenges	***HRD Challenges***
1. Globalising the organisation's operations 2. Developing new markets 3. Improving profitability 4. Market share growth 5. Managing ethical behaviour	1. Resourcing and developing talented people 2. Improving organisational capabilities 3. Developing leadership skills 4. Achieving high performance 5. Creating a Quality Work environment

Recent Scenario of Human Resource Development In India

Its no secret that employee's attitudes about their jobs, their benefits and their employers can range from exuberant to sour. What's less well known and harder to find out is exactly what matters to specific types of employees and how effective various types of HRD policies, practices, strategies and workplace characteristics are required in spurring employee productivity and retention.

Since human resource development and management is culture sensitive, therefore we shall examine the recent scenario of HRD in Indian context by having a brief preview of HRD scenario in the global context as discussed below:

More and more employers are assessing the value returned from each dollar spent on employees. They are targeting specific programmes and practice to the employees that value them the most and are becoming more important than ever. Determining what matters most to employees and aligning expenditures with priorities is a strategic challenge for HRD function. Employee change continuously due, in part, to changes in personal preferences but also in part to the chum that occurs as employees leave and new ones enter the organisation. However, it is neither cost effective nor practical to satisfy every employee. Therefore, understanding employees and issues they face holds the key to the function to respond quickly.

Discerning employee's priorities can pose immense difficulties. A Job Satisfaction Survey conducted by SHRM (Society of Human Resource Management) and CNNfn (Financial Network of CNN News Group) brings forth the followings:

RESULTS OF JOB SATISFACTION SURVEY	
ACCORDING TO EMPLOYEES (Rank wise)	**ACCORDING TO HRD PROFESSIONALS (Rank Wise)**
1. Benefits 2. Compensation/pay 3. Feeling safe in the work environment 4. Job security 5. Flexibility to balance work/life issues 6. Communication between employees and senior management 7. Relationship with immediate supervisor 8. Management recognition of employee job performance 9. Opportunities to use skills/abilities 10. The work itself 11. Overall corporate culture 12. Autonomy and independence 13. Career development opportunities 14. Meaningfulness of job 15. Variety of work 16. Career advancement opportunities 17. Contribution of work to organisation's business goals 18. Organisation's commitment to professional development 19. Job specific training 20. Relationship with co-workers 21. Networking	1. Relationship with immediate supervisor 2. Management recognition of employee job performance 3. Benefits 4. Communication between employees and senior 5. Compensation/pay 6. Opportunities to use skills/abilities 7. Flexibility to balance work/life issues 8. Career development opportunities 9. Job security 10. Organisation's commitment to professional development 11. Job specific training 12. Career advancement opportunities 13. Feeling safe in the work environment 14. The work itself 15. Relationship with co-workers 16. Overall corporate culture 17. Autonomy and independence 18. Contribution of work to organisation's business goals 19. Meaningfulness of job 20. Variety of work 21. Networking

Of the 21 factors in the job satisfaction survey, HRD professionals and employees differed on the relative importance of all but one. Now the question arises whether HRD professionals are out of touch with the attitudes among their own particular employees. Perhaps, in some organisations, HRD function is very much in tune with what their employees are thinking, while in some others the gap may be larger.

Finding out what really matters to employees so that the organisation can maximize its investment in human resources is not an incidental undertaking. There are costs involved in doing surveys and in analyzing their results and there are additional costs if an organisation does not show that it values the effort.

Thus, it is clear that core HRD tools, tactics and programmes remains the same however employee needs and priorities have changed and indeed changing. Employee's value greatly impact professional development, job specific training and learning, career development and empowerment more than anything else, except compensation. Employees are increasingly emphasizing opportunities for their development in order to enhance their productive contribution to the organisation and derive job satisfaction at the same time.

Hence, organisations understand, have adopted and implemented HRD programmes and practices as part of overall business planning. The difference however lies in the prioritization of various HRD issues and concerns. Now let us examine the HRD scenario in the Indian context.

With progressive developments in management science and practice, numerous programme, policies and systems has been designed to influence or adapt employee attitudes and behaviours to create capabilities and competencies. This is inevitable due to internalization, liberalization, growing competition and changing environment.

Post 1991, India started its phased economic restructuring to provide domestic organisations the time and competencies to face greater competition. The liberalization paved the way for integration of Indian economy with the global economy. It opened up many opportunities for growth through the removal of artificial barriers on pricing and output decisions, investments, mergers and acquisitions, joint ventures, technology imports, import of foreign capital, etc. This enabled Indian organisations an opportunity to expand, diversify, integrate and globalise more freely.

Liberalisation has resulted in sudden and increased levels of competition for Indian organisations from multinational firms, globalisation and internalization of domestic businesses, concerns for total quality management, incentives to export, demographic changes in the employee profile, retraining and redeployment of workforce, focus on performance appraisal and career management. Thus, with liberalization there is an increasing pressure on organisations in India to change from indigenous, costly, sub-optimal levels of technology to performance based, competitive and higher technology provisions.

Indian organisations have to develop the workforce capable of taking up the challenges thrown by the new economic environment. To tackle this challenging situation, Indian academics and practitioners have both advocated the adoption of the concept of human resource development (HRD). The adoption of professionalised HRD practices in India is a recent phenomenon, but has gained momentum in the past ten years. Organisations are now asking their HRD departments for innovative approaches and solutions to improve productivity and the quality of work life, while aptly coping with an environment of high uncertainty and intense global competition. This requires Indian organisations to develop a diverse workforce with competitive skill sets. This is difficult given the diverse socio-economic background of Indian workforce coupled with antagonistic nature of trade unions and colonial time cumbersome labour laws. The challenges for human resource development are:

- Changing workforce demographics;
- Competing in global economy;

- Eliminating the skills gap;
- Need for lifelong learning; and
- Need for organisational learning.

The scenario of human resource development in India is characterized by:

1. Lack of adoption of innovative HRD practices in unionized organisations due to lack of co-operative attitude among trade unionists.
2. Larger organisations have been able to adopt HRD practices fully due to various costs, resources and expertise involved. *Sparrow and Budhwar* (1997) in their study of 137 fully owned Indian organisations with more than 200 employees, located in North, Central and Western Indian states within six manufacturing sectors of food processing, plastics, steel, textiles, pharmaceuticals and footwear suggest that they are still not geared to adopt HRD programmes.
3. Organisations with foreign participation have more extensive and early implementation of HRD programmes and practices than public and family owned organisations. This is because private sector organisations in India are mostly family owned and operated and they want to concentrate on core competencies and focus on capacity enhancement while the public sector largely grapples with high degree of bureaucracy, red tapeism, high power distance between management and employees and low level of employee empowerment.
4. Indian organisations, which are trying to be competitive by involving the services of international management consultants, have been found to favour HRD programmes and practices. This is because international consultants propound those HRD strategies such as training, performance appraisal, career management; reward mechanisms, etc., which are key to performance improvement.
5. Organisations with stronger leadership have been able to implement HRD programmes and practices. This is because most of the Indian organisations seem to have rhetoric belief such as 'change is constant', 'only quality ensures survival', 'products, not people are paramount' and 'information is everything', etc. while the main challenges before the chief executives are to create flexible systems, to develop a culture of excellence, to facilitate teamwork and empower employees, and to speed up and decentralize data flows. A common feature of strong culture organisations in India has been the influential role of top management in development of human resources issues and institutionalizing practices.
6. Lack of professionally managed HRD department. This has resulted in lack of a strategic role in terms of ability to identify, develop and manage support resources

for adoption of HRD programmes and practices. This is primarily due to non-possession of current knowledge base and the ability to research new developments via methods of benchmarking and networking.

Hence, it is the institutional pressures that have influenced the adoption of HRD programmes and practices in the post liberalization scenario in India. However, the HRD scenario in India is not so grim. Due to liberalization of the Indian economy and subsequent opening of the Indian market to global competition has compelled many Indian organisations to embrace various HRD programmes. Most notable HRD organisations are L&T, SBI, HLL, IOC, ABB, ONGC, TISCO, etc.

However, even after 29 years of birth of professional HRD with L&T by IIMA professors (*Dr. T.V. Rao & Dr. Udai Pareek: 1975*) in India, still HRD is struggling and finding jargons to convince the managements about its importance and need in organisations. HRD has not been able to concentrate and work fully on the issues like:

- Specific contribution to the business challenges;
- Evolution of compatible and unique HRD systems and processes;
- Documentation of the need, process and expected results of each and every HRD systems (Justification on Investment- JOI); and
- Translating the outputs of HR systems into financial terms (Return on investment).

The generic functions of HRD like training, appraisal, career planning and development need to be executed more effectively with less manpower and more quality to meet the short-term strategies and goals of the organisation. Organisations which move in this direction of generic and strategic classifications will compete and survive in the markets with increased profits and global presence and obviously HRD function will move in the strategic direction of core culture management which facilitates the core competency of the organisation.

Being an intelligent and value adding HRD person one should always keep in mind that, what we see is not important but why we see? One should not go for a borrowed system and use peripheral coating systems in order to make the HRD presence felt by other departments. It should be properly studied, analyzed and then tested. One best practice in one organisation in a location may turns to be a worst in another part of the globe. All best HRD practices are 'evolved and not borrowed'. So every organisation should evolve their own systems and processes of HRD, which suits their culture and meets their business requirements.

It is worth noting that successful adoption and implementation of HRD programmes and practices is a critical determinant of organisational success and effectiveness in the Indian organisation's context.

Framework of Human Resource Development

Having discussed the nature, concept and various processes of Human Resource Development, we now look at the framework of human resource development as depicted in figure 1.28.

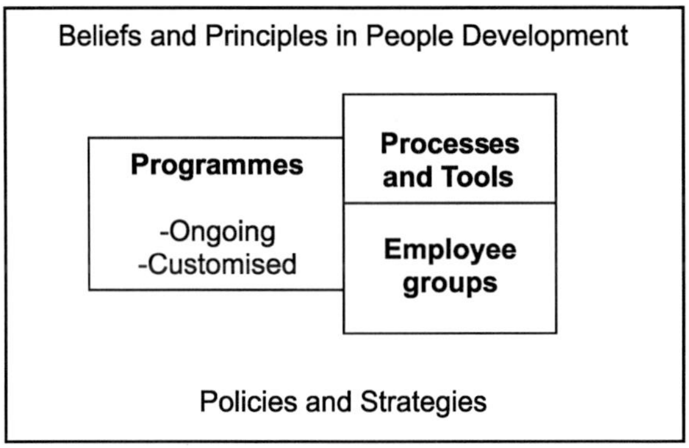

Fig. 1.28 : HRD's Framework

Programmes refer to the approaches to training, learning, performance improvement, methodologies, resources and monitoring activities for maintaining and improving core competences.

Processes and tools refer to the operational issues, individual needs, team needs, external changes, organisational manpower plans, and change initiatives and the ways to grapple with these.

Employee groups refer to various levels of employees such as line personnel, staff personnel, operatives, technical/professional personnel, etc. each group has different needs and therefore requires different programmes, processes and tools.

Human Resource Management and Human Resource Development

Nature and Concept of Human Resource Management:

Human resource management is a general term used to describe a variety of functions aimed at effectively managing an organisation's employees or human resources. Human Resource Management is the comprehensive set of managerial activities and tasks concerned with developing and maintaining a qualified workforce in ways that contribute to organisational effectiveness. It assists organisations to meet their strategic goals by attracting and retaining qualified employees, and managing them effectively while ensuring that the organisation complies with corporate social responsibility.

Due to increased complexity in global business, rapidly changing and highly competitive environment, effective human resource management is vital strategic concern for organisation's of today. The human resource function plays an increasingly important role in an organisation's ultimate success or failure. Where success was once dependent upon an organisation's ability to discover and manage natural resources, success today goes to the organisations that most effectively discover, develop and manage their human resources. In the new economy, raw materials and capital can be brought from anywhere at any time, organisational success will definitely depend on skills, creativity and ideas. There are four essential components of the human development paradigm as mentioned below:

1. Productivity:

Employees must be able to increase their productivity and participate fully in the process of wealth generation and remunerative employment.

2. Equity:

Employees must be able to access equal opportunities. All barriers to economic, social and political opportunities must be eliminated so that they can participate in them.

3. Sustainability:

Access to opportunities must be ensured for present and future generations. All forms of capital – physical, human and environmental must be replenished.

4. Empowerment:

Development must be by the employees and for the employees. They must participate fully in the decisions and processes that shape their lives.

Human resources are part of the overall business objectives and employees are not static resource; they can learn and create. Therefore, it is crucial to integrate HR systems and policies with strategic business planning to reinforce appropriate organisational culture (a pattern of shared basic assumptions that the group learned as it solved its problems of external adaptation and internal integration, that has worked well enough to be considered valid and, therefore, to be taught to new members as the correct way to perceive, think, and feel in relation to these problems, *Schein: 1992*. Organisation culture can be of four types:

1. Clan Culture: based on tradition, loyalty, commitment, teamwork, and socialization.
2. Entrepreneurial Culture: based on risk taking, creativity and dynamism.
3. Market Culture: based on financial goals, competitiveness and profit orientation.
4. Bureaucratic Culture: based on formalisation, rules, procedures and hierarchy.

Definitions:

Human Resource Management has been defined as:

1. "Human Resource Management is the proactive acquisition, retention, and development of human resources necessary for organisational success".

(Robert Kreitner)

2. "Human Resource Management is a strategic process and involves attracting, developing, and maintaining a talented and energetic workforce to support the organisation's mission, objectives and strategies"

(Schermerhorn: 2002)

3. "Human Resource Management is the comprehensive set of managerial activities and tasks concerned with developing and maintaining a qualified workforce – human resources – in ways that contribute to organisational effectiveness".

(Angelo S. DeNisi and Ricky W. Griffin: 2000)

From these definitions, we now look at overview of Human Resource Management as depicted in figure 1.29.

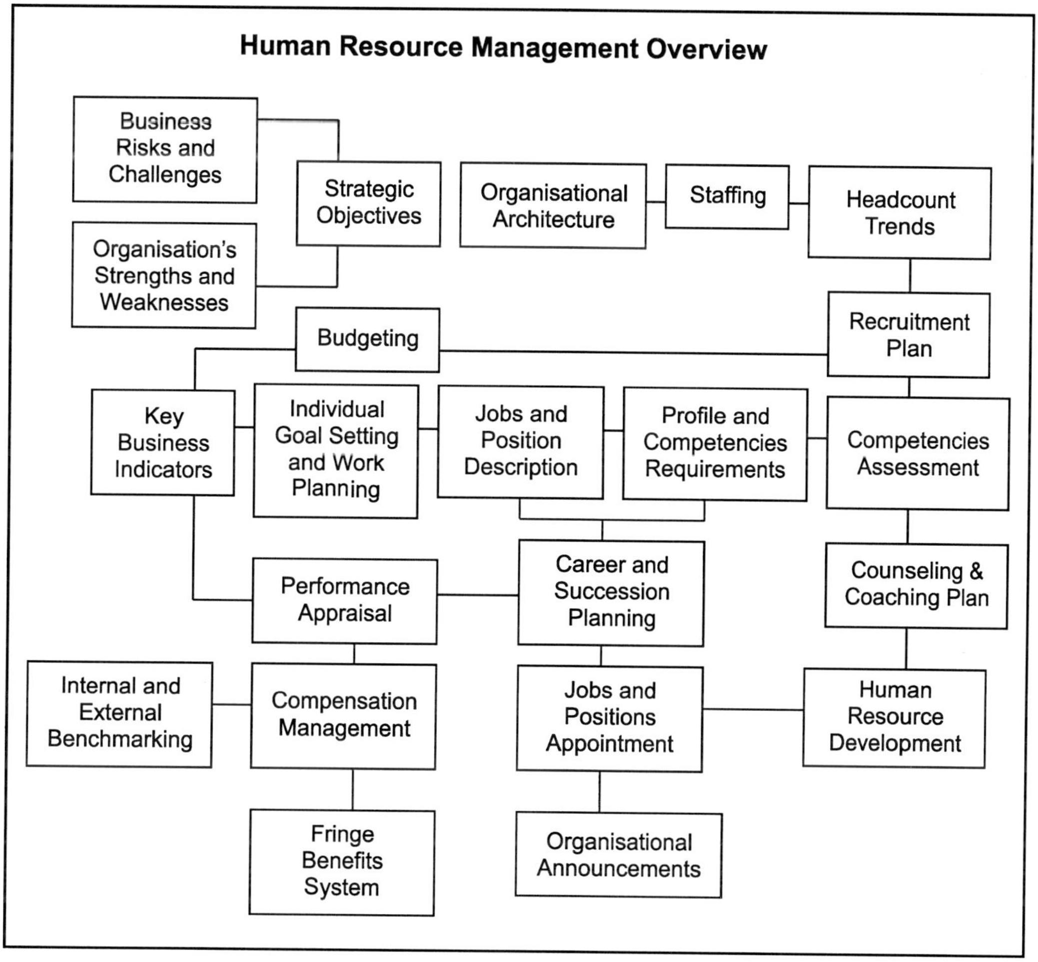

Fig. 1.29 : HRM Overviews

Human Resource Development is a part of Human Resource Management. Inter-linkages of Human Resource Management and Human resource Development is depicted in figure 1.30.

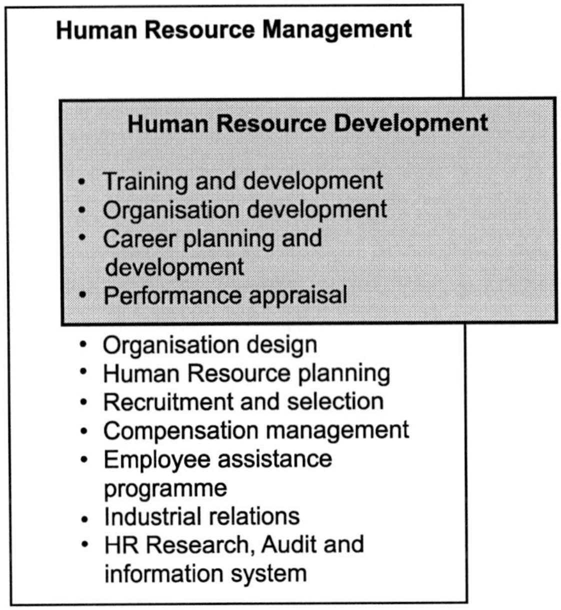

Fig. 1.30 : Interlinkage of HRM & HRD

Increasing complexity and uncertainty of business scenario demands total business performance of an organisation. Total business performance includes financial performance, market performance, and marketing effectiveness, investment in the organisation's future, wealth creation, asset management and effective human resource management. Today, human resource management is a key function to support business in a global and virtual economy and is fraught with extreme challenges and high requirements to continuously add huge value to organisations. A value added HR processes can ensure leadership quality, which develops competencies and commitment of employees for increasing human performance. Competent and committed employees can capture customer satisfaction and loyalty thereby bringing shareholder value and economic success. Thus, human resource management encompasses high commitment, high performance work system, innovative work practices and creative productivity for increasing total business performance.

Objectives of Human Resource Management:

Human Resource Management seeks to achieve the following objectives:

1. Organisational objectives:

- To contribute to organisational effectiveness;
- To help organisations to achieve business objectives; and
- To provide level of service appropriate to the organisation.

2. Societal Objectives:

- To respond to the needs and challenges of society;
- To minimize the adverse impacts on the organisation; and
- To reflect social and ethical concerns.

3. Employee objectives:

- To assist employees in achieving their personal goals; and
- To facilitate congruence of personal and organisational goals.

Human Resource Management Process:

Human Resource Management Process is depicted in figure 1.31.

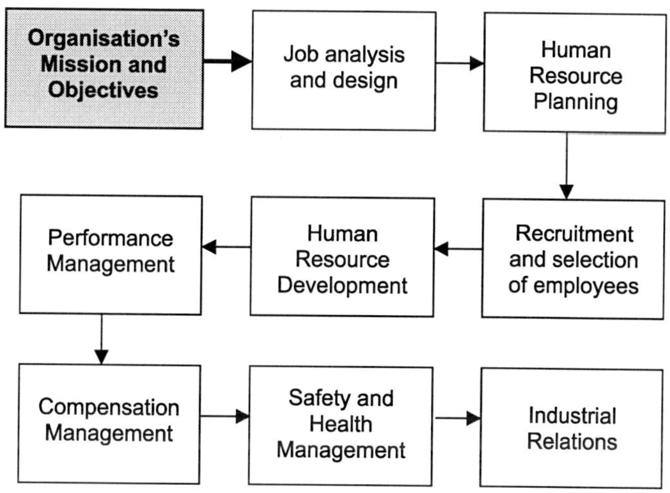

Fig. 1.31 : HRM Process

The various components of the human resource management process are described below:

1. Job analysis and design:

Organisation's objectives are achieved through a process of break up of various tasks, duties and functions. Adequate and competent manpower is required to handle these tasks, duties and functions. Now, to know what tasks, duties and functions are required to be performed for achieving the goals and objectives of the organisation and what kind of human resources are required for optimal performance of these jobs entail job analysis. Staffing begins with job analysis. Job analysis is the process and procedures used to collect and classify information about tasks the organisation needs to complete. It forms the basis for a job description and job specification. It helps in identifying employee characteristics needed to perform a given job or task successfully.

2. Human resource planning:

It is the most vital function of an organisation and is therefore the heart of human resource management. Human resource Planning is critical to the success of organisational strategy and planning. Human resource planning is the process of providing capable and motivated people to carry out the organisation's mission and strategy. Thus, human resource planning is the process of making decisions regarding the acquisition and utilization of human resources. It is a key element in the staffing function, which consists of:

- Recruitment.
- Selection.
- Socialization.

Planning activities is necessary to have the right number of people with the right skills at the right place at the right time. It involves:

- Anticipating the need for employees
- Anticipating the supply of employees
- Planning programmes to ensure that the organisation has the right number of employees with the needed skills when and where they are needed.

The scope of human resource planning varies according to various organisational and environmental factors: competitive practices, business or industry, rigor of business planning, etc.

The steps in human resource planning are:

I. Collecting Information.

II. Forecasting demand for human resources

III. Forecasting supply for human resources

IV. Planning and conducting needed programmmes for reconciling gaps.

The model of human resource planning process is depicted in figure 1.32.

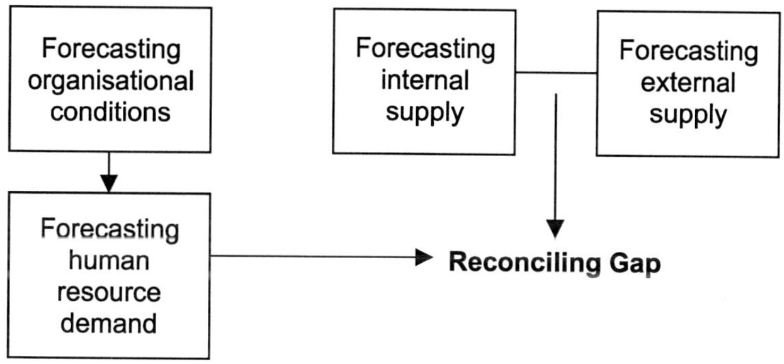

Fig. 1.32 : HRP Model

Human Resource Planning Model:

I. Collecting Information: It involves the following steps as follows:

It involves:

- Knowing about both the internal and external environments; and
- This step is conducted as part of the strategic planning process. Human resource management function is responsible to know it.

–External information: It includes informations on general economy, the industry, technology, and competition; labour market information and trends; unemployment rate; skill availability; and age, race, and sex distributions of the workforce.

–Internal information: It includes short- and long-term organisational plans and strategies as well as information on the current state of human resources in the organisation.

II. Demand Analysis: Forecasting:

It involves:

- Forecasting the demand for employees at various points in the future. Forecasts may be made for various scenarios;
- Forecasting the demand for employees is grounded in information about the past and the present and in assumptions (judgments) about the future of the organisation;
- Goal of forecasting: To determine how many and what type of employees will be needed in the future;

- Most demand forecasting methods will require certain assumptions regarding past trends or productivity ratios;
- Describing how many employees are needed in each job in the organisation and what each employee needs to do in that job; and
- Using Judgmental (Versus) Mathematical methods:

  –Delphi technique
  –Bottom up: Unit based forecasting
  –Top down: Managers or executives
  –Ratio analysis
  –Regression analysis

III. Supply Analysis: Forecasting:

i) Internal Supply Analysis:

It involves:

- The internal supply of employees consists of all individuals currently employed by the organisation;
- Skills Inventories. Skills inventories are manual or computerized systems designed to keep track of employee experience, education, and special abilities;
- The inventory provides information on the current internal HR supply;
- HRIS combines in one system all the information organisations typically keep on employees and on positions. It can be queried about characteristics of the current internal supply of human resources;
- An examination of the current internal inventory of employees and a forecast of internal supply assuming current activities are continued: common methods are:

➢ Markov Analysis (transition matrix)
  – Succession Planning

➢ Replacement Charting; Skills Inventory

➢ Forecast for whom:

➢ Aggregate level (jobs or job families)—below middle management level;

➢ Succession planning—for upper management positions

ii) External Supply Analysis:

It involves:

- A forecasting the quantity, productivity, and deployment of human resources focusing on the supply of employees projected to join the organisation from outside, assuming that current activities to attract and select employees are continued.
- External Demographic Trends
  - Applicant Pool Demographics
  - Applicant Flowcharting (yield ratios)

iii) Gap Analysis:

It is the reconciliation of employee supply and demand through setting objectives and choosing human resource activities:

–Setting objectives

–Generating alternatives

–Assessing alternative activities

–Choosing activity

IV. Planning and conducting needed programmes:

Having identified the gap in demand and supply of human resources, appropriate programmes for recruitment and selection are planned and conducted to fill the manpower gaps.

3. Recruitment and selection of employees:

Recruitment is the process of attracting the best-qualified individuals to apply for a given job. Typical recruitment steps are:

- Advertisement of a position vacancy;
- Preliminary contact with potential job candidates; and
- Preliminary screening to obtain a pool of candidates.

From application pool, selection is undertaken. Selection is a series of steps from initial applicant screening to final hiring of the new employee. Typical selection steps are:

- Completing application materials;
- Conducting an interview;
- Completing any necessary tests;
- Doing a background investigation; and
- Deciding to hire or not to hire.

4. Human resource development:

It is a process of learning, training and development of employees through an organized and systematic approach for achieving organisational excellence. For further details, please refer foregoing discussion.

5. Performance management:

Performance Management is a multi-step process of aligning employees' work behaviours with the strategy and goals of the organisation. It is the process of creating a work environment in which people are enabled to perform to best of their abilities. It is based on the principle of management by agreement rather than management by command. A performance management system is a tool for implementing strategic planning and achieving continuous improvement at all levels of an organisation.

Performance Management essentially consists of the following stages:

- Performance Planning
- Performance Development
- Performance Appraisal
- Reward and Recognition

6. Compensation management:

Compensation management is the strategic process of analyzing, developing, implementing, administering and performing ongoing evaluation of a total compensation system for all employee groups consistent with organisation's objectives and goals. It aims to support the recruitment process by attracting best professionals and retaining the existing talents. Designing of suitable compensation is necessary to keep employees motivated, satisfied and productive. Proper fitment of compensation strategy/design and business strategy of the organisation results in improved employee and organisational performance.

7. Safety and health management:

Safety and health management is the process of analyzing, developing, implementing, administering and performing ongoing evaluation of programmes, policies, practices and services to promote and preserve the physical and mental well-being of individuals in the workplace and to protect individuals and the workplace from unsafe acts, unsafe working conditions, hazards and diseases. Proper safety and health management system helps organisations in maintaining a satisfied, productive and capable workforce.

8. Industrial relations:

Industrial relation primarily refers to the relations between employees and management. It impacts employees, organisations, shareholders and customers. For maintaining harmonious industrial relations, it is essential to balance efficiency and equity between the interests/needs of management and workers. Good industrial relations help management to keep cost of production low and improve quality and productivity.

In the organisational context, human resource management performs the following functions:

1. Integration of traditional personnel management activities;
2. Increased involvement in overall organisational planning and change;
3. Partner in organisational change, creator of organisational culture, and facilitator of organisational commitment and the exercise of initiative;
4. Focus on individual employees rather than on collective management-trade union relations; and
5. Being broad and strategic, involves itself in all managerial functions, regards employees as the single most important organisational asset, being proactive in its responsibilities, and having the objective of enhancing organisational performance and meeting employee needs.

Human Resource Development fit within Human resource Management as depicted in figure 1.33.

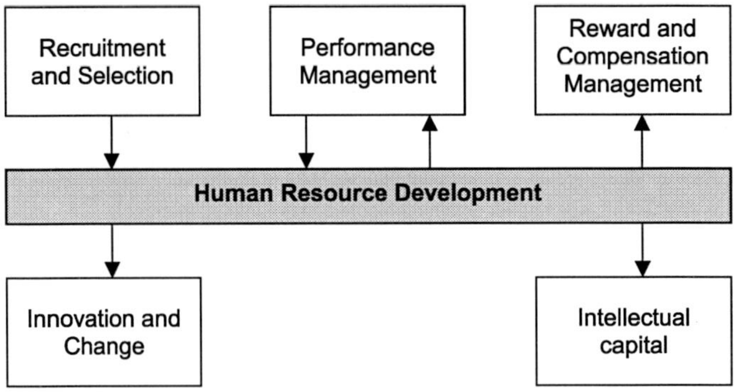

Fig. 1.33 : Fit of HRM & HRD

Code of Ethics For Human Resource Development Professionals

Human Resource Development as a profession is an emerging and interdisciplinary field. It is focused on systematic training and development, career development, and organisation development to improve processes and enhance the learning and performance of individuals, organisations, communities, and society.

As society becomes more dependent on knowledge power, human resource development (HRD) professionals involved in research and practice invariably come to assume greater responsibility, and logically, should be more accountable for their actions.

HRD professionals should aspire to norms of behavior that are well beyond the status quo or lead simply to avoid doing harm. It has to encourage conduct that promotes the welfare of the individuals and organisations being served as well as the betterment of communities and society as a whole. Such norms of behaviour provide moral ties among professionals and set a foundation for professional values.

Various professional bodies have developed codes of professional ethics for human resource development professionals. The most notable being the code of ethics called the Standards on Ethics and Integrity has been developed by Standing Committee on Ethics and Integrity (1999) of the Academy of Human Resource Development to establish the desired standards of behaviour and to bring an increased sense of professionalism to those engaged in HRD activities.

HRD professional being human resource developer should strive for excellence at all times and uphold the dignity of the profession and pride of the nation by practicing the following code of conduct:

1. HRD professionals should provide the highest quality of service in all activities relating to the development of human resources.
2. HRD professionals should maintain a reasonable level of awareness of current research and professional information in their fields of activity and undertake efforts to maintain competence in the skills they use.
3. HRD professionals should rely on professional knowledge while making decisions.
4. HRD professionals should provide appropriate prior information before undertaking any service.
5. HRD professionals should respect diversity of values, attitudes and opinions that differ from them.
6. HRD professionals should not exploit/harass any person or engage in discriminatory practices.
7. HRD professionals should act well within the framework of law and/or public standards.
8. HRD professionals should provide training, supervision and resources to their employees to see that they are able to perform their jobs responsibly, competently and ethically.
9. HRD professional should exercise honesty and integrity in the discharge of professional duties.
10 HRD professional should not take undue advantage of position, power and confidentiality entrusted.
11. If a conflict between professional ethics and organisational demands arises, then HRD professionals should seek to resolve the conflict in a way that permits the fullest adherence to these standards.
12. HRD professionals should co-operate in ethics investigations, proceedings, and the resulting activities of any professional organisation involved with performance improvement, training, instruction or learning.
13. HRD professionals should share knowledge and expertise with other HRD personnel for the enhancement of the image of the profession.
14. HRD professionals should constantly strive to practice the principles, values and skills of a professional human resource developer for the organisation.

15. HRD professionals should exercise honesty and integrity in the discharge of professional duties.

Professional codes of ethics are the foundation for responsible human resource development (HRD) research and practice and can help to define the field of HRD. As business and HRD in turn become more global, normative values and beliefs supported by a mono-cultural professional code of ethics may become problematic and may fail to represent the values, beliefs, and norms of international HRD.

Challenges of Human Resource Development

Human resource development operates in a business environment full of risks and challenges. Human resource development is increasingly in the forefront to enhance the competitiveness of organisations through development of the employees. The major challenges of human resource development are:

1. Changing workforce demographics:

The workforce's nature and composition has undergone significant changes in terms of employee qualifications, skills, and other personal characteristics. With increased spread of education, on one hand, more and more young people with higher qualification and skills are joining the ever-increasing workforce. They have higher aspirations and are highly career minded and want to achieve excellence in short span of time. And on the other hand, increasing number of women employees is making up significant proportion of the workforce. This group of employees have unique set of needs, aspirations and requirements.

Due to globalisation, our world has become borderless. More and more transnational employees are occupying key positions in the organisations. They bring with them unique values, ethics, systems, culture, and etc., which affects the organisational culture significantly. Human resource development has to grapple with this demographic challenge by becoming more focussed on cultural adjustment, better career management and people centric programmes.

2. Competing in global economy:

Globalisation has transformed the way organisation used to do business earlier. Highly complex, complicated and competitive environment has made organisation to focus on their last reliable source of competitive advantage i.e. human resources. Newer and innovative human resource development programmes, strategies and processes are required to continuously develop human competencies and enable people to adapt to a uncertain and complex business environment in order ensure the competitiveness and survival of the organisation.

3. Eliminating the skills gap:

Increasing customer orientation, fast changing technology, increased competition, etc. has resulted in fast obsceneness of skills of the employees. Organisations in their bid to stay afloat have to continuously develop and upgrade skills of their employees through various human resource development programmes. A skills gap can have devastating impact on the organisation's business in terms of lost business opportunity, losing industry leadership position, etc.

4. Need for lifelong learning:

In this new economy, knowledge and creativity is key to competitiveness. Organisations value people for bringing unique competencies to the organisation. Organisational learning has become vital to continuously develop employee skills and competencies for value addition to the organisation. However, organisations cannot meet all the learning requirements of the employees. Employees themselves have to take charge of their learning themselves. Self directed learning is more effective, meaningful and goal oriented. Learning provides knowledge, knowledge provides wisdom and wisdom provides direction, direction provides goal and goal provides will drives self-development, development embraces skill acquisition or upgradations and finally such help to achieve desired results both at individual as well as organisational level. Therefore, employees have to align skill-will matrix in order to have impact on self directed learning which will give competitive advantage to the organisation.

5. Need for organisational learning:

Every organisation intending to stay competitive and agile needs to become a learning organisation, where all employees are learners. Organisational learning is necessary to provide the tool to employees to adapt to fast changes in internal and external environment of the organisation such as competitor strategies, customer expectations, suppliers requirements, quality and productivity, etc. and technological changes, economic changes, political changes and cultural and social changes. Therefore, organisational learning is necessary in order to stay 'organic'.

Hence, human resource development has vital role to play not only to develop human resources but also to align the human resource development arena to the strategic business objectives of the organisation for excellence.

Review and Discussion Questions

Question 1: Trace out the changing paradigm of growth. Why has human resource development assumed greater importance in present times?

Question 2: Discuss the business risks and challenges facing today's organisations. What kinds of organisational changes have resulted from increased global competition and how the human resource development can help to contain those risks and challenges?

Question 3: Define and explain the nature and concept of human resource development. In your view which theoretical foundation of human resource development is more relevant today and why?

Question 4: Explain any three approaches to human resource development. How can human resource development improve performance of an organisation? Give examples from IT industry to support your answer.

Question 5: Enlist the role and responsibilities of a HRD Manager. What are the competencies necessary to effectively discharge the role and responsibilities?

Question 6: What are the newer ideas in human resource development?

Question 7: Explain the ethical dimension and issues in human resource development.

Question 8: Give a critical account of recent scenario of human resource development in India. What are the reasons of its slow progress in the Indian context?

Question 9: Define and explain concept and perspectives on Human Resource Management. Is there any difference between human resource management and human resource development? Justify you answer with examples.

Question 10: Write short notes on:

i) Globalisation
ii) Economic foundation of human resource development
iii) Talent management
iv) Code of ethics for HRD professionals

Exhibit : 1-A

Case Situation

- *Before attempting this section please read Chapter - 14 on Case Study.*
- *Please read the following case situations and answer the questions.*

Q 1. You have joined an old organization as HR Manager. The organization has personnel administration department. How would you market to the top management the necessity of establishing HRD department?

Q 2. You are working in very reputed organization and drawing handsome salary. You have been asked by your superior to manipulate the performance appraisal rating of one of the junior level employees (good performer) so that the employee (average performer) favoured by your superior gets a promotion. What would you do now?

Q 3. Once while you were passing unnoticed by your department (HRD), you overheard one of your subordinates talking face to face to a production supervisor as:

Production supervisor: What does HRD stand for?

HRD personnel: It means human resource department

Production supervisor: Oh! I thought it is human resource development

Being the HRD Manager, what do you conclude from this dialogue? What action plan do you intend to put into practice?

Exhibit: 1 – B

Case Study

- *Before attempting this section please read Chapter - 14 on Case Study.*
- *Please read the following case study and answer all the subsequent questions.*

Introduction to the organization:

The poultry supply company India Ltd. (TPSCIL) was established 25 years ago, to serve a specialized niche in the poultry supply industry. The Company is profit making and has been growing @ 15% per annum. Farmers grow chickens until they are in the right size for processing in the factory of the Company. The work although dirty requires certain skills as the birds must not be frightened or get injured in the process of transportation to the Company.

Its proprietors Mr. Ajit Ranjan Deb, Mr. P.N. Chakravarty and Mr. Sukumar Dutt own the Company. Gradually over time, Mr. P.N. Chakravarty started another business and left the business. Soon afterwards, Mr. Sukumar also left the business, as he got bored with the work.

Mr. Ajit Ranjan Deb, Chief executive with his one manager and 50 workers has been running the show since then.

Brief Description of the Problem:

After 5 years of taking sole charge, Mr. Ajit Ranjan Deb felt three needs for change:

• He could neither see any growth for his organization nor opportunity for personal development.

• He felt quite vulnerable to competition as his business had neither significant material asset nor had employed high technology.

• He wanted more from life and wished to leave the business, however not the same as his partners had gone.

Mr. Ajit Ranjan Deb reported to his wife that he was fed up and she suggested that he could go for an MBA at the local management institute.

After attending the programme, he felt that it was he who was blocking the development of his organization because all these years he has been practicing nice but manipulative management style and it needed change to nice, but open.

He decided and eventually ran a series of training workshops for his employees and hired the services of Mr. Sunil Pandya, a consultant for organization development work. These workshops were eye opener to Mr. Ajit Ranjan Deb as he came to know from his employees:

• 'the only time I switch off my brain is when I am at work'

• 'I have trouble transporting finished goods as many times the traffic cops demands money due to poor condition of the vehicle and I had to pay it as the organization pays no attention to quality of safety equipments being fitted'

- 'no opportunity for our training and development'
- 'no room for our suggestions as nobody is even willing to listen to us'

Questions:

1. What is the link between development of the chief executive and organization development in this case?
2. What is the fundamental problem with TPSCIL? How best can it be solved?
3. How has leadership affected change process in this Company?

CHAPTER

2 Designing HRD System and Developing HRD Strategies

Chapter Synopsis

Human Resource Development is a system within the organisational context. Therefore, HRD strategies can be developed for achieving the objectives of the organisation through various developmental interventions. Systems and strategies of human resource development facilitate effective achievement of mission and objectives of the organisation.

This chapter explains these concepts and strategies for achieving the mission and objectives of the organisation.

This Chapter contains:

HRD systems, HRD strategies, Designing HRD strategy, Future challenges to HRD strategy, HRD model, Review & discussion questions, Case situation and Case study.

Designing HRD System and Developing HRD Strategies

Human Resource Development System

Systems Theory is an interdisciplinary field, which studies systems as a whole. It sees the world in terms of 'systems', where each system is a 'whole' that is more than the sum of its parts, but also itself a 'part' of larger systems. It emphasizes that real systems are open to, and interact with their environments, and that they can acquire qualitatively new properties through emergence, resulting in continual evolution. Business organisations are open systems and that they have to take into account all the forces and factors of the environment within which they have to function. A system has its own objectives, components or elements and a process. It has inputs, outputs and a throughput.

The purpose of HRD system is to build the competencies and commitment of individuals, teams and the entire organisation as a whole through a variety of instruments. The instruments available for an organisation are put into subsystems and become HRD systems or subsystems. Followings are some of the instruments of the subsystems:

- Training;
- Performance appraisal;
- Potential appraisal and development;
- Employee counseling and coaching;
- Career planning and development;
- Mentoring;
- Quality circles and other team based activities;
- Role analysis;
- Organisation development;
- Team building activities; and
- Learning management.

The above instruments help to ensure maximum achievement of the goals of human resource development. For example, training attempts to provide necessary skills and competencies to employees for enhanced organisational effectiveness. The instrument of training is used efficiently, cost-effectively and appropriately, in line with the business strategy of the organisation. It becomes a system by formulating its own objectives; elements, inputs, output and processes, which in turn links to other subsystems of human resource development system.

Human resource development cannot be a series of ad-hoc decisions and practices. It has to be based on a set of predictable practices and measures. As per *Pareek and Rao*, HRD system consists of the following components:

1. Career system:

Employees can be developed through proper application of performance and potential appraisal, career planning and development activities. These activities should be linked to the business strategy of the organisation.

2. Work planning system:

Understanding of organisation's mission and objectives helps employees to plan and realize their work outputs effectively in order to achieve the mission and objectives of the organisation, which can then be reviewed for making appropriate improvements.

3. Development system:

Competencies and skills of employees needs to be continuously developed by the organisation through training, learning, coaching, etc. so that the present and future organisational requirements and challenges can be adequately met.

4. Self-renewal system:

Organisations being interactive social system must ensure their adaptability to their environment through feedback and research related activities. This requires role efficacy, team building, etc. activities for employees.

5. Culture subsystem:

A climate that sets norms, values and culture, and ensures a high level of motivation for employees constitutes culture-building subsystems.

The systems approach to human resource development helps in institutionalizing it and facilitates its contributions towards the mission and objectives of the organisation.

Human resource development being an organisational science, HRD strategies primarily deals with building competencies, commitment and culture in an organisation through various mechanisms/instruments. The maturity of HRD system plays a vital role in the degree of attainment of the mission and objectives of the organisation.

Dr. M.B. Athreya (of IIM-C fame) developed the following integrated model of HRD system* as a management consultant for a leading PSU in India as shown below:

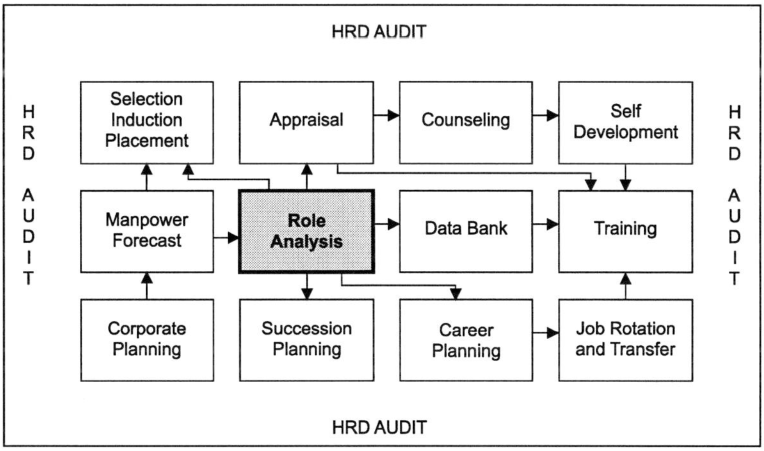

Fig. 2.1 : HRD System in Indian Oil Corporation Ltd.

Human Resource development system begins with role analysis. The various subsets of human resource development such as performance appraisal, counseling, coaching, mentoring, career planning and development, succession planning, training and development, etc. are interwoven around the role analysis system. Role analysis is conducted across the organisation at all levels to ascertain job description, job specification and subsequently employee specification (to fill vacancies) and a data bank is created which contains entire role descriptions of all employees. This provides the framework for analyzing gaps in actual and expected performance of employees and the needed human resource development interventions/initiatives such as creating greater employee commitment, enhancing productivity, ensuring human resource supply, promoting development, managing technologies and promoting customer focus to fill the identified gaps in skills and competencies.

The various subsystems of HRD system are described below:

1. Role analysis:

It is the process of collecting, analyzing and recording information about the requirements of roles in order to provide the basis for a role profile. Role analysis focuses on the demands made on roles holders (employees) in terms of what they

* HRD Audit has been added by the Author in Dr. Athreya's HRD Systems Model of IOCL.

need to know and be able (competency) to deliver as per the expected level of performance. Role analysis is a technique for maximizing human contributions to the organisations.

However, role analysis must be periodically conducted given changes taking place within the organisation's internal and external changes in order to keep role profile relevant to the needs of employees and organisation's strategic plans.

2. Data bank:

It is the process of maintaining systematic information about the individual employees, including history, characteristics, performance record, potential record, mobility and significant achievements.

This data bank becomes the foundations on which various subsets of HRD such as performance appraisal, career planning and development, succession planning, etc. are developed to enhance organisational improvement and effectiveness strategies. These data files are supplied to departments whenever solicited for various employee related decisions and actions.

3. Selection, induction and placement:

It is the process of determining which employee (present or potential) in the applicant pool posses the qualifications necessary to be successful on the job and then acclimatizing him with organisation's processes, people and systems and finally placing him on the relevant job/role. It includes promotion, counselling, compensation and reward administration.

4. Appraisal:

Appraisal is the process by which organisations evaluate the performance of the employees with respect to their suitability in present jobs and assessing potential for future jobs. It also provides a validated means of administering reward system in the organisation. It impacts manpower forecasting, training and development and career planning and development systems.

Summary of information of the performance is sent to data storage for further use.

5. Counseling:

It is the process of dealing with the emotional problems of employees with the general objective of decreasing the tension of the employee. Counseling may be many types and in many forms such as appraisal counseling, disciplinary counseling, career counseling, etc. Counseling facilitates the discussion of the steps the employee can take for improvement.

6. Self-development:

Self-development comprises the development of the self. The term may refer to traditional concepts of education or training but it is also associated with the new age movement through professional development business trainers who offer counseling and coaching of personal transformation and "inner pathways" to solve social and psychological issues.

Being oriented towards exploring and understanding all aspects of self and is vital to taking the initiative to grow and change. This entails asking deeper questions about self, actions, and impact on others. Being curious about what influences one's thinking, what triggers certain emotional reactions, and why one relates to others in a particular way. Having emotional and spiritual competencies provides groundedness, calm, clarity, and foresight in handling difficult situations. Having the courage to make personal changes that are needed, not just in surface behavior (which often doesn't last) but also in fundamental attitudes, beliefs, and underlying psychological structures (which leads to changed behavior that not only lasts but is much more effective). Holding a wider and more inclusive perspective on self, others, and the world around. Understanding how self-development impacts business results and change efforts. Knowing how to create organisational structures that support self-development in others.

7. Training:

Training refers to the systematic process of developing the job related competencies of employees for present and future roles and responsibilities in the organisation. It includes:

- Assessing employee training needs;
- Setting performance goals;
- Planning developmental strategies accordingly;
- Looking for available internal and external training aids;
- Developing training strategies, programmes and modules; and
- Evaluating training efforts.

Training programmes are designed to increase employee's knowledge, skills and abilities to foster job performance improvement.

8. Manpower forecast:

It is the process of determining the number of employees needed at some future time and estimating the number of current employees who will be available to fill various jobs at some future time. Manpower planning is completed based on forecast, internal search and manpower audit. It is vital to the very survival of an organisation.

9. Corporate planning:

It is the process of formulation of method/s by which organisation's goals and objectives are to be achieved. Corporate planning is the founding director of HRD system.

10. Succession planning:

It is the process of getting the right number of people with the right skills, experiences and competencies in the right jobs at the right time. Succession Planning is designed to ensure the continued effective performance of an organisation by working to ensure the development and replacement of key people over time.

11. Career planning:

Career planning is a process of systematically matching career goals and individual capabilities with opportunities for their fulfillment. It involves:

- Disseminating career information to all employees;
- Planning career paths for different groups of employees and individuals; and
- Planning developmental strategies with employees of low potential.

12. Job rotation and transfer:

Job Rotation is the process of systematically moving employees from one job to another with a specific objective.

However, organisations cannot improve performance continuously without periodic organisational diagnosis, team building, role development and job redesign. Since, the entire process of human resource development starts with self and extends to others, the role of organisation development is crucial to organisations. Simply putting, 'organisation development' = organisational growth + organisational change. *Ralph Stacy (1993)* defines Organisation Development as "a long-term programme of interventions in the social, psychological and cultural belief systems of an organisation. These interventions are based on certain principles and practices which are assumed to lead to greater organisational effectiveness". Organisation development is strategic tool used by organisations to maintain a state of fit between internal and external environment.

Role analysis creates a powerful framework for people proactively to the expectations of their stakeholders and also comfortably manages the difficult processes of goal setting, negotiation, performance review and counseling. The acquisition and development of employee skills and competencies through sophisticated and systematic selection, induction, training and appraisal has a positive impact on quality and productivity. It leads to better motivation within the organisation.

To maintain the effectiveness and utility of various subsystems of HRD, periodic HRD audit must be conducted to identify gaps, obsolescence, inappropriateness, etc. from time to time in order to maintain a coherent, vibrant and responsive human resource development system.

Human Resource Development Strategies

Organisations need to have an objective, mission and strategy to ensure its survival, development and growth. This requires a strategically aligned fitment of people, organisation and environment. Failure to integrate human resource strategies with objectives and mission of the organisation is very likely to result in failure of the organisation. The term strategy refers to the art or knack of commanding and maneuvering resources to attain a decisive advantage through fruitful exploitation of opportunities provided by the environment or keeping at bay certain threats witnessed by the environment.

For the human resource development function, the increasingly competitive business environment and the consequent streamlining of organisations have created both challenges and paradoxes. 'People are our greatest asset', is on the lips of many senior managers, yet the development budget is often the first target when economies are needed. Nor are human resource development professionals exempt from the pressures experienced throughout the organisation to do more with less, and do it faster. It is all too easy in such a context to work harder, yet achieve less, to launch initiative after initiative, confusing employees and exhausting the HRD resources. It is precisely when there seems no time to develop strategy yet a strategy is most needed. Far from being an intellectual or abstract exercise, it is a way of tackling quite pragmatic issues: prioritizing among conflicting demands for scarce resource or creating new, more effective ways of delivering value to the organisation.

Strategies are policies for action to achieve major goals; recipes for succeeding, which are planned, and emergent. They are the course of action chosen with a view to achieve certain objectives.

To implement a strategy means taking up series of tactical decisions and activities. Human resources need to be groomed well to ensure proper implementation because human resources are the means. HRD strategies are a plan that defines how the human resources would be utilized through the use of an integrated array of training, organisation development and career development efforts to achieve individual, group and organisational objectives.

HRD strategies are policies for action to achieve major and ongoing performance improvement and are apart of creating and sharing new knowledge:

–Not just formal written 'plans', updated each year, for allocating budgets- though these should exist.

–Reflect different systems and cultures appropriate to different organisations, and different levers for action.

HRD strategies deal with many aspects of human resource development such as training, learning, motivation, empowerment, counseling, etc. in order meet successfully various risks and challenges facing organisations in the context of human resource development.

The options for human resource development strategies are:

Business Relevance	Human Resource Development effort is invested in areas of greatest value-added for the business.
Value	The organisation obtains the best learning value for its development.
Synergy	Initiatives are integrated so that a learning culture can gradually be built and strengthened.

- The systematic training strategy; job analysis, training professionals and formal courses.
- Business orientation; business objectives, managerial involvement and performance review.
- Continuous development and learning environments self-development; of self and by self.

Human resources development strategy is integrated because it is not a stand alone strategy – it is integrated with our broader growth and development strategies in general and to initiatives aimed at employment creation in particular – and if it is to succeed it must remain so.

Benefits of human resource development strategy are:

Organisations plan and evolve human resource development strategy within their generic systems, culture and preferred modes of action. There may be a dominant strategy, but more often a mix combining elements of different approaches.

Sometimes an organisation wants a thorough review and reformulation of its human resource development strategy (e.g. a newly privatized organisation, an organisation facing a crisis). Some of the aspects of a human resource development strategy include:

1. Creating a response to a strategic business challenge e.g. developing greater international perspective among managers in an increasingly global business;
2. Improving the cost-effectiveness of development and learning approaches introducing more timely and flexible support for learning;
3. Equipping individuals to take greater responsibility for their own development;
4. Building a competency framework as a foundation for an integrated set of development processes; and
5. Developing a process to capture and priorities individual and organisational development needs.

It is essential that the human resource development strategy flow from a corporate strategy. Only then can the organisation proceed to measure whether it has the right people in place with the right competencies, knowledge, experience or capabilities necessary for both current and future responsibilities only then can real development and organisational progress be made. However with a corporate strategy in place a human resource development strategy can be created. Human resource development strategy in simplest terms refers to ways and means for effective resource utilization.

A human resource development strategy should contain aims or preferably **SMART** (Simple Measurable, Attainable, Realistic & time-bound) based objectives as mentioned below:

1. Helps to satisfy present and future organisation needs created by organisational growth and change, accelerating business technology and increasing competition;
2. It is only used where it is the most effective and efficient means of needs satisfaction;
3. It is designed to achieve the maximum possible learning in the shortest possible time; and
4. To ensure that training effectiveness is measured.

The human resource development strategy is based on four main principles as follows:

1. Promotion of employability.
2. Entrepreneurship.

3. Adaptability.

4. Equal Opportunities.

A human resource development strategy to achieve specified aims or SMART objectives could utilize a number of principal levels of attention, for example:

Level 1:

Assisting in defining the training needs of individuals required to fill all jobs successfully. Designing programmes of training and development that ensure people are available and have the necessary skills, knowledge and attitude to fill all jobs successfully.

Level 2:

Assisting in identifying training needs resulting from new investment programmes and new practices and procedures.

Designing and providing training programmes to increase the competence of the workforce.

Level 3:

Recruiting and training sufficient number of people having the ability to meet the organisation's short and long term resourcing needs.

Level 4:

Extending open learning and self-development facilities to encourage and enable employees to enhance their training and education programmes.

In order to be effective, human resource development strategies must:

1. Form an integral part of the corporate planning process. It cannot be an afterthought;
2. Have a direct relevance to products, services, policies and objectives;
3. Be regularly evaluated by line managers, who need to have a commitment to make human resource development part of their own management roles; and
4. Be adequately resourced with suitable forward planning in budgetary terms to ensure that initiatives do not come to a standstill because the funds are no longer availaible.

In particular, HRD must be closely linked with the Human Resource Management (HRM) and performance management processes of the organisation to ensure that people have the appropriate competencies to contribute to achieving organisation's goals and those effective strategies are in place to enhance individual and team performance.

Human resource development strategies contributes to winning employee commitment, motivation and devotion in creating a self disciplined workforce and responsive organisation.

HRD Strategies

Organisations today have to develop people strategies to deal effectively with globalisation and competitiveness. Generally, human resource development strategies relate to attracting, engaging, retaining, developing, motivating and utilizing employees and their competencies for effective organisational functioning, growth and excellence.

Therefore, it is essential to build a model of human resource development strategy on which the organisation's game plan will be based. A model for building HRD strategy (*Andrew Mayo:* 2004) is as under:

Major HRD strategies are as under:

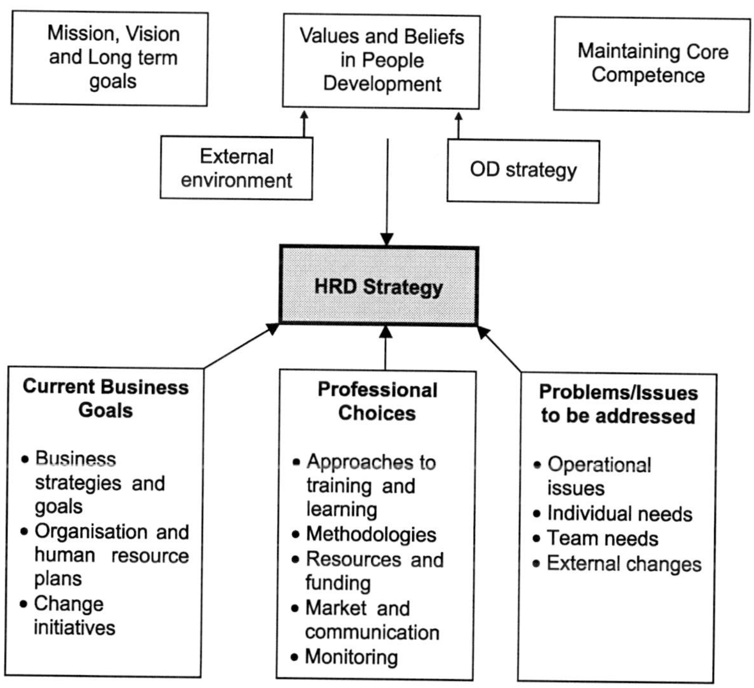

Fig. 2.2 : HRD Strategy Model

1. Communications strategy:

Continuous communication with employees, their family members and the society at large is crucial to an organisation. Given continuous changes, it is essential to educate and train employees about the need for change and seeking their commitment is critical factor in success of any change management process of an organisation. Organisations also need to integrate and develop the larger social systems they are part of.

2. Accountability and ownership strategy:

Employee accountability and ownership is vital to organisations intending to stay competitive. Employee's accountability and ownership leads to higher productivity and customer excelleration. Therefore, fostering accountability and ownership through various human resource development processes and systems such as performance appraisal, career planning and development, counseling and mentoring, quality of work life, etc. which must be linked to business plans, is essential to build a strong organisational culture for building and sustaining competitive advantage.

3. Quality strategy:

Quality is the foundation of any organisation. Quality is a mind set, which needs to be fostered in the employees through training and development. Quality should be promoted in everything an organisation does, through various quality management tools such as total quality management. Total Quality Management places emphasis on Quality that encompasses the entire organisation and involves:

- Continuous Improvement.
- Employee empowerment, quality circles.
- Benchmarking - best at similar activities, even if in different industries.
- Just In Time - requires quality of suppliers.
- TQM Tools - allow you to measure progress.

Quality improvement needs continuous commitment, support and ownership of employees at all levels at all times.

4. Cost reduction strategy:

Cost reduction strategy plays a significant role in the organisations. Employees need to see 'waste' everywhere. Every employee's contribution in savings is crucial as small contributions from each employee can be pooled by organisations to save substantial savings at the end of a given period and enhance its competitive strategy.

5. Intrapreneurship Strategy:

Every employee needs to be an intrapreneur i.e. independent entrepreneur who can generate ideas and bring them to reality by using the existing resources and support of the organisation to create innovative and creative products and services. This requires developing assertive risk taking in the employees. Organisations must enable their human resource development processes and systems to foster such an environment for its employees.

6. Culture building strategy:

Organisations valuing its employees have a sustainable competitive edge over competitors because employees are highly charged, motivated and commitment to the organisation. A strong culture fosters higher employee commitment towards the goals and objectives of the organisation.

7. Systematic training strategy:

Systematic training based on job analysis, organisational mission and objectives leads to improved return on investment. The planning and organisation of formal on-job training and off-job training leads to improving vital employee characteristics, build and sustain appropriate work culture and brings in more professionalism in action.

8. Learning strategy:

Continuous development and learning environments promote elf development of employees; of self and by self. It aim to achieve a 'learning organisation' necessary to equip employees with new skills and competencies on ongoing basis. It requires HRD processes and systems to focus on:

–Coaching and mentoring culture
–Self –directed systems
–Learner led

Economic liberalisation and globalisalisation have put pressures on Indian industry, to offer high quality products and services, backed by customer excelleration.

Designing Human Resource Development Strategy

The steps of designing human resource development strategy involve (see figure 2.3):

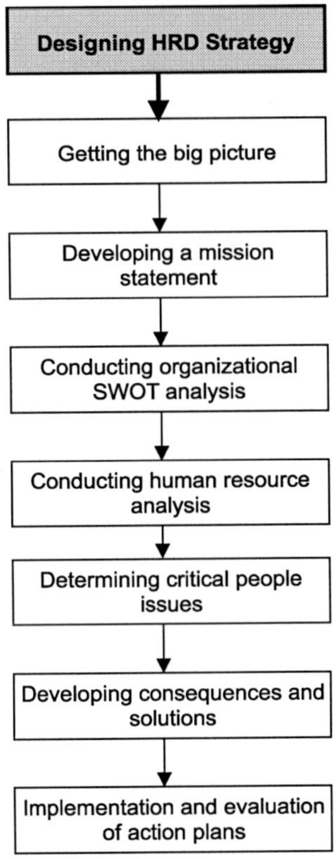

Fig. 2.3 : Designing HRD Strategy

1. Getting the 'big picture':

Understanding of business strategy is necessary to highlight the key driving forces of the business such as technology, distribution, competition, and the markets. Assessment of the implications of the driving forces for the people side of business is vital so as to identify the fundamental people contribution to bottom line business performance.

2. Developing a mission statement or statement of intent:

It is crucial to develop a mission statement or statement of intent that relates to the people side of the business. The words or references should not be idealistic statements - it is the actual process of thinking through the issues in a formal and explicit manner that is important.

3. Conducting a SWOT analysis of the organisation:

Focus should be placed on the internal strengths and weaknesses of the people side of the business such as the current skill and capability issues. Organisations must vigorously research the external business and market environment in order to highlight the opportunities and threats relating to the people side of the business.

From this analysis, review of the capability of human resource development function needs to be made. A complete SWOT analysis of the function embodying its current areas of operation, the service levels and competences of human resource development staff can be made.

4. Conducting a detailed human resources analysis:

It entails concentrating on the organisation's culture, organisation structure, people and COPS (culture, organisation, people, and systems). Then gap analysis can be undertaken by examining present status and desired status.

5. Determining critical people issues:

The business strategy is reviewed and examined against SWOT and COPS analysis to identify the critical people issues namely those people issues that must be addressed so as to have a key impact on the delivery of business strategy. Then prioritization of the critical people issues is to be shaped up keeping in view efforts and available resources.

6. Developing consequences and solutions:

For each critical issue the options for managerial action generated needs to be highlighted, elaborated and created. This is an important step as frequently people jump for the known rather than challenge existing assumptions about the way things have been done in the past. Various courses of action need to be evaluated carefully. Consideration of the mix of human resource development systems needed to address the issues such as ways to improve communications, training or career development and the implications for the business and the human resource development function is important.

Once this process is over, it should then be possible to translate the action plan into broad objectives. These will need to be broken down into the specialist human resource development systems areas of:

i. Employee training and development.

ii. Career planning and development.

iii. Organisation development.

iv. Performance appraisal.

v. Employee counseling, coaching and mentoring.

vi. Employee empowerment.

Action plan around the critical issues is to be developed with set targets and dates for the accomplishment of the key objectives.

7. Implementation and evaluation of the action plans:

The ultimate purpose of developing a human resource development strategy is to ensure that the objectives set are mutually supportive so that the reward and payment systems are integrated with employee training and career development plans. There is very little value or benefit in training people only to then frustrate them through a failure to provide ample career and development opportunities.

Future Challenges to Human Resource Development Strategy

Resources may be wasted by neglect, depleted by consumption, destroyed by misuse or enhanced by developmental intervention. The human being is indeed the resource of all resources. No one, therefore, would ever think of wasting, depleting, or destroying this prime resource. And yet, humans do face such a predicament. This predicament, it is argued, is primarily because of the absence of an appropriate ideology or set of values in those who are the in-charge.

The challenges could be viewed in the broader perspective of the ever-evolving HR knowledge corpus, rather than from a narrow, technical and operationalised human resource development practice. The 21st century challenges are as follows (see figure 2.4):

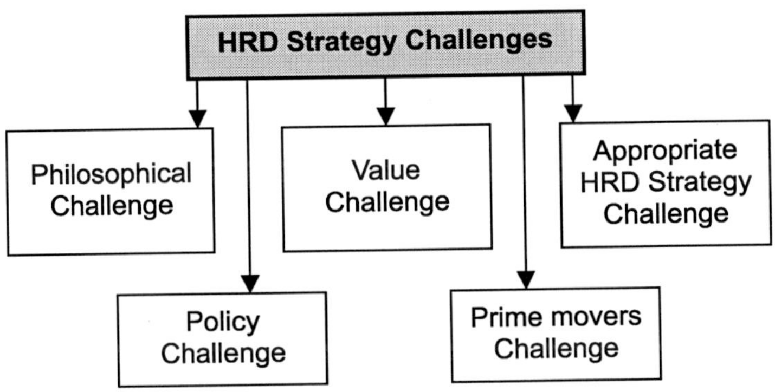

Fig. 2.4 : Future Challenges to HRD Strategy

1. The Philosophical challenge:

The need is to have a holistic understanding of human resource development as a hallmark of organisational excellence. Organisational excellence refers to excellence in whatever endeavour an organisation undertakes to achieve organisational objectives. There is a great need to understand that business success emanates from people – who are fully developed, committed, motivated and satisfied, and who can do value creation and value addition to the organisation, simply because employees are not just an organisation's greatest asset but they are the greatest asset of customers of the organisation. Organisations must have a free, just and fair culture and practices to respect diversity, divergence and risk taking capabilities.

2. The values challenge:

The issue is between nature and nurture. Nature is a matter of potentialities, talents and gifts and nurture is a matter of trainability or educability. It is possible that 60 per cent of the support staff in an organisation could not have a university degree because there were no opportunities given to them and due to the elitist policy for higher education. However, now society is moving towards the democratization of education. Therefore value is core to human resource development. For instance, values of ageism. After people have retired, there is no more use of them. In some society, they pay for the education of retired people and for the overall development of old people.

3. The challenge of appropriate HRD strategy:

Organisations have to devise appropriate human resource development strategy in conjunction with its business strategy, which leverages individual goals and aspirations with that of the organisation resulting in maximization of business impact for corporate success. Senior leadership must understand people side of the business and imbibe it with business of the organisation treating people as a strategic resource of the organisation with limitless potential.

4. The challenge of policy:

Human resource development policies must be comprehensive and integrated so that key elements are included resulting in maximum development of employees so that they are able to create an agile and responsive sets of competencies for maximizing both individual wants and needs and that of goals and objectives of their organisations.

5. The challenge of prime movers (Champions)

All the systems and sub-systems of an organisation should interactive and communicative with each other so that human resource development becomes an integrated organisational approach and a way of doing great business.

Human Resource Development Model

Human resource development is not only an organisation science, but also a key business strategy of the organisation. For organisations intending to excel, human resource development programmes and practices offers immense scope for enhancing its competitiveness. Therefore, a model of human resource development needs to be developed on which various instruments and mechanisms can be based in order to make the organisation an organic and competitive system.

A generic model of human resource development is depicted below:

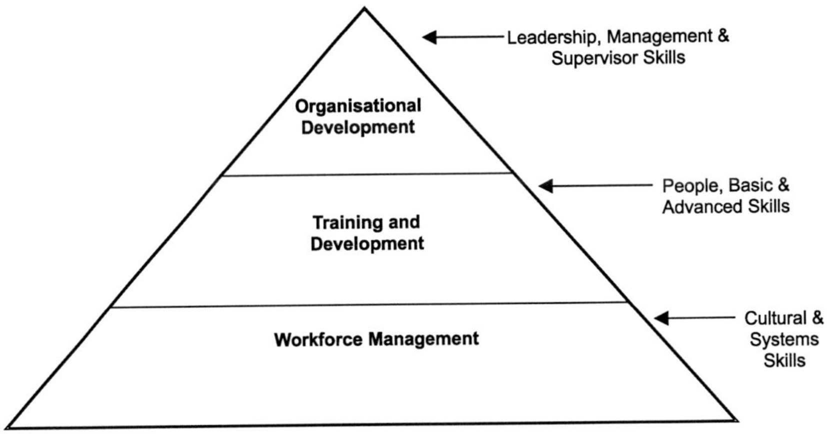

Fig. 2.5 : Generic HRD Model

The various components of human resource development model are as under:

1. Organisational Development:

Those responsible for direction, management and/or supervision, including ownership, directors and officers must posses the following attributes in order to make human resource development an agile and responsive system as enumerated below:

- Leadership skills.
- Management skills.
- Supervisory skills.

2. Training and Development:

All employees, including leaders, are part of the workforce producing a product or service needs to posses certain key skills for making human resource development programmes and strategies successful as enumerated below:

- People skills.
- Basic skills.
- Advanced skills.

3. Workforce Management:

All individuals or groups must consider themselves part of the organisation, which can be harnessed and/or nurtured through the following skills of line managers as enumerated below:

- Cultural skills.
- Systems skills.

HRD is a strategic weapon for achieving competitive advantage for which organisations must become self-renewing. HRD professionals/managers should enhance the maturity levels of all the subsystems of human resource development for building competitive advantage through the development of human resources and their competencies on continuous basis. It must be noted that human resource development is ultimately about developing people for achieving corporate excellence.

Review and Discussion Questions

Question 1: Define and explain the HRD systems in the organisational context. Give an example to support your answer. In your opinion, which subsystem of HRD system needs to be emphasised in present day business scenario and why?

Question 2: What do you understand by HRD strategies? Give a model of HRD strategy in the organisational context.

Question 3: How would you design a HRD strategy? Discuss with examples each step of designing a HRD strategy.

Question 4: What is the need of having HRD strategies in an organisation? Enlist the future challenges to HRD strategy.

Question 5: Explain the generic model of human resource development.

Question 6: Write short notes on:

i) Philosophical challenge
ii) Communication strategy
iii) Role of SWOT analysis in designing HRD strategy

Exhibit: 2 – A

Case Situation

- *Before attempting this section please read Chapter - 14 on Case Study.*
- *Please read the following case situations and answer the questions.*

Q 1. You have joined a traditional organization as HR Manager. The organisation has workers, staff and managers who are essentially rank promotees with low education and professional trainings. The CEO has the vision of taking the organisation from a sales turnover of 45 crores to 200 crores per annum in a span of three years through HRD programmes. What specific systems and strategies will put in place to realize the CEO's vision?

Q 2. You are working in HRD function in an expanding automobile company. You have the task of developing HRD Strategy to support Corporate Strategy. Outline the approach you would adopt and the HRD Strategies you would seek to develop to support a new Corporate Strategy to achieve competitive advantage.

Q 3. You are a HRD Consultant. Recently a CEO of a merged organization approaches you to help him in increasing productivity in his organization. The merged organisation's employees are reeling heavily under FUD – fear, uncertainty and distrust, as informed by the CEO. What strategic advice you would like to give the CEO before embarking on productivity improvement programmes?

Exhibit: 2 – B

Case Study

- *Before attempting this section please read Chapter - 14 on Case Study.*
- *Please read the following case study and answer all the subsequent questions.*

Introduction to the organisation:

The auto comp. Ltd. (ACL) made constructive work under environmental threat. The company was not doing well quite some time. The company is in the business of manufacturing and marketing automobile components such as tube connectors, and pressurized die-casting components for automobile majors and replacement market. The management decided to hire the services of a new CEO, Mr. Tarun Suri. He is a hard-core operations man with 30 years of professional credibility to his standing. After taking charge, he called a meeting of senior management and representatives of employees and informed that his main task is to create a new work culture for organisation through various HRD mechanisms and instruments for developing people, raising their morale and commitment care and training and building achievement oriented work system, transforming the rank and file for empowering them and setting right competencies to create competitive advantage for the organisation in order to come out of the blues.

Brief Description of the Problem:

The main problems are – sagging employee morale, low productivity, high sales outstanding, and accumulated loss of 45 crores. CEO decided to introduce HRD strategies based on survey feedback. First a diagnostic study was conducted to understand the state of mind of the employees across the levels of hierarchy, with the objective of formulating people orientation in addition to task orientation. As the next step, organisational structures were revamped and made more agile. Restructuring of reward management system, career management systems, training and development system, succession planning system and appraisal system was undertaken. These were the major HRD strategies being implemented by the CEO.

Within two years, the company started doing well. The organisation's sales had picked up by 30%. The accumulated losses came down from 45 crores to 25 crores. All this happened without adding even a single employee and any additional investment.

The sales outstanding came down from 60 days to 7 days and share price went up from Rs. 50 to 120.

The employees were highly motivated and charged and were quite sure that they will make the company profitable in the next 3 years.

Questions:

1. What is major reason of revival of this sinking company? Who, do you think is/are responsible for this transformation?
2. What HRD strategies had the CEO employed to drive the organisation on the path of profitability and success?
3. Can the organisation sustain its present improvement in the next three years? What more in your opinion should be done to strengthen the HRD strategies?

CHAPTER

3 Training and Development

Chapter Synopsis

Training and development refers to those activities that provide learning situations in which an employee acquires additional knowledge, skills and abilities to increase job performance.

Training and development is needed to facilitate the life long learning of employees that will characterize the business in the future. Therefore, it is important to:

- Assess employee training and development needs
- Set performance goals
- Plan developmental strategies accordingly

This chapter explains these concepts and strategies to meet the goals of the organisation and aspirations of individual employees.

This Chapter contains:

Training: Concept of training, Definitions of training, Features of training, Objectives of training, Training paradigms, Training category, Training process – planning, designing and evaluating, Training feedback questionnaire, Cost of training, Types and methods of training, Responsibility for training, Ingredients of a good training programme, General model for training intervention;

Development: Concept of management development, Definitions of management development, Objectives of management development, Principles of management development, Strategies to support management development, Identification of needs of management development, Designing management development programmes, General model of management development, Recent scenario of training and development – trends and experiences, Review & discussion questions, case situation and Case study.

Training & Development

Training

Training constitutes a basic concept in human resource development. It is the systematic modification of behaviour through learning, which occurs as a result of education, instruction, development and planned experience. It is concerned with developing a particular skill to a desired standard by instruction and practice. However, there are three issues or concerns:

1. Training is not the same as human resource development. It is a misconception to equate one with the other.

2. Training function often fails to deliver quality service in terms of meeting increasing standards and expectations of organisations and employees.

3. Training function suffers from structural and managerial limitations, which hampers its contribution in enhancing individual and organisational performance.

Nevertheless training is a highly useful tool which can bring an employee into a position where he can do his job correctly, effectively and conscientiously: a) correctly, in that he can apply whatever he has been taught, b) effectively, in that he may be in a position where he can perform to the expected standards, and c) conscientiously, in that the behaviour of the trainers can bring the trainees to the position where they can put their maximum effort at the right time.

A training programme should constitute a key feature in a formal development programme, and this could be a standard offering by various specialist bodies or in-house courses developed for the organisation's specific needs. Increasingly, these options are being combined so that there is the possibility of an externally provided course tailored to suit an organisation's particular needs.

Most training schemes and processes are based on the following model:

1. Identification of training needs and the setting of training objectives;
2. Designing of a training and development programme;
3. Identification and selection of training and development methods;
4. Implementation of the programme; and
5. Evaluation of the programme.

However, all training and development programmes must be linked to the business strategy of an organisation. Business Strategy is an integrated body of plans that covers all aspects of business activities and aims to achieve organisational goals and objectives.

The process of training is depicted through the Training Pyramid (see figure 3.1):

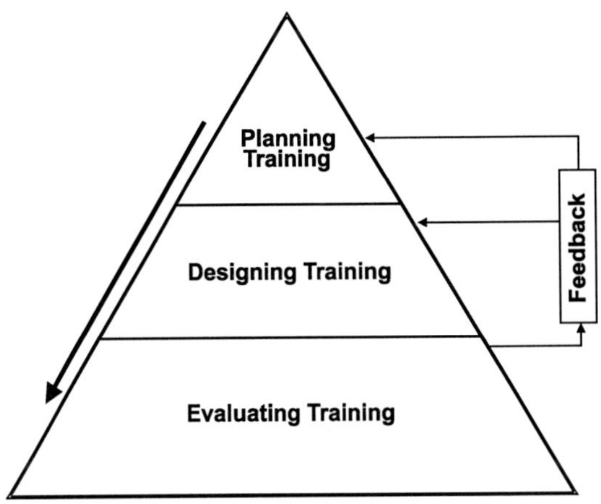

Fig. 3.1 : Training 'Process' Pyramid

Definitions:

A few noteworthy definitions of training are as follows :

1. "Training is a set of activities that provides the opportunity to acquire and improve job-related skills.

(Schermerhorn, Hunt and Osborn: 2004)

2. "Training is a process of altering employee behaviour and attitudes in a way that increases the probability of goal attainment".

(Irwin: 2004)

3. "Training is the process of acquiring the skills necessary to do the job".

(Robert N. Lussier: 2002)

4. "Training is one of several responses that an organisation can undertake to promoted learning".

(Reynolds et al: 2002)

5. "Training is a planned effort by a Company to enable employees to learn job related competencies".

(Noe: 2002)

6. "Training and Development is the process of developing expertise for the purpose of improving performance".

(Swanson and Holton: 2001)

7. "Training is the systematic modification of behaviour through learning which takes place as an outcome of education, instruction, development and planned experience".

(Michael Armstrong: 1998)

8. "Training is a learning experience in that it seeks a relatively permanent change in an individual that will improve the ability to perform on the job. We typically say training can involve the changing of skills, knowledge, attitudes, or behaviour. It may means changing what employees know, how they work, their attitudes towards their work, or their interaction with their co-workers or supervisor".

(De Cenzo and Robbins: 1996)

9. "Training is a planned process to modify attitude, knowledge or skill behaviour through learning experience to achieve effective performance in an activity or range of activities. Its purpose, in the work situation, is to develop the abilities of the individual and to satisfy the current and future manpower needs of the organisation".

(British Manpower Services Commission: 1981)

From an analytical study of the above definitions, we may conclude that:

Training is the process of identifying, assuring, and developing, through planned activities, the knowledge, skills, and abilities that employees need to help them perform their current and future job responsibilities in organisations to the greatest extent possible.

Training focuses on mastering knowledge, skills and behaviours that enable the implementation of the organisational strategy. This broader perspective is known as High Leverage Training.

Training supports adaptive, productive workplaces that capitalize on investments in both technology and workforce skills to boost productivity. Training is organisation focused and is a key element of an organisation's overall performance improvement plan. Training assists an organisation to achieve:

- Effective utilization of technology and resources;
- Decentralized decision- making;
- Improved work processes by measurably improving employee knowledge, skills, and ability; and
- Full customer satisfaction and profitability. It links technical, occupation specific skills development with broad-based foundational skills such as teamwork, problem-solving, leadership and initiative, resource allocation, customer service, communications, and commitment to lifelong learning to meet the requirements of today's and tomorrow's workplace.

In large organisations, internal staff often provides training; in small and mid-sized organisations, third party agency (outsourced) usually provides training.

Features of Training

1. Training objectives are tied to organisation's business objectives and industry skill standards.
2. Training objectives are derived from and continuously aligned with the organisations overall performance objectives and specific job requirements.
3. Training success is tied to the attainment of performance-based, measurable learning objectives that are linked to industry skill standards.
4. Programmes are developed with input from management, supervisors, and employees or their representatives.
5. Training curricula, structure, and delivery methods reflect the workplace and its requirements.
6. Training curricula, structure, and delivery methods are appropriate to the organisation's organisational structure, work processes, and culture; and training activities incorporate and draw on an organisation's work processes, tasks, and materials.
7. Training addresses both occupational skill requirements and the academic or foundational knowledge, skills, and behaviours that underlie them.

8. Training supports forms of work organisation that emphasize broadening employee skills and empowering employees.
9. Training activities are interactive and experiential, and include regular opportunities to integrate the knowledge and skills learned into solving problems commonly encountered on the job.
10. Training is modular so it can be adapted to workplace schedules.
11. Training is delivered "just in time."
12. Training uses technology and materials that are comparable to those used on the job.
13. Training is reinforced on the job once trained employee's return to their workplace.
14. Training is tailored to trainee needs and learning styles.
15. Training is developed based upon an assessment of the target employee's knowledge, skills, and abilities.
16. Training meets individual skill development needs as reflected in an individualized development plan (based on each trainee's own skill levels and training goals).
17. Training uses a variety of instructional methods and media, allowing for differences in the learning styles of individual employees.
18. Training structure allows employees to learn at their own pace.
19. Training builds the learner's ability to transfer his skills to different work settings.
20. Training builds employee's understanding that learning is an integral and ongoing component of successful work performance.
21. Successful training completion results in a portable credential for the learner.
22. High quality assessment is an integral part of the training.
23. Assessments used are valid and reliable indicators of job performance.
24. Expected performance outcomes and assessment methods are clearly communicated to trainees.
25. Learner needs are assessed prior to training and inform the learner's individualized training plan.
26. Trainees are provided regular, ongoing feedback concerning their progress while in the training programme.

27. Trainees are assessed at the completion of training to ascertain learning gains and overall training programme performance.
28. Training staff is highly skilled and well trained.
29. Trainer is well versed in job performance requirements and has industry-based experience.
30. Evaluation is used to assure training quality.
31. Training is evaluated based on both performance outcomes and the quality and effectiveness of the training process.
32. Management, supervisors, employees, and, in unionized workplaces, union representatives participate in evaluating programme effectiveness and its responsiveness to their needs.
33. Evaluations are conducted regularly to ensure that the training programme remains on track.

Objectives of Training

The main objective of training is to help the organisation achieve its objectives by adding value to its key assets – the people it employs. Training means investing in human resources to enable them to perform better and to empower them to make the best use of their natural abilities. The main objectives of training are to:

1. Develop the competencies of employees and improve their performance.
2. Help people grow within the organisation in order that, as far as possible, its future needs for human resources can be met from within.
3. Reduce the learning time for employees starting in new jobs on appointment, transfer or promotion, and ensure that they become fully competent as quickly and effectively as possible.

Training is a dynamic process made up of three major components: *planning, designing, and evaluation.* Organisations should continuously plan for and support training that is linked to their mission, goals and objectives; assess current and future training needs of all employees; ensure that appropriate training activities are provided; and evaluate and utilize the results.

Training, Development and Education are often used interchangeably, but they are different and meet different needs. Because they are often linked, overlapping nested, and conducted simultaneously, agreement on their basic differences is important to training and development professionals. They can be refined or deepened, but they need to be identified as different processes in the continuous maximization of human potential. Training is primarily concerned with attainment of specific skills necessary to perform present jobs, Development is concerned with attainment of maximum personal competencies for performing not only present, but future jobs and education is concerned with completing curriculum-based fixed time achievements aimed at building professional capabilities. Education may be defined at two levels: At Individual level: developing the capacities and potential of the individual so as to prepare that individual to be successful in a specific society or culture. From this perspective, education is serving primarily an individual development function. At societal level: the process by which society transmits to new members the values, beliefs, knowledge, and symbolic expressions to make communication possible within society. In this sense, education is serving a social and cultural function.

The difference between Training, Development and Education is depicted below:

Headcount	Training	Development	Education
Focus	Skill	Process	Concept
Benchmarks	Behavioural	Readiness	Capacity
Time Span	Short to medium	Medium to long	Long
Duration	Continuous	Milestones	Fixed
Measures	Bottom-line	Competencies	Professionalism

However, training, development and education are interlinked and change in one will bring change in another. Dr Leonard Nadler had given the following equation, linking all the three aspects as under:

$$\text{Training} + \text{Education} = \text{Development}$$

To understand how training should be developed and operated within an organisation, the first requirement is to appreciate learning theory and approaches to providing learning and development opportunities in organisations.

Training Paradigms

The paradigms of training are depicted below:

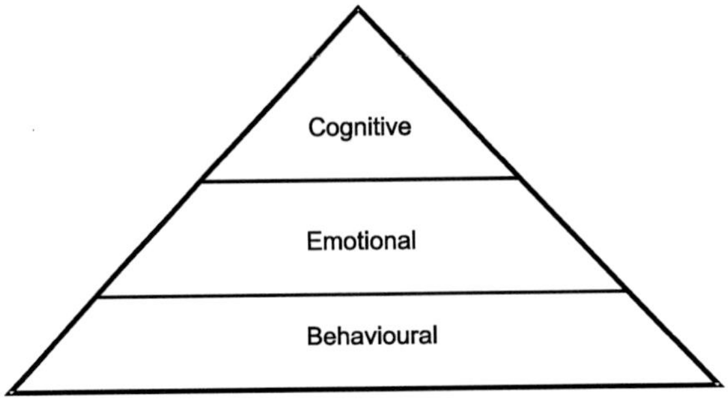

Fig. 3.2 : Training Paradigms

Cognitive paradigm refers to culture specific training, language training.

Emotional paradigm refers to social skills training, coaching on prejudices and communication programmes.

Behavioural paradigm refers to culture assimilator, social skills training. It focuses on intercultural situations.

Training Category

Broadly speaking, there are two categories of training as depicted below:

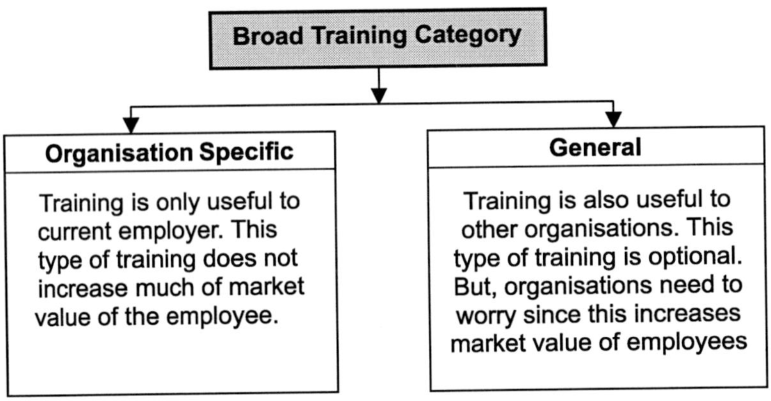

Fig. 3.3 : Broad Training Category

If the employees were to be laid off, he would be unable to reap the benefits of the organisation-specific training. So the employee would not be willing to bear all the costs of the training. If the employees were to quit, the organisation would lose its investment in the human resources. So the organisation would not be willing to bear all the costs of the training either. So the employee and the organisation share both the costs and the benefits of the training.

Thus, training can be classified as : organisation specific and general. The training is specific to an organisation if an employee can't "take it with him" so the organisation is willing to pay for it, but then reaps some of the benefits of the increased productivity post-training. Such training results in development of skills that add value only within a specific organisation.

Example: proprietary software or product knowledge.

Implications of organisation specific training are:

- The employee has invested in the organisation and the organisation has invested in the employee;
- Employees with organisation specific training are less likely to quit and less likely to be laid off than employees with no training or only general training; and
- Organisations will be concerned with the employment stability of an employee hired with such training in mind.

An organisation will be less willing to invest in an employee if it is uncertain that it will reap sufficient benefits of the training. Thus, if an organisation thinks that an employee may turnover, it is less likely to train that employee. If an employee expects a discontinuous workforce experience, the benefits of specific training will be reduced. Furthermore, if the employee is uncertain that he will be able to get back his old job with the higher compensation from training, the benefits are reduced even further. Consequently, an employee who expects a discontinuous workforce experience will be less likely to invest in organisation specific training.

General training is the training in which employees can use training to increase productivity at many organisations. So organisations won't pay; employee must pay with reduced wages during training but then benefits with increased wage after training. Such training results in development of general skills that add value to any organisation.

Example: management or sales skills.

An individual will invest in general training if the benefits are sufficient to compensate for the costs. An organisation should be willing to pay for specific skills but less willing to pay for general skills. Employees who receive general training can quit and receive a wage/compensation premium in the market.

Since the employee can leave and take the skills to other organisations, the organisation will not be willing to pay the costs of general training. So the employee pays the costs by initially accepting compensation below what could be obtained elsewhere without training. The compensation is the employee's productivity net of training costs. As the employee becomes more skilled, his earnings catch up and eventually exceed what he could have earning without training. The amount by which earnings exceed what could have been made without training represents the benefits of the training. The organisation receives benefits by paying less than the employee's productivity with training.

Training Process

Training process involves – planning, designing and evaluation of training as discussed below:

I. Planning Training:

Planning is the process of establishing the sequence and relationship of a series of operations prior to commencing work.

Training is the process of identifying, assuring, and developing, through planned activities, the knowledge, skills, and abilities that employees need to help them perform their current and future job responsibilities in organisations to the greatest extent possible. Training planning is a strategy for employees to develop workplace expertise, both general and specific.

Training must be planned so that the priority needs of the business can be met, whilst making the best possible use of organisational resources.

Training is a process for developing individual skills and effectiveness; therefore, rarely it is a process of organisation or group development. Individual effectiveness, in terms of skills, knowledge and attitude, is one of the essential building blocks towards achievement of the wider goal of improved organisational efficiency and effectiveness. The development of the individual and the organisation are therefore inextricably linked. Thus, Planning Training is the determination of the goals and objectives of an organisation's endeavour to improve performance and the selection, through a systematic consideration of alternatives, of the policies, programmes and procedures for achieving them. An activity devoted to clearly identifying, defining, and determining courses of action on training, before its initiation is necessary to achieve predetermined goals and objectives of the organisation.

Planning of training is essential if both short and long-term objectives of the organisation are to be achieved at the right time. Planning Training is a critical task, which involves the sequence of step, as depicted in figure 3.4.

Fig. 3.4 : Steps of Planning Training

Details of each step are as follows:

1. Setting strategic direction:

Setting strategic direction means the assessment of current competency of human resources and comparing it with the desired competency levels based on the strategic business plan of the organisation to identify gaps in competency i.e. Strategic Direction = Competency Model - Current State = Gaps. It is depicted in figure 3.5.

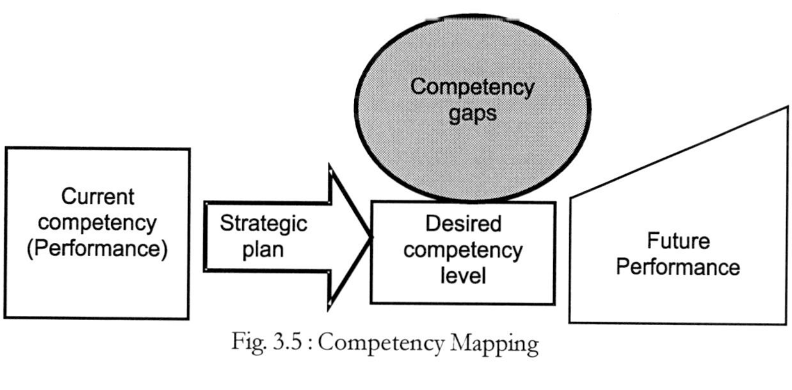

Fig. 3.5 : Competency Mapping

The strategic plan contains the blue print for transforming the organisation's current performance into the desired future state. The performance plans include incremental goals that lead toward the achievement of the longer-term strategic goals. Training ensures that any competency gaps within the workforce are addressed appropriately so as to equip the workforce with required competency that will enable human resources to accomplish long-term organisational goals and objectives.

2. Training needs assessment:

After competency gaps have been identified, it is then analysed to determine where training could enhance goals achievement. This requires the assessment of training needs of the workforce for appropriate training intervention. Before conducting a training needs assessment, it is important understand as why training is contemplated in the organisation. Since training enhances the specific skills and competencies of the employees to effectively achieve organisational objectives and mission, therefore understanding of the organisations competitive position in terms of its strengths, weaknesses, opportunities and threats needs to be carried out. A Training SWOT analysis will show what specific skills and competencies needs to be developed for employees in line with the business strategy of the organisation. This will facilitate in efficient and effective goal attainment of the organisation and yield higher return on training investment for the organisation.

Organisation SWOT Analysis for Training	
INTERNAL	
Organisation's Strengths refers to areas in which organisation is doing well. Organisation's Weaknesses refers to areas on which organisation need improvement	
Organisation's Strengths	**Organisation's Weaknesses**
• A distinctive competence	• No clear strategic direction
• Adequate financial resources	• A deteriorating competitive position
• Proven management	• Lack of managerial talent
• Competitive advantage	• Plagued with internal operating problems
• Acknowledged industry leader	• Financial difficulties
• Well conceived functional strategies	• Competitive disadvantage
EXTERNAL	
Organisation's Opportunities refers to areas in which organisation can expand. Organisation's Threats refers to forces (external and internal) that prevent the organisation from full effectiveness	
Organisation's Opportunities	**Organisation's Threats**
• New market or segment open for entry	• Slow market growth
• Diversification options	• Adverse government policies
• Complacency	• Growing competitive pressure
• Fast market growth	• Vulnerability to recession
• Weak competitors	• Adverse demographic changes
• Expansion to meet broader market range	

Training Needs Assessment:

Training has always been important. In recent years, however, the process of training is more important than ever in order for organisations to cope with accelerating change which affects existent training needs (e.g. inefficient job performance) and future training needs (e.g. responding to the continuous progress of technology).

Training must have a purpose and that purpose can be defined only if the learning needs of the organisation and the groups and individuals within it have been systematically identified and analyzed. Training needs can be identified at the individual and the organisation level through a process of analysis. Data for identification of training can be assessed through:

- Evaluation of personnel.
- Analysis of work.
- Analysis of skills.
- Observation.
- Changes in the organisation or job.
- Interviews between superiors and subordinates.
- Analysis of data.

Training Needs Assessment outlines a step-by-step process for identifying training needs at the organisational, occupational, and individual levels as mentioned below:

Step One - Obtaining needs assessment data through questionnaires, surveys, advisory groups, focus groups, interviews, etc.

Step Two - Analyzing data for discrepancy or gap between the desired knowledge and skills and those currently possessed by the employees.

Step Three - Defining performance problems such as changing technologies, etc.

Step Four - Conducting research on performance solutions by locating agencies that are doing; determining costs of training and non-training solutions; through involvement of all affected employees.

Step Five - Determining best approaches to resolving problems and issues.

Step Six - Conducting a cost/benefit analysis or business case for selected approach to project what financial benefit will result from the investment of money on training.

A model of training needs assessment is given below:

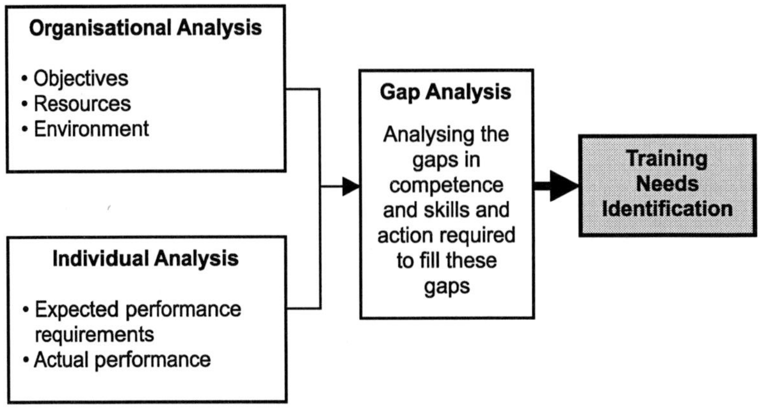

Fig. 3.6 : Training Needs Identification

Training needs assessment occurs at two levels:

A. At the individual level:

Identification will need to begin with the job description. This will provide a list of the skills and knowledge required. It can be compared with the actual skills and knowledge that the jobholder processes.

Another approach could be to look at critical incidents over, say, the past three months that were particularly challenging or stressful. The training can then be directed at the areas that are most relevant.

Managers will also be able to identify training for their subordinates. One of the best ways of achieving this is through the appraisal interview, where agreed training needs can be identified.

Individuals may request training that they perceive will equip them for a change of job, either laterally or through promotion.

B. At the organisational level:

Training needs may be identified through the performance appraisal system. This may provide the key channel for feeding back individual needs. The information should be processed by a human resource development department in order to plan the overall needs of the organisation.

The management team may identify areas from the corporate plan that they want to include in the training plans.

The most common methods of diagnosis of organisational training needs are the following:

1. Evaluation of personnel:

The director (or a team) evaluates the personnel's performance. This process takes place periodically with an evaluation form. That form contains questions in which the ability to take good knowledge and the abilities of organizing, leadership and progress are reported.

2. Analysis of work:

Every step, which takes place during the work performance, is examined in order to determine if it is really needed. After determining the necessary steps, the areas in which employees needs training is identified.

3. Analysis of skills:

The trainer must first identify the differences between new and experienced employees, in relation to their effectiveness. These differences will show the depth or level of the training need for the new employees.

4. Observation:

Observation can help the trainer find out what an employee does not do correctly and and it becomes the basis of determining the training needs.

5. Changes in the organisation or the job:

The creation of new job positions, the abolition of old positions and the integration of positions are some important changes which often take place in an organisation and accordingly generates the need for training.

6. Interviews between superiors and subordinates:

Very often, when the superior and the subordinate discuss matters, which concern the organisation, it is a good opportunity to discuss training needs as well. These interviews can be formal or informal.

7. Analysis of data:

Selecting data from departmental records such as personnel statistics, accident records, training reports, and employee's appraisal forms also helps to identify training needs.

Also, the following factors can indicate training or development needs of employees:

- Trainee or intern training plans.

- Career enhancement plans.
- New supervisors.
- Performance problems.
- Production problems.
- Safety problems.
- New equipment or programmes.
- Managerial competency assessments.
- Mission changes.
- State certification.
- Inspection deficiencies.
- Employees' requests.
- Laws and regulations.
- Modernization of equipment.
- Reassignments.
- Realignments.
- Competition.
- Recent competition results.
- Competition behaviour.

3. Developing training strategy:

There are many ways to provide training such as on-the-job training and off the job training, whether training will occur in a classroom, through electronic system or in the workplace. A large number of alternatives for imparting training for addressing competency gaps need to be generated keeping in view the strategic and performance goals that would be advanced by training. Then, the cost and benefits are to be assessed for selecting most appropriate approach. Also, the consequences to the strategic and performance goals are to be analyzed if training is not conducted. Thereafter, the business case for the selected approach is to be built. Developing training strategies, which support the achievement of business strategies involves:

- Analyzing and identifying corporate and occupational training needs;
- Developing proposals on how these needs should be satisfied;
- Preparing plans and budgets for training activities; and
- Identifying external training resources, selecting external training providers, specifying what is required from them and ensuring that their delivery of training meets the specification.

Formulation of training strategy is impacted by the philosophy of the organisation pertaining to the training and development of its human resources. The training philosophy of an organisation expresses the degree of importance it attaches to training. Organisations with a positive training philosophy understand that they live in a world where effectiveness is achieved by having higher quality people than other organisations and that this need will not be satisfied unless they invest in developing the skills and competencies of their employees. They also recognize that actual or potential skill shortages can threaten their future prosperity and growth. In hard economic terms, these organisations are convinced that training is an investment that will pay off. They understand that it may be difficult to calculate the return on that investment but they believe that the tangible and intangible benefits of training will more than justify the cost.

It is not enough, however, to believe in training as an act of faith. This belief must be supported by a positive and realistic philosophy of how training contributes to the bottom line. Underpinning this belief is the need to set concrete objectives for training in terms of a return on investment, in the same way as other investments have to demonstrate a pay-back. The main areas in which such a philosophy should be developed are the following:

A strategic approach to training: this takes a long-term view of what skills, knowledge and levels of competence employees of the organisation need;

Relevance: Training must be relevant to identify appropriate training needs;

Problem-based: Training should be problem-based in the sense that it should be planned to fill the gaps between what employees can do and what they need to do, now and in the future;

Action-orientated: Training philosophy should stress that training exists to make things happen, to get employee into action, and to ensure that they can do things they are doing now better, or will be able to do things that they could not do before;

Performance-related training: A performance-related training philosophy involves training specifically to performance and competence requirements; and

Continuous development: Learning is a continuous process and, therefore, a policy of continuous development should be pursued.

Training strategy is depicted in figure 3.7.

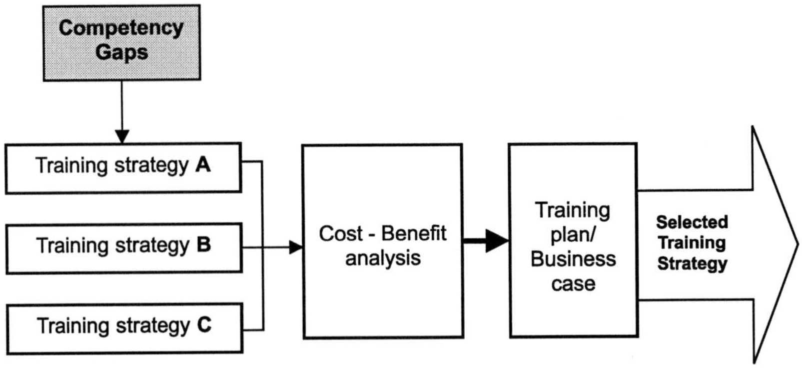

Fig. 3.7 : Training Strategy

4. Developing training policies, plans and procedures:

After selection of most suitable training strategy, training plans and procedures are to be drawn up. Training policies provides guidelines on the amount of training needed, the amount of money that should be allocated to training, the scope and aims of training schemes, and the allocation of responsibilities for training. The purpose of a training plan is to identify the work to be carried out to achieve agreed objectives. Training plans should be drawn up to identify long-term objectives as well as short-term plans for the future. The first stage of preparing a training plan is to gather background information about employees and the objectives for the forth-coming period.

Thereupon, procedure of the training programmes is to be determined. The purpose of training procedure is to establish the general requirements for the work process of identifying, providing and tracking employee training. It specifies the requirements for the training and how each requirement will be addressed. Questions such as how the training will be communicated to employees, who will be the trainers, what will be the medium and manner of conducting training, how the employees will be selected for the training, what will be the ideal trainee group size, how the line managers will relieve the trainees, etc. forms the basis of defining training procedure.

5. Identifying training resources and earmarking funds and staff:

Training resources, budgets and staff is to be determined for carrying out the training programmes. Training resources includes: trainers, training place, infrastructural facilities, course materials, support services required, etc. all these involve costs, which has to provide for by earmarking appropriate funds. This is called as training budget. Generally training budgets are obtained for a year. The amount of sanctioned funds depends on number, cost and time frame of training programmes. It may be given on lump sum basis or as percentage of the sales or the net profits.

Trainers constitute the key for the successful holding of a training programme. It is really difficult for an organisation to succeed effective training if the trainers do not have the necessary abilities for that. According to *Peel (1994)*, possible trainers can be:

- Inside the company trainers.
- Outside consultants.
- Managers.
- Colleagues.

Many employees of the same organisation can be excellent with their work but it can be proved that they are not relevant to be trainers. According to *Stout* (1993), the ideal trainer must be:

- Knowledgeable about the organisation.
- Able to communicate effectively and listen carefully to others.
- Able to analyze and solve problems.
- Flexible in the use of training methods.

The old saw, "When revenue is down, training gets cut," is for many organisations. When tough economic times slash or burn training budget, that doesn't mean training should be stopped. It means one has to work harder to keep training going. Therefore, human resource development function should exercise cautious approach while drawing up training budget and finally investing in training.

6. Developing training calendar:

Training calendar is to be prepared so that training is conducted in systematic and phase-wise manner. A training calendar consists of name of the training programme, employee group for whom is meant, duration, tentative date of commencement and completion of the training, tentative name of the trainer/s, etc., which would be adhered to by the organisation. Training calendar is issued by the human resource development function prior to the start of training year.

II. Designing Training:

Training design is needed to execute the training plans. Training needs to be designed individually, and the design will continually evolve as new learning needs emerge, or when feedback indicates that changes are required. Before designing and implementing training certain decisions are necessary in the following areas:

Objectives: The objectives need to be considered against the desired results. The end-result will be the acquisition of a new skill or changed behaviour. Skills and behaviours can be learned. A skill can be learnt in isolation whereas a behavioural change will lead to permanent change in the values and behaviours held. That means, teaching the skill of juggling to people who cannot juggle is achievable.

Location: Training may be conducted on-site as well as off-site and can be conducted by internal and external trainers.

Timing: The optimum time, duration and planning pilot courses of action needs to be determined.

Level: If the training is to be just conceptual, are the trainees experienced enough to be able to relate it to the work situation?

Techniques: Consideration should be given to elements of technique. Is it appropriate to use case studies or role-plays? What are the objectivity level of the trainer and the expectation of the trainee? There are a variety of training techniques that can be used. The techniques can be divided into:

- *On-the-job techniques*: which are being practiced on a-day-to-day basis or as part of a specially tailored training programme. These techniques include demonstration, coaching, job rotation, planned experience and mentoring.
- *Off-the-job techniques*: which are used in formal training courses away from the place of work? These techniques include lectures, talks, discussions, the discovery method, case study, role-playing, simulation, group exercises, team building, distance learning, outdoor learning and workshops.

Designing training involves the following steps as discussed below (see figure 3.8).

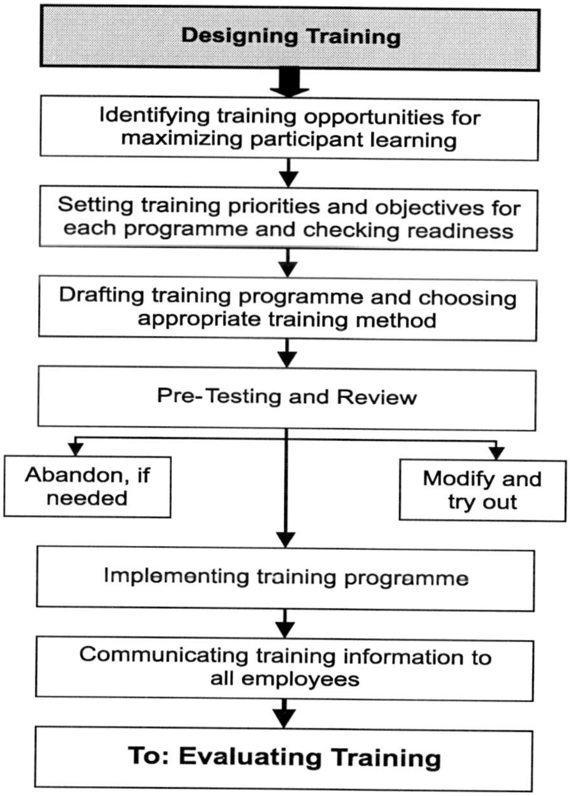

Fig. 3.8 : Steps of Designing Training

1. Identifying training opportunities for maximizing participant learning:

Proper combination of training methods and adequate resources must be employed to facilitate the maximum possible learning of the participants/employees. Therefore, analysis of the profile of the participants assumes importance here. It is desirable to put participants of almost same or comparable background, qualification, intellectual capability, and hierarchical level to facilitate the trainer and the individual participants to capitalize on the benefits of the training to the maximum. Maximum participant learning will increase the probability of increased application at the workplace.

2. Setting training priorities and objectives for each programme and checking readiness:

Training must reflect the training priorities of the organisation. Otherwise it may be possible that low significant training programmes gets more priority than highly significant training programmes. Training needs are prioritized based on these criteria:

- The number of employees experiencing a deficiency in a particular skill;

- The severity of the deficiency;
- The importance of the skill for meeting organisational goals; and
- The extent to which skill improvement can be achieved through training.

Objectives of each training programme must be clearly stated based on the training needs priority so that participants are clear about the return expected from them through a given training programme. However, it is important to check the readiness of the participants to absorb the learning, given individual differences, retain them and put effectively into workplace to enhance the impact of the training. Readiness means to increase motivation by including trainee in decisions about training programme, increasing cognitive ability and building high self-efficacy leads for training success.

Clear guidelines on what is expected of them and an indication of the time it will take should be given.

3. Drafting training programme and choosing appropriate training method:

In this step, training materials are drafted and the method of training is decided. Depending on the method of training – on the job and off the job, the training course curriculum will vary. For example, in on the job training the requirements of drafting training course material will be negligible. However, for off the job training such as classroom training, drafting of training course materials will be generally elaborate and methodical. Drafting training programmes requires meticulous planning, ideations, hard work, intuition and experience on the part of the trainer. The contents must be in conjunction with the training objectives. The draft should help participants to meet the objectives.

4. Pre-testing and review:

Useful feedback on the effectiveness of training programme contents can be gleaned from the pilot stage as to whether it is realistic and achievable or not? Thereupon it can be decided which activity can be improved and which need to be withdrawn. This implies that certain activities are to be suitably modified and tried out again on the colleagues or participants before including it in the training programme.

5. Implementing training programme:

After successful piloting, training programme is ready for implementation. Trainer/s is ready to conduct the programme. Training should continually be monitored to ensure that they are proceeding according to plan and within the agreed budget and second; all training should be evaluated after the event to check on the extent to which it is delivering the required results.

There are, however, a number of considerations which affect the conduct of training for specific occupations, and those concerning managers and team leaders, sales staff, skilled workers and office staff are the following:

- Management and team leader training.
- Sales training.
- Technical and skill or craft training.
- Training office staff.
- Team building training.
- Meeting the training needs of special groups.

6. Communicating training information to all employees:

Training time, duration, venue, name of trainers and participants, objectives, topic and general administrative guidelines are to be communicated to concerned employees through suitable media such as general circulars, training communication bulletin, personal letters, e-mails, etc. so that the participant employees can reach the training center and training can be successfully implemented.

III. Evaluating Training:

One of the most nebulous and unsatisfactory aspects of training programmes is the evaluation of their effectiveness. *Hamblin* (1974) defines Evaluation as "any attempt to obtain information (feedback) on the effects of a training programme, and to assess the value of the training in the light of that information". Evaluation leads to control which means deciding whether or not the training was worth the effort and what improvements are required to make it even more effective. Training Evaluation is of vital importance because monitoring the training function and its activities is necessary in order to establish its social and financial benefits and costs. Evaluation of training within work settings can assist a trainer/organisation in learning more about the impact of training. It is important to understand the purpose of evaluation before planning it and choosing methods to do it. Some advantages of using evaluations are difficult to directly witness, but when done correctly they can impact organisations in positive ways.

Evaluation feedback assists in improving efficiency and effectiveness of:

- Training content and methods;

- Use of organisation budget, staff, and other resources;
- Employee performance; and
- Organisational productivity;

Through evaluation, trainers:

- Recognize the need for improvement in their training skills;
- Are given suggestions from trainees for improving future training; and
- Can determine if training matches workplace needs.

According to *Hamblin*, there are five levels at which evaluation can take place:

1. 'Reactions of trainees' to the training experience itself;
2. "Learning evaluation requires the measurement of what trainees have learned as a result of their training;
3. "Job behaviour, evaluation" is concerned with measuring the extent to which trainees have applied their learning on the job;
4. "Organisational unit evaluation" attempts to measure the effect of changes in the job behaviour of trainees on the functioning of the part of the organisation in which they are employed; and
5. "Ultimate value evaluation aims to measure how the organisation as a whole has benefited from the training in terms of greater profitability, survival or growth.

Training evaluation can done based on certain pre-determined evaluation criteria and also based on evaluation level which must be followed with testing for the purpose of determining validity and regular follow up studies should be conducted to keep evaluation relevant and training effective as depicted in figure 3.9.

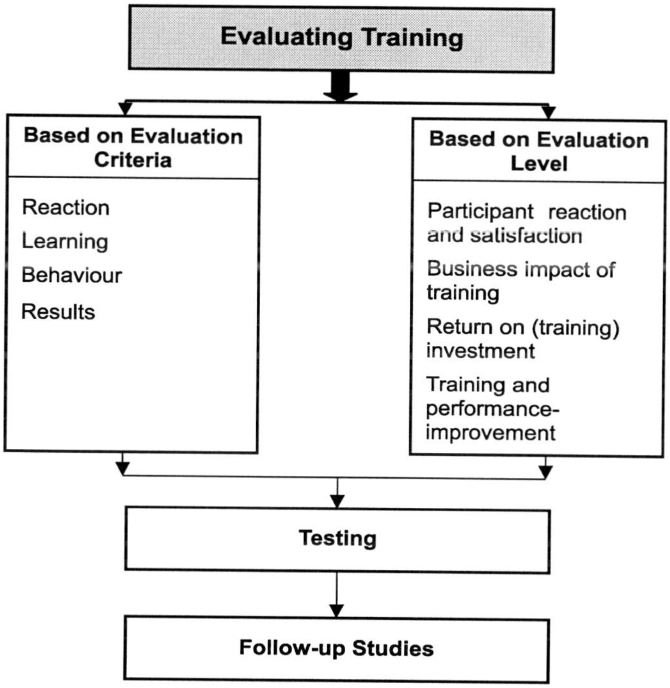

Fig. 3.9 : Steps of Evaluating Training

A. Evaluation Based on Criteria:

Donald Kirkpatrick has developed a very popular evaluation model that has been used since the late 1950s by the training community. The focus is on measuring four kinds of outcomes that should result from a highly effective training programme.

Kirkpatrick's model includes four levels or steps of outcome evaluation:

- **Level 1 Evaluation—Reaction**
- **Level 2 Evaluation—Learning**
- **Level 3 Evaluation—Behaviour**
- **Level 4 Evaluation—Results**

Details are as under:

Level 1—Reaction:

The goal is to measure participants' reactions to the training programme. Here the reaction of the participants immediately after the training programme is carefully observed and noted. Level one evaluation should not just include reactions toward the overall programme (e.g., Did you like the programme?); it should also include measurement of participants' reactions or attitudes toward specific components of the programme, such as the trainer, the topics, the presentation style, the schedule, audiovisuals, etc. Furthermore, each of these components can be further broken down into sub-components for evaluation to evaluate specific characteristics of the instructor, the presentation, etc. In short, level one evaluation is far more than just the measurement of overall customer satisfaction.

Learning (Level two outcomes) and transfer of learning (Level three outcomes) are unlikely to occur unless participants have positive attitudes toward the training programme. Therefore, it is important to determine participants' reactions to the training programme. Also, positive reactions are important because employees are more likely to eliminate unpopular training programmes. Finally, the measurement of specific aspects of the training program can provide important information about what aspects of the training programme can be improved in the future.

Level one evaluation relies on the measurement of attitudes, usually through the use of a questionnaire. It is important to include closed-ended items (including rating scales) as well as open-ended items on the questionnaire.

The following point applies to all four levels of Kirkpatrick's outcome evaluation, evaluators should establish performance standards on the outcomes, when possible, so that the four steps in the logic of evaluation can be utilized and evaluative judgments can be made. Also, it is important to communicate the results because utilization of evaluation results will not happen without dissemination and communication.

Here are a few advantages of level one evaluation:

- Trainer will know how the participants felt about the training event.
- It may point out content areas that participants felt were missing from the training event.
- It will tell the trainer how engaged the participants felt by the training event.
- It can provide information about overall participant reaction as well as participant feedback and evaluation of specific aspects of the training event.

Level one evaluation can provide formative evaluation information that can be used to improve future versions of the training programme.

Level 2—Learning:

Here goal is to determine what the training programme participants learned during the training event. Because the trainer should have specific learning objectives, one hopes to find clear learning outcomes. Learning outcomes can include changes in knowledge (e.g., what are the key differences between Windows 95 and Windows NT?), skills (can the participant upload a new operating system to a computer), or attitudes (have participants' attitudes toward computers improved?). Some training events will emphasize knowledge, some will emphasize skills, some will emphasize attitudes, and some will emphasize multiple learning outcomes. The evaluation should focus on measuring what was covered in the training event (i.e., the learning objectives).

Level two evaluation should be done immediately after the training event to determine if participants gained the knowledge, skills, or attitudes. Important issues here are (a) how shall one measure knowledge, skills, and attitudes, and (b) what research design should be use to demonstrate improvement in level two outcomes?

First, let's talk about the measurement of level two outcomes. Knowledge is typically measured using already available or trainer constructed *achievement tests* (i.e., tests designed to measure the degree of learning that has taken place). In the training environment, these tests are usually criterion-referenced. *Norm-referenced tests* are traditional standardized tests that are constructed to maximize individual differences and to allow comparison of individuals to an external norming group. A normal curve often characterizes the performance distribution of the norming group. In contrast, *criterion-referenced tests* are constructed to determine whether learners have mastered one or more learning objectives and these tests include a cutoff point (pass/fail). The results of criterion-referenced tests often take the form of a negatively skewed curve, where the vast majority of the learners have reached or surpassed the criterion or cut-off point (i.e., the point at which one must reach in order to pass the test) and only a few learners have lower scores. In constructing a criterion-referenced test, trainer should develop a pool of items potentially measuring the content, have a panel of experts examine the items, pilot test the selected items, and analyze each item for item difficulty (i.e., the percentage of people who answer the item correctly), item discrimination (i.e., the high performers should be more likely to get the item correct than low performers if it is a good item), and distracter effectiveness (are the distracters working well?). Items with poor performance on difficulty (i.e., items that are too hard or too simple) should be eliminated, discrimination (i.e., items that the low/less knowledgeable performers are more likely to get correct than the high/knowledgeable performers), and items whose distracters do not work well (e.g., an item where all incorrect responses are for only one distracter).

Skills typically require some kind of motor or manual response on the examinee's part, or some kind of manipulation; therefore, a *performance test* is used. A performance test is just a test that requires the test taker to create a product or demonstrate a process. Obviously the goal is to determine whether each person can perform the skills they have been taught in the training event. For example, if the learning objective were to learn to make repairs to computers, a performance test would be required to determine whether a person could install a power supply or a computer chip in a computer. If the learning objective were to learn how to make effective public speeches, the participants would need to be evaluated on actual speeches that they give to the group. Some performance elements can be included on traditional paper-and-pencil tests (e.g., essay writing, drawing skills, etc.). In the training environment, performance tests are likely to be criterion-referenced (i.e., participants' scores are compared to a cutoff point).

Attitudes are measured with questionnaires similar to the questionnaires described for level one evaluation based on Likert's summated scale i.e. participants to give their ratings for various items (responding with Strongly Agree, Agree, Neutral, Disagree, or Strongly Disagree or with other rating scales).

Level 3—Behaviour:

Here goal is to find out if training programme participants have changed their on-the-job-behaviour (OJB) as a result of their having attended and participated in the training programme. If the behaviour change does not occur, then it must be found why the change did not occur. Level three evaluation specifically involves measuring the transfer of knowledge, skills, and attitudes from the training context to the workplace.

Learning is likely to transfer only if the conditions in the work setting are favourable for transfer. In addition, there are obviously many things that trainers can do to increase the likelihood of transfer. In other words, transfer is affected by "training factors" before participants go back to their workplace as well as "workplace factors" that operate in their workplace when they return. Here are two sets of factors that make

Programme→Reactions→Learning→Behaviour→Productivity→Increased profits.

transfer more likely to occur:

A. These are some factors in the training programme that can help facilitate transfer of learning:

- The training or learning environment or context or culture is made to be similar to the actual work environment or context or culture of the organisation (this is called *situated learning*). Learning that takes place in "authentic" contexts is more likely to by used later;
- Providing real world examples and actual experience performing and practicing the behaviours;

- Ensuring participants understand the general principles behind the behaviours (called "transfer through principles"); and
- Explaining the importance and applicability of the future on-the-job behaviours (i.e., motivate the participants)

B. These are some factors in the receiving organisation that can help facilitate transfer of learning:

- The organisational culture and climate that support change.
- The participant's direct supervisor and others with whom he works support and/ or facilitate the participant's new behaviours through direct extrinsic rewards such as help, encouragement, praise, increased freedom and responsibility, pay increases, and recognition;
- The participant gains intrinsic reinforcement from applying his new knowledge, skills, or attitudes (i.e., he likes what was learned and enjoys performing the new related behaviours); and
- The participant has the opportunity to use his or her new knowledge or skills on the job.

Level three is often harder than level one and level two evaluations because behaviour changes at the workplace are often harder to measure than reaction and learning directly after the training event.

Level 4—Results:

Here goal is to find out if the training programme led to final results, especially business results that contribute to the "bottom line" (i.e., business profits). Level four outcomes are not limited return on training investment (ROI). Level four outcomes can include other major results that contribute to the well functioning of an organisation. Level four includes any outcome that most people would agree is "good for the business." Level four outcomes are either change in financial outcomes (such as positive ROI or increased profits) or changes in variables that should have a relatively direct effect on financial outcomes at some point in the future.

Here are some examples of different kinds of level four outcomes:

- Improved quality of work.
- Higher productivity.
- Reduction in turnover.

- Reduction in scrap rate (i.e., less wasted resources).
- Improved quality of work life.
- Improved human relations (e.g., improved vertical and horizontal communication).
- Increased sales.
- Fewer grievances.
- Lower absenteeism.
- Higher worker morale.
- Fewer accidents.
- Greater job satisfaction.
- Increased profits.

Level four evaluations is difficult in the sense that it is quite difficult to establish firm evidence that a training programme was the key or only source that produced the level four outcomes. For example, time has to elapse after the training programme in order for these outcomes to occur. Other factors may also occur during that time period. Second, it is hard to isolate the effect of the training programme because there are usually many additional causal variables operating on the level four outcome variables (i.e., the training event is just one of many potential causes). Level four outcomes are often more distal outcomes, rather than proximal outcomes of a training programme. For these reasons, the evidence obtained from level four evaluations is usually weaker than the evidence obtained from lower level evaluations, especially levels one and two, which are relatively easy to document.

Level four outcomes (increased productivity and profits) is a potential outcome line that ends with the level four results. Often, level four outcomes tend to fall far down outcome lines, which mean that many intervening factors must take place in order for the level four outcomes to take place. This means that we should not be overly optimistic in expecting large level four outcomes from single training programmes.

Critical appraisal of Kirkpatrick's training evaluation model:

Evaluating at different Kirkpatrick levels is affected by different variables. The evaluation ought at least to be cognizant of these, as they can affect the ability of one level to affect the level that follows it. A critical appraisal of Kirkpatrick model is given below (level wise):

Reaction:

At the reaction level, research has shown that there is relatively little correlation between learner reactions and measures of learning, or subsequent measures of changed behaviour. It has been suggested that 'satisfaction' is not necessarily related to good learning and sometimes discomfort is essential. Mixed results may indicate that what is measured at the reaction level stage might be important, and more focused reaction level questionnaires may be more informative about the value of training.

Learning:

There is much literature encouraging the use of before-and-after questionnaires to gauge learning gain from courses. Some have urged caution, raising concerns that a trainee might be able to repeat what they have learnt but may not be able to apply it, that performance during training may not be a predictor of post-training performance, that testing may not be appropriate for measuring the attainment of soft skills, or indeed for skills in general.

Behaviour change:

There are a wealth of studies that comment on the failure of training to transfer into the workplace and which have identified a range of organisational factors that inhibit success. Some have identified the importance of organisational culture and learning confidence. The more difficult an individual finds the training, the less likely they are to be able to apply it; the more supportive line managers are, the more likely the application of learning. Other important factors are perceived usefulness and job autonomy and commitment.

Similarly, there are a number of individual factors that influence transfer and application of learning; self-efficacy, motivation to learn, and general intelligence have all been associated.

Not surprisingly, several researchers have suggested that evaluation of behaviour change needs to become much more complex to take account of these factors. There have been suggestions of using manager- and self-assessment, but with concerns that they are not always accurate.

Organisational results:

Whilst this is probably the most difficult level of evaluation, many writers have expounded the view that training must be evaluated using hard outcome data. The difficulties of doing so tend to be dismissed by these researchers. Others, however, express caution, pointing out the many assumptions that are made, or the inherent difficulties in linking soft skills training to hard results, the time delays that are rarely taken into account, and that hard measures miss much that is of value.

Five Levels of Training Evaluation

- Training approach, methods, and learner's reaction to these.
- Actual learning, meaningfulness for the individuals and ability to meet the training objectives.
- Changes in job performance stemming from the training experience.
- Changes in organisational performance as a result of training.
- Increase in contribution of the organisation.

B. Evaluation Based on Level:

It encompasses the following criteria:

1. Participant reaction and satisfaction:

The focus is on the training programme and the instructor, revealing what the learner thinks about the programme and his reaction to the training and trainer. Most training programmes are evaluated at this level, usually through questionnaires.

This type of evaluation on training effectiveness is mostly subjective because reaction data is not measurable.

2. Business impact of training:

Training can yield both objective and subjective data, which produces an impact on business results. Business impact data is also not measurable, but it does influence organisational performance.

- Cost savings.
- Increased output.
- Time savings.
- Quality improvements.
- Increased employee satisfaction.
- Reduced conflicts and stress.
- Improvements in response time to customers.
- Customer satisfaction.
- Learning results.

The focus is on the participant. This type of evaluation measures if the knowledge, procedures, and skills have been learned.

Learner results data is measurable. Measures of learning need to be objective, with quantifiable indicators of how competencies are understood and skills are applied.

3. Return on (training) investment:

The ROI process creates a balanced evaluation by collecting, measuring, and reporting data on all levels of evaluation.

- Learning must take place.
- Performance must improve as a result of training.

Let us examine a technique that turn observed behaviour into a metric that can be used to calculate ROI:

360-Degree or 180-Degree Evaluations:

This type of evaluation allows multiple observers (360-degree) or an employee and his manager (180-degree) to rate a common set of observed competencies, usually on a scale:

- Is able to coach others in skill.
- Can perform skill independently.
- Can perform skill with guidance.
- Conceptually understands the skill.
- Little ability in the skill.
- No ability in the skill.

This type of instrument can be used to establish a baseline skill set prior to training and can be used after the training to determine the impact on the individual's actual job performance. In order to generate a metric that can be used for an ROI calculation, a group of supervisors who manage the position in question need to assign a value or weight to the skill. Once this has been done, any improvement in the skill can be shown as an economic benefit.

3. Training and performance improvement:

Initiatives must be integrated into the overall strategic and operational framework of the organisation. They cannot be isolated, event-based activities, unrelated to the mainstream functions of the business.

Performance-Learning-Satisfaction Evaluation System (PLS)

Another model thought to be useful in evaluating how well training has improved executive or supervisor performance, the Performance-Learning-Satisfaction Evaluation System model embraces the domains of performance, learning, and satisfaction. It is thought to be both rigorous and flexible: rigorous in terms of core questions, techniques, and reporting results, and flexible enough for most applications. It also includes an auxiliary data processing programme (*Swanson and McClernon*: 1996). When using this system, performance is considered in terms of two factors: (a) business results at the organisational, process, or individual levels; and/or (b) financial results or benefits in terms of money or monetary ratios. *Swanson and McClernon* asserted that most business results could be "monetized" and expressed as financial data. The general financial results goal of the model is to have benefits exceed the costs by a 2:1 ratio. Once the 2:1 return on investment goal is achieved, it can be said that the programme achieved 100% of its goal. In that sense it appears to have more application value than 360-degree feedback.

In the Performance-Learning-Satisfaction Evaluation System, learning has two components: (a) knowledge demonstrated on tests and other measurements, and/or (b) expertise in demonstrating simulated or actual workplace environments. Satisfaction is seen in terms of perceptions of the behaviours that are demonstrated. Participants (trainees) are expected to meet learning and expertise standards. If the standard were a rating of two on a one-to-three scale, an average score of two by the participants would represent 100% attainment of the goal. Attention to rising the goal should occur only after there is clear evidence that existing performance and learning goals are being reached. The Performance-Learning-Satisfaction Evaluation System method does not seem to have been used much in recent years.

Summary of Training Evaluation Techniques

- **Reactions**

-One-to-one and group reactions.
-Direct and indirect feedback.
-Survey methods (rating against criteria + open-ended responses)

- **Learning**

-End of training.
-Tests, demonstrations, examinations, simulators, role-play.
-Job behaviour (transfer and application).
-Incidents, staff appraisal reviews, project outcomes.

- **Organisation**

-Improved production and service quality indicators.
-Survey feedback of organisational climate/culture.

- **Overall Value**

-Cost-benefit reviews.
- Human resource accounting.

TRAINING FEEDBACK QUESTIONNAIRE

Name of Training Programme: **Date:**

Name of Trainer:

Participants requested to rank the following aspects of the training programme on a scale from 1 (poor) to 10 (excellent).

Training Aspects **Score Assigned** **Remarks**

The Instructor:

1. Effectiveness of trainer

2. Trainer's coverage of concepts in a clear and concise manner

3. Confidence and preparation level of the trainer

4. Understanding of the training material

5. Trainer's spoken clarity and audibility
6. Pace of teaching of the trainer
7. Trainer left room for questions and answered each thoroughly

The Facilities:

1. The facilities were clean, comfortable, and pleasant
2. The location was convenient
3. The equipment was adequate and functional
4. The support staff was friendly and helpful
5. The meals and beverages were plentiful and satisfying

The Training:

1. The training topic was timely and relevant
2. The training content met my expectations
3. The training materials were of high-quality
4. The training materials were useful
5. The training was just the right length of time

General Considerations:

1. This training was reasonably priced
2. This training met my expectations
3. This training will improve my professional capabilities
4. I would recommend this training to my colleagues
5. I would be interested in attending future training of this trainer

OVERALL

Cost of Training

The decision for the implementation of a training programme must be carried out only after careful consideration of the organisation's training needs. When a training programme is properly organized and meets the training needs, the organisation must not hesitate to undertake the cost.

According to *Torrington and Hall* (1998), the cost of a training process can be compared against performance improvement to give a cost-benefit analysis. Costs amount to far more than the money equivalent of the participant's time off the job.

The cost of these programmes includes cost of materials, facilities, support staff and employee time off the job where appropriate. The costs which may be estimated, includes absence costs, turnover costs, productive costs, and costs of field visits. These outcomes look attractive to the organisations, but clearly identifying the impact of training programmes on these, as opposed to other factors, is no easy matter.

Organisations must retain employees in the organisation over a specified period of time to recover training costs.

Thus, the two main components of training costs are:

Direct Costs: development, instructor, and materials costs.

Indirect Costs: employee salary paid while being trained, salary of other employees who provide the training (instructors, evaluators), administrative overhead costs.

The true cost of training is depicted (ice berg) below:

The hidden part (*shaded*) of the iceberg – the alignment of training with the organisation's vision and values, the assurance that the training is effective (actual changes on the job knowledge or behaviour), the delivery of training when it can be immediately used and provision of on the job reinforcements to reinforce the learning.

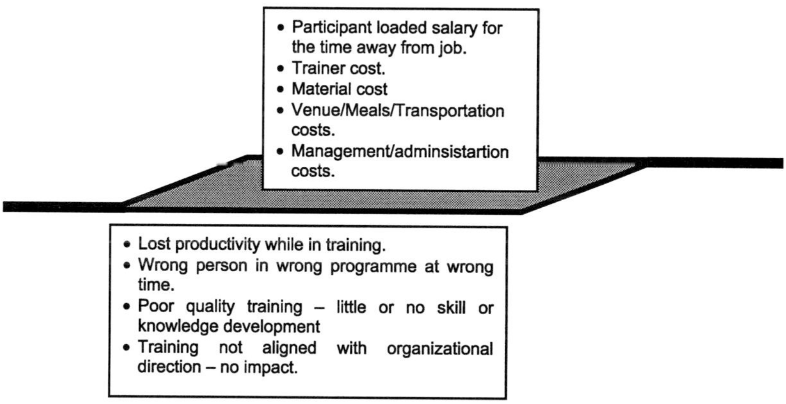

Fig. 3.10 : Training Cost

Training can be viewed as a "Make or Buy" decision. One can avoid training costs by "buying" a trained employee in the market. Human resource development function can generate significant savings for an organisation by keeping training business oriented and results focused.

Types and Methods of Training

Training is process and therefore involves a sequence of interlinked activities. There are two types of training as depicted in figure 3.11.

1. Systematic Training:

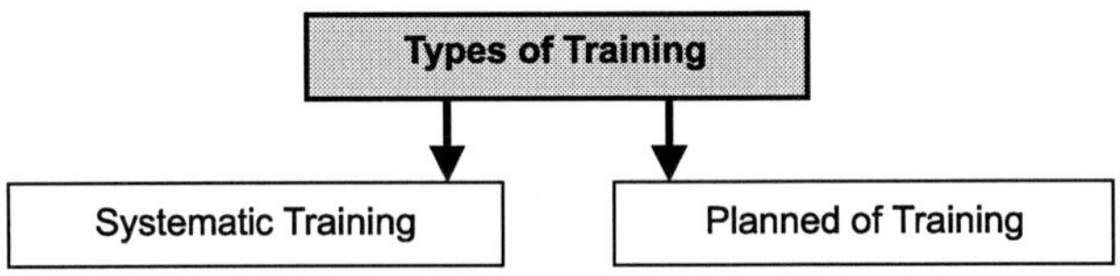

Fig. 3.11 : Types of Training

Systematic training is training which is specifically designed to meet defined needs. It is planned and provided by people who know how to train, and the impact of training is carefully evaluated. It is based on a simple, four-stage model expressed as follows:

- Defining training needs;
- Deciding nature of training required to satisfy these needs;
- Using experienced and trained trainers to plan and implement training; and
- Evaluating training to ensure its effectiveness.

The model of systematic training provides a good basis for planning training programmes, but it is often oversimplified – training is a more complex process than this. Another drawback of systematic training is that insufficient emphasis is placed on the responsibilities of managers and individuals for training. The concept of planned training provides a more comprehensive description of the training process.

2. Planned Training:

Planned training is a deliberate intervention aimed at achieving the learning necessary for improved job performance. The process of planned training consists of the following steps:

- Identifying and defining training needs;
- Defining the learning required.

- Defining the objectives of training;
- Planning training programmes;
- Deciding who provides the training; and
- Implementing the training.

Training is conducted for workers, supervisors and managers in an organisation. There are many ways of classifying training such as on the job and off the job training, individual and group training, cognitive and behavioural training, etc.

Here we shall discuss some of the major methods of training as depicted in figure 3.12.

Fig. 3.12 : Training Methods

1. Orientation Training:

Orientation training is designed to acquaint new employees with their new organisation, their place in the organisation, and the part the organisation plays in carrying out the mission(s). Every person entering an organisation or unit for the first time needs orientation training. Before people can become enthusiastic about their work, they must know something about the organisation and feel a sense of pride in being a part of it. Generally, new people are apt to be more attentive, open-minded, and eager to learn than the "old hands"; and what they learn is more likely to remain indelibly fixed in their minds. Therefore, a good orientation is important to new people.

2. Apprenticeship Training:

An apprenticeship is a formal agreement between an individual who wants to learn a skill and an employer who needs a skilled worker. Apprenticeship training is an "earning while learning" arrangement for a required term. Training occurs under the supervision of an experienced person; an apprentice receives knowledge and develops skills associated with a designated trade through on the job training. The skills an apprentice learns on the job are supplemented with a required number of weeks each year of technical training. Upon successfully completing an apprenticeship programme, the trainee is eligible for applying for permanent job in an organisation subject to availability of vacancy.

3. Introductory Training:

Introductory training is a method to bring familiarity or awareness about people, processes and systems in an organisation. At the beginning of the training, for purposes that may include one or more of the following:

- Encouraging involvement and active participation;
- Getting the group acquainted;
- Facilitating networking;
- Stimulating thought about concerns and expectations;
- Setting the tone for interaction; and
- Building teamwork and cooperation.

4. On-the-job Training:

This is the most common method of training. On-the-job training relies on current employees to train new recruits; results depend on trainer's skill in training. The trainee is placed on the job and the supervisor or the manager shows the trainee how to do the job. To be successful, the training should be done according to a structured programme that uses task lists, job breakdowns, and performance standards as a lesson plan. It involves job instruction Technique and coaching/mentoring.

However, this method is not standardized for employees. There is often a tendency to have a person learn by doing the job, providing no real training.

5. Demonstration with Practice Training:

This method of training is used to show trainees how to perform a task correctly and to provide them an opportunity to learn by doing. It is basically on the job training.

It can be used by:

- Placing group so all can see in correct perspective;
- Pointing out principles that are illustrated; and
- Asking questions to check understanding after each key point.

However, demonstration, alone, is ineffective for improving participant skills.

6. Vestibule Training:

Vestibule training is a method that combined the benefits of the classroom with the benefits of on-the-job training. The classroom is located as close as conditions allowed to the department for which the employees are being trained. It is furnished with the same machines as used in production. There were normally six to ten trainees per trainer, who are either skilled workers or supervisors from the organisation. Vestibule training takes place in simulated environment.

There are many advantages of vestibule training. The employees are trained as if on the job, but it does not interfere with the more vital task of production. Transfer of skills and knowledge to the workplace is not required since the classroom is a model of the working environment. Classes are small so that the trainees receive immediate feedback and can ask questions more easily than in a large classroom. Its main disadvantage is that it is quite expensive as it duplicates the production line and has a small.

7. Upgrading Training:

Upgrading training is a method to help employees (usually frontline workers) to improve the supervisory skills and keep abreast with latest developments and changes in skill requirements in the organisation. It is given to those employees who either need to strengthen their supervisory skills or they lack it since some employees are promoted from non-supervisory position to supervisory position.

8. Seminars and Conference Training:

Seminars and conferences combine several other training methods: lectures, discussions, and demonstrations. This training method is a good problem-solving approach wherein a specific problem or issue is taken up for discussion by experts and facilitates interaction of trainer and trainees to clarify issues.

However, it can be difficult to control a group. Opinions generated at the seminar and conference may differ from the manager's ideas, causing conflict.

9. Computer Based Training:

Courses conducted online; flexible timetable; can be done at own pace; requires self-discipline on trainees to achieve training objective. This method includes interactive guided learning in which the training material is presented to the trainee through the use of a computer. It is a method of programmed instructions.

However, clarifying individual doubts can pose problems in this method.

10. Refresher Training:

Refresher training helps participants to ensure knowledge retention and work procedure compliance. It also teaches them about any changes in methods or techniques.

However, this method requires continuous effort and support of top management.

11. Training by Lecture:

This method of training uses the trainer's oratory skills to provide knowledge and skills to the employees through intensive study materials. It invoves programmed instruction material, which is to be learned, is presented in small, sequential steps with self-instruction.

Communication is primarily one-way: from the instructor to the learner. It provides a great deal of information quickly to a large group of trainees.

It can be used by:

- Trying to involve the audience;
- In the beginning, explaining when questions will be answered;
- Asking the trainees to share experiences;
- Using visual aids including charts, diagrams, and pictorials coupled with preparatory comments and explanations;
- Providing copies of all overhead transparencies;
- Using instant attention-getters to illustrate a point;
- Providing examples related to group's experiences to illustrate concepts;
- Providing notes of key points with space for writing;
- Used in combination with other approaches;
- Using catchy words and phrases; and
- Pausing for desired effect.

However, this method is least effective for retaining and applying information and the trainees looses attention easily.

12. Simulation Training:

A training method that represents a real life situation, with trainee's decisions resulting in outcomes that mirror what would happen if trainee would have been on the job. Experiential training suitable for cross-cultural relations, team building, empowerment, problems solving in real work conditions such as trading in financial instruments. Trainees participate in a reality-based, interactive activity where they imitate actions required on the job. It is a useful technique for skills development.

However, this method is time-consuming and requires great deal of skill and practice.

13. Brainstorming Training:

Osborn defined brainstorming as 'using the brain to storm a problem'. This method uses ideation as the basis for developing and sharpening of problem solving and analytical skills of the employees/trainees. It involves:

- To generate many alternative solutions to a problem;
- To come up with new uses for things or design new products;
- When participants represent many different backgrounds;
- When you want to create equity within a group (break through traditional, established roles);
- To encourage all group members to speak; and
- To obtain the best and fullest intelligence and creativity from a combined group.

It can be used by:

- Establishing rules: Round robin, one idea per person, be wild and creative, no interruptions, no evaluation of others' comments, individuals may pass;
- Stating a problem or open-ended question to focus participants' ideas;
- Giving group a few moments to jot down their own thoughts before starting the round robin;
- Recording all ideas on flip chart paper;
- When brainstorm is complete, have group help to merge items and narrow to a manageable few;

- Using voting to narrow and prioritize ideas;
- Moving to action planning once the top 2 or 3 ideas have been identified; and

14. Case Studies Training:

A Case Study is a methodological approach in training in which an actual or fictitious scenario is used to engage trainees in active learning of concepts, facts and/or problem-solving skills. It's a story with a practical message. Effective cases portray real people in moments of decision, faced with a need to take action and accept its consequences. The trainees recommend solutions based on the content provided

It can be used by:

- Doing skills training;
- Hands-on, practical application exercise is desired;
- To focus the trainees on the recipients of service;
- To build team cohesiveness;
- Ensuring adequate information is included for trainees to work with;
- Allowing time for participants to read and reflect on cases;
- Works well with any size group; divide large crowds into smaller groups of 7 to 8;
- Facilitation is helpful, but not required; and
- Effective with interdisciplinary group.

However, it can be frustrating if not enough time provided to adequately problem solve.

15. Facilitating Group Work Training:

This method of training is used when there is a task to be done and the focus is to make the group's work efficient. Basically it is a team based training approach. Any group size can be used but optimal size is 5 to 9 trainees at a time.

It can be used by:

- Establishing and publicizing group guidelines;
- Facilitator should be neutral, with no personal investment in the content of the work;

- Establishing group objectives and outcome;
- Creating an open, trusting, safe, productive climate to enhance the group's efficiency;
- Understanding and monitoring group dynamics (e.g., group roles, communication patterns, participation, conflict management, etc.);
- Trying to start with an opening activity that creates a "norm equity state," or equalizes group members for the business at hand. Such an activity involves each person speaking in turn, possibly answering the same question about the content of the task, or his or her participation in the group;
- Respecting the group members;
- Monitoring individual contributions to avoid certain group members dominating the discussion;
- Frequently summarizing the group's work; and
- Using a "group memory" system to record the group's output.

However, use of unskilled facilitators can be a detriment to productivity.

16. Role Playing:

During a role-play, the trainees assume roles and act out situations connected to the learning concepts. It may be structured, spontaneous, single, multiple, rotational. Trainees can learn possible results of certain behaviours in a classroom situation. They get an opportunity to practice people skills. It is possible to experiment with many different approaches to a situation without alienating any actual customers.

However, this method requires that trainers must be skilled and creative in helping the class learn from the situation.

17. Behaviour Modeling:

Involves presenting trainees with a model who demonstrates key behaviour to replicate and provides trainees with the opportunity to practice the key behaviours.

However, it may be noted that behaviour is a dynamic concept, which means that it has to be modeled again and again requiring complicated set values.

18. In-basket Exercise Training:

In this method of training, trainees are given in-tray of a manager containing various kinds of mails and correspondences, which requires decision-making. Trainees go through each mails and correspondence and gives his decision. This is good method to develop analytical thinking and decision-making capabilities of the trainees.

19. Training the Trainers:

This is special type of training meant for the trainers. The trainers may be in-house specialist or outsides experts. The objective of this training is to sharpen and update the knowledge and skills of trainers with changing times. We live in a dynamic business environment wherein the domain of knowledge, skills and competencies change very fast requiring use of new tools, techniques and methods which the trainer needs to be well aware of as he is the link between new knowledge and the trainees.

20. Supervisory Training:

Supervisors are front line managers in an organisation who lead and direct employees in work towards the organisation's objectives. Supervisors stand in between the employees on the one hand and the top managers on the other hand. They manage and are managed and often they feel caught in between and get beaten on both sides. The supervisor's duties and responsibilities are complex and divergent since they are accountable to top managers as well as to employees and trade union/s. Supervisors have to balance the needs, aspirations and demands of both the management and employees aptly. Thus, they must have many skills, leadership, technical and human relations skills.

The specific training needs of supervisors can be ascertained through job analysis, organisation structure, promotion charts, etc. asking the supervisors themselves as to what are their training needs is one of the methods. But this method has certain drawbacks, since most persons may not be knowing what their needs are, even if they are aware of their needs, they may not reveal the true picture. However, the following may be the training areas for supervisors:

1. Training in general management area. Supervisors are front line managers and get work done through employees. As management personnel they need to know the basic management process, practice and skills of planning, organizing, directing, controlling, budgeting and coordinating;
2. Orientation in organisational policies, plans, programmes, activities, nature, future, opportunities, duties and responsibilities enjoined upon and expected on the part of supervisors by the organisation, their authority and decision making range;

3. Job performance methods training needs to given to supervisors. It includes – the break of work into details, steps and procedures involved at each stage including material handling, work flow, hand and machine works, the person, place and period of each work, equipment design and layout, simplification of work and events, new methods of task performance, etc. with the willing cooperation of employees.
4. Job relations training is another training that supervisors need. Job relations include –the relation between jobs and departments, sequential, and time and event, relationship between different jobs and human relations in the workplace. The supervisor must be able to understand the human psychology, behaviour and aspirations.
5. Job instruction training comes next. The supervisors must be trained in imparting instruction to employees in carrying out their assigned jobs. They must be apt in communication skills and therefore need training in better communication methods, so that the employees understand the instructions properly. Also, supervisors need to be trained on safety measures to be adopted by the employees while working in the workplace.

Organisations can no longer afford to provide training and development for its own sake and like any investment it must be measurable and deliver demonstrable benefits against organisational requirements as well as individual needs. Organisations need to provide training to their employees on ongoing basis, using a suitable combination of several training methods as discussed above.

The American Society for Training & Development's 2004 State of the Industry Report (18/01/2005) is based on data from 344 U.S. companies that detailed how they invested in and delivered learning to their employees in 2003 and their estimates for 2004. Annual training expenditure per employee has held steady at about $820 since 2002 investing in employee learning continues to be a priority for business leaders. Organisations are linking learning to performance and the bottom line; they understand the relationship between creating a skilled workforce and achieving organisation-wide success.

Thus, employees must be trained and developed in the context of an organisation's vision, mission and strategy.

Responsibility for Training

The responsibility for training is a shared responsibility between line managers, human resource development professional and learning specialist. This relationship is depicted in figure 3.13.

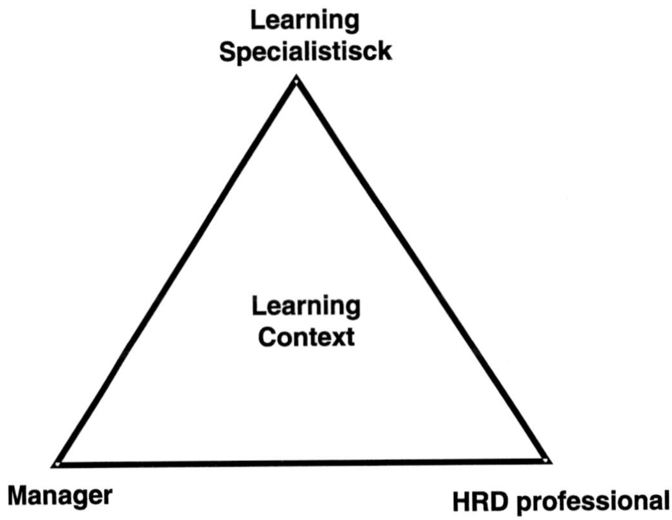

Fig. 3.13 : Training Responsibility

It is believed that most learning occurs on the job through coaching, planned experience and self-development. The onus is on managers and individuals to ensure that it takes place. Senior management must create a learning environment in which managers recognize that training and development are a key part of their role and one on which their performance will be assessed.

The role of human resource development function is generally to provide advice and guidance to managers on their training responsibilities. Some of the responsibilities of a training function are the following:

- Advising on external training courses for individuals or groups;
- Organizing internal courses and training programmes, but often relying on outside help for the whole or part of formal training courses;
- Training managers, supervisors and mentors in their training responsibilities;
- Providing help and guidance to individuals in the preparation and implementation of personal development plans; and
- Monitoring and evaluating the effectiveness of training throughout the organisation.

The Ingredients/Economics of a Good Training Programme:

The major ingredients of a good training programme are;

1. Maximizing similarity between the training and the job;
2. Providing as much experience as possible;
3. Providing a variety of examples;
4. Labeling or identifying important task features;
5. Understanding general principles enhances transfer;
6. Rewarding trained behaviors and ideas;
7. Designing training content for meaningful and practical applicability; and
8. Using questions to guide trainee's attention.

According to Svenson and Rinderer (1992), organisations expect their trainees to accomplish the following upon their return from training:

- Develop skills and knowledge for improving job performance;
- Support organisational culture change;
- Support the introduction of new systems, new technology and new products;
- Support the organisation's quality goals;
- Bring new employees promptly to a basic level of competency; and
- Provide a systematic measure for employees, managers and the organisation to manage competence.

Bibliographical Reference

Sevenson, R.A. and Rinderer, M.J., 1992, *The Training and Development Strategic Plan Workbook*, Prentice Hall, New Jersey.

In addition to the above, a good training programme should be able to deliver value to the organisation and employees (trainees) in terms of training deliverability i.e. Economy (Cost), Quality and Convenience as depicted below:

Economy	Quality
• Lower up front implementation costs • Reduced content development costs • Low on going management costs • Reduced time away from job • Reduced travel costs	• Consistency • Blended learning • Employee empowerment • Qualifications and standards based • Enhanced commitment
Convenience	
• Automatic generation of training records • Flexibility, scalability and stability • Learning fit with personal goals • Personal support • Tailored training resources	

Fig. 3.14 : Ingredients/Economics of Training Programme

Training is an investment in *Excellence*. Organisations must make continuous learning one of its goals in order to achieve organisational excellence.

General Model for Training Intervention

The generic model of training intervention (self-explanatory) is depicted below:

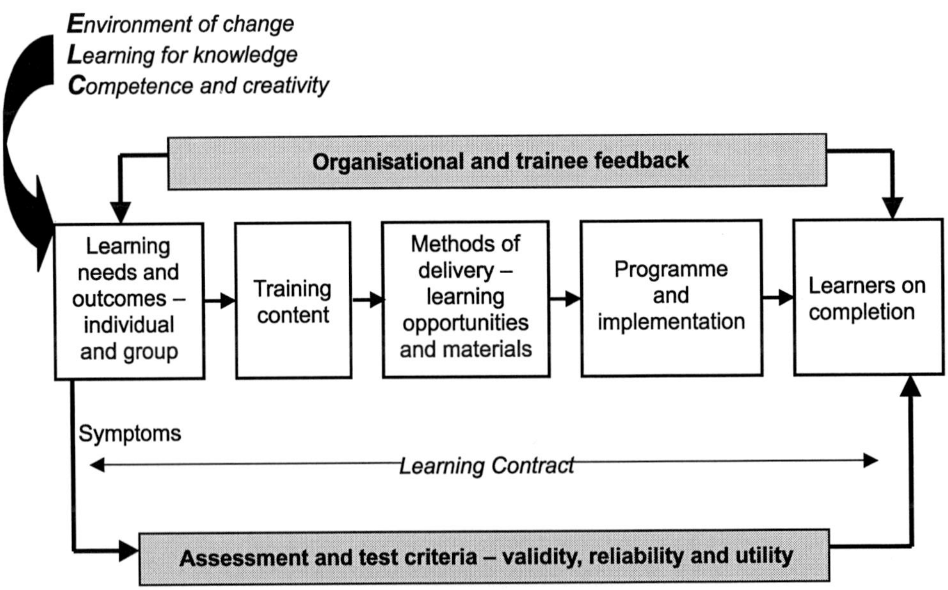

Fig. 3.15 : General Training Intervention Model

Management Development

The management and leadership development process is flexible and continuous, linking an individual's development to the goals of the job and the organisation. Management development programmes provides the opportunity to develop a broad base of skills and knowledge that can be applied to many jobs in the organisation. Management development curriculum is changing. The overarching goal is a comprehensive curriculum for managers to develop the necessary core competencies to become excellent leaders. Expanding management core competencies will enable managers to keep pace with the demands of a changing organisation.

There are seven competencies required by today's Managers:

1. Global perspective.
2. Local responsiveness.
3. Synergistic learning.
4. Transition and adaptation.
5. Cross-cultural interaction.
6. Collaboration.
7. Risk taking.

Definitions:

A few noteworthy defines of Management Development are as follows:

1. "Development is ongoing education to improve skills for present and future jobs".

(Robert N. Lussier: 2002)

2. "An organisation's conscious effort to provide its managers (and potential managers) with opportunities to learn, grow, and change, in hopes of producing over the long term a cadre of managers with the skills necessary to function effectively in that organisation."

(DeSimone et al: 2002)

3. "Management Development teaching managers and professional employees broad skills needed for their present and future jobs".

(Thomas S. Bateman and Scott A. Snell: 2002)

Objectives of Management Development

The main objectives of management development are:

1. To provide effective managerial resources to the business at all levels now and in the future as well as to provide opportunities for self-development and career growth.
2. To develop a set of personal attributes which are required to understand customer's present and future needs, create innovative products and services, mobilize energy and commitment of people and effective strategy execution and are related to potential such as analytical skills, leadership skills, vision, etc.
3. To develop managerial talent necessary for meeting present as well as future organisational manpower needs, especially at top positions.
4. To attract and retain best professionals in the organisation.
5. To enable managers to develop management skills and competencies needed to achieve excellent levels of performance in both present and future jobs. Fundamentally, the competencies can be grouped into four heads:

- Communication related competencies
- Task effectiveness related competencies
- People oriented competencies
- Strategic and conceptual competencies

6. To develop intrapreneurship and facilitate transfer of skills and learning to other employees of the organisation such as new joinees.

Principles of Management Development

The principles of management development are:

1. Encouraging growth and career development of employees as per the philosophy of human resources development;
2. Improving skills and knowledge that can be immediately applied at work;
3. Increasing motivation and job satisfaction of managerial personnel;
4. Creating a network of colleagues for problem solving and support; and
5. Promoting communication and planning throughout the organisation and department networks.

Strategies to Support Management Development

The followings strategies are noteworthy:

1. Modeling and encouraging the desired behavior that fits well with organisation's mission, vision, values, objectives and culture;
2. Discussing and creating a development plan during the performance planning cycle;
3. Endorsing employees attending classes and activities that support development plans and goals;
4. Discussing what the employee learned in classes and support integrating new ideas/methods to workplace issues;
5. Providing timely behavioural feedback on performance and discussing ways to improve and develop further; and
6. Providing opportunities for employees to develop through mentoring, cross training, internships, professional associations, committee and task force assignments, skill assessment programmes, and university extension programmes.

Identification of Needs of Management Development

Identification of developmental needs of managers is crucial to organisation's success and competitiveness. Therefore, a systematic method for identifying their performance, potential, own wishes and future development needs to be assessed as depicted in figure 3.16.

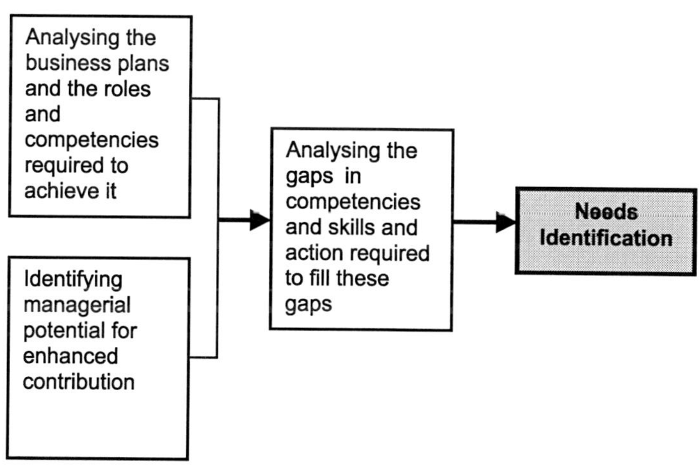

Fig. 3.16 : Management Development Needs Identification

However, management development need identification must focus on:

1. A clear link to business plans and strategies;
2. Seamless integration of personal, professional and organisational goals;
3. A global orientation;
4. Individual learning occurs within a framework for organisational learning;
5. Recognition of the organisational culture;
6. Focus on career development, leadership development and succession planning activities; and
7. A focus on core competencies of the organisation.

Three main strategies used to provide management development are:

1. Management education
2. Management training
3. On-the-job experiences

For details of methods of management development, please refer 'Training Methods' in the previous section.

Designing Management Development Programmes

A good management development must entail the followings:

1. Management development must be tied to the organisation's strategic plan;
2. A thorough needs analysis is essential;
3. Specific objectives should be established for each component;
4. Senior management involvement and commitment in all phases is critical;
5. A variety of developmental opportunities should be used;

   -Formal (programmes)

   -Informal (on-the-job)
6. Ensuring that all participants are motivated to participate; and
7. The regular evaluation updating of all programmes is essential.

General Model of Management Development

The generic model of management development (self-explanatory) is depicted in figure 3.17.

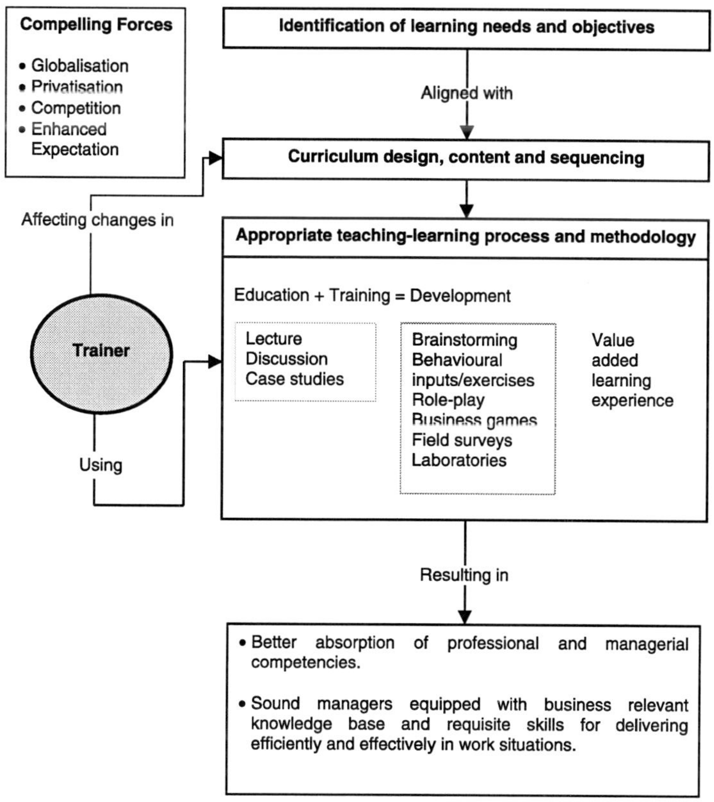

Fig. 3.17 : General Management Development Model

Recent Scenario of Training and Development - Trends and Experiences

Globally, today's organisations are undergoing significant change as they struggle for improvement and, in some cases, survival. Success often hinges on their ability to adjust to external forces and changes. Training and human resource development professionals are being required to play a critical role in guiding organisations through the change process.

The changes occurring in business, government and education influence the training function in many different ways. Business is becoming global which implies that individual organisations have to be internationally competitive. Mergers, acquisitions, and closures abound. With increasing complexity in the business arena, the value of the competent individual is going to become even more important. Hence, those in the talent development function have great opportunities, as well as heightened responsibility.

The training and development functions in most organisations face similar challenges and opportunities. Monitoring and reacting to trends is an essential part of developing an effective training and development policy and practice. Trends are not solutions in search of a problem or tools and techniques in search of a prescription. Trends represent important changes that must be followed and addressed.

These trends include changes in the focus of the traditional training function and in the use of different terminology to label the function. Although many global organisations still prefer to use the words *education* and *training* to represent the process of improving job-related skills and preparing individuals for future jobs, others prefer the terms *learning* and *learning solutions* as they become an important part of developing a *learning organisation.* Still others find learning restrictive and prefer to focus on *performance* or *performance improvement*, where the overall focus of training has been broadened to become the performance improvement function.

A significant shift in focus is that trainers need to become faster and more responsive to the needs of the learners than ever before. The most challenging aspect, however, is that the learner has undergone a lot of change. He can no longer be expected to accept whatever is offered as a training programme, module, lesson, or any other form of learning input as a given. Learners are more experimental in their approach. They are more versatile in seeking out information on their own (this is supported by new technologies opening up information on an unprecedented scale), are more comfortable with sophisticated technology, and are more ambitious with respect to their career growth. Another significant trend is that the learner is not the regular employee in an organisation who needs developmental inputs to perform the job better. The "new learner" is less loyal to the organisation, seeks and is more comfortable with change, and will offer his services and expertise to the organisation or person who values his expertise as well as provides the desired chunk of experience to add to his portfolio of experiences. This implies that the learner is more elusive and less willing to be tied to one place and organisation. On the other hand, organisations are on the constant search for the competent individual. There is a premium for the most talented and competent individual to give the necessary boost to an organisation. Today organisations are in a "war for talent" and have introduced progressive retention strategies to keep their talented and ambitious employees.

Most organisations typically do a poor job preparing for the future and understanding which trends and forces are particularly important to the way they do business. Moreover, most people do a poor job of forecasting. History is replete with examples of smart people, organisations, and governments that all fail to perceive warning signs of new developments. Human resource development professionals have, for the most part, failed to anticipate evolving needs and major changes. At an individual level, this has resulted in decreased job security and missed professional opportunities for many trainers. At an organisational level, it has meant minimization or less strategic involvement.

It is essential that trainers and human resource development professionals focus on the future. At a time when one has the greatest need to become attuned to change, it is too tempting to ignore the future because of immediate demands. Trainers need to stretch their imaginations, change their mental models, and promote new insight. Certainly, these new insights are not going to come from being internally focused. Learning for trainers can be hidden in opportunities in the most unexpected and unrelated areas. They need to look outside their immediate environment, to professional material, organisations, industries, and geographic areas, not within their immediate needs. Trends in other professions too can imply similar trends for training. For instance, we find an increase in the individualization of processes and products to meet individual needs. In medicine, the possibility of making individual prescriptions of medicines according to a person's biological make-up, can spell similar possibilities for individualizing the learning processes.

The rationale for examining trends is to take action, if needed. The appropriate action may come in the form of a complete restructuring, reengineering, or repositioning of the training and development function. In other situations, specific steps may be needed for only a few trends. Trends always have the seeds of counter trends within. Thus, while being aware of any trend, we do not slavishly have to follow it. Once we know what is happening, we still need to think through what is best for us. Having a better grasp of developments to come allows us to do our jobs better, have more impact in the work we do, and decrease the personal and organisational trauma of many significant changes.

Given globalisation there is an urgent need for human resource development systems such as training, performance appraisal system, etc. to be redesigned to attain world-class standards. The paradigm shift being experienced by the business world to face global competition has a tremendous effect on the way employees are trained, and prepared to meet global competitive challenges. It no longer suffices to provide traditional skill upgradation training or ad-hoc training. Organisations have to gear their employees for continuous learning and be able to transfer their skills across geographic borders. Since managers enjoy a higher level of participation in learning at work than their subordinates, management development has a greater potential to contain some clues for good practice that can be generalized to other employees. The principles of the learning organisation as had been applied to management development across a number of organisations from mining, clothing, chemical manufacturing, and aerospace industries the world over. The resurgence of interest in learning organisation is primarily due to three factors. First, there is a general recognition that organisations must become more adaptable and responsive to change. Second, technological developments behind product and process transformations are having a profound impact on organisations, demanding faster learning to facilitate accelerated restructuring. Third, the concept of learning has 'broad analytical value' as a dynamic, integrative concept that can unify various levels of analysis: individual, group, corporate, which is particularly helpful in reviewing the cooperative and community nature of organisations. The quest for knowledge is an important preoccupation for individuals and organisations alike. The challenge for organisations is to harness the knowledge inherent within its organisational members and processes and convert them to a sustainable competitive advantage. The evolving discipline of Knowledge Management is a multi-disciplinary function, which aims to create, capture, refine, store, retrieve, and distribute explicit as well as tacit knowledge. Although, technology has a key role to play in supporting this function, the human resource development function too has a tremendous role to play in supporting this effort. Based on the organisation's structure and circumstances, it is suggested that the organisation in India can take the necessary steps to move towards achieving the ideal goal of the learning organisation.

The process of performance audit should be applied for trainers. The performance audit process when applied to training needs analysis is a better option for trainers. The audit process is better equipped to uncover performance problems. It is in many ways ahead of training needs analysis, in the sense it sets the stage for further analyses and a substantially robust solution system aimed at performance improvement, whereby training is only one kind of solution.

Instructional design is an important part of the training activity, rather the very core of the process. Due to several trends influencing the human resource development function, the instructional design process is undergoing a paradigm shift. This shift is from a trainer or teacher-centered instructional design model to a learner-centered model, which is necessary to meet the learning needs of the 21st century learner. This is not to say that the traditional models of instructional design would no longer be useful, but that these models have to be adapted keeping in perspective two things - learning principles such as constructionism, heutagogy, and multiple intelligences, and secondly the needs of today's learners. Today's learners need more control over the process of learning. The trend is towards self-directed learning. Hence their requirement is to learn how to learn. For this to happen, instructional design has to be engineered to meet the pace, learning style, and individual requirements of the learner in a timely fashion i.e., just-in-time.

The modus operandi that had worked for training departments in the past is not going to work anymore. As too many people require too much training, and that too which is individually idiosyncratic, the traditional approach to training has to move beyond the buzzword phase and become a major force in employee training. To meet the vast amounts of just-in-time learning needs of today's employees, the organisation has to strive to achieve the goal of the learning organisation. This implies that the notion of self-directed learning has to be converted into a reality. For organisations, the self-directed mode of learning requires a sheer leap of faith as it involves giving more control to the learner. For employees, the challenge for the learner is to take more control over his learning. Those who take greater charge of their learning are also more likely to climb the corporate ladder faster.

Some human resource development professionals have predicted action learning to be the next big movement in training. The process of action learning offers several advantages over the more traditional forms of training - the transfer of learning to the job is highly enhanced, they are very relevant and meaningful to participants, offer great flexibility in the process itself focuses on learning what to do in the real world rather than becoming aware of how to do. This latter aspect of action learning is what sets it apart. Action learning is a structured process, originally coined by *Reg Revans*, action learning offers the feasibility to be used in all organisational contexts and at all levels of the organisation. Those in the corporate and academic fields who have used action learning have realized tremendous benefits. This process is being increasingly applied in MBA programmes by making business students take on real-life work challenges.

E-learning has grown tremendously over the last 6-7 years. E-learning comes with its issue and challenges such as the issues of bandwidth, hardware and software incompatibilities, human and technological issues, and the growth of the 'learning object'. IBM has realized several measurable benefits through its e-learning programmes. It saved US$ 166 million and achieved an ROI of 2284% from its Basic Blue e-learning programme. It has emerged as the company with the largest number of employees enrolled into e-learning courses in 2002. Overall, it found that the delivery of training through the electronic mode was much more effective than the traditional mode. Based on the success of its e-learning programmes, IBM has started offering e-learning products to other organisations as well. In addition, it plans to widen the scope of the e-mode to other HR systems, such as payroll administration.

Cost-competitiveness is a major concern for all businesses. The current business scenario is rife with examples of industry consolidation, mergers and acquisitions, and other innovative forms of organisations, whose main aim is to reduce costs and increase synergies from existing operations. In this background, the training and development function is facing the pressure of justifying costs incurred for employee development. The trend toward measuring the return on investment of training is being fueled by these and other reasons. The most important aspect of this process is to translate every qualitative variable (amply documented in the past) into quantitative measures (a prime requisite for trainers of the future).

The drive for increased cost-effectiveness in all operations is prompting more organisations to outsource their entire human resource development function, or large portions of it. It is estimated that within the next 10 years, half of the trainers will be working for outsourcing partners. With the increased focus on "core competencies", outsourcing partnerships are becoming more common in traditionally corporate "cost centers", including human resource development. The trend towards outsourcing of training by businesses usually is due to the perception of training being a non-strategic function. While this line of thinking leads to insecurity for trainers, they can, on the other hand, take a more proactive role by leading the outsourcing of certain training activities, thereby helping the organisation to leverage better benefits in terms of quality and cost. In any case, outsourcing of training should not imply shifting the entire responsibility of training and development to a training consultant but to have a more strategic approach to training.

In view of current and emerging business trends, it is no surprise that survival is very much on the minds of employees, and trainers are no exception. Increasingly employees are facing the issue of job insecurity and even their employability. Trainers face certain unique challenges. They have to not only adapt to the needs of changing times but also have to also deal with, and correct, the misconceptions held by many managers about training being a non-strategic, non-valuable, and expensive function.

Review and Discussion Questions

Question 1: Define and explain the concept of training. What are the key features of training?

Question 2: What is training? Discuss the process of training.

Question 3: Why is evaluation of training essential? Discuss any two methods of training evaluation.

Question 4: What are the different methods of training? Critically examine any two methods.

Question 5: Indicate how will you diagnose the training needs in your organisation?

Question 6: Training effectiveness is crucial for the success of the training department. How will you ensure it? Design an evaluation model for the training programme that you have attended or conducted recently.

Question 7: What is the significance of training policy? How will you integrate training strategy and business strategy?

Question 8: The choice of training method depends on the objectives of training programme. Do you agree? Please explain.

Question 9: Define and explain perspectives of management development. What are essential features of a good training and management development programme?

Question 10: Give an account of recent scenario of training and development. Give example to support your answer.

Question 11: Write short notes on:

i) Broad categories of training
ii) Performance learning satisfaction evaluation system model
iii) Cost of training
iv) Training Budget
v) Training Strategy
vi) Training Needs Assessment (TNA)
vii) Steps of designing training programme

Exhibit: 3 – A

Case Situation

- *Before attempting this section please read Chapter - 14 on Case Study.*
- *Please read the following case situations and answer the questions.*

Q 1. You have responsibility for putting forward suggestions for training and development of both managerial and non-managerial staff. Outline various methods of training and development which you would use and why?

Q 2. Create a training programme for listening skills programme:

–List your objectives.
–What training method(s) will you use?
–How many people will you train at once?
–How long will the training program last?
–How will the programme be evaluated?

Q 3. Your boss is very angry that one month after orientation training programme, seventy percent trainees have left the organisation blaming that the training is away from the reality. What will you do now?

Exhibit: 3 – B

Case Study

- *Before attempting this section please read Chapter - 14 on Case Study.*
- *Please read the following case study and answer all the subsequent questions.*

Introduction to the organisation:

The Modern Appliances Company Ltd. (MACL) is an existing profit making FMCG Company. The company has 600 personnel and has branches all other the country. It has a separate training department with a Training Manager, Mr. A.P. Mohan as its head who is supported by two qualified training officers. Mr. Mohan has been in the company for the last 8 years and is very efficient.

Brief Description of the Problem:

Mr. Mohan wants to leave the organisation. He is fed up with organisational politics. He is dissatisfied and infact frustrated. There are several reasons attached to it. First and foremost is that he is not paid adequately despite the fact that he has brought 120% growth in revenue to the company. Second reason is that he is not consulted and constantly neglected while making decisions on training aspects. Lastly, he considers himself to be a victim of politics played in the organisation. Production Manager is constantly hurting him and interferes with his work. Dr. Ashok Sarao, boss of Mr. A.P. Mohan does not want him to leave the organisation, as he knows that the efficiency will come down if he leaves. Dr. Ashok tries to convince Mohan that he should adjust himself with the environment and also talk of how Mohan is constantly neglected. He talks of how politics is played in the organisation and strengths and weaknesses of Mohan but does nothing to convince Mohan. Rather he says that they have to adjust, as they are part of family run business. In this setting, personal equation rather than merit works. Mohan is not convinced, and says he is leaving.

Questions:

1. Why a high performer like Mr. Mohan decided to leave the organization he has been long part of?

2. How does his boss, Dr. Ashok Sarao fared in convincing Mohan to stay back in the organisation? What was missing in his convincing?

3. Do you think Mr. A.P. Mohan took the right decision to leave the organisation? What would you have done if you were in his shoes?

CHAPTER

4 Learning and Learning Organisation

Chapter Synopsis

In today's rapidly changing business world, continuous learning throughout an organisation is vital for flexibility, responsiveness and innovation necessary to quickly adapt to a rapidly changing business environment in order to survive and prosper. To do so entails the need to learn by recognising the value of individual, team and organisational learning. By encouraging individuals and teams to accept responsibility and authority for their actions, and by encouraging risk-taking, businesses are more likely to reap rewards of innovation, creativity and improved employee motivation and performance.

This chapter explains these concepts and strategies to meet the goals of the organisation and aspirations of individual employees through learning.

This Chapter contains:

Learning: Concept of learning, Definitions of learning, Components of learning, Theoretical perspectives of learning, Learning cycle, Learning pyramid, Learning model, Approaches to and process of learning, Learning process, Learning approaches, Business priority of learning and Pitfalls of learning.

Learning Organisation: Concept of learning organisation, Definitions of learning organisation, Organisational learning culture, Learning in learning organisation, Human resource development in learning organisation, Role of human resource development function in learning organisation, E-learning, and Self-directed learning. Review & discussion questions, Case situation and Case study.

Learning and Learning Organisation

Learning

Human resource development goes beyond the traditional concepts of training and development in a dog-eat-dog business world. This requires organisations to look at the methods that are most appropriate for achieving the desired learning and encompasses and includes, but is not limited to, on-the-job training, placements, rotations, research, seminars, mentoring, coaching and counseling which requires one or other type of learning. Learning is a relatively permanent change in behaviour or knowledge brought about by practice or experience. Indeed, without this broader framework, most training ends up as wasted money. Thus, human resource development should accelerate learning in all forms and enable productive application of that learning.

A traditional training course is not always the most appropriate method of learning as it is often the case that the potential learning that the employees are supposed to have gained are quickly lost due to a lack of follow up or the opportunity to practice the learning and cement the knowledge transfer. Managers must provide employees with the opportunities to practice and discuss what they have learnt. The follow up to learning requires both managers and employees to plan how this will be undertaken - forward planning ensures that no one is forgotten. Although important in all organisations, it is especially true in a small organisation where "repeat" training is not financially feasible. Learning is at the heart of training and development as shown in figure 4.1.

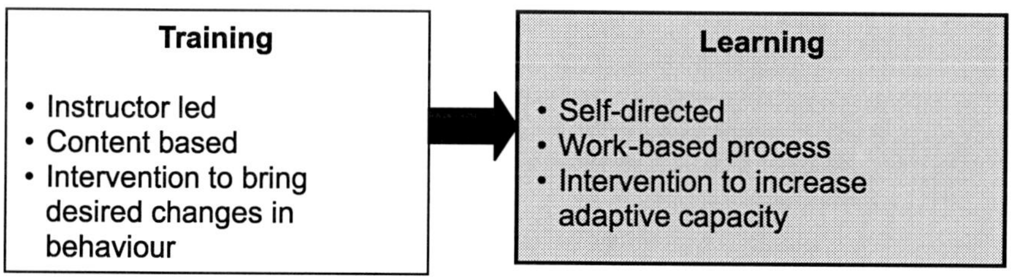

Fig. 4.1 : Changing Paradigm : From Training to Learning

This changing view of learning has far-reaching consequences for line managers, who are expected to manage the workplace as a place fit for learning, for instance, by fostering a learning climate, and by coaching employees. In addition, it considerably affects the role and tasks of human resource development professionals, who are involved in organizing learning activities for the organisation. Their role changes from that of 'trainer' to 'performance consultant' or 'learning specialist.' Also, this shift impacts upon employees who are now expected to take greater responsibility for their own learning.

Learning is emerging as a critical enabler of enhanced organisational performance as follows:

Enabler of Enhanced Organisational Performance
Human Capital has replaced physical capital as the source of competitive advantage.
Many employees' posses outdated skills and competencies and lack the requisite educational background to effectively perform their jobs.
Organizations recognize that training and development extend beyond corporate walls.

Managers, therefore, must identify the most appropriate method of learning. This may range from the use of traditional training courses to internal discussions or seminars, from rotational opportunities and mentoring to including junior/new employee so that they can observe more experienced employees at meetings. Not all learning methods cost money - sometimes it "only" requires lateral thinking and an expenditure of effort and minor inconvenience. Further study is an important component of a learning organisation's repertoire.

Definitions:

A few noteworthy definitions of Learning are as follows:

1. "Learning is the process by which a person constructs knowledge, skills and capabilities".

(Martyn Sloman: 2004)

2. "Learning is a relatively enduring change in the potential to engage in a particular behaviour resulting from experience with environmental events specifically related to that behaviour".

(M. Domjan: 2000)

3. "Learning is the process by which skills, knowledge and attitudes are acquired and translated into habitual forms of behaviour and performance, whether by design or through the natural passage of time".

(Harrison: 1993)

4. "Learning is a relatively permanent change in the ability to exhibit behaviour: this change occurs as the result of successful or unsuccessful experience".

(S.B. Kline: 1987)

From analytical study of the above definitions, we may conclude that:

Learning is relatively permanent change process and always refers to some systematic change in behaviour or behavioural disposition that occurs as a consequence of experience in some specified situation over a period of time.

In Learning, strategic is the key word. It involves:

1. Strategically relevant learning solutions for each job family within an organisation.
2. A learning organisation functions as the umbrella for an organisation's total education requirements - for all employees and the entire value chain, including customers and suppliers.
3. Employees build individual and organisational competencies, thereby improving the organisation's overall performance.

Evolving strategies for learning involves:

-Evolution of the systematic learning.

-Evolution of the business orientated learning.

-Evolution of e-learning.

Lifelong learning has become, and will remain, an important endeavour for all organisation, as the world develops into a "learning society". Organisations are becoming important partners in this learning society, as they provide more and more opportunities for continuous learning to their employees with the objective to optimise organisational learning as a whole. This new focus on employee learning changes the role of human resource development function in facilitating employee learning on a continuous basis and thus supporting the strategic learning processes of the organisation.

Components of Learning

Learning is not something that requires time out from being engaged in productive activity; learning is the heart of productive activity. To put it simply, learning is the new form of labour. Therefore, learning is a strategic process and consists of essentially three different components as depicted in figure 4.2.

Fig. 4.2 : Learning Components

The Components of Learning are as follows:

1. Strategic learning planning:

Organisational strategy spells out the learning requirements of the organisation. What employees are supposed to learn, and ensuring that this is communicated to employees is a vital part of planned strategic learning activity. Learning seeks to help employees to do a job in a better way or do it differently or work for a higher standard in order to effectively achieve mission and objectives of the organisation.

2. Business relevant learning:

For improving organisational performance, learning must support its strategy. Employees should be provided business relevant learning so as to improve its performance in order to build or maintain its competitiveness. Relevant data about needed skills and competencies expected of employees for smooth achievement of organisation's strategies must be analyzed and put into effective use.

3. Learning effectiveness measurement:

Since people learn in various different ways, therefore it is vital for the organisation to develop systematically different methods of learning for its employees. Differences in methods and approaches relate to differences in the nature of learning experiences, which in turn impact the extent and nature of the learning that takes place.

The impact and result of learning in improving overall employee performance and ultimately organisational performance needs to be measured by using suitable metrics to verify the effectiveness and utility of different methods and approaches employed for fostering learning. Measuring effectiveness of learning involves taking a hard and calculated look at:

- *Efficiency*: of any planned learning activity in terms of use or intended use of resources and its commitment.

- *Effectiveness*: of planned learning in terms of the outcomes and effect of the use and application of organisational resources.

Theoretical Perspectives of Learning

There are four main theoretical perspectives of learning as briefly described below:

1. **The Behaviourist theory,** which equates the human being with a machine stimulated into learning by positive or negative reinforcement.

2. **The Cognitive theory,** which equates the human being to a brain and stresses the importance of critical thinking and problem solving.

3. **The Gestalt theory,** which involves the whole personality and stresses that the whole (the gestalt) is more than the sum of the parts. A gestalt begins to form when the individual experiences a physical and/or psychological need in relation to the environment. This moves the individual away from equilibrium in the direction of action to satisfy a need. Equilibrium is only re-established when the learning problem is solved.

4. **The Humanistic theory,** which maintains that all individuals have the capacity to learn and, therefore, that the purpose of learning is to encourage each individual to attain his/her full potential.

Whatever be the assumptions of learning, essentially there are two facets of learning as depicted in figure 4.3.

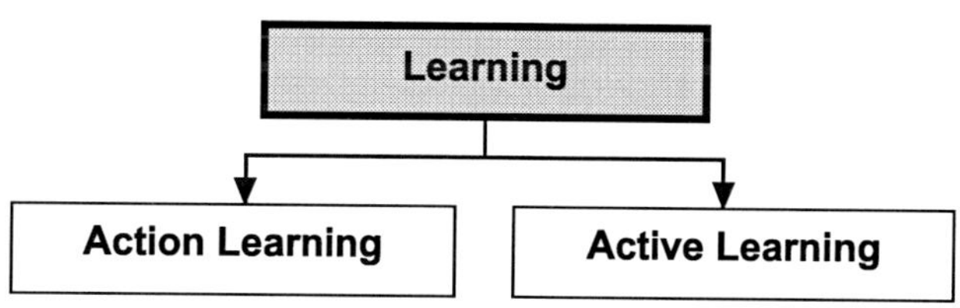

Fig. 4.3 : Learning Facets

Action Learning

This is a continuous process of learning and reflection with the intention of getting something done. It does not use project work, job rotation, or any form of a simulation such as case studies or business games (see active learning). Learning is centered on the need to find a solution to a real problem. Most action learning programmes take from four to nine months to complete. Learning is voluntary and learner driven, while individual development is as important as finding the solution to the problem.

Active Learning

A process of learning new ideas, skills and attitudes through what an employee does at work or in other behavioral situations. It is about learning from doing, performing, and taking action. The action can be either mental (e.g. reflection) or physical (e.g. case study). It uses such devices as games, simulations, introspection, role-playing, etc.

Learning Cycle

David Kolb gave the idea that learning is a circular process with a distinctive number of stages are as follows (figure 4.4):

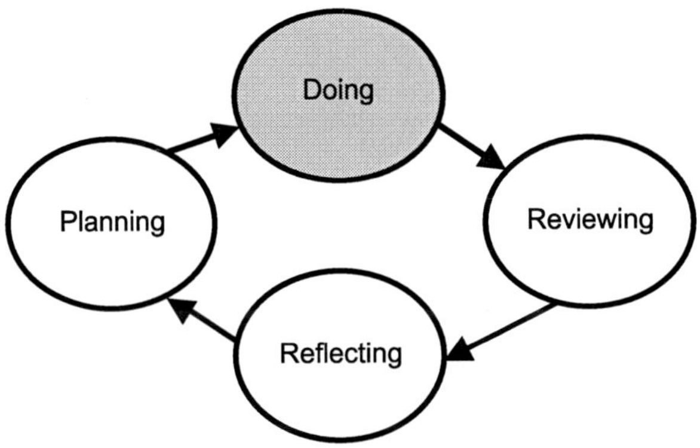

Fig. 4.4 : Kolb's Learning Cycle

1. Doing:

Immersing oneself in the "experiencing" of a task is the first stage in which the individual, team or organisation simply carries out the task assigned. The person engaged is usually not reflecting on the task at this time, but carrying it out with intention.

2. Reviewing:

Involves stepping back from task involvement and reviewing what has been done and experienced. The skills of attending, noticing differences, and applying terms help identify subtle events and communicate them clearly to others. One's paradigm (values, attitudes, values, beliefs) influences whether one can differentiate certain events. One's vocabulary is also influential, since without words, it is difficult to verbalize and discuss one's perceptions.

3. Reflecting:

It involves interpreting the events that have been noticed and understanding the relationships among them. It is at this stage that theory may be particularly helpful as a template for framing and explaining events. One's paradigm again influences the interpretive range a person is willing to entertain.

4. Planning:

Enables taking the new understanding and translate it into predictions about what is likely to happen next or what actions should be taken to refine the way the task is handled.

The timing of the learning cycle is particularly important. If one waits until after a task is completed, there is no opportunity to refine it until a similar task arises. However, continual reflection leaves the person spending more time on thinking than getting the task done – these must be balanced. In general, the learning cycle should be used during initial framing of a problem to see whether past experience may offer an approach; during natural breaks in tasking such as the end of meetings or workdays; when progress is noticeably going well or poorly; or when a crisis occurs that disrupts the process.

The logic of the learning cycle is to make many small and incremental improvements, which when done by many people, constitute major improvements over time. The model can also be applied to teams:

Doing: the team members are engaged in team task and interaction

Reflection: Team members use public reflection and open dialog to share perceptions of what has occurred, how they interact, and evaluate facilitative and no facilitative team processes

Interpretation: The team increases cohesiveness and develops a common culture by constructing shared meanings about the events.

Planning: The team engages in joint planning, deciding, and express commitment to action.

Learning Pyramid

Learning consists of data, information, knowledge and wisdom. Data is a representation of facts, concepts, or instructions in a formalized manner suitable for communication, interpretation, or processing by humans or by automatic means. Data helps in collecting information about the kind of learning that is required for the human resources of an organisation. Information is a term with many meanings depending on context, but is as a rule closely related to such concepts as meaning, knowledge, instruction, communication, representation, and mental stimulus. Often used very broadly to encompass all ideas, facts, and imaginative works; can also be used to mean a single data element. Information helps an organisation to analyse various options and methods of learning that can be employed. Knowledge refers to what one knows and understands. Knowledge is sometimes categorized as unstructured, structured, explicit or tacit. What we know we know is explicit knowledge. Knowledge that is unstructured, understood and not clearly expressed is implicit knowledge. If the knowledge is organized and easy to share then it is called structured knowledge. To convert implicit knowledge into explicit knowledge, it must be extracted and formatted. This refers to a body of information relevant to job performance. It is what people have to know to be able to perform a job, such as knowledge of policies and procedures for a HR professional. The ability to recall the underlying principles and theories, and the names of the parts, tools, resources, and forms required to perform a task. Knowledge is increasingly important, as a source of competitive advantage. Knowledge creation leads to continuous innovation, which in turn results in competitive advantage. Wisdom is the ability and desire to make choices that can gain approval in a long-term examination. In this sense, to label a choice "wise" implies that the action or inaction was strategically correct when judged by widely held values. Having experience, knowledge and understanding together with the power of applying all three with prudence, practicality, discretion and common sense.

The learning pyramid is depicted in figure 4.5.

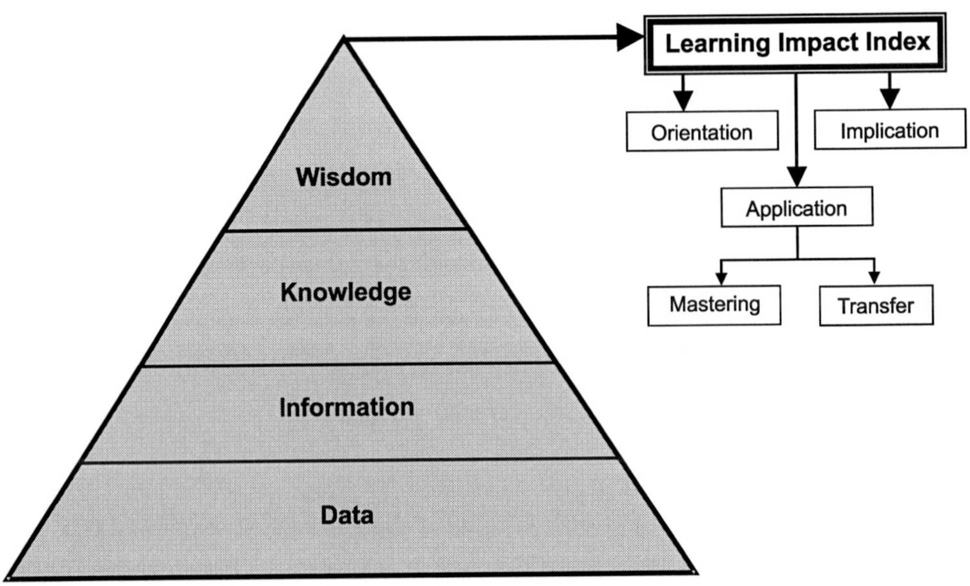

Fig. 4.5 : Learning Pyramid

Wisdom facilitates the application of appropriate learning tool in the organisation to gain competitiveness because the ability of the organisation to learn faster than its competitors is the only source of sustained competitive advantage. Now, the degree of wisdom will depend on the learning absorbed by the employees and employed productively at the workplace. Therefore, it is essential to measure the impact of learning through index: (*i*) orientation *i.e.*, how well employees have grasped skills, competencies and desired behaviours, (*ii*) implication i.e. what are the benefits of learning anticipated such as improvement in quality, customer service, productivity, cost saving, etc. and application *i.e.* (*iii*) mastery of learned knowledge, skills and behaviours and their productive transfer to workstations and other employees for improving the performance of the organisation.

Learning Model

Learning is the process by which skills; knowledge and attitudes are acquired and translated into desired behaviour and performance by design. Therefore, learning encompasses a specific process in the organisational context as depicted in figure 4.6.

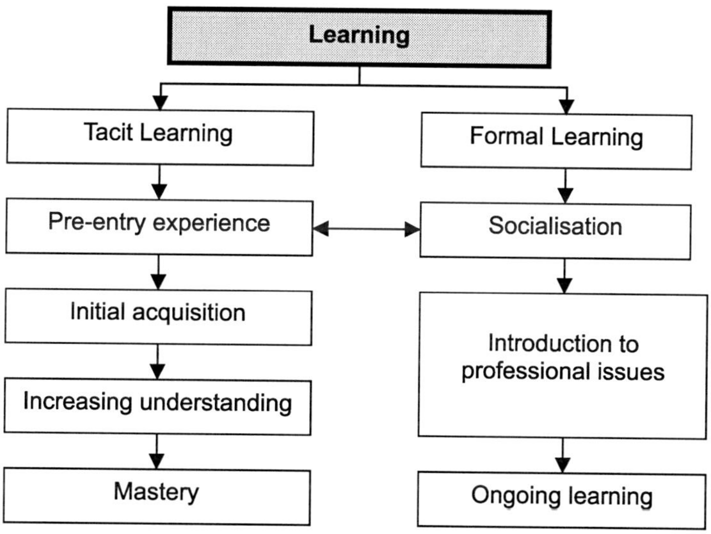

Fig. 4.6 : General Model of Learning

Tacit learning is defined as "learning by doing". The process of acquiring knowledge is best done through tacit learning. It involves classroom learning and applying on the shop floor. It facilitates employees to use their talents to best apply the learning concepts to improve business processes. Every employee (except freshers) has specific idea various concepts, tools and techniques associated with a job owing to their prior work experience. They have knowledge as to how to do a particular assignment and/ or a project. Learning provided by the organisation to the employees helps in bringing in the initial acquisition of knowledge, skills and competencies, which the employee's will correlate to their previous experiences. This helps in increasing understanding of the specific needs of skills and competencies required by the organisation. Employees then practices the learning acquired in their workplaces and gradually develops mastery.

Formal learning is planned learning that derives from activities within a structured learning setting. Formal learning is enrolling on a programme of study, attending lectures, and preparing coursework, engaging in seminar/discussions etc. Formal learning provides opportunities to employees, especially the new ones, to get acquainted with the culture, philosophy, morals and values of the organisation. This helps employees in preparing ground for application of learning within the organisational parameters in a focused manner. Employees also come to know about various professional issues confronting their work through the process of socialization from other senior employees/peer group. Employees gears themselves to effectively pursue professional issues and this require continuous learning so as to stay abreast with the challenges posed by environment. With ongoing learning, employee's keep sharpening their skills and competencies to provide thrust to the strategic planning activities of the organisation. Learning is essentially a process of maturing, which may start from a stage of no formal learning opportunity to learning organisation. Competitive pressures on organisations and strategic planning of the organisation forces organisations to establish learning management approach, which must be consistently applied and must enhance the competencies of the learners/employees. However, learning process must be linked to the strategic planning of the organisation so as to facilitate the attainment of competitive advantage by the organisation. As the organisation starts leveraging its strategic learning system, it reaps benefits and institutes more learning activities and encourages all employees to learn ... learn ... and learn thereby making the organisation a 'learning organisation'.

Learning Maturity Model Stages is depicted in figure 4.7 summarizes the above discussions.

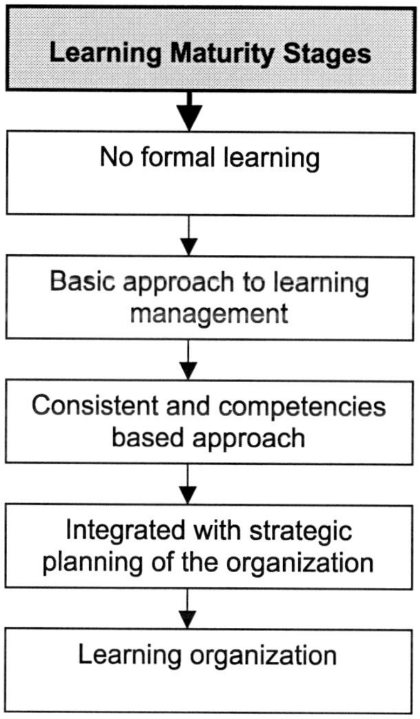

Fig. 4.7 : Stages of Learning Maturity Model

Approaches to learning

There are two ways, which have dominated learning over the years. Specifically; these approaches are as follows:

1. Operant conditioning:

This way views learning as a behavioural change brought about by a function on its consequences. It can be described as a type of conditioning in which behaviour leads to a reward or prevents punishment. Operant conditioning focuses on learning from external sources, as opposed to learning that takes place from within. In operant conditioning, there are four ways in which behaviour can be shaped:

- Positive reinforcement, which provides a pleasant response to an individual's actions;
- Negative reinforcement, which involves an unpleasant reward; and
- Punishment, which penalizes employees for specific undesirable behaviours.

2. Social learning theory:

This theory views learning as a continuous interaction between individuals and their environments. According to this theory, learning occurs through observation and direct experience. Social learning theory focuses on what individuals observe, and the importance of their perceptions in learning. In social learning, four processes have been found to influence an individual as follows :

(*i*) Attentional processes:

People only learn from models when they recognize and pay attention to their critical features.

(*ii*) Retention processes:

A model's influence will depend on how well the individual remembers the model's action.

(*iii*) Motor reproduction processes:

After a person has seen a new behaviour by observing the model, the observation must be converted to doing.

(*iv*) Reinforcement processes:

Individuals will be motivated to exhibit the modeled behaviour if positive incentives or rewards are provided.

Learning Process (Organisational Learning Process)

A learning process is fundamental to the individual and organisational existence. Much of what people learn is the result of subconscious cognitive process which connect the person with their environment and takes place almost independently of the intentions and desires of the individual. Thus, learning will take place always irrespective of incentives or circumstances surrounding an individual.

The learning process is depicted in figure 4.8.

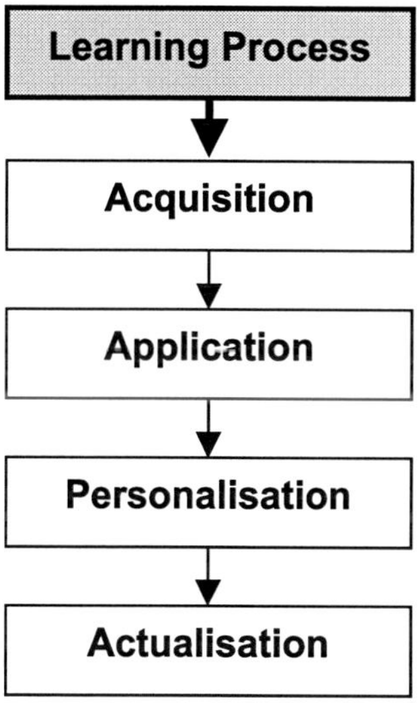

Fig. 4.8 : Learning Process Steps

1. Acquisition:

Employee acquires knowledge and understands the knowledge acquired. This stage presents the employee with information that may later serve as the basis for desired behaviour, learning integration and self-actualization.

Capturing learning occurs by thinking about self-preferences and review or consideration of alternatives. The process of capturing learning is depicted in figure 4.9.

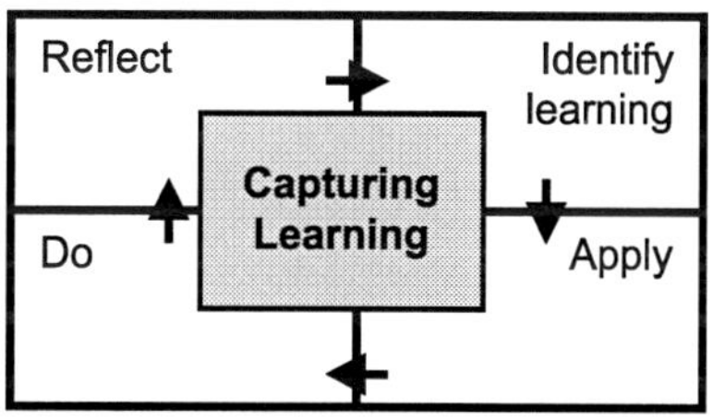

Fig. 4.9 : Capturing Learning

2. Application:

Employee demonstrates acquisition by putting into action knowledge acquired. Moving from the dimension of knowing into the dimension of know-how characterizes this stage.

3. Personalisation:

Employee integrates acquired and applied knowledge and re-examines and evaluates that knowledge. At this stage, employee will either make the learning of his own or reject it.

4. Actualisation:

At this stage, employee is approaching full potential. Transforming, inventing, conceptualizing and creating occur at this stage.

However, research indicates that learning process is affected by the following factors:

- National culture;
- Current knowledge;
- Motivation to learn;
- Learning orientation; and
- Learning styles.

In the organisational context, learning style takes the following shape as depicted in figure 4.10.

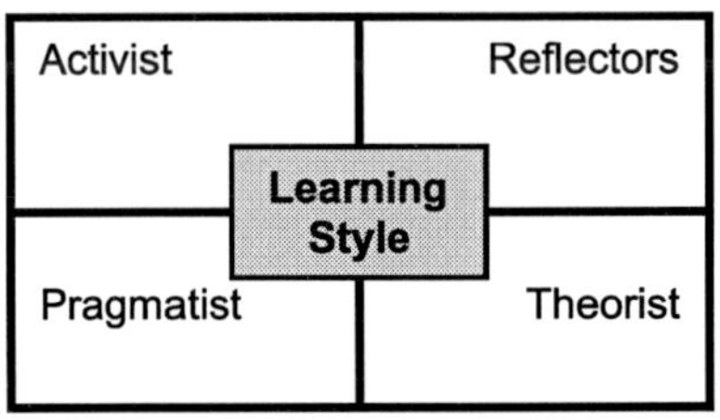

Fig. 4.10 : Learning Styles

1. Activist:

'Hands On' learners, who prefer to have a go and learn through trial and error.

2. Reflectors:

'Tell Me' learners, who prefer to be thoroughly briefed before proceeding.

3. Theorist:

'Convince Me' learners, who want reassurance that a particular project makes sense.

4. Pragmatists:

'Show Me' learners, who want a demonstration from an acknowledged expert.

Therefore, while designing a learning system, the following factors must be incorporated as mentioned below:

- Indirect factors;
- Strategic orientation;
- Organisational culture;

- Key stakeholders;
- Resources;
- Designer's personal frame of reference;
- An overview of the design process;
- A holistic view; and
- The HR developer as designer.

Mr. Ronesh Puri, MD, Executive Access, Asia's premier search Company, says "People are looking for a greater learning experience and is especially true for those between 30-40 years. They want to be CEOs by 45 years and prefer a job profile that helps them to move to the hot seat. They are looking at their careers in a more mature way".

Learning Approaches

Different organisations have different models or approaches to learning, depending on organisation's mission and objectives, leadership styles, organisational climate and culture, quality of personnel, strategic planning imperatives, nature of competition, general environment of business, etc. learning may be formal as well as informal, however the focus remains on increasing organisational competitiveness through appropriate deployment of knowledge made possible by suitable leverage to learning.

A generic model of learning approach is depicted in figure 4.11.

LEARNING CONTEXT	LEARNING APPROACHES: Formal	LEARNING APPROACHES: Informal
Developmental	• Skills • Curriculum • Prescription	• Counseling • Mentoring • Coaching
Work-based	• Workflow support • Performance support	• Collaborative learning • Action learning

Fig. 4.11 : Learning Approaches

Business priority of Learning

Learning is critical to achieve organisational excellence. A strategically aligned learning system in the organisation contributes immensely towards its success over a long period of time. Learning takes place at individual, group/team and organisational levels. To leverage the advantage of learning, it must be aligned with the strategic imperative, goals and objectives of the organisation. Learning at each level must be reciprocal and ultimately contribute to organisational effectiveness and excellence as depicted in figure 4.12.

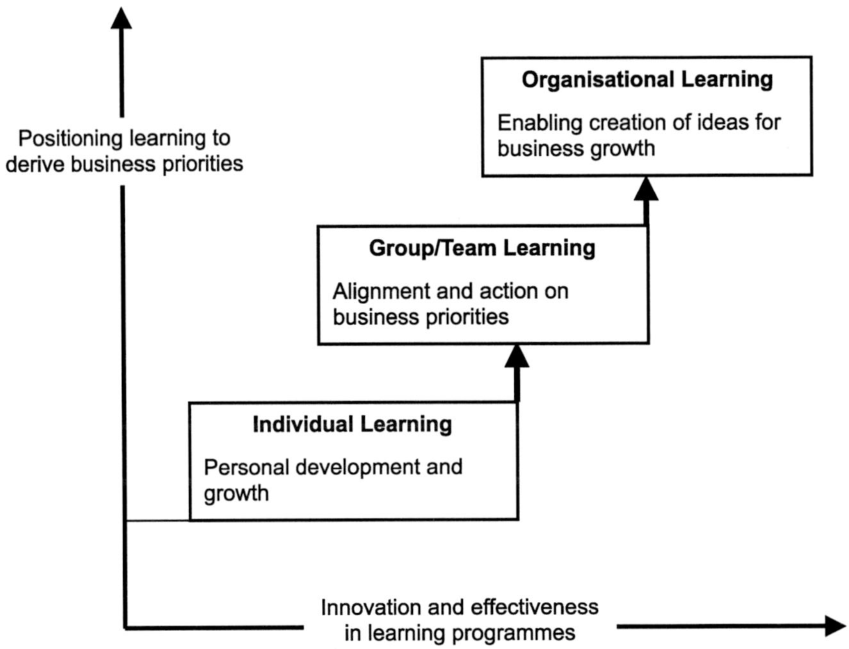

Fig. 4.12 : Learning Stages

Pitfalls of Learning

Learning sometimes becomes a frustrating experience due to lack of feeling of having learnt something or lack of appropriate reward for learning. Establishing the reasons of learning failures is critical to learning activity.

Some of the major pitfalls of learning are:

1. Learners are uncertain about the new behaviours they are expected to learn.
2. Lack of managerial ability to differentiate between a genuine learning need from lack of motivation or conflicting behavioural requirements adds to learning failures.
3. Difficulty in measuring quantitatively the learning because learning is difficult to see or observe;
4. Although learning fosters permanent changes in behaviour, however over time these changes can be diluted or completely lost; and
5. Some learners do not want to learn for a number of reasons, which causes problems in learning.

Learning Organisation

As organisations struggle to survive and prosper in the increasingly competitive environment, it is necessary to enhance the potential of the 'human asset' to achieve sustainable competitive advantage and cope with change. One approach is to constantly identify learning opportunities for individuals and the organisation (as a collection of individuals), share the learning from these and continuously transform the organisation. This requires re-thinking structures, working practices, communication systems and management styles.

Increasingly the business leaders believe that the ability to learn faster than competitors may be the only sustainable competitive advantage. The concept of learning organisation has emerged from the need of knowledge development for gaining or sustaining competitive advantage. A learning organisation can be described as one, which facilitates the learning of all its employees and continuously transforms itself as a whole. It is the skill in creating, acquiring, and transferring knowledge and modifying its behaviour which reflects new knowledge and insights. The concept of the learning organisation has the underlying idea of transforming an organisation through an open learning approach to present and future performance. It refers to an organisation's adaptability to a changing environment. Learning organisation continuously expands its capacity to create its future.

The learning organisation needs to have a formal way of asking questions, seeking out solutions and reflecting on them. Members of the organisation must be encouraged to challenge traditional ways of doing things and suggest improvements.

All successful organisations are good at doing certain things. This is their knowledge and skills base. This base must be developed to match changing conditions. Learning is not just the acquisition of new knowledge, it is, rather, a collective process of observation, experimentation and experience, which can be mobilized to deal with new opportunities or threats.

It is necessary for organisations to 'make space' in meetings, workshops and conferences, so that employees can reflect on what they have learned and need to learn. But what needs to be learned cannot always be taught. Human resource development programmes must therefore help people to learn from their experience. HRD professionals should understand that learning cannot be left to chance.

As organisations develop into learning organisations, this has a profound impact on the relationship between work and learning. Whereas learning used to be primarily equalled to training, it is now becoming predominantly associated with learning from experience, and self-directed learning. This changing view of learning has far-reaching consequences on the role and tasks of Human Resource Development function onward in the future.

Definitions:

A few noteworthy definition & Organisational Learning are as follows:

1. "Organisational learning is the process of acquiring knowledge and utilizing information to adapt successfully to changing circumstances".

(Schermerhorn, Hunt and Osborn: 2003)

2. "A Learning Company is an organisation that facilitates the learning of all its members and consciously transforms itself and its context".

(Pedler et al: 1997)

3. "By the term organisational learning we mean the changing of organisational behaviour. The changing of organisational behaviour is a collective learning process".

(Swieringa and Wierdsma: 1992)

4. "Learning organisation is an organisation which facilitates the learning of all its members and continually transforms itself".

(Pedler, Boydell and Burgoyne: 1989)

5. "Learning organisation as one that both learns and encourages learning in people. It creates space for people to question, think and learn, and constantly reframes the world and their part in it.

(Handy: 1989)

From analytical study of the above definitions, we may conclude that:

Organisational learning is a culture of continuous learning to maximize performance and capacity at individual, team and organisation level. However, *Senge (1995)* has emphasized that it is the individuals and not organisations that learn.

Characteristics of Learning Organisations

The main characteristics of learning organisations are:

1. Systematic problem solving;
2. Experimentation with new approaches;
3. Learning from own experiences and past history;

4. Learning from experiences and best practices of other organisations;
5. Transferring knowledge quickly and efficiently throughout the organisation;
6. Encourages people to identify and satisfy their own learning needs;
7. Provides individuals with regular reviews on performance and learning needs;
8. Provides feedback on performance and achieved learning;
9. Provides new experiences from which people can learn; and
10. Facilitates the use of training on the job.

A learning organisation engages in the following actiuities:

- It learns collaboratively, openly and across boundaries;
- It values how it learns as well as what it learns;
- It invests in staying ahead of the learning curve in its industry;
- It gains competitive edge by learning faster and smarter than competitors;
- It turns data into useful knowledge quickly and at the right time and place;
- It enables every employee to feel that every experience provides an opportunity;
- It exhibits little fear and defensiveness and learns what goes wrong;
- It takes risks but avoids endangering the basic security of the organisation;
- It supports people and teams who wish to pursue action-learning projects; and
- It depoliticizes learning but not penalizing individuals for sharing information.

Organisational Learning Culture

Given the dynamic and competitive nature of business, organisations have to develop an environment and provide resources so as to enable all employees (including top notch managers) to engage in learning in order to acquire new competencies both for individual growth and development and to effectively achieve the objectives and mission of the organisation (see figure 4.13).

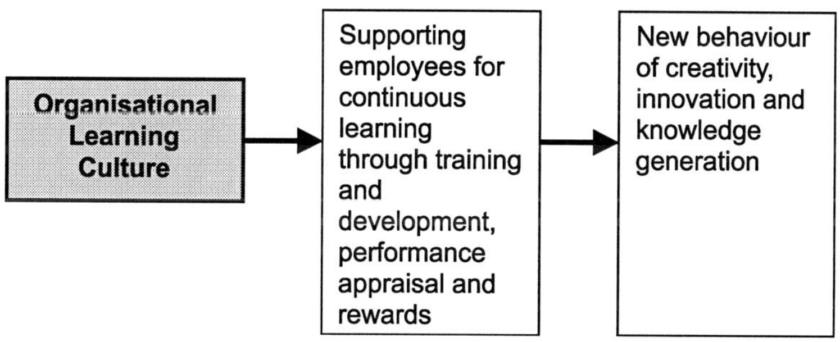

Fig. 4.13 : Organizational Learning Culture

Learning in the Learning Organisation

As a result of the ever-increasing rate of technological change induced by developments such as globalisation and the current 'explosion of knowledge', the organisational learning capabilities are pinpointed as the key strategic factors for contemporary organisations.

Argyris and Schön (1978) suggested that organisational learning is a process in which members of an organisation detect error and correct it by restructuring organisational theory of action, embedding the results of their inquiry in organisational maps and images. This learning can occur at two levels. The first level is that of single-loop learning, which means that the organisation makes small adjustments in its actions, but doesn't radically change them. Double loop learning involves detecting errors, but finding solutions outside the current ways of thinking and acting – there is a change in the system itself. A third level of organisational learning is labeled as "deuteron learning". This refers to the capacity of organisations to learn how to carry out, and how to optimize its single and double-loop learning processes. In other words, it refers to "learning how to learn".

For learning on an organisational level, organisations depend on the learning of their employees, since they embody the capacity to acquire or create new knowledge for the organisations, disseminate this knowledge to others within the organisation and apply the new knowledge within the organisation. Organisations deliberately set out to create learning structures for employees, believing that they need 'learning individuals' to realise 'organisational learning'. However, employee learning in it is not enough to ensure learning at an organisational level. Also an adequate communication (to transfer to other levels), and a certain amount of empowerment of employees within the operational core (to make improvements in the workplace) are important in this respect.

Considering the above, a learning organisation can be described as an organisation that responds to (and anticipates) changes in its environment by fostering learning on a strategic level. Moreover, it deliberately aims at improving its ability to learn by single loop and double loop learning. It makes use of the learning of all employees; therefore this employee learning is enhanced at all hierarchical levels (deuteron-learning). A learning organisation accepts both the environmental turbulence and the fact that it cannot predict which changes will occur. The concept is more adequately described as a metaphor or an ideal; it is a way of looking at organisations wherein the process of organisational learning is the centre of attention.

Organisations should focus on creating opportunities for employee learning with the long-term goal of becoming a learning organisation, wherein facilities for employee learning (on-the-job as well as off-the-job) are created. Moreover these organisations stimulate employees not only to attain new knowledge and skills, but also to acquire skills in the field of learning and problem solving and thus develop their capacity for future learning. One could say that becoming a learning oriented organisation is the first stage in the growth process towards a learning organisation.

Human Resource Development in Learning Organisations

As organisations develop into learning organisations, the transformation has profound impact on the relationship between work and learning. Whereas learning used to be primarily equaled to training, it has now become predominantly associated with learning from experience, and self-directed learning, necessary to cope with changing demands in the organisational environment. Similarly, learning is no longer regarded solely as a classroom activity. This changing view of learning has far-reaching consequences for line managers, who are expected to manage the workplace as a place fit for learning. In addition, this shift has an influence upon employees who are now expected to take greater responsibility for their own learning. Finally, it considerably affects the role and tasks of human resource development professionals, who are involved in organizing learning activities for the organisation and ensuring that work culture facilitates application.

Role of Human Resource Development Function in Learning Organisation

The role, which is generally contributed to human resource development practitioners, is the role of consultant towards line management on how to facilitate and stimulate employee learning in the workplace, and how to link this learning to organisational needs and goals. The word 'trainer' is really no longer an adequate label for their function. The new role of human resource development practitioners will be that of a strategic learning facilitator, performance consultant and change agent. In general, the field of human resource development seems to be moving from a reactive, isolated business function to a more strategic factor.

More specifically, the vision of human resource development function in learning organisations with regard to their own role can be characterized by three basic principles:

The first working principle is the broadened view of human resource development function's own work field. It's not limited to training, but stretched to facilitating and supporting learning processes within the organisation, with the aim to contribute to meaningful organisational learning processes. As a result, the human resource development function not only fosters formal learning, but also strives to enhance informal and even incidental learning. Next to that, the department not only focuses on individual learning, but also aims at facilitating the collective learning of groups and organisational learning.

The second working principle is that 'learning' is a shared responsibility of management, employees and the human resource development function. The human resource development department regards its own role in this respect as primarily supportive (e.g. the role of consultant). This implies a shift away from the idea that training is primarily the responsibility of the training department.

Thirdly, the processes of learning and working are very much intermingled. Learning is being regarded as a normal part of everyday work and working is seen as a rich source for learning. On-the-job learning is stimulated as much as possible. Therefore, a considerable amount of training takes place on-the-job. Off-the-job training activities will remain important, but they are no longer the dominant way to organize the learning processes. They fulfill a supportive role with regard to the learning and training, which takes place on the job.

The "learning organisation" is an important metaphor for human resource development. Role of human resource development professionals in learning organisations are:

1. Developing collective intelligence within organisations and organisational forms supporting such a need thus eliminating the holding of knowledge in separate compartments at different levels;
2. Understanding the importance of knowledge and in particular tacit knowledge, which has to be recognized and valorized insofar as it is embedded in human resources;
3. Moving from training-based development policies towards new policies fostering learning in different ways (support for competencies development, learning networks, learning self-assessment in the communities of practice);
4. The main motivator for wanting to become a learning organisation is the desire to become more customer (internal & external) centered by continuous improvement and innovation. However, more people-oriented reasons such as improving the quality of working life seem to play a role as well;
5. The envisioned role of human resource development professionals within learning organisations is to:

   –Support the business;

   –Support (informal) learning;

   –Support knowledge sharing (as a special form of supporting informal learning); and Develop and coordinate training.

6. Change human resource development practices. Although human resource development professionals consider that this is still their main responsibility, managers and employees are important active partners in supporting learning, and are expected to become more so in the future. Their role is predominantly one of identifying learning needs, stimulating and supporting informal learning, ensuring the continuous learning of themselves and others. Human resource development professionals will continue to provide support like organizing training and supporting informal learning efforts;

7. Human resource development training-related strategies still fulfill a significant role, with instruments and initiatives to increase employee responsibility for learning, being of least importance. Some barriers to change are:

–Insufficient time for learning on the part of the employees;

–Insufficient time for performing human resource development tasks on the part of the managers; and

–Lack of clarity on the role of human resource development.

8. The type of organisation does not influence the way in which the organisation envisage the role of human resource development; the strategies they employ to implement human resource development activities and the factors that facilitate the attainment of the envisioned role of human resource development.

9. There is no one single model for human resource development, although there are subtle but meaningful differences as to the philosophies, strategies, and practices on human resource development across the organisations and cultures.

10. Line-managers should increasingly take a role in the development of human resources due to the convergence of management of organisational competences (aimed at internal effectiveness and competitive advantages on the market) and the management of individual competencies (based on explicit and tacit knowledge) results in new ways of organizing organisations.

E-Learning

There has been a growing global interest in E-Learning. E-Learning may be defined as 'A way of working, studying and problem solving that reflects the growing connectivity of people and learning resources".

The paradigm of E-learning has changed drastically in recent years as depicted in figure 4.14.

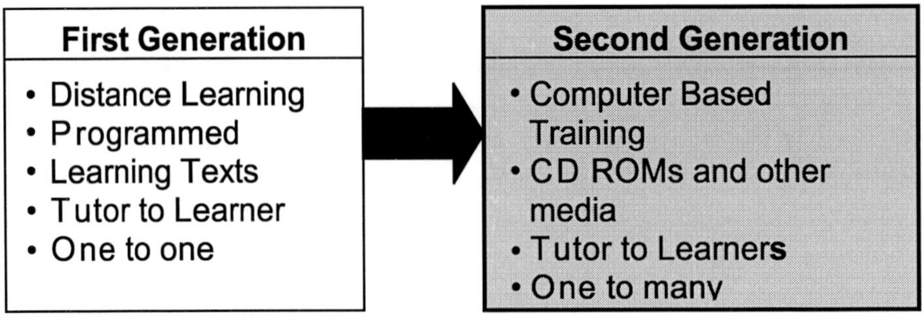

Fig. 4.14 : Changing Paradigm of E-Learning

Self-directed learning

The idea that personal development is distinct from formal training is subject to self-management is one that has received increasing attention and support in recent times. According to *Sambrook and Stewart* (1999), there is a need to move away from organisational directed learning, as the individual start to take more control of their own development needs. Due to the differences in organisational needs, cultural context organisational structure and resources available, the concept of the individual taking more responsibility for his development is a significant shift away from earlier ideas.

Additionally, there has been a shift in the last decade from off-the-shelf training to meet competence voids, towards a more learning environment that relies on experiential learning and self-direction. It is argued, such an approach, does not limit itself to training, but stretches to facilitating and supporting learning processes within the organisation, with the aim to contribute to meaningful organisational learning processes. This clearly has an impact on the concept of human resource development and any approach it may take within an organisation. It can therefore be argued, that a key role of human resource development is to create and/or maintain a learning organisational environment as the foundation to any training and learning within an organisation.

The concept of self-directed learning involves encouraging individuals to take responsibility for their own learning needs, either to improve performance in their present job or to satisfy their career aspirations. It can be based on a process of recording achievement and action planning which involves individuals reviewing what they have learnt, what they have achieved, what their goals are, how they are going to achieve those goals and what new learning they need to acquire. *Mumford* (1994) suggests that self-directed learning can be carried out as follows:

- Identify the individuals' learning style;
- Review how far their learning is encouraged or restricted by their learning style;
- Review core learning skills of observation and reflection, analysis, creativity decision-making and evaluation, and consider how to use them more effectively;
- Review the work and other experiences in which they are involved in terms of the kind of learning opportunity they offer;
- Look for potential mentors in the self-development process;
- Draw up learning objectives and a plan of action; and
- Set aside some time each day to answer the question 'What did I learn today?'

Self-directed learning is based on the principle that people learn and retain more if they find things out for themselves. There is a need to create a climate of awareness about the opportunities for learning and development and to design training events to develop training styles and skills.

The organisation can encourage self-directed learning by ensuring that learners:

- Define for themselves, with whatever guidance they may require, what they need to know to perform their job effectively;
- Receive guidance on where they can get the material or information which will help them learn;
- Prepare a learning plan and programme as part of a learning contract; and
- Prepare a personal development plan setting out what they need to learn, how they should develop and the actions they need to take to achieve learning and development goals.

Hence, it can be concluded that training is still an important strategy, but it is complemented by strategies to support other types of learning and by activities meant to ensure a close link between training and organisational strategy. Important to that human resource development function is not only to provide opportunities for learning, but also deliberately try to change attitude towards learning.

Eight Trends in workplace learning

According to Colteryahn and Davis (2004), the eight trends are :

According to Colteryahn and Davis (2004), the eight trends are :

- HRD/Training and Development must help organisations to create and innovate for higher efficiency and effectiveness with less money;
- Streamlining and becoming more flexible (outsourcing);
- Globalization–work done off-site, out of country;
- Diversity–not experienced workers, retirement workers, lifestyle and ethnic backgrounds, need for skilled and educated workers;
- Change– adaptability–quick. Combining e-learning in person;
- Security;
- Technology; and
- Ethics.

Bibliography :

Colteryahn, K. and Davis, P., "Trends you need to know now", T&D Magazine, January 2004, Pp. 28-36.

Review and Discussion Questions

Question 1: Define and explain the concept of learning in the organisational context. What are the components of learning?

Question 2: Give a brief account of theoretical perspectives of learning. Which theory do you find more relevant in today's business scenario and why?

Question 3: How is learning pyramid constructed? Also, explain the learning process.

Question 4: What are the essential approaches to learning? Give a generic model of learning approaches in organisational context.

Question 5: How can be linked to business priority of an organisation?

Question 6: Define and explain the concept of learning organisation. Name some Indian 'learning' organisations.

Question 7: How organisational learning culture can be instituted?

Question 8: What is the role of human resource development function in a learning organisation?

Question 9: Give a critical account of recent scenario of learning organisation in India. What are the reasons of its slow progress in the Indian context?

Question 10: Explain the meaning of self-directed learning.

Question 11: Write short notes on:

i) Pitfalls/shortcomings of learning
ii) E-learning
iii) HRD in learning organisation
iv) Learning model

Exhibit: 4 – A

Case Situation

•*Before attempting this section please read Chapter - 14 on Case Study.*

•*Please read the following case situations and answer the questions.*

Q 1. You have joined a start up small company as CEO. What measures would you take to foster business relevant learning processes and build learning culture?

Q 2. Julie, Head-Human Resources for a large manufacturing firm, is concerned that 40% of the clerical staff hired last year lacked basic reading, writing and filing skills. She thinks that these staff should be terminated as early as possible. Do you agree to this? What would you do if you had been in her place?

Exhibit: 4 – B

Case Study

• *Before attempting this section please read Chapter - 14 on Case Study.*

• *Please read the following case study and answer all the subsequent questions.*

Introduction to the organisation:

Nihant Sofwares Ltd. (NSL) is into the business of software development with significant market share. The company has grown consistently by 20% per annum and is known for the quality of its software packages.

The CEO wants to spread head further growth to tap huge overseas market for software products. The organisation intends to build a learning culture, which is a crucial weapon in the hand of CEO to give impetus to the growth plans.

Brief Description of the Problem:

The organisation intends to put up training and learning center to strengthen the learning culture in the organisation. It has identified the followings as key to developing an organisational learning culture:

- Learning is crucial to the company's success.
- The organization and individual employees through appropriate mix of training and learning initiatives can develop competencies, crucial to competitive advantage.
- Selection of E-learning as the most cost effective and efficient method.

The CEO decided that training shall be outsourced but the content outlines shall be based on in-house guidelines. Special reward shall be given to employees who acquire business relevant software skills and/or higher qualification, which can contribute to the bottom line of the organisation. CEO calls a meeting of all employees and explains his game plan to them and seeks their active cooperation.

Emphasis in communicating special learning incentives was placed by the CEO and Head-Human Resources and how it will benefit the organisation and individual employees was also explained.

Annual review was conducted to assess the effectiveness of learning initiatives. It was found that within one year, the company had accomplished 15% rise in business volume primarily from overseas market. 35% of the employees have acquired new skills of their own either through workshops/training or higher education which has helped the organization to grow.

Questions:

1. What are the major reasons of CEO seeking to build a learning organization culture?

2. How self-directed learning has helped the organization to grow?

3. Why e-learning method was chosen?

CHAPTER

5 Career Planning, Career Development and Career Strategy

Chapter Synopsis

Career Planning, Development and Strategy are necessary to attract, engage and retain the best professionals in the organisation for its increased competitiveness. Best employees attach great value to career for their personal and professional development.

This chapter explains these concepts and strategies to align the goals of the organisation and developmental aspirations of individual employees for organisational excellence.

This Chapter contains:

Nature and concept of career planning, Definitions of career planning, Characteristics of career planning, Objectives of career planning, Importance/Benefits of career planning, Nature and concept of career development, Definitions of career development, Characteristics of career development, Objectives of career development, Importance of career development, Principles of career development, Theories of career development, Strategies to support career development, Role of HRD function in career planning and development of employees, Career banding, Nature and concept of career strategy, Career strategy process, Review & discussion questions, Case situation and Case study.

Career Planning, Career Development and Career Strategy

Career Planning

A career is a sequence of work-related positions occupied by a person during a lifetime. Career is the sequence of attitudes and behaviours associated with work related activities experienced by individuals over the span of their working lives.

Career may be defined as:

1. "A sequence of jobs that constitute what a person does for a living".

(Schermerhorn: 2002)

2. "Career is a succession of related jobs arranged in a hierarchy of prestige through which the person moves in an ordered predictable fashion".

(Wilensky: 1960)

A career is the sum total of all the work — paid and unpaid – a person has done and will do in his lifetime. At any given time, a person has exerted conscious effort to provide goods or services to benefit to him or others and has been engaged in work. Paid or unpaid, volunteer or reluctant, he plays many work roles: student, homemaker, citizen, manager, worker, etc. in his life time.

Career path is a chart showing the possible directions and career opportunities available in an organisation; it presents the steps in a possible career and a plausible timetable for accomplishing them. Every career path has a plateau also. Career plateau is a position from which someone is unlikely to move to a higher level of work responsibility.

A persons' career influences and gets influenced by a number of factors. Major career influences are:

- Influence of other people such as superior, subordinate or peer group;
- Major work achievements;
- Success and satisfiaction at work;
- Risks taken; and
- Helping others to grow and succeed.

Career Planning is a process to gain insight into what a person is, where he is and where he wants to go in his career. The process may include identifying what is important to him in career, identifying what career path is best for him and skill building to improve his career possibilities. Career planning today is characterized by:

- Rapid change;
- Complex nature of work in today's organisations;
- Wide work options;
- High diversity of people;
- Gender issues; and
- Availability of career resources and guidance.

Definitions:

a few noteworthy definitions of Career Planning are as follows:

1. "Career planning is a process of systematically matching career goals and individual capabilities with opportunities for their fulfillment".

(Schermerhorn, Hunt and Osborn: 2003)

2. "Career planning is the process of enhancing an employee's future value".

(Schwind, Das and Wagar: 2004)

Thus, a career plan is an individual's choice of occupation, organisation, and career path.

The career planning encourages individuals to explore and gather information, which enables them to synthesize, gain competencies, make decisions, set goals and take action. Each individual varies in their progress through each of these stages for many reasons. Some advance rapidly through each or all of the stages while others progress more slowly. Individuals may repeat all or parts of the career development process at various points throughout their lives as values, interests, abilities, and life circumstances change.

Career planning is a crucial phase of human resource development because career planning provides employees with strategy for work-life balance. Work-life balance refers to the process by which people balance career demands with personal and family needs. Progressive organisations support a healthy work-life balance.

Career planning as process of identifying and matching the needs of individuals and organisations is depicted in figure 5.1.

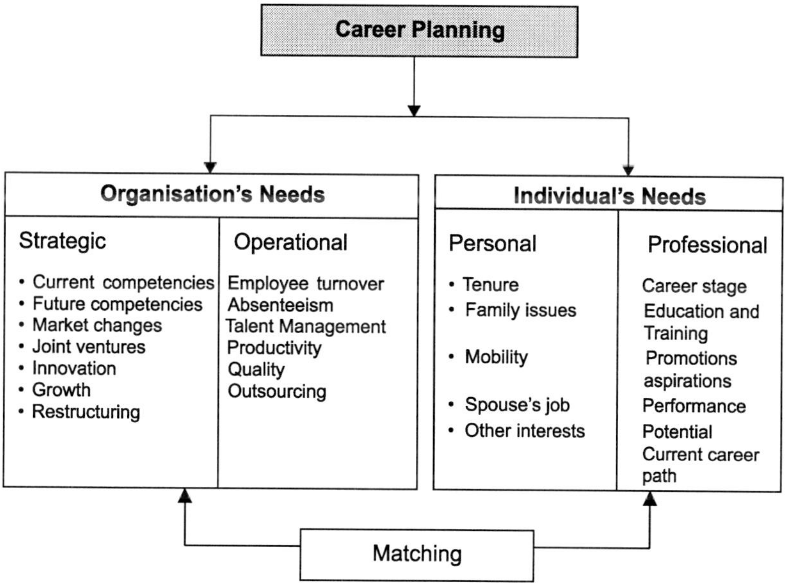

Fig. 5.1 : Matching Career Needs of Organization & Individual

Characteristics of Career Planning

The main characteristics of career planning are:

1. It is an ongoing process;
2. It develops and shares a personal life-career model/timeline;
3. It defines life career, abilities, and interests of employees;
4. It describes the various roles an individual may have as part of his career in the organisation;
5. It helps individual to develop skills required to fulfill different career roles, within or outside an organisation;
6. It strengthens work-related activities in the organisations; and
7. It charts out occupational/professional directions as they relate to career goals.

Objectives of Career Planning

The major objectives of career planning are:

1. To develop an awareness of each employee's uniqueness;
2. To identify positive characteristics about employees, which can be harnessed for organisational development;
3. To identify personal qualities and events that has influenced employee's self-concept;

4. To identify personal interests, abilities, strengths and weaknesses and how they relate to careers;
5. To get an understanding of the relationship between personality and occupational/ professional goals and how they can be aligned to organisational mission and objectives;
6. To explore personal value systems of employees and how they relate to organisational culture;
7. To recognize differences in the way people see the abilities of others;
8. To foster effective team building skills;
9. To develop respect for the feelings and beliefs of others;
10. To create healthy ways of dealing with conflicts, stress, and emotions in self and others;
11. To attract, engage and retain talented professionals in the organisation; and
12. To develop higher motivation, commitment and competence amongst the employees.

Importance/Benefits of Career Planning

Career planning needs to begin early to optimize the range of career options that will be available when each employee begins his career in an organisation after selection process. The success of an organisation depends on the caliber of its human resources. It is the quality of the people that determines the continued survival and growth of the organisation. As the organisation grows, thought must be given not only to the recruitment, selection, development and retention of human resources but also for the organisation to direct its attention towards career planning.

In the past, many organisations adopted a benevolent and paternalistic attitude, assuming responsibility for the career pathing and growth of their employees. The organisation or rather the senior management would decide to what position, and at what pace employees would advance in their careers. This system could work in situations of stability or very steady growth.

The dynamic nature of business today, however, has presented problems for this system. Many organisations today have realized that they cannot take total responsibility for the career growth of their employees. Neverthless, career planning is important because the consequences of success or failure are linked closely with each individual's self-concept, identity, and satisfaction with work and life.

Career planning entails a process by which an individual employee chooses and sets his career goals and identifies the means to achieve them. The focus is to match the individual's personal preferences and goals with the opportunities that are realistically available. This means that career planning does not necessarily concentrate only on promotion and advancement opportunities. In fact the concept of career success has changed tremendously over the years and is no more as simple as it was in the past. The concept of career success and how a person views his career depends not only on the individual but also on many other factors. It is generally the case that people want more from their jobs than just money to survive on.

People today have achieved a standard of living that places them sufficiently well off to the point that they have the security to explore non-traditional models of career success and they are confronted with a variety of alternatives. Not everybody may want to be a manager. There may be some engineers, for example, who would prefer to be working on their technical problems. Today it is also recognized that from a practical standpoint, there are just not enough openings or opportunities to make promotion available for everyone. In fact, as more organisations opt for a flat structure, the coming years will see less promotion opportunities and this will cause frustrations and more job-hopping.

Organisations will need to look for alternatives means of satisfying employees' career aspirations. Ultimately career planning cannot be defined as just about promotions alone, each organisation will need to define it in terms of the career programmes it creates and by the individuals in terms of their own perspectives and needs.

Although career planning is the primary responsibility of the individual, the organisation should take an active interest in an employee's career planning. From the organisation's point of view, career planning involves a deliberate attempt to maximise an employee's potential contributions. The human resource plans of the organisation will indicate its future employment needs and the related career opportunities. With career planning, the organisation will be able to develop the employees so that when the time comes; there will be adequate supply of the right types of skills and abilities needed to enable the organisation to achieve its objectives.

There are many benefits for the organisation in undertaking career planning programmes. Some of these are:

1. Career planning develops promotable employees. Career planning ensures that the organisation has a constant supply of promotable employees;
2. Career planning reduces employee turnover. It helps in increasing the employees' loyalty because they will feel that the organisation has a genuine interest in their development;
3. Career planning encourages employees' growth and development. Employees will be motivated to grow and develop their potential abilities;
4. Career planning reduces hoarding. Career planning will discourage selfish managers from hoarding their key subordinates and suppressing their growth to the point that they stop doing their best, develop negative attitudes, or leave the organisation;
5. Career planning will ensure that senior management will become aware of the

interests, skills and qualifications of these employees who have better chances of moving upwards; and

6. Career planning can help the organisation prepare certain categories of employees for more important jobs and thus contribute to succession planning for the organisation.

Career Planning Process

Career planning process encourages individuals to explore and gather information which will enable them to synthesize, gain competencies, make decisions, set goals and take action. Each individual varies in their progress through each of these stages for many reasons. Some advance rapidly through each or all of the stages while others progress more slowly.

The steps of career planning are discussed as follows (see figure 5.2):

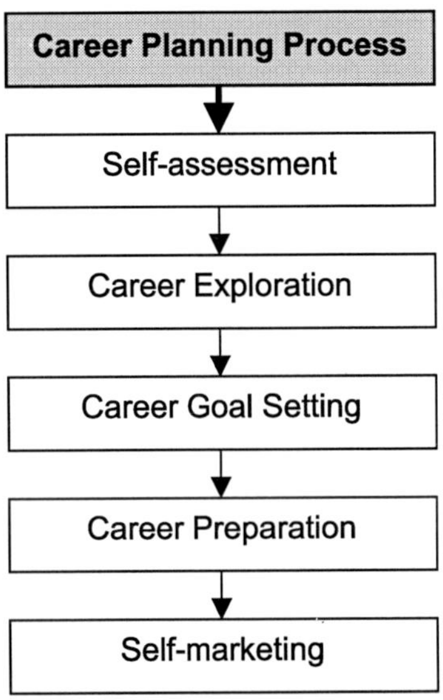

Fig. 5.2 : Steps of Career Planning Process

1. Self-Assessment:

The first step in career planning involves gathering information about an employee to assist him in making a decision about his career. The employee should develop an understanding of self-including values, interests, aptitudes, abilities, personal traits, and desired life style, and becoming aware of the interrelationship between self and occupational choice. It can be started by:

- Learning interests, abilities, skills, and work values;
- Listing accomplishments;

- Understanding physical and psychological needs;
- Assessing aspirations and motivation level; and
- Deciphering personal traits and characteristics.

A simple process of self-assessment is depicted in figure 5.3.

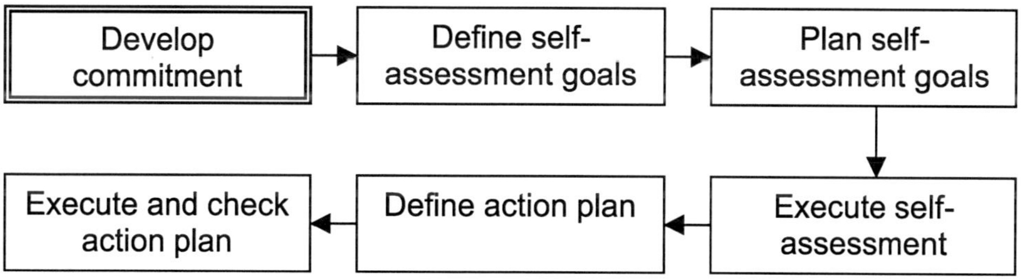

Fig. 5.3 : Steps of Self Assessment

Self-assessment is increasingly important for organisations that want to empower their employees to take control of their careers whether done through workbooks or workshops, Self-assessment usually involves doing skills assessment exercises, completing an interest's inventory, and clarifying values as depicted in figure 5.4.

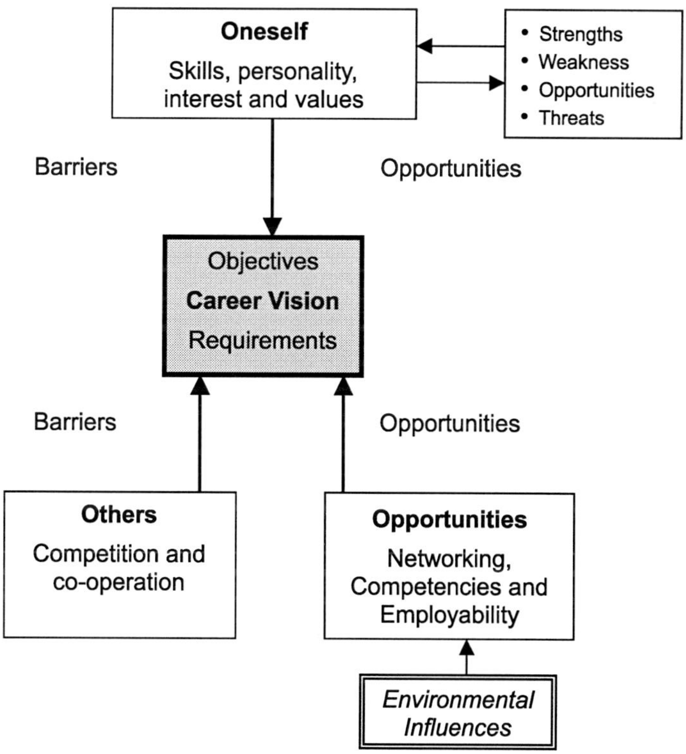

Fig. 5.4 : Career Needs - Opportunity Assessment

One of the modern and scientific methods of self-assessment is SWOT analysis. This key tool of strategic planning process can also be applied to career planning. A SWOT analysis focuses on the internal and external environments, examining strengths and weaknesses in the internal environment and opportunities and threats in the external environment. Self-assessment can be made through SWOT Analysis as mentioned below:

Career SWOT Analysis

INTERNAL

Employee's Strengths refers to Internal positive aspects that are under control and upon which an employee may capitalize in planning. Employee's Weaknesses refers to internal negative aspects that are under the control and upon which an employee may plan for improvement

Employee's Strengths	Employee's Weaknesses
▶ Work experience	▶ Lack of work experience
▶ Proper education	▶ Lack of proper education
▶ Strong job knowledge	▶ Lack of job knowledge
▶ Transferable skills	▶ Weak skills
▶ Positive personal characteristics	▶ Negative personal characteristics
▶ Good networking	▶ Poor networking

EXTERNAL

Employee's Opportunities refers to positive external conditions that are not under control and upon which an employee may take advantage. Employee's Threat refers to negative external conditions that are not under the control but the effect of which has to be lessened by an employee.

Employee's Opportunities	Employee's Threats
▶ Buoyancy in HR market	▶ Downslide in HR market
▶ Cashing on new/higher education	▶ Competition from fellow Professionals
▶ Skill shortages	▶ Competitors with superior skills
▶ Increased self-knowledge	▶ Competitors with better job hunting skills
▶ Increased professional development	▶ Limited professional development
▶ Good networking	▶ Poor networking
▶ Possess unique skill sets	▶ Possesses general skill sets

To construct a Career SWOT analysis is to set a course for employee's own career planning, examination of current situation is necessary in terms of his strengths and weaknesses, strategies for capitalizing on strengths and overcoming weaknesses in relation to the external opportunities and threats in one's chosen career field.

Employee should not only explore his own self-perception of strengths, but also put himself inside an organisation's (prospective or current) head keeping in view strong points. While doing so, false modesty must be avoided, as one needs to be brutally honest and realistic about himself.

One of the greatest strengths can be affinity for the work one is doing. Learning to "follow bliss" should be a critical component of managing career. Some people know from an early age what kind of work will make them happy. For others, nailing down the self-knowledge that leads to career fulfillment comes from a process of exploring interests, skills, personality, learning style, and values. Career assessment tools and tests can be taken to examine the kind of work that will give satisfaction to a person.

In assessing weaknesses, thinking about what prospective employers might consider being critical area has to be charted out for possible improvements. Facing frailties now can give a huge head start in career planning.

As humans, we find it relatively difficult to identify the areas where we are weak. But this assessment helps to identify areas where one needs to improve. If a skill has been identified in a chosen field, but he is weak in that skill area, he needs to take steps to improve that skill. Past performance appraisals and feedback can also provide valuable insight.

After having analyzed strengths, weaknesses, threats, and opportunities, an employee should use that information to plan how to market himself.

The marketing planning process entails a three-step process:

- Identifying objectives:
  - Determining objectives.
  - Developing marketing strategies.
  - Strategizing an action programme.
- Identifying development needs:
  - Feedback from others.
  - Praise and constructive criticism.
  - Knowing strengths and development needs.
  - Plan of action for development.

- Organisational Assessment:

Some of the tools traditionally used by organisations in selection are also valuable for career development. Among these are:

- Assessment centers.
- Psychological testing.
- Performance appraisal.
- Promotability forecasts.
- Succession planning.

Another crucial area pertains to assessment of competuey. Competency means an interrelated set of abilities, behaviors, attitudes, and knowledge needed by an individual to be effective in most professional and managerial positions. It can be measured against well-accepted standards and can be improved through training and development. There are three types of competencies viz. Contributing competencies, Journey competencies and Advanced competencies as depicted in figure 5.5.

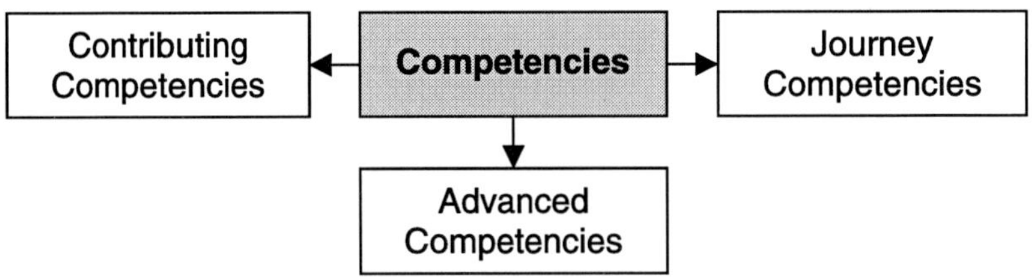

Fig. 5.5 : Types of Competencies

Following the method as depicted in figure 5.6, competency can be assessed:

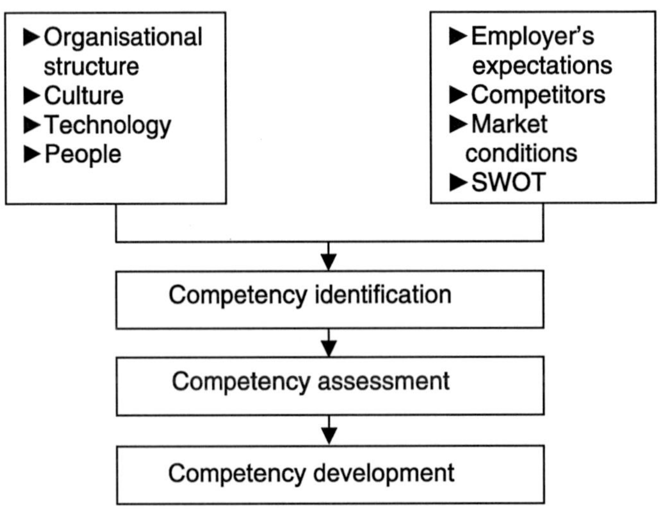

Fig. 5.6 : Compentency Assessment Steps

As an employee begins to understand himself, he will gain the following competencies:

- Gaining self-awareness.
- Improving self-confidence.
- Understanding time and stress management.
- Developing personal/professional management skills.

Strategies for gaining self-assessment competencies needs to be devided. Strategies are those concrete items that lead to acquiring a specific goal or competency. The Road map to building employee core competencies is:

- Step One: Understanding which core competencies are important to a career.
- Step Two: Meeting manager about the need for professional development.
- Step Three: Establishing a record of accomplishments.
- Step Four: Determining targets level of development.
- Step Five: Establishing Individual Development Plan using the applicable core competencies.
- Step Six: Execution.

The following list gives concrete examples of ways to gain competencies for self-assessment:

- Exploratory endeavours;
- Attending workshops for study skills, time management and stress management;
- Identifying symptoms of stress;
- Identifying personality style;
- Identifying work values;
- Demonstration of interpersonal skills in expressing feelings and ideas;
- Demonstrating skills in overcoming self-defeating behaviours; and
- Completing Strong's career Interest Inventory, Self Directed Search, and/or MBTI.

2. Career Exploration:

The second step allows individuals to investigate the world of work in greater depth, narrow a general occupational direction into a specific one through an informed decision making process.

An employee will begin to identify potential careers, gather information about those careers, and match the career information with the results from self-assessment. It can be started by:

- Learning academic and career entrance requirements;
- Learning related majors and careers to one's interests;

- Investigating education and training required;
- Learning skills and experience required;
- Planning academic and career alternatives; and
- Learning job market trends.

This requires identifying competency areas and devising appropriate strategies.

Identifying competency areas includes:

- Gaining research and investigative skills;
- Practicing decision-making, problem solving and critical thinking skills;
- Enhancing internal locus of control; and
- Increasing understanding of how abilities, interests, and values match career/ academic requirements.

Strategies for gaining competencies includes:

- Investigating careers in the HR market;
- Conducting informational Interviews to acquire required information;
- Spending time with professionals in different careers;
- Seeking information from academic advisors and career counselors;
- Taking courses or attending workshops in areas where transferable skills can be gained (i.e. communications, computer knowledge, foreign languages, diversity and international studies); and
- Attending Job/Career Fairs and/or Career Panels.

3. Career Goal Setting:

In this step, individuals evaluate occupational choices and gain practical experience through internships, cooperative education, relevant industrial training, work experiences and campus activities. This is depicted in figure 5.7.

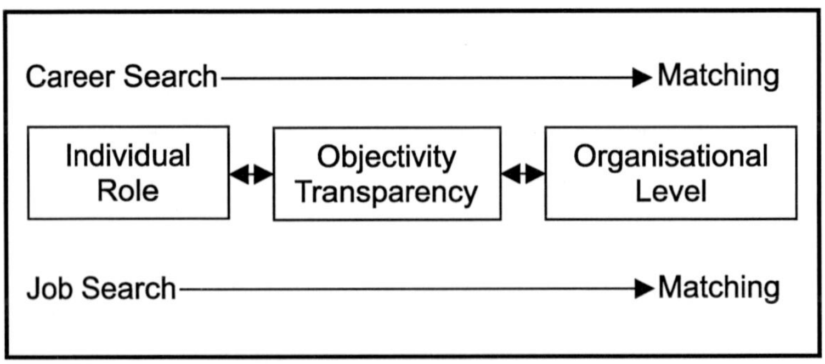

Fig. 5.7 : Career Goal Setting

In addition, more specific decisions about occupational choices can be made through:

• *Individual Career Counseling:*

This refers to one-on-one sessions with the goal of helping employees examine their career aspirations.

• *Information Services*

Information services provide career development information to employees through:

- Job-posting systems.
- Skills inventories.
- Career paths.
- HR department.

Competency areas:

- Improving interpersonal, written and oral communication skills;
- Gaining an appreciation for working with individuals from diverse cultures;
- Understanding and practicing ethical behaviour;
- Gaining supervisory/leadership/teamwork skills;
- Enhancing self-management skills;
- Obtaining work related, transferable skills; and
- Developing conflict management skills;

Strategies for gaining competencies:

- Participating in the alumni external programmes for networking;
- Choosing courses to compliment career goals;
- Conducting informational interviews.
- Attending career/job fairs;
- Attending relevant conferences and seminars.
- Becoming familiar with work settings and job descriptions; and
- Joining a professionally managed organisation.

Choosing development activities involves:

- Projects and planned work assignments.
- Coaching.
- Observing experts.
- Working alongside specialists.
- Interviewing people.
- Role play or rehearsal.
- Secondments/ out posting.
- Networking.

- Membership of professional bodies.
- Computer based training.
- Distance learning programmes.
- Reading materials, including books, journals and newspapers.
- Videos, audio tapes.
- Website browsing.

4. Career Preparation:

Acquiring the additional skills, knowledge and education is needed for starting new career. It can be done by learning how to prepare saleable resume and cover letters, and complete employment applications, implementing job search strategies and practicing skills for appearing interviews successfully.

Organisations should provide the following services to employees:

- *Mentoring:*

Mentoring relationships generally involve advising, role modeling, sharing contacts, and giving general support for developing an individual holistically.

- *Coaching:*

Employee coaching consists of ongoing, sometimes spontaneous, meetings between manages and their employees to discuss the employee's career goals and development.

- *Job Rotation:*

Job rotation involves assigning employees to various jobs so that they acquire a wider base of skills.

- *Career Assistance Programmes:*

Organisations should offer career assistance programmes to support their employees' education and development.

- *Managing self-development:*

Employees should initiate the followings:

- Analysis of strengths and developments;
- Looking for opportunities elsewhere;
- Taking positive actions;
- Preparing personal development plan;
- Monitoring progress;
- Updating plan;

- Selecting a suitable mentor;
- Identifying ways of increasing knowledge and skills; and
- Seeking new skills development.

5. Self-marketing:

This step is crucial to career planning process. Without self-marketing strategies, all the career goals, efforts and preparation are useless. Employees have to adopt strategies to attractively package and market themselves to their present or prospective organisation so that the employee can attain his career vision with ease (see figure 5.8).

	Promotes others to a low extent	Promotes others to a high extent
Promotes Self to a low extent	Independent	Team Player
Promotes self to a high extent	Promoter	Strategist

Fig. 5.8: Self Marketing

Different employees have different levels of motivation, which influences their career choices and aspirations. High performance employees tend to have differing career vision than marginal performance employees as high performance employees have high ambition, motivation, competencies and drive for achieving success and upscale career ladder fast. The difference between the two types of employees is depicted in figure 5.9.

Career Development

Career development involves making decisions about an occupation/profession and engaging in activities to attain career goals. Career development has been defined as "the interaction of psychological, sociological, economic, physical and chance factors that shape the sequence of jobs, occupations/professions or careers that a person may engage in throughout a lifetime". Career development is a major aspect of human development. It includes one's entire life span and concerns the whole person. Career development involves a person's past, present, and future work roles. It is linked to a person's self-concept, family life, and all aspect of one's environmental and cultural conditions.

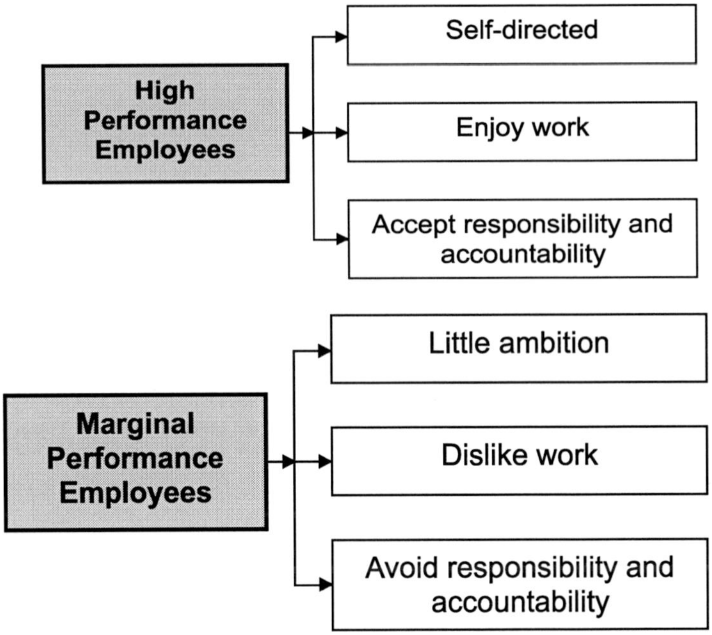

Fig. 5.9 : Characteristics of High & Marginal Performance Employees

Career development is about growing through life and work; about learning, experiencing, living, working and changing; about creating and discovering pathways through one's life and work. When international, career development is about actively creating the life one wants to live and the work one wants to do.

Thus, career development is an ongoing and formalized effort that focuses on developing enriched and more capable employees.

Definitions:

A few noteworthy definitions of Career Development are as follows:

1. "Career Development is an on-going process that occurs over the life span; includes home, school, and community experiences".

(Pietrofesa and Splete)

2. "Career Development is self-development over the life span through the integration of the roles, settings, and events of a person's life".

(Gysbers and Moore)

3. "Career Development is total constellation of economic, sociological, psychological, educational, physical, and chance factors that combine to shape one's career".

(Reardon, Lenz, Sampson,and Peterson; Sears)

4. "Career Development is implementing a series of integrated career decisions over the life span".

(Peterson, Sampson, Reardon, and Lenz)

From an analytical study of the above definitions, we may conclude that:

Career development is a process wherein the organisation provides a supportive environment in terms of inputs, which the employee uses to develop competencies (knowledge, skills, attitudes and behaviours) and values for realizing his full potential in consonance with the organisational mission and objectives.

Thus, career development is the ongoing acquisition or refinement of skills and knowledge, including job mastery and professional development, coupled with career planning activities. Job mastery skills are those that are necessary to successfully perform one's job. Professional development skills are the skills and knowledge that go beyond the scope of the employee's job description, although they may indirectly improve job performance.

Effective organisations closely integrate the learning of relevant competencies with the processes of career development for the relevant individuals and the formulation and implementation of new organisational strategies and policies. Since career development is an ongoing, dynamic process, employees may need encouragement and support in reviewing and re-assessing their goals and activities. Managers are in a key position to provide valuable feedback and learning activities or resources. Formal training and classes away from the job are effective in providing new information, but adult learners also needed to practice new skills. Therefore, managers can contribute significantly to their employee's career development by supporting career development activities within the department.

Planning for career development involves:

- Self-knowledge;
- Knowledge of the organisation; and
- Establishing clear cut goals and steps to attain these goals.

While evaluating career (job) offers, a thumb rule can be followed as mentioned below:

FACTS =

- **F** = Fit
- **A** = Advancement
- **C** = Compensation
- **T** = Training
- **S** = Site

While making self-career decisions, following points are noteworthy:

- Self marketing is crucial to achieving success.
- Choosing appropriate area of interest and then developing some expertise in it.
- Building on existing skills and abilities.

Characteristics of Career Development

The major characteristics of career development are:

1. It is an ongoing process;
2. It develops and shares transferability of skills and competencies;
3. It aligns individual goals with organisational goals for increased satisfaction of employees;
4. It helps individual to develop skills and competencies required to fulfill present and future leadership roles within an organisation; and
5. It strengthens professional work culture in the organisation.

Objectives of Career Development

Career development provides an understanding of career development and related life factors, including all of the following:

1. Career development theories and decision-making models;
2. Career, vocational, educational, occupational and labour market information resources, visual and print media, computer-based career information systems, and other electronic career information systems;
3. Career development programme planning, organisation, implementation, administration, and evaluation;
4. Interrelationships among and between work, family, and other life roles and factors including the role of diversity and gender in career development;
5. Career and educational planning, placement, follow-up, and evaluation;
6. Assessment instruments and techniques that are relevant to career development and decision making;
7. Technology-based career development applications and strategies, including computer-assisted career guidance and information systems and appropriate worldwide web sites;

8. Career counseling processes, techniques, and resources, including those applicable to employees; and
9. Ethical and legal considerations.

The major objectives of career development are:

1. To understand career development from a developmental and multicultural perspective;
2. To devise intervention strategies for developing, engaging, rewarding and retaining talented personnel;
3. To be able to discuss and apply models of career counseling that is appropriate for use in an organisational set up;
4. To identify developmentally appropriate and culturally sensitive strategies for addressing the career development needs of employees;
5. To understand the use of assessment procedures in career development interventions;
6. To understand how to use technology in career development interventions;
7. To facilitate understanding of personal, social, economic, and other factors related to the world of work for employees throughout their organisational lifespan;
8. To plan, design, and implement life-long career development programmes;
9. To locate, identify, evaluate, and disseminate career and educational information to employees, in line with organisational needs and opportunities; and
10. To evaluate the career development programme and use the results to effect organisational and employee improvements.

Importance of Career Development

The importance of career development is:

1. Career development helps in developing skills and competencies of employees for initiating, expanding and managing an organisation effectively with focus on real life business situations and business practices;
2. Career development develops in developing entrepreneurship spirit and potential amongst the employees in order to make them successful innovators;

3. To facilitate the acquisition of requisite skills, knowledge and competencies for organisational excellence;
4. To develop and create a pool of talented people to successfully execute the business strategies of the organisation;
5. To devise and implement a talent management system in the organisation; and
6. To facilitate succession planning and development to ensure long-term growth and success of the organisation.

Principles of Career Development

Organisational support for career development is important to the process of career development. Some of the major principles of career development are:

1. Dissemination of current information about the organisation and future trends helps employees create more realistic career development goals;
2. Focus on skill development by providing learning opportunities;
3. Opportunities for promotion and/or lateral moves contribute to the employee's career satisfaction;
4. A greater sense of responsibility for managing one's own career contributes to self-confidence;
5. Career planning and development clarifies the match between organisational and individual employee goals;
6. Its cost-effective to use current employee talent to provide career development opportunities within the organisation;
7. Career development increases employee motivation, quality and productivity;
8. Organisational attention to career development helps to attract top professionals and retain valued employees; and
9. Supporting career development and growth of employees is the founding philosophy of human resources development.

Theories of Career Development

Career developments theories provide a rationalized set of assumptions or hypotheses that allows explaining the past and predicting the future. As such, they provide direction and expand knowledge on career movements. There are two types of career development theories: structural and developmental.

I. Structural Theories:

These theories focus on individual characteristics and occupational tasks. The major structural theories are described below:

1. Traits and Factor Theory:

This theory began with Parsons, who proposed that a choice of a vocation depended upon (*i*) an accurate knowledge of self, (*ii*) thorough knowledge of job specifications, and (*iii*) the ability to make a proper match between the two. There are three broad factors: (*a*) a clear understanding of self, aptitudes, abilities, interests, ambitions, resources, limitation; (*b*) a thorough knowledge of the requirements and conditions of success, advantages and disadvantages, compensation, opportunities, and prospects in different lines of work; and (*c*) true reasoning on the relations of these two groups of acts.

Two major assumptions of this theory are: (*i*) that individuals and job traits can be matched, and (*ii*) that close matches are positively correlated with job success and satisfaction. These ideas are still part of our career development system today.

2. Vocational Personalities and Environment Theory:

This theory was developed by John Holland to organize the voluminous data about people in different jobs and the data about different work environments, to suggest how people make career choices and to explain how job satisfaction and vocational achievement occur. Holland suggested that people can function and develop best and find job satisfaction in work environments that are compatible with their personalities. Holland based his theory of personality types on several assumptions. People tend to choose a career that is reflective of their personality. Because people tend to be attracted to certain jobs, the environment then reflects this personality. He classified these personality types and work environments into six types which he labeled realistic, investigative, artistic, social, enterprising, and conventional. Therefore, closer the match between personality and job, the greater will be the job satisfaction.

This theory places emphasis on the accuracy of self-knowledge and career information necessary for career decision-making. Although the theory appears to be applicable to both male and female workers, there is some question of gender bias in that most females frequently tend to score predominately in three personality types: artistic, social, and conventional. Holland suggests that in our society, females will display a greater interest in female-dominated occupations.

3. Socioeconomic Theory:

Sociologist and economists provide detailed explanations and descriptions of how one's culture, family background, social and economic conditions and other factors outside an individual's control strongly influence one's identity, values, and overall human and career development. Socioeconomic theory is also known as the "chance" or "accident" theory. This approach to understanding career development suggest that many people follow the path of least resistance in their career development by simply falling into whatever work opportunities happen to come their way.

II. Developmental Theories:

Developmental Theories focus on human development across life span. The major developmental theories are described below:

1. Super's Theory:

Donald Super (1957) and other theorists of career development recognize the changes that people go through as they mature. Career patterns are determined by socioeconomic factors, mental and physical abilities, personal characteristics and the opportunities to which persons are exposed. People seek career satisfaction through work roles in which they can express themselves and implement and develop their self-concepts. Career maturity, a main concept in Super's theory, is manifested in the successful accomplishment of age and stage developmental tasks across the life span. Self-concept is an underlying factor in Super's model. Self-concept develops through physical and mental growth, observation of work, identification with co-workers, general environment, and general experiences. As experiences become broader in relation to awareness of world of work, the more sophisticated self-concept is formed.

Super's contribution was the formalization of stages and developmental tasks over the life span:

Stage	Age	Characteristics
Growth	Birth - 14	Form self-concept, develop capacity, attitudes, interests, and needs, and form a general understanding of the world of work.
Exploratory	15-24	"Try out" through classes, work experience, hobbies. Collect relevant information. Tentative choice and related skill development.
Establishment	25-44	Entry skill building and stabilization through work experience
Maintenance	45-64	Continual adjustment process to improve position.
Decline	65+	Reduced output, prepare for retirement.

Although Super originally presented the stages and tasks in a sequential manner, he later added that we 'cycle' and 'recycle' throughout our life span as one adapts to changes in oneself as well as to the trends in the work place. Understanding these ages and related stages of career development helps the organisation to select appropriate responses and activities.

Super and Thompson (1979) identified six factors in vocational maturity: (*a*) awareness of the need to plan ahead, (*b*) decision-making skills, (*c*) knowledge and use of information resources, (*d*) general career information, (*e*) general world of work information, and (*f*) detailed information about occupations of preference.

Super also looked at the different roles we play during our lifetimes and the relative importance we give to those roles at different times in our lives.

2. Krumboltz's Social Learning Theory:

Much growth takes place as a result of learning and imitating the behaviour of others. *Krumboltz* developed a theory of career decision-making and development based on social learning, or environmental conditions and events, genetic influences and learning experiences. People choose their careers based on what they have learned. Certain behaviours are modeled, rewarded and reinforced.

3. Decision-Making Theories:

Some decision-making theories hypothesize that there are critical points in people's lives when choices are made that greatly influence their career development. These decision-making points are such events as educational choices, entry-level job positions, changing jobs, etc. Other decision-making theories concerned with ongoing choices across the life span. The decisions made are influenced by person's awareness of the choices that are available to him and his knowledge of how to evaluate them. Others address the complex environment. For example, *H.B. Gelatt* (1991) says, "We make our decisions based upon what is actual and what is actual is never static"

4. Cognitive Theories:

Cognitive theories of career development are built around how individuals process, integrate and react to information. The ways in which individuals process information are determined by their cognitive structures. These structures influence how individuals see themselves, others and the environment. Cognitive theories suggest ways to help clients build or refine a hierarchy of thinking skills and decision making skills that influence career development.

Summary of theory of Career Development

- Formulated from positivist > interpretative viewpoints.
- Focus on objective > subjective experience.
- Emphasise intra-individual vs. contextual factors.
- Disregards gender, race and class.

Strategies to Support Career Development

The following strategies can be adopted to support career development of employees in an organisation:

1. Conducting periodically (at least annually) an individual development plans and career discussion with employees with the help of managers;
2. Holding managers accountable for supporting employee development efforts;
3. Creating programmes and activities to provide skill development, such as job rotation, cross training, mentoring, internships, coaching, and career strategy to employees;
4. Supporting requests for alternate work schedules from employees;
5. Serving as a model employer by participating in career and professional development opportunities of all employees;
6. Encouraging employees to put applications for other positions as a healthy sign of a dynamic workplace;
7. Supporting lateral moves within the organisation;
8. Referring employees to the staff internship programme to explore opportunities to apply for career development internships or self-initiate an internship in an area of special interest; and
9. Creating job vacancy listings that allow for the most diverse applicant pool while honouring transferable skills.

Role of Human Resource Development Function in Career Planning and Development of employees

Human resource development function plays a vital role in planning and development of careers of employees in an organisation in order to foster motivated, committed and competent workforce who can meet aptly the business risks and challenges.

The role of human resource development function is depicted in figures 5.10.

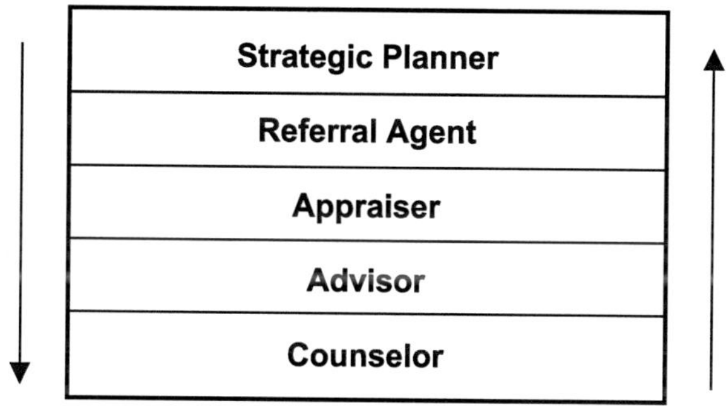

Fig. 5.10 : Role of HRD in Career Planning & Development

1. Counselor:

Human resource development function helps employees in identifying strengths, weaknesses, interests, and values by maintaining open, effective communication and ongoing encouragement. It can assist employees by:

(*i*) Encouraging two-way dialogue;

(*ii*) Showing employees how to identify their skills, interests, and values; and

(*iii*) Scheduling uninterrupted career development discussions.

2. Advisor:

Human resource development function provides organisational information, realities, and resources to employees. It can assist employees by:

(*i*) Helping employees develop realistic career goals based on organisation's needs and their individual development plans;

(*ii*) Helping employees understand the current opportunities and limitations of the organisation; and

(*iii*) Advising employees on the feasibility of various career options.

3. Appraiser:

Human resource development function facilitates the evaluation of employees' performance in an open, candid way and relating to potential opportunities. It can assist employees and managers to improve their appraisal skills by:

(*i*) Providing frequent feedback in a way that fosters development;

(*ii*) Conducting performance appraisals that define strengths, weaknesses, and career development needs;

(*iii*) Relating current performance to future potential in realistic ways; and

(*iv*) Using an individual development plan as a tool for continual feedback and development.

4. Referral Agent:

Human resource development function can help employees in meeting their goals through contacts with people and resource centres. It can assist employees by:

(*i*) Helping employees formulate development plans and consulting on strategies;

(*ii*) Providing opportunities for experience, exposure, and visibility, such as committees and task forces;

(*iii*) Using known personal resources to create opportunities; and

(*iv*) Help in seeking employees' lateral or vertical placement.

5. Strategic Planner:

Strategic planning is one of the most important activities in the life of any organisation. Human resource development function helps in identifying the current state of the organisation, including an analysis of strengths, weaknesses, opportunities and threats – a SWOT analysis. It then provides a forum to envision and articulate the desired future, define goals, and develop strategies and action plans to attain these goals.

A recent online poll of 17000 people by an online job site has shown that a majority of job seekers are willing to change jobs for a more challenging one, rather than for more pay. A snapshot of the results are as under:

- 33% of job seekers plan to change jobs if the new job offers more challenges;
- 31% want a better work/life balance;
- Just 24% said they were looking for more pay; and
- 12% were looking to relocate.

Thus, **Career Planning and Development** may be defined as:

"The deliberate process through which a person becomes aware of personal career-related attributes and the lifelong series of stages that contributes to his or her career fulfillment".

Career Banding

A career band is designed to place an employee into banded classes where:

–Career paths are identified; and
–Career development continues to be emphasized.

Banded classes are based on:

–Similar jobs in the labour market;
–General nature of the work;
–Competencies needed to perform the job; and
–Type of training and experience needed.

Hence, the basic goal of career planning and development is to create **'Career Self Reliance'** i.e. the development of autonomous employee in the organisation.

Career Strategy

Career Strategy is the process of highlighting an organisation's greatest resource, its human resources, for developing them for future career and business opportunities within the organisation for benefit of employees as well as the organisation.

Previous generations were familiar with a vastly different employment picture. One that included jobs for life, jobs that answered to set management, a well defined career plan that allowed one to climb up the corporate ladder, jobs that did not require keen attitudes and interests, careers that were well defined, within organisations that were stable and had long term prospects. Today's picture is vastly different. There are no more "jobs for life", management is flexible and ever changing, employees are expected to change along with the organisation and its operating environment, and organisations are not stable entities with mergers, acquisitions, and attrition resulting from increased global competition.

In this environment, employees need to be better prepared for change, including drastic, life changing events that can occur at any time. Employees could also use this as a tool as the HR market is expected to remain tight, especially in the skilled and service fields. The knowledge economy is no longer a panacea, and those who can better themselves through hard work and continuous education should reap the rewards. What is needed is a change in attitudes, towards the job market. People create their own careers; this is not only from their hard work and learning, but also from their personal ingenuity and attitudes. Attitudes must transform from personal focus to a team focus, for an organisation is akin to a team whose goal is to perform even as it replaces players and managers/coaches as the needs arises. This leads to the most daunting task for employees - the lack of job security.

So in an environment that embraces continuous change, the need to stay competitive, in more important than ever. This can mean both good and bad things for employees, depending on the economic cycle, their qualifications and the needs of an industry. As more people enter the job search market and do so with more frequency, it is essential for job seekers (employees) to circumvent the traditional job search avenues in order to gain an edge. The person who can network their way to a decision maker has the best chances of landing even the most highly sought after job position. Once in the job, employees must start the cycle once again of adapting to new environment and continually improving by adding new skills and qualifications.

Career Strategy Process

As already stated career strategy is the process of highlighting an organisation's greatest resource - its employees for developing them for future career and business opportunities within the organisation for benefit of employees as well as the organisation.

For employees, the organisation helps to identify career options and development opportunities they can apply across it. Organisation should provide a framework for each employee to develop knowledge, skills, and competencies.

Choosing a career direction is perhaps the most important decision an employee (present or potential) will have to make. The choices made now determine much about how the rest of his life will unfold, influencing family, health, income, and leisure time. The job search journey entails hard work. But it can also be a gratifying-and crucially important-process of self-discovery by assessing own strengths, gather information, target opportunities, explore new directions, set goals, and, ultimately, launch career. Through careful choosing and planning, career can be the vehicle that leads to a life of many rewards.

There are five steps of career strategy, each step providing resources and tools for successful navigation of the career search process (see figure 5.11) :

1. Discovering:

In order to manage job search successfully and attain career goal of meaningful employment, employees must first conduct a self-assessment process. Knowing oneself is the foundation for developing a successful career management and job search strategy. This step is perhaps more important than any other step, because it establishes the foundation for everything that is to follow. It determines how to market oneself, whom to market, and what career direction to pursue by considering:

(*i*) Existing career assets;

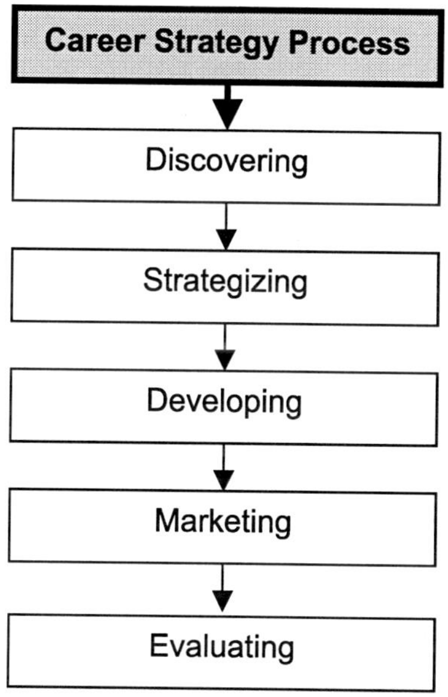

Fig. 5.11: Steps of Career Strategy Process

(*ii*) Current skills, abilities and experiences vis-à-vis the job market;

(*iii*) Career mission;

(*iv*) Personal values;

(*v*) Career goals and plans for a year, five years or ten years; and

(*vi*) Degree of earning urge;

Identifying and understanding business interests, reward values, and abilities will give a head-start in identifying and exploring business career options to help individual employees develop an enhanced awareness of their interests, skills, and abilities.

2. Strategizing:

Strategizing is the art of devising or employing plans or stratagems towards the attainment of a goal. This step affords a valuable opportunity to grow-deliberately, intelligently, and systematically, rather than by chance-in the direction of career goals.

In this step, an initial career management strategy is defined and a plan is created for enhancing career assets. Knowing and managing own strengths and weaknesses helps to identify industries, job functions, and organisations where career assets will be valued.

3. Developing:

In this step, employees need to focus on developing the knowledge, experience, and skills necessary to market self to prospective organisations. This is the time to sharpen the job search assets that will move career search forward-and maximize opportunities of launching and/or re-launching one's career.

Networking expands career options, sometimes in unexpected ways. Through networking, jobs are sometimes created where there weren't any before. Networking helps to uncover the hidden job market and can reveal positions that have not been posted or publicized. Significant percent of job seekers with experience find their jobs through networking. Sharpening one's networking skills, then, can make the difference between success and failure in career search process.

Despite the emphasis placed on it, however, networking remains one of the most misunderstood dimensions of the search process. While for some lucky people, networking seems to come naturally; the process intimidates many job seekers.

The job market today requires that employee market himself effectively to prospective organisations. An effective résumé works as a key sales tool. While the résumé alone can never replace the other critical aspects of the career search process-such as identifying skills and abilities, learning about career fields, researching prospective employers, networking, etc. A well-prepared résumé serves several vital functions such as:

(*i*) Focuses effort to assess own skills and abilities;

(*ii*) Raises self-confidence about one's value in the job market;

(*iii*) Acts as a "sales brochure" to stimulate the interest of prospective organisations;

(*iv*) Reminds a prospective organisation of employee's interest; and

(*v*) Helps to get job interviews done.

One of most important tools for self-marketing, the résumé, should be flawless and compelling. It should clearly and concisely highlight achievements and experience, and communicate what employee has to offer to the prospective organisation.

4. Marketing:

In this step, employee has to convey to prospective organisations a dynamic and accurate portrait of oneself, desires, and the experiences and skills that will add value to the organisation.

Resources available to use includes:

(*i*) *Networking to market:*

Having identified target organisations and contacts, marketing materials and networking targets has to be developed. The principle here is the known person gets the job. Because many people get jobs through networking therefore, it pays to take a proactive approach in networking efforts. The purpose in networking is to publicize a candidate's availability, get advice and information about trends in a particular industry, to uncover other useful contacts, and to get potential job leads.

To network effectively, a good place to start is by developing a master contact list of people to talk to, ranking them and building rapport with such people. While making rapport, it is advisable to contact the known persons first and then contacting the unknown persons.

(*ii*) *Finding available positions:*

The developed network of contacts can be used to identify job opportunities.

(*iii*) *Preparing for the Interview:*

The candidate who gets the job is not necessarily the person who is most qualified; often it is the one who is best prepared. Preparation leads to quiet confidence; quiet confidence speaks volumes about relevant competence. But job interviews can be intimidating, especially when entering the job market for the first time. The steps to successful interview preparation include:

1. *Knowing yourself.*
2. *Knowing the job wanted.*
3. *Researching the organisation and industry.*
4. *Preparing specific questions to ask at the interview.*
5. *Practicing interviewing for confidence.*

5. Evaluating:

Having completed self-marketing successfully to prospective employers, it is time to analyze new options within current organisation, and then choosing a new direction that will help move career forward and career assets.

The decisions taken at this stage will influence many aspects of an employee's life. These are not, therefore, judgments that should be made in haste. A careful analysis of career and position alternatives should be done to determine whether they represent a good match with career assets and long-term career strategy. Other considerations will bear substantially upon the quality of life and the level of job satisfaction, includes:

-The lifestyle associated with the position.

-Personal values;

-The level of responsibility;

-The organisation culture;

-A team versus an independent work environment;

-Learning opportunities;

-Role and expected level of contribution to the decision-making process; and

-Compensation package offered, including benefits.

It must be noted that better the articulation skills of career assets, the greater the probability of reward and status, position, money, and perks.

Often people confuse between career management and career planning, development and strategy and treat them same. However, it is not so. Career management is concerned with specific activities such as recruitment, selection, induction, placement and performance appraisal purporting to facilitate career development. It conveys three perspectives:

- Individuals focusing on themselves (self-management of career).
- Organisations focusing on individuals (managing individuals according to their career/age/stages/profiles).
- Organisations focusing on their own maintenance and growth (employee movement, up, down, over, relocation).

Review and Discussion Questions

Question 1: Define and explain the concept of Career Planning. How can the needs of individual and organisation be matched?

Question 2: Enlist the importance and benefits of Career Planning in today's business organisations.

Question 3: What is the process of Career Planning? Explain in detail.

Question 4: Define and explain the concept of Career Development of employees.

Question 5: Enlist the principles of Career Development.

Question 6: Explain various theories of Career Development. How can these theories be applied to the Indian industry?

Question 7: What strategies should be adopted by progressive organisations to support Career Development in an organisation?

Question 8: What are the roles of human resource development department in Career Planning and Development of employees, particularly talented people?

Question 9: Give a critical account of recent scenario of Career Planning and Development in India. What are the reasons of its slow progress in the Indian context?

Question 10: Define and explain the concept and perspectives on Career Strategy. Illustrate your answer with suitable examples.

Question 11: Write short notes on:

i) Structural Theories of Career Development
ii) Career Strategy Process
iii) Self-marketing
iv) Objectives of Career Planning

Exhibit: 5 – A

Case Situation

- *Before attempting this section please read Chapter - 14 on Case Study.*
- *Please read the following case situations and answer the questions.*

Q 1. You have joined a biotechnology company as HR Head. The organization enjoys leadership position in its industry. The company employs mostly at entry level as Trainee Biotechnologist. Thereupon, after one year eligible trainees are absorbed as Officers. For the last five years, these scientific personnel are working like this as Officers. Of late the turnover of scientific staff has increased by 30%. What do you think are the reasons of increased turnover and how best can you control it?

Q 2. A talented Finance Executive (C.A.) has submitted his resignation letter citing reason that there is only basic Accounts job and there isn't any Finance work. What would you do to retain this guy? Give specific HRD measures you would apply.

Q 3. Make career plan for a fresh MBA-HR professional for the next 10 years.

Exhibit: 5 – B

Case Study

- *Before attempting this section please read Chapter - 14 on Case Study.*
- *Please read the following case study and answer all the subsequent questions.*

Introduction to the organization:

RD Elevators is into the business manufacturing and marketing of passenger lifts with significant market share. The company has grown consistently by 12% per annum and is known for the quality of its products.

The company has a total strength of 600 personnel. One Manager – Personnel & Administration, duly assisted by two Personnel Officers and two Personnel Assistants, mans its HR department. To give further impetus to its ambitious growth plans, the management has decided to hire an Assistant General Manager-HR.

Mr. Alok Saxena joined the company as Assistant General Manager-HR, having rich experience in different facets of HRD.

Brief Description of the Problem:

One the first day itself, the Executive Director calls on Mr. Alok Saxena and shares with him one major/pressing problem being faced by the company: high executive turnover.

Mr. Alok Saxena decided to conduct some field studies/surveys with resigned as well as existing executives. The study revealed the following issues:

- High turnover was due to better compensation being paid in other competitor companies.
- High turnover was due to 'better environment'.
- High turnover was due to lack of variety and challenge in jobs.

Based on these revelations, Mr. Alok Saxena embarked on the following HRD measures to arrest high executive turnover:

- Redesigned executive jobs and enriched them.
- Modified performance appraisal embodying self-appraisal.
- Integrated jobs with organizational structure with the involvement of individual executives.

Annual review was conducted to assess the effectiveness of HRD measures. It was found that within one year, the company had accomplished 100% retention of executives.

Questions:

1. What are the major reasons of high executive turnover?
2. What steps were taken by Mr. Alok Saxena to accomplish 100% retention of executives?
3. In your opinion, can the organization sustain its 100% retention rate in the next 3 years?

CHAPTER

6 Performance Appraisal and Potential Appraisal

Chapter Synopsis

Performance Appraisal is concerned with evaluating the performance of the employees with respect to their suitability in present jobs and assessing potential for future jobs. It also provides a validated means of administering reward system in the organization.

A good performance appraisal system is most crucial for customer satisfaction because only competent employees will be able to provide customer excelleration. However, although a performance appraisal system exists to help everyone succeed, but unless employees work WITH management, it can't work well.

This chapter explains these concepts and methods to meet the performance goals of the organization and reward needs of the individual employees.

This Chapter contains:

Concept of performance appraisal, Definitions of performance appraisal, Performance appraisal model, Objectives of performance appraisal, Elements of performance appraisal, Purpose of performance appraisal, Uses of performance appraisal, Designing performance appraisal, Performance appraisal process, Appraisal interview, Appraisal interview questionnaire, Employee feedback, Methods of performance appraisal – rating, comparative, narrative and behavioural/objective methods, Alternative performance assessors, Performance appraisal failures, Essentials of a good performance appraisal system, Types of performance appraisal, Benefits of performance appraisal, Performance appraisal in future organizations, Potential appraisal, Model of organizational excellence, Review & discussion questions, Case situation, case study, and Sample performance appraisal forms – KRA and trait based for managerial and non-managerial cadres.

Performance Appraisal and Potential Appraisal

Human resource development is the process by which management stimulates the motivation of employees to perform effectively. Accordingly organisations have to create conditions where skill, will and resources, the three important ingredients for performance, are matched appropriately as in figure 6.1.

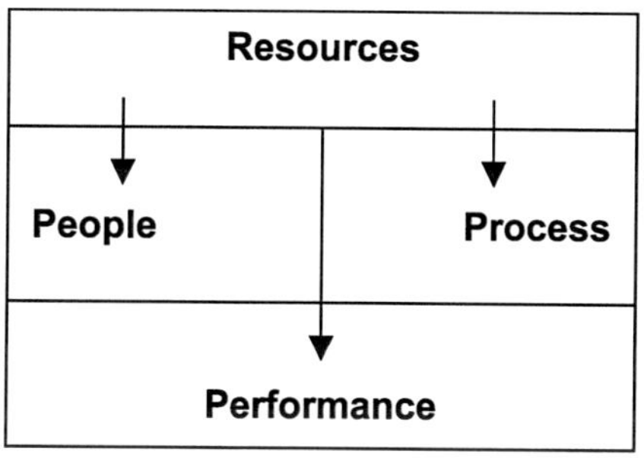

Fig. 6.1 : Ingredients of the performance

Performance appraisal is a part of Performance Management. Performance management is a multi-stage process of identifying, planning, developing, supporting, appraising and rewarding employee performance and involves the following key considerations:

- Sharing mission and objectives of the organisation with the employees;
- Clarifying organisation's performance imperatives and expectations from the employees;
- Linking organisational and departmental objectives with individual job goals;
- Helping employees in setting performance goals (or targets);
- Establishing performance metrics (or measures) that reinforce organisation's strategy, processes, stakeholders expectations and culture;
- Provide ongoing feedback to employees about their performance;
- Assessing and rating actual performance of the employees in conjunction with their performance goals (or targets);

- Improving performance of the empolyees through coaching, counseling and mentoring programmes;
- Determining and realizing development plan (not merely some courses) that are needed to enhance employee performance for sustained competitive advantage of the organisation.
- Documenting empolyee performance for various HR actions, future reference and legal purposes;
- Administering differentiating rewards for achieving performance goals (or targets) by the empolyees;
- Planning for future career planning and organisational goal linkage; and
- Evaluating and ehnancing the effectiveness of performance management process.

Performance management essentially consists of the following cycles:

- Performance Planning
- Performance Development
- Performance Appraisal
- Reward and Recognition
- Performance Management Audit

Performance appraisal is an important tool to successfully realize performance management process. Performance appraisal may be defined as "the process by which an employee's contribution to the organisation during a specified period is assessed". It is an important strategic management tool. The term performance appraisal can be split up as:

Performance Appraisal = Performance + Appraisal

Performance refers to the achievement of positive results (Rothwell et. al). Performance consists of seven dimensions:

- Effectiveness
- Efficiency
- Quality
- Productivity
- Quality of work life
- Innovation
- Profitability

Further, the term "performance" can be split as:

- PERFOR – MAN – CE *i.e.* 'Perform' 'Men' Like 'Core Entrepreneur.'

Appraisal can be defined in terms of:

- Process of measurement of facts, figures, and means. Measurement is a decision support system for management and is an integral part of the management process.

- Analysis of verifiable components of a given job.

A good performance appraisal possesses the following characteristics:

- It is based on evidence;
- It is highly individualized;
- It is a joint activity'
- It strives for understanding;
- It creates commitment;
- It maximizes self analysis and self discovery; and
- It results in improved performance.

Definitions:

A few noteworthy definitions of Performance Appraial are as follows :

1. "Performance appraisal is a process of systematically evaluating performance and providing feedback upon which performance adjustments can be made".

(Schermerhorn, Hunt and Osborn: 2004)

2. "Performance Appraisal is a comparison of actual performance with expected to assess an employee's contributions to the organisation".

(Nelson: 2004)

3. "Performance Appraisal may be defined as evaluating individual job performance as a basis for making objective personnel decisions".

(Robert Kreitner: 2004)

From an analytical study of the above definitions, we may conclude that:

Performance appraisal is concerned with formally assessing an employees work accomplishments and providing feedback. An overview of performance appraisal is in figure 6.2.

Performance appraisal and training goes hand in hand. Integration of training and performance improvement initiatives in the overall strategic framework of the organisation can be achieved by:

1. Developing and delivering programmes with the end result in mind;
2. Programme objectives are stated not only in terms of learning, but also what the emp is expected to do in the work setting and the impact it should have on business performance;

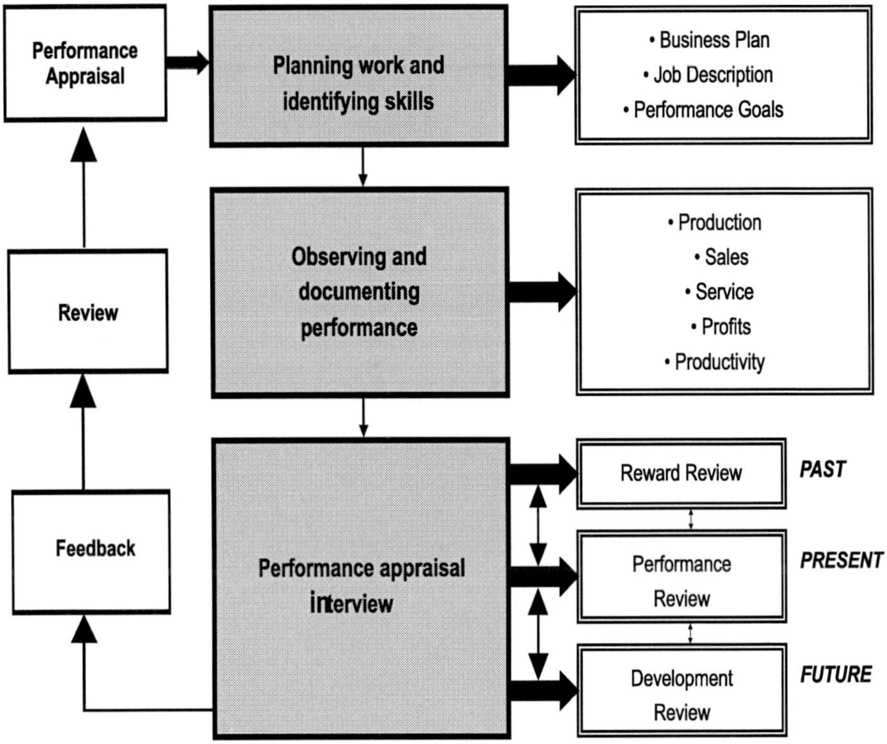

Fig. 6.2 : Overviews of Performance Appraisal

3. Employees understand what is expected from them as a result of each programme. They expect to be held accountable for learning and for applying what they learn;
4. Evaluation is in place for each training programme;
5. Training support is in place to help achieve results from training; and
6. All stakeholders carry out their responsibilities in creating a performance culture that initiates and continues the learning process.

There are three basic elements to evaluation of performance that are helpful in attaining and evaluating human resources development as mentioned below:

• CAPACITY

Personal abilities necessary to perform tasks and assignments such as mental, physical, social, and spiritual capacities.

• SKILLS

Behavioural competencies necessary to perform tasks and assignments such as comprehension, tactical, verbal, and interpersonal.

• MOTIVATION

Willingness to perform tasks and assignments -intrinsic and extrinsic.

Performance Appraisal Model

A conceptrual model of performance appraial is depicted in figure 6.3.

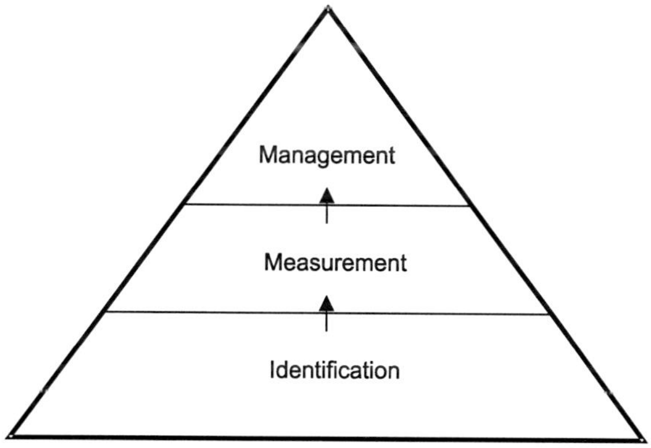

Fig. 6.3 : Model of Performance Appraisal

Performance appraisal is the identification, measurement, and management of human performance in organisations. Performance is the result of individual competencies, efforts and motivation to excel. However, performance does not happen in isolation to other organisational conditions and factors. An employee shall be motivated to perform if he knows that such an effort shall lead to better performance and a better performance shall, in turn, lead to better rewards. The higher the effort-performance-reward linkages, higher shall the attractiveness of the process to perform better and better. This is confirmed by theory (Expectancy Theory) and Research (Scholars and Practitioners). Victor H. Vroom states that receiving a promotion will be more rewarding to persons who did not expect it than to those who did. Similarly, failure to receive a promotion might be less frustrating to those who did not expect it than those who did. The leverages, as discussed above, are depicted in figure 6.4.

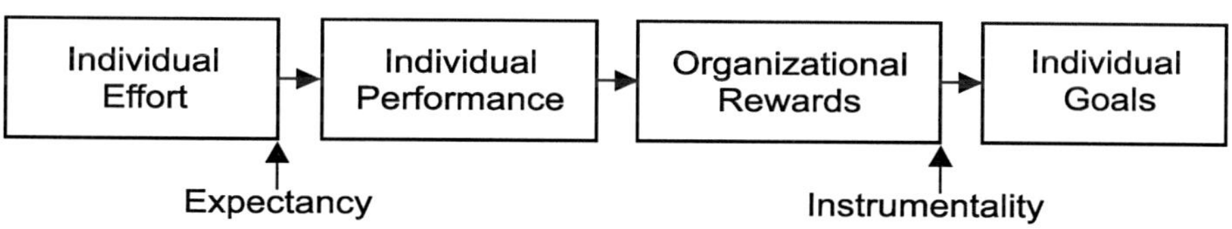

Fig. 6.4 : Interlinkage of Individual Effort & Goal

Therefore, performance appraisal system ensures that:

1. Performance standards and objectives are set;
2. Performance results are assessed regularly; and
3. Actions are taken to improve future performance.

Objectives of Performance Appraisal

The main objectives of performance appraisal are to improve the performance of the organisation through improved employee performance. The goal of performance appraisal is to allow an employee the opportunity to progress to their full potential in order to meet organisational needs and his personal development goals. Through this process, teamwork and maximum performance can be achieved. The foundation of the performance appraisal is improved communication between the employee and the manager. It is worth noting that performance goals should be:

SMARTER

S - goals must be **Specific**

M- goals should be **Measurable**

A - goals should be **Adjustable**

R - goals must be **Realistic**

T - goals should be **Time based**

E - goals should be challenging and **Exciting**

R - goals should be **Recorded**

SCCAMP

S - goals must be **Specific**

C - goals should be within the **Control** of the employee

C - goals are **Challenging**

A - goals must be **Attainable**

M- goals should be **Measurable**

P - goals are **Personal**

Performance Appraisal offers several advantages at the following level:

(a) *Individual*

- Recognition of past effort.
- Developmental requirements can be uncovered.

(b) *Team*

- Alignment of effort with objectives.
- Motivation of team members.

(c) *Organisation*

- Development of human resources.
- Achievement of key objectives.
- Best and focused utilization of human resources.

Objectives of performance appraisal are depicted in figure 6.5.

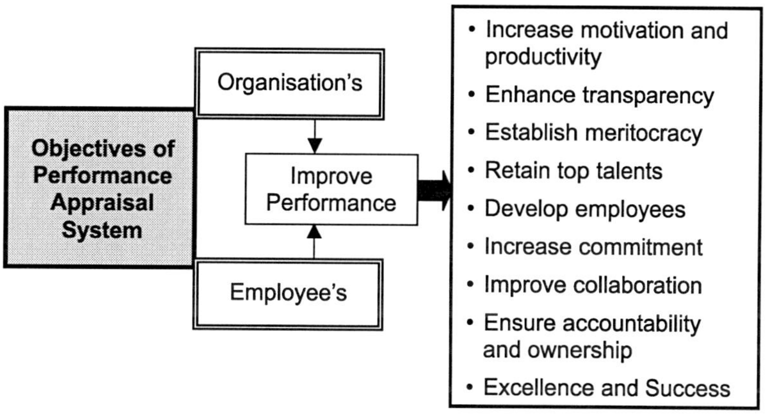

Fig. 6.5 : Performance Appraisal Objectives

1. To increase motivation and productivity:

Performance appraisal helps employee to plan work and identify skills in order to achieve them. Employee is motivated as there is clarity of what he is required to do in a given period. Increased clarity brings greater focus on job related activities, which in turn facilitates better performance, efficiency and commitment. This increases the productivity of the individual employees and the organisation stands benefited out of improved performance of employees.

2. To enhance transparency:

Setting of performance targets/objectives, agreement on measurement criteria and organisation's expectation of desired performance level brings in transparency to the appraisal process. Since every employee knows his performance requirement and the associated standards, therefore credibility of the appraisal system increases as being perceived to be free and fair.

3. To establish meritocracy:

Performance appraisal gives an opportunity and impetus to employees to continually improve and develop their performance. The gaps, if any, are rectified through various performances improvement techniques such as training and development programmes. This encourages meritocracy in the organisation, as performance becomes the prime basis for growth and career development of an employee in the organisation, including compensation increase decisions. Employees engage in healthy competition and strive hard for reaching peak performance.

4. To retain top talents:

Performance appraisal help organisation in taking people related decisions such as career planning, career development, promotions, training and development opportunities, and succession planning. Meritorious employee are rewarded better with increased compensation, promotions, leadership grooming opportunities, job rotations, etc. and help retain top talents in the organisation by satisfying their growth and development needs.

5. To develop employees:

Performance appraisal accords an opportunity to develop employee through the identification of gaps in skills and competencies. Once deficiencies in skills and competencies has identified, suitable training and development programmes can be established for rectifying the gaps/deficiency. This results in personal and professional development of employees.

6. To increase commitment:

Employee's involvement in planning of work and identification of skills helps to bring greater self-awareness and increases his commitment to the objectives of performance appraisal activities. The performance appraisal provides an opportunity to communicate performance feedback, review the job description, plan upcoming goals and objectives and develop an individual development plan. This requires effort by both the employee and manager to identify strengths and improvement opportunities from a performance and development point of view.

7. To improve collaboration:

Performance appraisal brings a sense of unity of purpose (organisation's mission and objectives) amongst the employees and manager and fosters a collaborative work culture in the organisation. This is because all jobs in an organisation are not only interlinked but also inter-dependent on each other. Collaboration is the only way through which every employee can achieve his performance objectives and effectively accomplish his work.

8. To ensure accountability and ownership:

Performance appraisal casts high responsibility on the individual employees to accomplish work objectives effectively. It induces employee's to put their heart and head into improving performance for which they are accountable to their managers. Since he is clear of performance goal and requirements, therefore owns the appraisal as a good way to improve his career prospects in his organisation.

Elements of Performance Appraisal

Performance appraisal consists of the following elements:

1. Goal Setting:

Managers should set performance objectives or standards for individual employees keeping in view the business objectives of the organisation.

2. Measures:

Tasks or levels of performance should be used to gauge whether an employee has achieved his goals or not and to what extent.

3. Feedback:

Comparison of performance to goals is usually provided at end of performance period.

4. Performance Rating:

Manager judges overall performance and gives numeric rating.

5. Performance Pay:

Pay increase given is based on performance rating and market price for position.

Purpose of Performance Appraisal

The purpose of performance appraisal is many fold. However, there are two broad purpose of performance appraisal as depicted in figure 6.6.

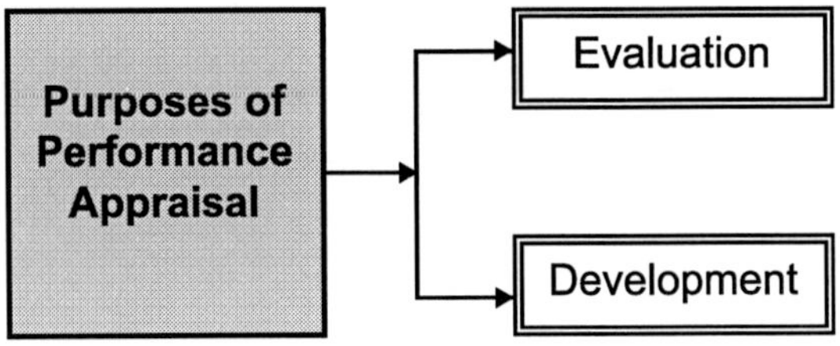

Fig. 6.6 : Purpose of Performance Appraisal

1. Evaluation:

Evaluation of performance involves letting employees know where they stand relative to performance objectives and standards. An effective evaluation entails the followings:

- Establishes performance standards that are clearly related to the organisation's mission and objectives;
- Sets mutually acceptable and measurable performance standards;
- Provides continuous feedback to employees about their performance;
- Objectively measures performance;
- Compares actual performance with performance standards; and
- Develops employee where necessary or take corrective action where appropriate.

2. Development:

Development oriented performance appraisal assists in training and continued personal development of people. Developed employees are more motivated, committed and competent to achieve their work roles and goals. They can contribute effectively in improving the organisation's effectiveness.

Uses of Performance Appraisal

Performance appraisal is crucial tool in the hands of the management to bring about greater agility and responsiveness in the human resources of an organisation. Performance appraisal is the foundation of many human resource decisions. Therefore, it has multifarious uses as depicted in figure 6.7.

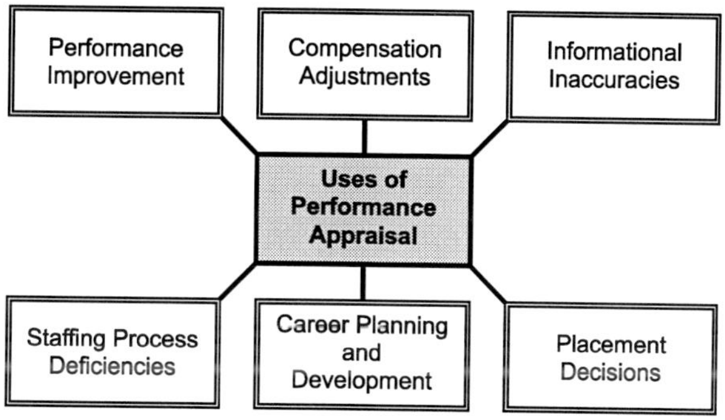

Fig. 6.7 : Uses of Performance Appraisal

Major uses of performance appraisal are as detailed below:

1. Performance Improvement:

Performance appraisal is used as a developmental tool by organisations. It helps in improving the performance of employees through work planning, skill identification and potential development. Employees are given reward for improved performance to reinforce improvement efforts and also feedback is given to efficiently and effectively achieve the strategic goals and objectives of the organisation. Training, learning and developmental activities are undertaken to fulfill gaps in employee's performance as shown in figure 6.8.

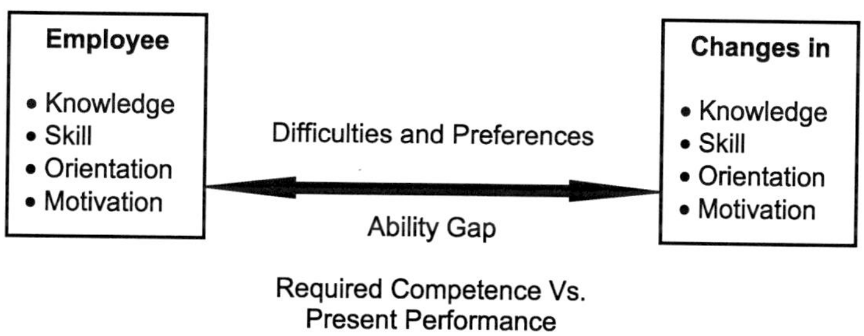

Fig. 6.8 : Filling Performance Gaps

2. Compensation adjustment:

Performance appraisal's most popular outcome is its linkage to compensation adjustment. Employees exhibiting superior performance are rewarded through increase in their compensation to motivate them to further excel in their jobs. Employees showing weaker performance are given lesser compensation raises. Therefore, appraisal differentiates compensation of employees for performance variation.

3. Informational inaccuracies:

Performance appraisal provides opportunity to employees and their managers to share information, ideas, requirements, expectations, and feedback to remove any misconception and/or misunderstanding between the manager and the employee. This fosters greater bondage between the employees and managers and results in increased employee commitment to organisational mission and objectives. Also, poor performance may indicate errors in job analysis information, human resource planning, or other parts of the human resource information system. Reliance on inaccurate information may have led to inappropriate hiring, training or counselling decisions.

4. Placement decision:

Performance appraisal is used as a tool for making decision on employee placements such as promotion, demotion, transfer, relocation, reassignment, etc. performance appraisal is considered to be the most valid and reliable basis for placement decisions.

5. Career planning and development:

Performance appraisal provides reliable data and information on the current performance level, potentialities and developmental needs of employees. Based on it career planning and developmental needs are identified. Organisations can take decision on competence to shoulder present responsibilities and potential to handle higher and/or key responsibilities in future based on need-opportunity alignment.

6. Staffing process deficiencies:

Since performance appraisal helps in identifying present performance and potentialities for future development of employees, therefore the accuracy and reliability of recruitment and selection process can be judged. It helps in finding whether right man for the right job has been adhered to or not? Organisations can take appropriate decision for rehabilitation or separation of wrongly selected and posted employees so that operational inefficiencies can be eliminated. Thus, appraisal is test of reliability and validity of selection process and appropriate adjustment can accordingly be undertaken.

Designing Performance Appraisal System

Every organisation has to institute a performance appraisal system for increasing the efficiency and effectiveness of the human resources so as to enable it achieve its goals and objectives. The process of designing performance appraisal system in an organisation is depicted in figure 6.9.

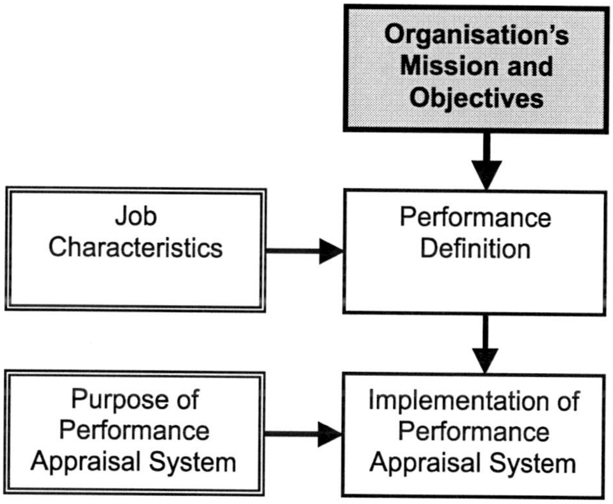

Fig. 6.9 : Designing Performance Appraisal System

Designing performance appraisal system starts with an examination of the mission and objectives of the organisation pertaining to production volume, sales turnover, service deliverability, profits anticipated and productivity expected. It provides a general guideline and direction to follow. Based on the mission and objectives of the organisation, the performance standards expected of employees to effectively achieve its goals and objectives are identified and systematically defined for each and every job. The job characteristics influence the definition of performance because every job is different and requires different knowledge, skills and competencies of the employees. Thereupon, purpose of performance appraisal system is determined. The purpose states that objectives performance appraisal pertaining to the organisation, teams and individual employees will serve such as improving individual and departmental performance, attaining job accountabilities and aligning individual performance goals with organisation's objectives. Having completed that, these are documented and communicated to the employees for implementation of the performance appraisal system.

Performance Appraisal Process

The objectives of performance appraisal process are:

1. Appraisers (Managers): To recognize and reward top performers;

2. Appraisee (Employees): To obtain honest, timely feedback, development and coaching;

3. Organisation: To ensure that performance of the employees improves and is helpful in the attainment of the goals and objectives of the organisation. Also, compensation is being allocated according to performance of the employees; and

4. HRD Manager: To identify top performers and plan for their development and succession keeping in view the present and future organisational needs.

The performance appraisal process is depicted in figure 6.10:

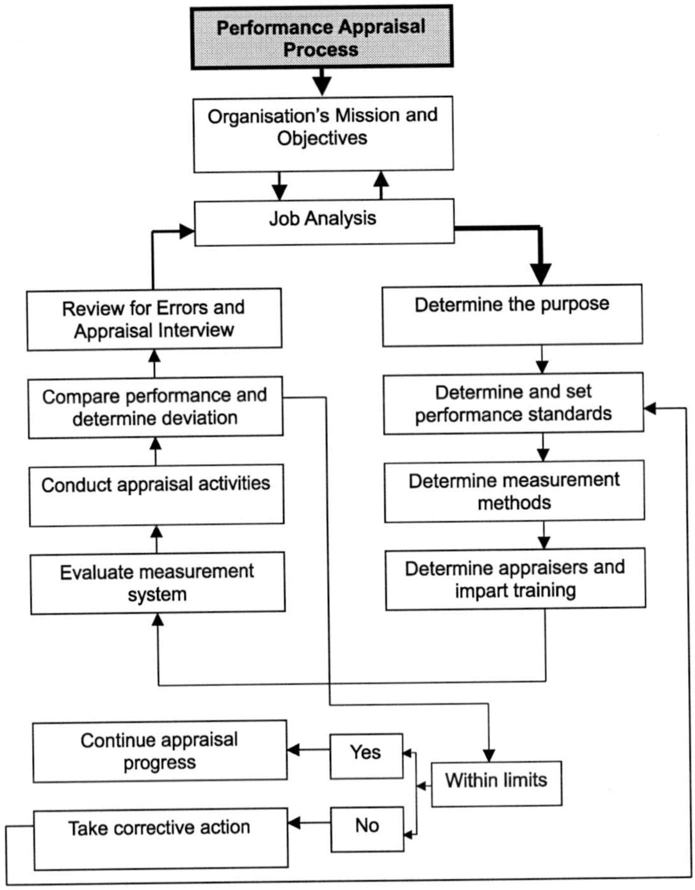

Fig. 6.10 : Steps of Performance Appraisal Process

1. Organisation's mission and objectives:

Performance appraisal is a strategic management tool to achieve the mission and objectives of the organisation. How the organisation intends to stay competitive, attain competitive advantage and continually grow and develop spells the objectives of performance appraisal. Human resources are the means of attaining organisational goals and objectives and therefore without strategic linkage, performance appraisal will not be useful for the organisation.

2. Job analysis:

Organisations objectives are achieved through a process of break up of various tasks, duties and functions. Adequate and competent employees are required to handle these tasks, duties and functions. Now, to know what tasks, duties and functions are required to be performed for achieving the mission and objectives of the organisation and what kind of human resources are required for optimal performance of the tasks, duties and functions entails job analysis. Staffing begins with job analysis. Job analysis is the process and procedures used to collect and classify information about tasks the organisation needs to complete. It forms the basis for a job description and job specifications. It helps in identifying employee characteristics needed to perform the job effectively.

3. Determine the purpose:

The purpose of the performance appraisal system is to be determined and stated clearly. Without a valid purpose, performance appraisal system is a fad. The purpose is to increase communication, motivation, skills and competencies of employees so as to enable them to improve their performance and discharge their job responsibilities and accountabilities efficiently for organisational effectiveness.

4. Determine and set performance standards:

Performance standards reflects what a satisfactory employee can accomplish. Performance standards are the measurements used to assess whether an employee is meeting expectations. Standards should be realistic, attainable, measurable, and specific. Performance may be measured by quality, quantity, time and frequency. Standards are necessary to achieve mission and objectives of an organisation in efficient and effective manner. Standards form the basis on which actual performance of employees will be compared to assess the deficiencies, if any, for appropriate training, learning and development intervention for the purpose of improving performance of the employees. Performance standards help in increasing individual employee's effectiveness on the job and make him more productivity through realistic targets and goal setting. However, great care is to be taken while determining performance standards. It should have strategic relevance i.e. it should be linked to the mission and objectives of the organisation, it should have appropriate performance criteria i.e. it should be based on objective and job relevant performance criteria, it should be reliable and valid *i.e.,* it must seek to measure what it intends to measure based on strategic relevance and should be applied consistently, and must provide for adjustment of criteria deficiency *i.e.* standards must be flexible to make for aspects of actual performance that are not measured due to oversight at the criteria defining stage.

Actual performance must be measured based on relevant performance factors. It is depicted in figure 6.11 for clarity.

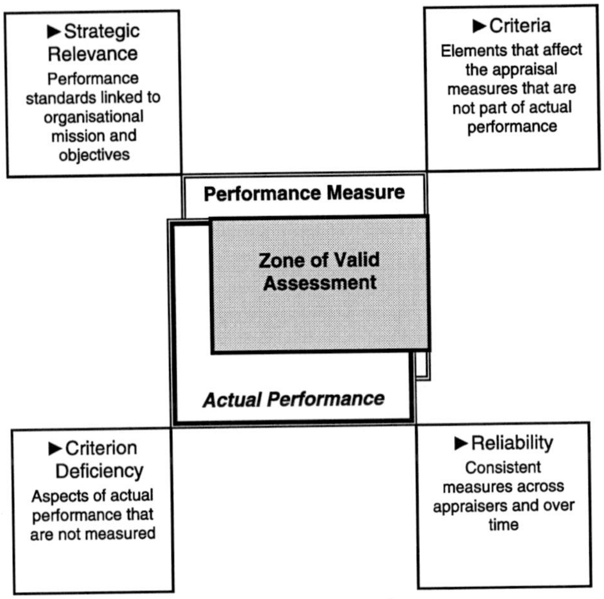

Fig. 6.11 : Valid Performance Assessment Framework

5. Determine measurement methods:

Having determined the performance standards, the next task is to identify a suitable method of performance appraisal. A variety of methods for appraising employee performance are available which can be broadly classified as ranking methods, comparison methods, narrative methods and behavioural/objective methods. No single method is appropriate and an intelligent combination of more than one method could yield better results. The choice of method/s will depend on organisational characteristics, employee characteristics, environmental characteristics and competition behaviour. Based on these characteristics, organisation will determine which method/s to employ.

6. Determine appraisers and impart training:

Determination of correct number and level of appraisers is critical for the success of the performance appraisal system. Only competent and experienced managers should be selected. It is not enough to select a suitable performance manager, but also to impart training to the managers on how to administer the appraisal. Human resource development function should conduct training sessions on performance appraisal system to enable the managers to understand and administer it effectively so that appraisal can attain its purpose.

7. Evaluate measurement system:

The measurement system is to be evaluated for ease of use, practicability, reliability and validity of the performance appraisal system.

8. Conduct appraisal activities:

Performance appraisal activities are to be conducted to evaluate the performance of the employees. It generally involves assessment of performance objectives, various inhibiting and facilitating factors, resources utilized and results achieved. For this purpose, prescribed performance appraisal forms are filled-in by the managers (appraiser) and the employees (appraisees) to complete the appraisal activities.

9. Compare performance and determine deviation:

The actual performance exhibited by the employees is compared with the performance standards determined for every job to see how well (or poorly) employees have faired in their performance. By comparing with standards, deviations are noted for further discussions and agreed for performance improvement initiatives by the managers. For employees exhibiting performance deviation to lower order, manager must continue appraisal progress and track performance with a view to strengthen performance of the employee where he has fumbled a little. For marginal performance employees, immediate corrective action has to be initiated, while at the same time performance standards for the employee has to be examined to assess whether performance problem is due to organisational factors or due to personal factors. After careful analysis, corrective action to improve the performance standards for a particular employee or performance of the employee has to be improved, as the case may be, through counseling, coaching and mentoring techniques.

However, it may be noted that performance appraisal is affected by motivation, reinforcement, and organisation behaviour modification factors as depicted in figure 6.12:

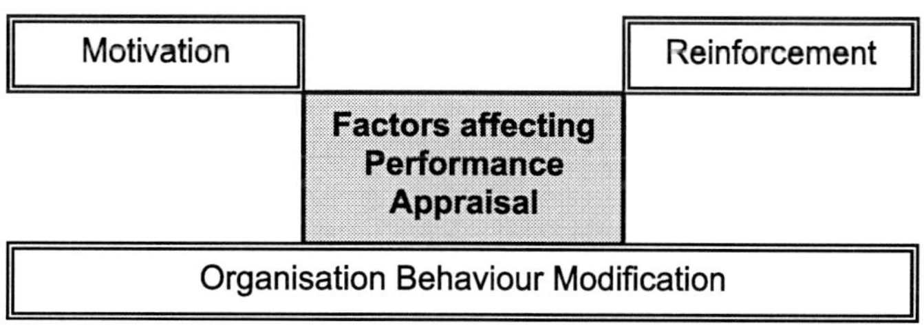

Fig. 6.12 : Factors Affecting Performance Appraisal

(*a*) Motivating for performance:

Motivation are the forces that energize, direct, and sustain an employee's efforts. Highly motivated people, with adequate ability and understanding of the job, will be highly productive and therefore managers must know what behaviours they want to motivate people to exhibit.

(*b*) Reinforcing performance:

Behavior that is followed by positive consequences probably will be repeated. This is known as 'Law of Effect'. Reinforces lead to positive consequences that motivate behaviour.

(*c*) Organisational behavior modification:

Application of reinforcement theory in organisational settings can be made. People's behaviour and performance can be improved by systematically managing work conditions and the consequences of people's actions.

10. Review for Errors and Appraisal Interview

Errors that might have inadvertently crept in the appraisal activities and evaluation must be analyzed for appropriate rectification. Certain task and behaviour related to performance issues needs discussion to foster understanding and clarity and for future action between the manager and his employees. This is because appraisal is primarily a two way communication process. This necessitates appraisal interview.

Appraisal interview is also known as Performance Review Discussions, Appraisal Meeting, Performance Appraisal Discussion, etc. Performance appraisal interview is the process of initiating performance dialogue with an objective to improve performance of an employee.

In an appraisal interview, the appraiser (Manager) assumes the role of coach, leader and communicator, all rolled into one. The appraiser has to look into the following aspects before planning and conducting a performance appraisal interview as depicted in figure 6.13.

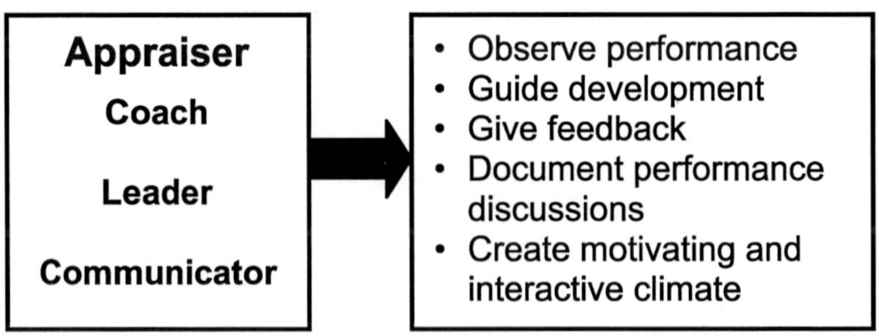

Fig. 6.13 : Facets of an appraise

Performance Appraisal Processes often fails due to:

1. Performance Appraisal process only operates for part of the yearnot meaningful if goals are not monitored;
2. Ratings are based on manager's opinions only include what managers remember;
3. Managers avoid honest feedback to prevent conflict;
4. Organisations try to meet too many objectives (feedback, development, compensation raises, etc.); and
5. Employees believe criteria are vague, subjective; can be demoralized by ratings, especially when pay is involved.

Appraisal Interview

Performance Appraisal Interview is the systematic process of giving feedback to employees about their past performance or future potential. Therefore, it should be a positive, performance-improving dialogue between the manager and the employee.

For many managers, the formal performance appraisal interview is one of the most dreaded activities. Managers often have no problem evaluating the outstanding performer. The problem is with everyone else. Often providing information to an employee that runs contrary to the employee's own self-evaluation or self-image is difficult. This can lead to a number of outcomes that many managers would prefer avoiding.

Nevertheless, it is necessary to carry out the interview, as this is indeed one of the most important part of a manager's jobs.

Appraisal Interview is conducted as depicted in figure 6.14.

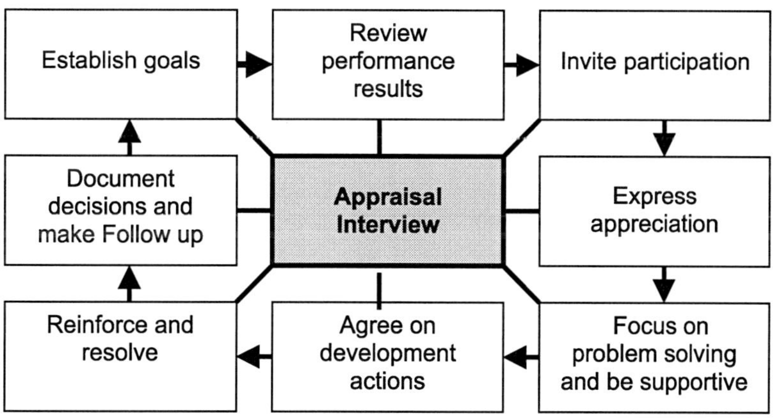

Fig. 6.14 : Steps of Appraisal Interview Process

Involves the following steps

1. Establish goals:

A fruitful performance discussion between the manager (appraiser) and his employee (appraise) can only take place when there are clear goals for appraisal interview. The manager while preparing for the actual dialogue with the employee must take time to review completed performance appraisal form including self-appraisal form of the employee. He should plan what topics/critical elements will be discussed in the interview, jotting down the major issues to be discussed to identify relevant/sensitive issues, anticipating areas that the appraisee will raise and some strategies to focus on, preparing some (awareness-raising) questions – this is where the reflection occurs and arranging protected time and privacy.

Walking into a performance appraisal interview without thinking about the goals will lead to an ineffective interview.

2. Review performance results:

Manager should go over the employee's performance, own interactions, the history of the employee; if the employee reports to a number of supervisors, then it must be ensured that input from all relevant sources has been obtained. Manager should try to identify the assumptions and blind spots that may have concerning this employee (for example, performance fine but he just doesn't like the "style" of the employee). Next is to identify the root cause of employee's problems.

Manager should create an open and accepting climate for the employee to reduce his anxiety and tension and explain the overall purpose and process of the appraisal interview *i.e.* telling the employee how he is doing. There are four approaches for giving performance feedback as mentioned below:

- **The tell-and-sell interview:**

  Communicate to employees about their performance as accurately and directly as possible with little return feedback, which can lead to defensiveness on the part of employees.

- **The tell-and-listen interview:**

  Communicate to employees about their strengths and weaknesses, but also allows for return feedback. This creates an environment that is less defensive and stressful to the employee.

- **The problem-solving interview:**

  Playing the role of helper more so than judge, the manager creates an environment through which the employee can discover his or her own developmental needs.

- **The mixed-model interview:**

  Allows for the problem-solving interview in the beginning, where the subordinate leads off, and finishes with the tell-and-sell or tell-and-listen approaches if the subordinate has missed some important areas of his or her performance.

The performance review should be restricted to the employee, his job and his performance only. The employee should also be productive, understand the role of the manager, and should do his preparation.

3. Invite participation:

The manager should ensure full participation of the employee in the performance discussions. He should accord an opportunity to the employee to put forth his views and comments on various facilitating and inhibiting factors that has affected his performance and on any new tasks or additional responsibilities, new procedures, training, etc. which the employee is eager to shoulder. Employees should participate with their managers in the creation of their own performance goals and development plans. Mutual agreement is a key to success. A plan wherein the employee feels some degree of ownership is more likely to be accepted than one that is imposed. This does not mean that employees do not desire guidance from their manager; indeed they very much do.

Lack of participation by the employee in the appraisal interview will result in communication break down and make the interview ineffective.

4. Express appreciation:

The manager should really try to understand the employee and ask him broad and general questions. He must praise his achievements and provide clear and specific feedback on performance of the employee. He should also appreciate at the outset that his contributions to the organisation's mission and objective and convey that it is being valued by the organisation. Managers need to learn about deep feelings and values of the employee so as to foster mutual agreement and understanding about the problems and goals for improvement.

5. Focus on problem solving and be supportive:

Manager should provide effective feedback with a descriptive and specific objectives aimed at solving problems of the employee. He should discuss at length the employee's problems and suggest appropriate solutions. If specific resources are required to improve the performance of the employee then the manager should be committed to make available the same, of course within his/organisation's means. Appraisal interview must focus down on evidence – this makes the appraisal robust.

6. Agree on development actions:

Manager should develop developmental plans with the employee to improve his effectiveness on the job through various training and learning developmental interventions. The specifications of the employee's learning need is to be identified, the process of realizing the needs and ways of measurement of achievement of outcome is to be emphasized. Skills pertaining to time management, stress coping, and informational needs is to be focused. Manager should facilitate the employee for taking more responsibility and explore opportunities for delegation. It is important for the manager to get the commitment of the employee to the development plan.

7. Reinforce and resolve:

Manager should develop some joint conclusions together with the employee based on the discussion and the developmental needs that have been identified. He should summarize the discussion and reaffirm the plans and action mutually agreed upon.

8. Document decisions and make Follow up:

Manager should record the appraisal interview in the prescribed manner with the details of specific improvement area, developmental plans and action needed. This forms basis for future reference and records. However, it must be noted that appraisal interview does not end here. Manager has to continuously make follow up to assess the progress made and other inputs as necessary to realize the mutual goals being agreed upon in the appraisal interview.

Properly prepared managers and well-planned appraisal interview can be a positive experience for both the employee and the manager. A sample appraisal interview questionnaire is given below:

Appraisal Interview Questionnaire

Appraisal Interview Form

Appraisal Year: Form No.:

NAME: DATE/TIME:

The appraisal interview is an annual working session where both appraiser and appraisee will give systematic feedback as regards performance, cooperation and working relationships, and set objectives for next year's achievements. The interview will address long-term conditions, which are difficult to address on a daily basis. The appraisee will benefit most from the interview if he is well prepared and has thought through the interview topics.

This form is meant to prepare the appraisee and to help organize the appraisal interview. If you want to discuss issues related to your work situation, which are not covered by the items in this form, please raise them at the beginning of the interview. The interview and the preparations are personal and concern the working relationship between appraiser and appraisee. The information shall be kept confidential unless otherwise explicitly agreed in the conclusion.

This form will be marked for destruction no later than when the working relationship between the appraiser and the appraisee comes to an end, unless otherwise agreed.

Follow-up from previous appraisal interview (unless this is the first):

Has the agreement been implemented?

Why not?

1. Please describe your tasks/duties on a separate, attached, sheet:

- Please list the tasks you are in charge of and/or take part in as part of your work and deliver it to your superior no later than 7 days prior to the appraisal interview.

- Please indicate the amount of work and time consumed for each task or type of task.

2. Which tasks or type of tasks went particularly well?

Why did they go so well?

3. How do you feel about the content of your work/your area of work?

Do the distribution and prioritizing of tasks work well?

How are your qualifications, skills and experience employed at work?

4. How could your current job be further developed?

Do you have any suggestions for new tasks you would like to undertake?

Are there any current tasks you would like to be exempted from?

Do you have any suggestions for improvements?

What are your objectives or suggestions for the next year as regards professional development and training?

5. How do you feel about the working relationship between you and your manager (your appraiser)?

(If you do not want to write anything under points 6, 7 and 8, you may choose to address them orally during the interview.)

6. How do you feel about the working relationship between you and your subordinates? (Applicable for managers)

7. What is your opinion of the working relationship between you and your colleagues?

Do you have any suggestions for improvements?

8. Are your physical working conditions satisfactory?

Do you have any suggestions for improvements?

9. Any other relevant circumstances?

Are there any other circumstances you would like to mention which influence your work situation?

Domestic circumstances?

Honorary posts, etc?

Circumstances at your work place not covered by previous items?

Conclusion

Appraiser and appraisee shall keep one copy each of this sheet.

Follow-up from previous appraisal interview:

Appraisee's responsibilities (indicate time limit):

Appraiser's responsibilities (indicate time limit):

Date:

---------------------------	---------------------------
Appraisee's signature	Appraiser's signature

After the Interview,

- Make sure you receive a completed appraisal form so you can insert your comments.
- Ensure you receive a final copy of the appraisal with the reviewer's comments.
- Make sure you understand what you have agreed to do.
- Do it.
- Make sure you understand what the appraiser agreed to do.
- Discuss any changes to your job as they occur, and the effect this may have on your objectives.
- Use the appraisal reviews and the annual interview to look for ways in which to become better at your job and enjoy it more.

Performance Feedback

Performance feedback is given in order to improve the performance of employees. It is an informal discussions to instruct, direct, or prompt the employee to improve performance. Providing feedback and models of the behaviour and/or skills needed to improve performance ensures success for the employee and the organisations.

Providing feedback involves the followings factors:

- Focussed on specific behaviour;
- Impersonal;
- Goal oriented;
- Well timed; and
- Understanding fostered.

There are two types of performance feedback, depending on the goal of appraisal interview, appraisee and actual performance exhibited as depicted in figure 6.15.

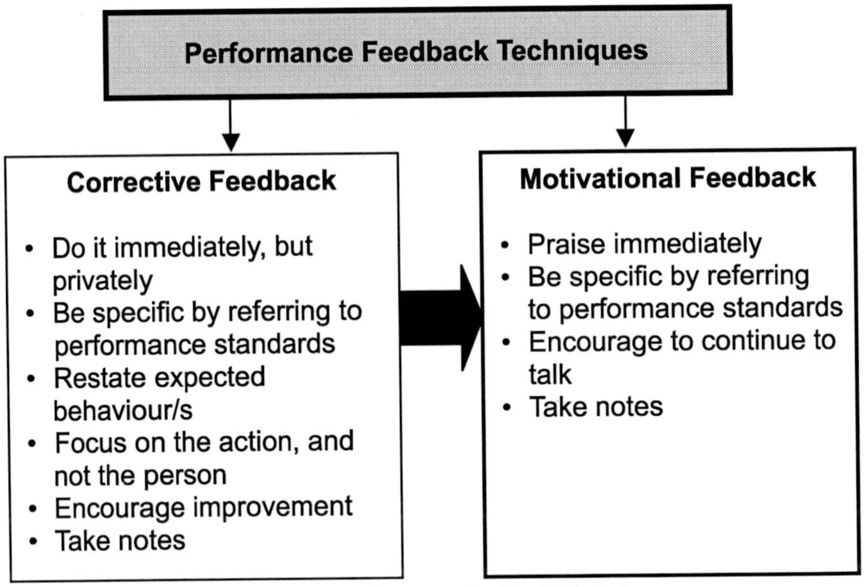

Fig. 6.15 : Performance Feedback Techniques

Methods of Performance Appraisal

There are various methods of performance appraisal depending on the size and nature of the organisation. Broadly speaking, the methods of performance appraisal may be divided into four *viz.* Rating method, Comparative method, Narrative method and Behavioural/Objective method as discussed below (see figure 6.16).

I. Rating Methods:

These methods rely on putting employees on certain pre-defined scale to asses their performance. Two common rating methods are:

1. Checklist Method:

Under this method, a list of statements or words are given to the appraiser and is asked to check statements representing the characteristics and performance of each employee. The statements may carry yes/no alternative or + and–sign representing possession or non-possession of required characteristics and performance.

This method poses a lot of difficulty in assembling, analyzing and weighing a number of statements about employee characteristics and contributions.

2. Graphic Rating Scale Method:

Under this method, employee characteristics and performance are evaluated through a graph. This technique is more consistent and reliable. Typically, a graphic scale

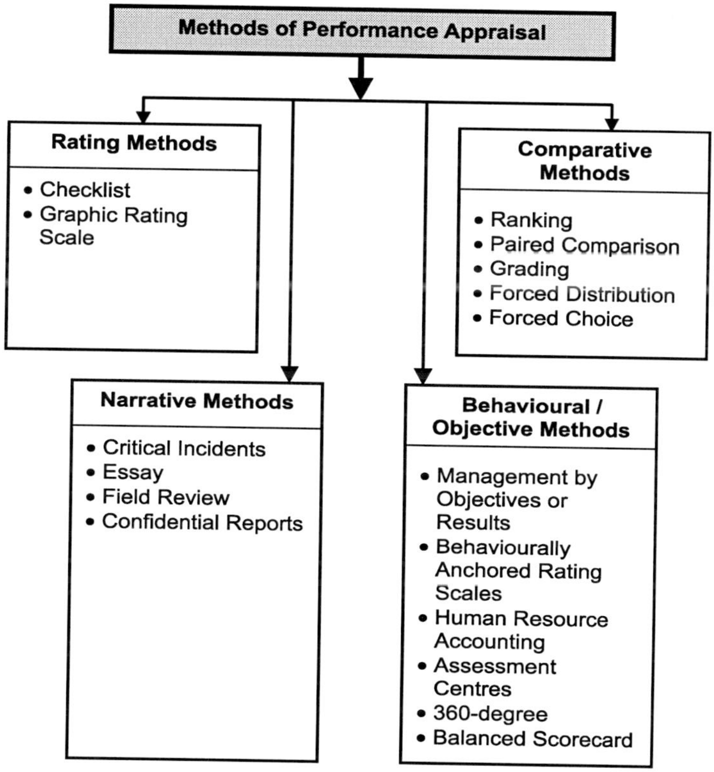

Fig. 6.16 : Performance Appraisal Methods

assesses an employee on the quality and quantity of his work (is he outstanding, above average, average, or unsatisfactory?) and on a variety of other factors that vary with the job but usually include personal traits like reliability and cooperation. It may also include specific performance factors like oral and written communication.

The graphic scale has come under frequent attack, but remains the most widely used rating method. In a classic comparison between the "old-fashioned" graphic scale and the much more sophisticated forced-choice technique, the former proved to be fully as valid as the best of the forced-choice forms, and better than most of them. It is also cheaper to develop and more acceptable to raters than the forced-choice form. For many purposes there is no need to use anything more complicated than a graphic scale supplemented by a few essay questions.

II. Comparative Methods:

These methods rely of relative comparison and ranking of employee performance based on certain criteria or characteristics of performance. Five common comparative methods are:

1. Ranking Method:

In this method, the names of employees are listed on the left-hand side of a sheet of paper – preferably in random order. A manager is asked to choose the "most valuable" employee on the list, cross his name off, and put it at the top of the column on the right hand side of the sheet. Next, the manager selects the "least valuable" employee on the list, crosses his name off, and puts it at the bottom of the right-hand column. The ranker then selects the "most valuable" person from the remaining list, crosses his name off and enters it below the top name on the right-hand list, and so on.

This method is very simple and inexpensive. But it's reliability and validity may be open to doubt.

2. Paired Comparison Method:

This technique is probably just as accurate as ranking and might be more so. But with large numbers of employees it becomes extremely time consuming and cumbersome. To illustrate the method, let us say we have five employees: A, B, C, D and E. We list their names on the left-hand side of the sheet. We compare A with B on whatever criterion we have chosen, say, present value to the organisation. If we feel A is more valuable than B, we put a tally beside A's name. We then compare A with C, with D, and with E. The process is repeated for each individual. The man with the most tallies is the most valuable employee, at least in the eyes of the rater; the man with no tallies at all is regarded as the least valuable employee.

Both ranking techniques, particularly when combined with multiple rankings (i.e., when two or more people are asked to make independent rankings of the same work group and their lists are averaged), are among the best available for generating valid order-of-merit rankings for salary administration purposes.

3. Grading Method:

Under this method, different grades of performance are determined in advanced such as excellent, very good, good, satisfactory and poor. Employees are placed in any of these grade according to their performance.

4. Forced Distribution Method:

Under this method, the employees are appraised according to the pattern of a normal curve (bell shaped) in order to check tendency of appraisers to rate most of the employees around high points. This method forces the appraisers to spread their employee evaluations in a prescribed distribution. The distribution in general is as under:

20% of employees = excellent performers

60% of employees = average performers

20% of employees = poor performers

This method is based on questionable assumption that all groups of employees will have the same distribution of excellent, average and poor performers.

5. Forced Choice Method:

This technique was developed to reduce bias and establish objective standards of comparison between individual employees. Although there are many variations of this method, the most common one asks raters to choose from among groups of statements those which best fit the individual being rated and those which least fit him. The statements are then weighted or scored, very much the way a psychological test is scored. Employees with high scores are, by definition, the better employees; those with low scores are the poorer ones. Since the rater does not know what the scoring weights for each statement are, in theory at least, he cannot play favourites. He simply describes his employees, and someone in the human resource development department applies the scoring weights to determine who gets the best rating.

In practice, however, the forced-choice method tends to irritate raters, who feel they are not being trusted. They want to say openly how they rate someone and not be second-guessed or tricked into making "honest" appraisals.

A few clever raters have even found ways to beat the system. When they want to give average employee a high rating, they simply describe the best employee they know. An additional drawback is the difficulty and cost of developing forms. Consequently, the technique is usually limited to middle and lower-management levels where the jobs are sufficiently similar to make standard or common forms feasible. Finally, forced-choice forms tend to be of little value and probably have a negative effect when used in performance appraisal interviews.

III. Narrative Methods:

These methods rely on written statements to indicate the performance level of employees and involve great deal of linguistic skills of the appraisal designer. Four common narrative methods are:

1. Critical Incidents Method:

The discussion of ratings with employees has, in many organisations, proved to be a traumatic experience for managers. Employees who receive honest but negative feedback are typically not motivated to do better and often do worse after the appraisal interview. Consequently, managers tend to avoid such interviews, or if forced to hold them, avoid giving negative ratings when the ratings have to be shown to the employee. One stumbling block has no doubt been the unsatisfactory rating form used. Typically, these are graphic scales that often include rather vague traits like initiative, cooperativeness, reliability, and even personality. Discussing these with an employee can be difficult. The critical incident technique looks like a natural to some people for performance appraisal interviews, because it gives a manager actual, factual incidents to discuss with an employee. Managers are asked to keep a record, a "little log book," on each employee and to record actual incidents of positive or negative behavior. Instead of arguing over traits, the discussion now deals with actual behaviour.

There are, however, several drawbacks to this approach. It requires that managers jot down incidents on a daily or, at the very least, a weekly basis. This can become a chore. Furthermore, the critical incident rating technique need not, but may, cause a manager to delay feedback to employees. And it is hardly desirable to wait six months or a year to confront an employee with a misdeed or mistake. Finally, the manager sets the standards. If they seem unfair to an employee, might he not be more motivated if he at least has some say in setting, or at least agreeing to, the standards against which he is judged?

2. Essay Method:

In its simplest form, this technique asks the rater to write a paragraph or more covering an individual employee's strengths, weaknesses, potential, and so on. The assumption is that an honest and informed statement either by word of mouth or in writing from someone who knows an employee well, is fully as valid as more formal and more complicated methods.

The biggest drawback to essay appraisals is their variability in length and content. Moreover, since different essays touch on different aspects of an employee's performance or personal qualifications, essay ratings are difficult to combine or compare.

3. Field Review Method:

When there is reason to suspect rater bias, when some raters appear to be using higher standards than others, or when comparability of ratings is essential, essay or graphic ratings are often combined with a systematic review process. The field review is one of several techniques for doing this. A member of the human resource development department meets with small groups of raters from each supervisory unit and goes over each employee's rating with them to *(a)* identify areas of inter-rater disagreement, *(b)* help the group arrive at a consensus, and *(c)* determine that each rater conceives the standards similarly.

This group-judgment technique tends to be fairer and more valid than individual ratings and permits the human resource development staff to develop an awareness of the varying degrees of leniency or severity as well as bias exhibited by raters in different departments. On the negative side, the process is very time consuming.

4. Confidential Reports Method:

Under this method, the manager appraises the performance of the employee based on his observations, judgments and intuitions and reports it confidentially. The employee is not allowed to see or discuss the appraisal.

IV. Behavioural/Objective Method:

Behavioural/objective methods of performance appraisal are based on the following propositions:

(a) Evaluations are not conducted for raises, promotions, or bonuses instead for development and communication; and

(b) Most important aspect in all is multilateral communication between employee, managers, and others, rather than one-way communication.

Six common behavioural/objective methods are:

1. Management by Objectives or Results Method:

Peter F. Drucker put forth the concept of management by objectives in 1954. It is George Odione, Valentine and Humble who refined it and made it an appraisal technique. It is one of the most promising appraisal techniques particularly for managerial personnel. Under this method, employee (subordinate) and manager (superior) of the organisation jointly identify verifiable objectives, define individual's major areas of responsibility in terms of results expected and use these measures on guides for operating and measuring individual contributions. The model of MBO based appraisal process is depicted in figure 6.17.

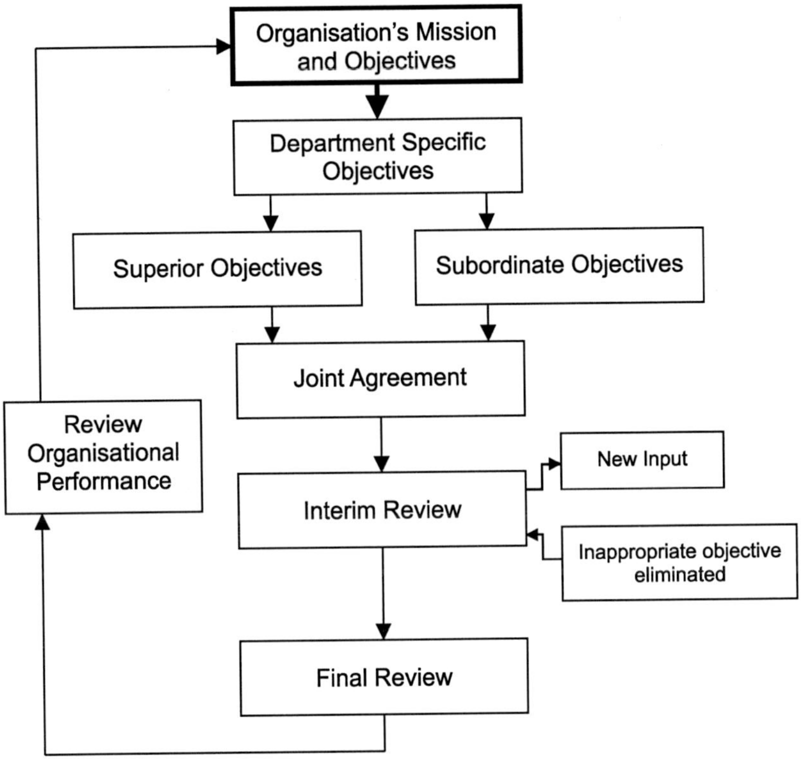

Fig. 6.17 : Steps of MBU Based Performance Appraisal

The various steps involved in appraisal by objectives or results are as under:

1. CEO decides the business strategy of the organisation, duly approved by Board of Directors and accordingly the departmental objectives are defined by managers;
2. Manager then defines his own objectives in light of the departmental objectives. He advices the employees of his department to prepare their blue print of major responsibilities and contributions in their respective job domains. The manager also prepares a blue print of the major activities to be undertaken to achieve the departmental objectives with tentative list of hands for shouldering the planned activities;
3. Manager and the Employee decide and define the major performance objectives and evaluation criteria under mutual consultation;
4. Manager appraises the performance of the employee at the end of the performance cycle on the basis of mutually agreed evaluation criteria against each performance objective; and

5. Manager discusses the results of appraisal with the employee for corrective actions, if any, and defines the jointly decided performance objectives for the next performance cycle.

Merits:

1. Quantitative method of appraising performance through achievement of contributions of the individual employee;
2. Performance objectives are target oriented and can be set up easily in terms of production figures, reduction of wastages and spoilages, sales figures, etc which ensures more objective evaluation of performance; and
3. Employees know beforehand the performance standards, measures and criteria which help them to stay focused.

Demerits:

1. Participative approach of this technique may not suit all leadership styles as prevalent in different organisations;
2. All jobs cannot be quantified and hence do not fit into this appraisal technique well; and
3. It is difficult to make a comparative assessment of all employees given the fact that each employee has different evaluation factors.

2. Behaviourally Anchored Rating Scales (BARS) Method:

BARS combine elements of rating scales and critical incidents methods that are related to specific job dimensions. Under this method, effective and ineffective job behaviours are described more objectively. The various steps involved in construction of BARS are as under:

1. Performance measures for effective job performance are identified and clustered into a small set of key performance dimensions for a given job. These measures are identified usually from superiors, employees and HR department;
2. Those behaviours, which are essential/critical for effective job performance, are identified;
3. The critical behaviours/incidents identified are reclassified to form the definition of job dimension and the best ones are kept for further development, keeping in view job dimensions;
4. The critical behaviours are assigned numerical scale values usually from 1 to 7, with each point demonstrating the perceived level of performance; and

5. The result of arranging various scales for different dimensions of the job (known as behavioural anchors) produces a series of vertical scales (one for each dimension) anchored (measured) by the final incidents. Each incident is positioned on the scale according to its mean value. This scale is used for performance appraisal.

Merits:

1. High participation and hence acceptance of the technique by superiors and subordinates.
2. Differentiates among behaviour, performance and results; and
3. Technique is valid and reliable as it identifies observable and measurable behaviours of specific jobs.

Demerits:

1. Identified critical behaviours are activity directed rather than result directed;
2. Construction of BARS is expensive and time consuming; and
3. Research does not support the high gain claims of BARS.

3. Human Resource Accounting Method:

Under this method, cost and contribution of human resources are measured and compared. Cost of human resources include recruitment & selection cost, induction & placement cost, training & development cost, compensation & benefits cost, etc. and contributions include the value addition made by the employee to the organisation to further the goals and objectives of the organisation.

This appraisal technique has not developed and still it is in transition stage.

4. Assessment Center Technique:

An assessment center is a comprehensive, standardized procedure in which multiple assessment techniques are used to evaluate individual employees for a variety of decisions.

This method was first applied in German Army in 1930 and was subsequently applied by British Army in 1960. Under this method, various experts using various techniques do assessment of several individual employees. A technique can be considered as assessment centre only if it meets the following requirements:

(*i*) Multiple assessment techniques must be used, one of which must be a simulation;

(*ii*) Multiple trained assessors must be employed;

(*ii*) Judgments must be based on pooled information from all assessors;

(*iv*) Evaluation must be made at a time separate from the observation of behaviour; and

(*v*) The dimensions, attributes, characteristics, or qualities evaluated by the programme must be determined by an analysis of relevant job behaviour.

The main tools used in assessment center are:

(*a*) Psychometric Tests: Three types of tests or questionnaires such as aptitude tests, ability test and personality test are employed. These tests are selected keeping in view:

- Measurement objectives
- Reliability and validity
- Time required for administration
- Cost involved

(*b*) Interviews: Structured interviews are used to probe background, critical incidents, and situational and behavioural event of the employees.

(*c*) Leaderless Group Discussions (LGD): A small group of employees (participants) are given a problem to solve and are instructed to arrive at a group decision within a specified time frame.

(*d*) In-basket Exercise: The in-basket or in-tray represents day to day decision making situation which a manager is likely to face in the written form from various sources and are give to the employee to assess his activity level, problem analysis skills, planning and organizing skills, time management, delegation, etc. The in-tray materials are given keeping in view the job duties and competencies required (or shall be required) of each employee.

(*e*) Management Games/Simulation Exercises: A real life situation such as running a manufacturing operation, stock trading, etc. is simulated to the entire group of employees. The complexity varies in these games; the common denominator is the relatively unstructured nature of interactions among the participants and the variety of actions that can be taken by all participants.

The interactive nature of the business game provides opportunities to assess dimensions such as strategic planning, teamwork, team skills, leadership, analytical ability, etc.

(*f*) Role Playing: It is a method of adopting roles from real life, other than those being played by the person concerned and understanding the dynamics of the role. Role playing tends to evaluate the human relations processes and personal attitudes and behaviour in a particular role such as conflict management, leadership skills, group problem solving, team skills, communication, interpersonal skills, etc.

(g) Presentations: Presentations on vision, organisational issues, case studies, etc. are extensively used for assessing employees/participants.

Assessment Center procedure is as under:

1. During exercise the one assessor observes and records the behaviour of the employee/participant and no final interpretations are arrived at;
2. Once the individual assessors have prepared the reports, they are followed by assessor discussion to carry out a comparative analysis. After the discussions, final rating (average) is arrived at;
3. The role of facilitator in assessment center technique is critical to the success of the technique. He provides inputs on various areas such as job competencies, training on the assessment center technique, assessor's selection, etc; and
4. CEO plays a vital role in supporting and propagating the concept and ensuring that it is in line with the organisation's objectives.

Companies such as RPG, TISCO, AV Birla Group, Castrol (India), ONGC, Wipro, etc. have assessment centers in India.

5. 360-Degree Method:

The 360-degree feedback can be used as a tool for assessment. This technique was first developed and administered by General Electric Company (GEC) of USA in 1992. It is a process of gibing performance feedback that combines self-appraisal with ratings made by co-workers at the same level, above, and below the target person in the managerial hierarchy and customers as depicted in figure 6.18.

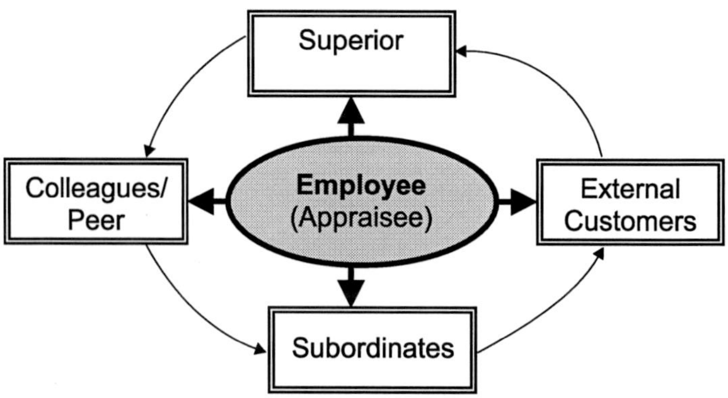

Fig. 6.18 : Components of 360 Degree Appraisal

This technique is used to collect feedback on various managerial and behavioural dimensions. Such feedback is then compiled to prepare a profile of the assessee (employee). Such a profile highlights the following:

- How well he is performing various roles.
- His strengths and areas of improvement as perceived by himself and others.

On the basis of the above feedback, the assessee can then prepare action plan to improve his managerial effectiveness and have positive impact at the workplace. The various components of this technique are discussed below:

(*a*) Appraisal by Superior: The superior appraises the performance of the employee on various job dimensions since he is familiar with subordinates job profile, is responsible for getting the work done and understands employee's performance and related factors.

(*b*) Appraisal by Colleagues/Peer: Colleagues/peers are in a better position to evaluate certain aspects of the behaviour and competencies of the employee as they are closely linked to the employee (appraisee).

(*c*) Appraisal by Subordinates: Subordinates appraise the employee in terms of guidance, resourcefulness, delegation, and management of interpersonal conflict and showing of fair play at workplace.

(*d*) Appraisal by External Customers: The employee's performance is also evaluated by the customers (end customers, vendors, suppliers, etc.) who interact with him regularly and has fair knowledge of the work and it's requirements as performed by the employee.

Merits:

(*i*) Provides a well-rounded view;

(*ii*) Avoids individual bias;

(*iii*) Can have more impact than a single source; and

(*iv*) Can establish consensus.

Demerits:

(*i*) Responses from colleagues and external customers may be biased or simply the result of trade-offs (give and take);

(*ii*) It ignores performance in terms of achieving goals; and

(*iii*) The rate may deny the truth of negative feedback.

6. Balanced Scorecard Method:

This new approach was developed in the early 1990's by Dr. Robert Kaplan (Harvard Business School) and Dr. David Norton. They named this system as 'balanced scorecard'. Recognizing some of the weaknesses and vagueness of previous management approaches, the balanced scorecard approach provides a clear prescription as to what organisations should measure in order to 'balance' the financial perspective.

The balanced scorecard is a management system (not only a measurement system) that enables organisations to clarify their vision and strategy and translate them into action. Strategy is the way an organisation seeks to achieve its vision and goals. The balanced scorecard identifies and prioritizes critical activities in an organisation's daily work and measures progress along the way. It provides feedback around both the internal business processes and external outcomes in order to continuously improve strategic performance and results. When fully deployed, the balanced scorecard transforms strategic planning from an academic exercise into the nerve center of an enterprise.

Kaplan and Norton describe the innovation of the balanced scorecard as follows:

"The balanced scorecard retains traditional financial measures. But financial measures tell the story of past events, an adequate story for industrial age companies for which investments in long-term capabilities and customer relationships were not critical for success. These financial measures are inadequate, however, for guiding and evaluating the journey that information age companies must make to create future value through investment in customers, suppliers, employees, processes, technology, and innovation."

The Balanced Score Card (BSC) may be defined as a conceptual framework for translating an organisation's vision into a set of performance indicators distributed among four perspectives: Financial, Customer, Internal Business Processes, and Learning and Growth. Indicators are maintained to measure an organisation's progress toward achieving its vision; other indicators are maintained to measure the long-term drivers of success. Through the BSC, an organisation monitors both its current performance (finance, customer satisfaction, and business process results) and its efforts to improve processes, motivate and educate employees, and enhance information systems–its ability to learn and improve.

Three metrics are used to determine whether they're meeting customer demand:

- Percentage of projects completed on time and on budget.
- Percentage of projects released to the customer by the agreed-upon delivery date.
- Customer satisfaction as indicated by customer surveys.

Balanced Scorecard enables linkage of strategy to management actions by placing the organisation's key performance indicators on manager's desktops. By illustrating the cause-and-effect relationships between KPIs, Balanced Scorecard gives managers a clear understanding of how their decisions impact both their direct area of responsibility, as well as the organisation's overall strategy.

With BSC, the organisation can:

- Link strategy to quantifiable and measurable metrics;
- Provides organisation-wide deployment capabilities; and
- Create rapid prototyping.

A balanced scorecard is a central list of numbers, which show each key part of an organisation's success, such as financials, people, operations, suppliers, customers, and support systems. The numbers should measure not just important outcomes, but also the factors, which influence, or drive, those outcomes.

The balanced scorecard suggests that we view the organisation from four perspectives, and to develop metrics, collect data and analyze it relative to each of these perspectives (see figure 6.19).

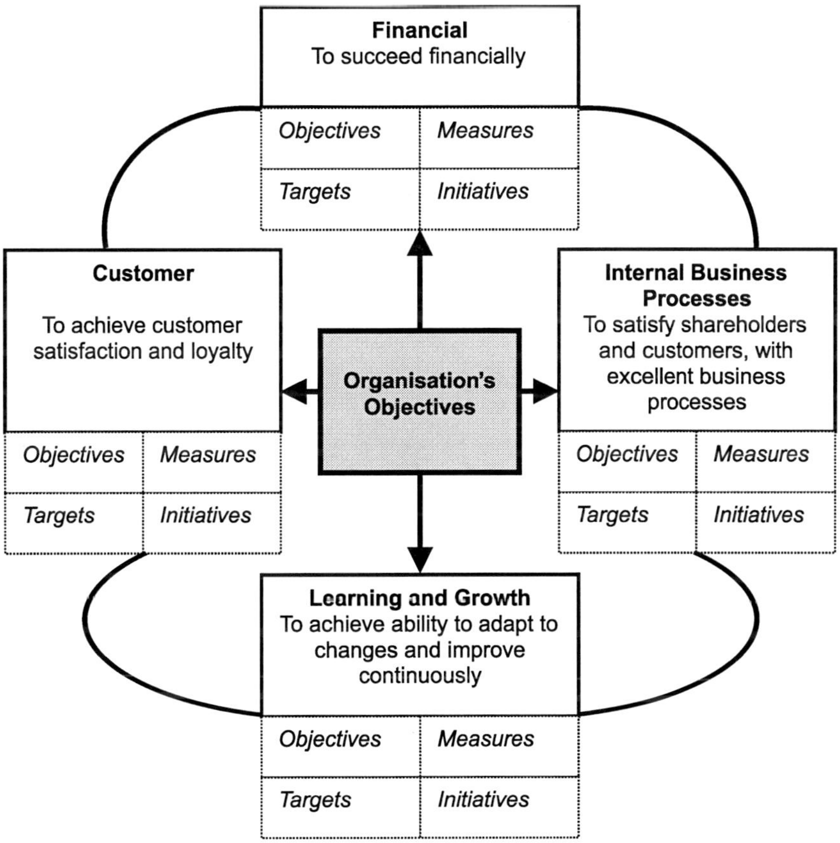

Fig. 6.19 : Components of Balanced Scorecard

1. The Learning and Growth Perspective:

This perspective includes employee training and corporate cultural attitudes related to both individual and corporate self-improvement. In a knowledge organisation, people – the only repository of knowledge are the main resource. In the current climate of rapid technological change, it is becoming necessary for knowledge workers to be in a continuous learning mode. Organisations often find themselves unable to hire new technical workers and at the same time is showing a decline in training of existing employees. This is a leading indicator of 'brain drain' that must be reversed. Metrics can be put into place to guide managers in focusing training funds where they can help the most. In any case, learning and growth constitute the essential foundation for success of any knowledge-worker organisation.

Kaplan and Norton emphasize that 'learning' is more than 'training'; it also includes things like mentors and tutors within the organisation, as well as that ease of communication among workers that allows them to readily get help on a problem when it is needed. It also includes technological tools; what the Baldrige criteria call "high performance work systems."

2. The Business Process Perspective:

This perspective refers to internal business processes. Metrics based on this perspective allow the managers to know how well their business is running, and whether its products and services conform to customer requirements (the mission). These metrics have to be carefully designed by those who know these processes most intimately; with unique missions these are not something that can be developed by outside consultants.

Additionally, two kinds of business processes may be identified: a) mission-oriented processes, and b) support processes. Mission-oriented processes are the special functions of the organisation, and many unique problems are encountered in these processes. The support processes are more repetitive in nature, and hence easier to measure and benchmark using generic metrics.

Internal measures should stem from the business processes that have the greatest impact on customer satisfaction: cycle time, quality, employee skills, and productivity. The organisation should also identify critical core competencies and try to guarantee market leadership;

3. The Customer Perspective:

There are increasing realization of the importance of customer focus and customer satisfaction in any business. These are leading indicators: if customers are not satisfied, they will eventually find other suppliers that will meet their needs. Poor performance from this perspective is thus a leading indicator of future decline, even though the current financial picture may look good.

In developing metrics for satisfaction, customers should be analyzed in terms of kinds of customers and the kinds of processes for which we are providing a product or service to those customer groups.

4. The Financial Perspective:

Timely and accurate funding data will always be a priority, and managers will do whatever necessary to provide it. In fact, often there is more than enough handling and processing of financial data. With the implementation of a corporate database, processing can be centralized and automated. But the point is that the current emphasis on financials leads to the "unbalanced" situation with regard to other perspectives.

Formal systems for appraising performance are neither worthless nor evil, as some critics have implied: Nor are they panaceas, as many managers might wish. A formal appraisal system is, at the very least, a commendable attempt to make visible, and hence improvable, a set of essential organisation activities. Personal judgments about employee performance are inescapable, and subjective values and fallible human perception are always involved. Formal appraisal systems, to the degree that they bring these perceptions and values into the open, make it possible for at least some of the inherent bias and error to be recognized and remedied.

By improving the probability that good performance will be recognized and rewarded and poor performance corrected, a sound appraisal system can contribute both to organisational morale and organisational performance. Moreover, the alternative to a bad appraisal programme need not be no appraisal programme at all, as some critics have suggested. It can and ought to be a better appraisal programme. And the first step in that direction is a thoughtful matching of practice to purpose.

Alternative Performance Assessors

An alternate performance assessment is suggested below as depicted in figure 6.20.

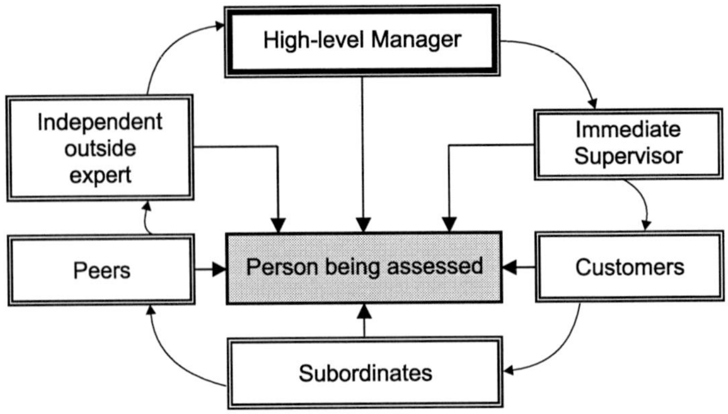

Fig. 6.20 : Alternative Performance Assessment Loop

Here, seven different appraisers assess the performance of a person. In addition to the immediate supervisor, peers, subordinates and customers, a high level manager such as CEO/COO and an independent outside observer such as a management consultant/subject matter expert also overseas the appraisal of the person. This can help to make the performance appraisal activities more objective and the person concerned has more sources of reliable feedback. This also reduces various types of rater errors.

This system has the potential for future success. But the major problem is the large number of appraisal points which may be very time consuming, expensive and difficult to administer.

Performance Appraisal Failures

Performance appraisal is the most critical human resource development/management tool in the hands of the management as well as employees. Being a human process, a number of errors and problems creep into making it less objective and reliable. The major reasons of failure of performance appraisals are as under (see figure 6.21):

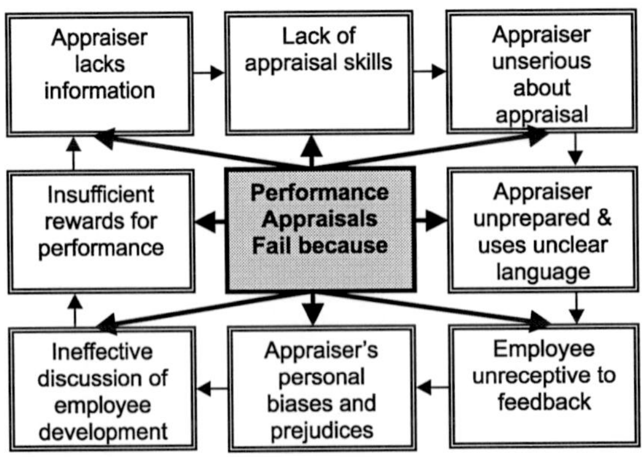

Fig. 6.21 : Reasons of Performance Appraisal Failures

1. Appraiser lacks information:

Due to lack of knowledge and training of appraiser on performance appraisal system, it may fail to deliver intended results. Also, the manager may have limited knowledge of job characteristics, job demands, job conditions, performance standards, etc. which adds to the reasons of the failure of performance appraisal system.

2. Lack of appraisal skills:

Performance appraisal requires great managerial skills because a manager has to be skillful in appraising the performance of the employee by examining the work plans, required skills, performance goals, facilitating and inhibiting factors, past performance results and has to then appraise the performance of the employee. He must have also procedural knowledge of appraisal system, purpose of the appraisal system, and mission and objectives of the organisation to do justice to appraisal.

3. Appraiser unserious about appraisal:

One of the most common mistakes managers makes in the practice of performance appraisal is to perceive appraisal as an isolated event rather than an ongoing process. Where performance appraisal fails to work as well as it should, lack of support from the managers is often cited as a major contributing reason. Opposition may be based on political motives, or more simply, on ignorance or disbelief in the effectiveness of the appraisal process. It is crucial that they believe in the value of appraisal and express their visible commitment to it. Managers are powerful role models for employees.

Many managers treat performance appraisal as a form filling ritual and just find time to complete and submit it to human resource development department. They think with this their responsibility is over. They do not place high importance on the appraisal's role in improving not only individual performance, but organisational performance also. It must be understood that performance appraisal plays a key role in developmental activities of the employees. Developed and competent employees can only bring competitive advantage to an organisation.

4. Appraiser unprepared and uses unclear language:

Many managers have a natural reluctance to "play judge" and create a permanent record, which may affect an employee's future career. This is the case especially where there may be a need to make negative appraisal remarks. They are not prepared to do handle the responsibility bestowed on them by the performance appraisal system. Also, the bane of any performance appraisal system is the manager who wants to "play it by ear". Stressing the importance and technical challenge of good performance appraisal should actively discourage such attitudes.

There is a suspicion among many managers that a poor appraisal result tends to reflect badly upon them also, since they are usually the employee's supervisor. Many appraisers have a vested interest in making their employees "look good" on paper. When this problem exists (and it can be found in many organisations), it may point to a problem in the organisation culture. The cause may be a culture that is intolerant of failure. In other words, appraisers may fear the possibility of repercussions both for themselves and the appraisee and therefore uses unclear language.

5. Employee unreceptive to feedback:

Many employees are not receptive to the feedback given to them. Some employees consider it to be undue criticism, some make stony faces and take it casually and still some believe that feedback is useless and wastage of their time. This attitudinal problem of some employees makes the appraisal system ineffective. Larson (1989) has described a social game played by poor performers. Many supervisors will recognize the game at once and may have been its victims. The game is called feedback seeking. It occurs where a poor performing employee regularly seeks informal praise from his manager at inappropriate moments.

Often the feedback seeker will get the praise they want, since they choose the time and place to ask for it. In effect, they "ambush" the manager by seeking feedback at moments when the supervisor is unable or unprepared to give them a full and proper answer, or in settings that are inappropriate for a frank assessment.

The supervisor may feel "put on the spot", but will often provide a few encouraging words of support. The game seems innocent enough until appraisal time comes around. Then the manager will find that the employee recalls, with perfect clarity, every casual word of praise ever spoken!

This places the manager in a difficult situation. Either the manager lied when giving the praise, or least, misled the employee into thinking that his performance was acceptable (in fact, this is the argument that feedback-seekers will often make).

The aim of the game is that the feedback seeker wants to deflect responsibility for their own poor performance. They also seek to bolster their appraisal rating by bringing in all the "evidence" of casual praise. Very often the feedback seeker will succeed in making the supervisor feel at least partly responsible. As a result, their appraisal result may be upgraded.

The truth of the matter is that they have been "blackmailed" by a subtle social game. But like most social games, the play depends on the unconscious participation of both sides. Making managers aware of the game is usually sufficient to stop it. They must learn to say, when asked for casual praise, "I can't talk about it now... but see me in my office later."

This puts the manager back in control of the appraisal process.

6. Appraiser's personal biases and prejudices:

Managers own value system and personal characteristics affect the appraisal system. His personal biases and prejudices adversely impact the effectiveness of performance appraisal thereby making less reliable. They may dislike any employee or any group, which will result in their lower rating than warranted. Many managers do a little fudging; they actually defend it as a tactic necessary for effective management. The fudging motives of appraisers have, at times, certain plausibility. For instance, a manager who has given an overly generous appraisal to a marginal performer might claim that their 'legitimate' motive was the hope of encouraging a better performance. On the other hand, fudging motives can be a lot less admirable and sometimes devious: the appraiser who fudges to avoid the possibility of an unpleasant confrontation, the manager who fudges to hide employee difficulties from senior leadership, the manager who fudges in order to punish or reward employees. Managers will, for all sorts of reasons, deliberately distort the evaluations that they give to employees.

Common rater biases (errors) that can negatively influence the performance appraisal are:

- **Halo Effect:** Draws on one specific characteristic/accomplishment to excessively influence performance review. Or applies favorable ratings to all job duties based on impressive performance in one area.
- **Pitchfork Effect:** Bases ratings on the rater's dislike for a particular trait in an employee.
- **Invalid Criteria:** The use of criteria other than performance as basis of ratings.
- **Recency Error:** Tendency to use a particular recent event or behavior that occurred closer to the performance review as the basis of rating.
- **Leniency Error/Loose Rater:** In an effort to avoid conflict the rater has the tendency to be overly generous in judgment. Typically, is reluctant to point out weaker areas of an employee's performance.
- **Central Tendency Error:** Instead of rating each person individually based on merit, the tendency is to rate everyone as average. Both the "excellent" and the "needs improvement" categories are avoided.

- **Strictness:** Tendency to be overly harsh when judging performance. This may be a case where the standards of performance may be too high or unrealistic.

The following will help to avoid rater biases:

- Keeping a personnel file on each employee to keep documentation of his performance throughout the year;
- Reviewing documentation that manager has gathered throughout the review cycle; and
- Rating performance based on established performance standards.

7. Ineffective discussion of employee development:

Sometimes managers get busy with giving feedback especially negative feedback and there is very little time or inclination to discuss developmental plans. Such managers feel that giving feedback to employees is their responsibility and develop necessary skills, competencies and desirable behaviours is the responsibility of the employee and they have no business on that. However without training, learning and development plans and interventions, the very purpose of performance gets defeated because the main goal of performance appraisal is to develop the human resources of an organisation as depicted below in figure 6.22.

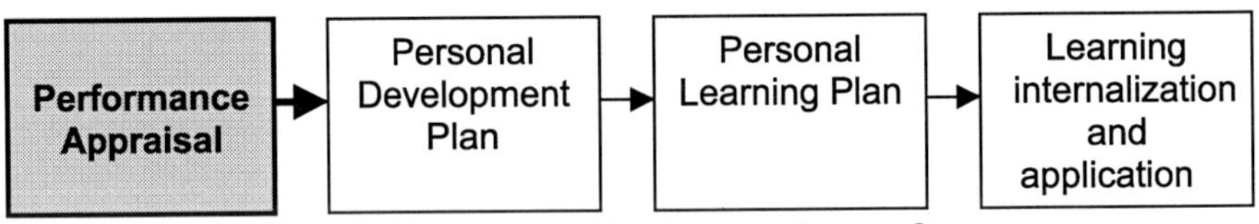

Fig. 6.22 : Performance Development Process Steps

8. Insufficient rewards for performance:

An employee shall be motivated to perform if he knows that his effort shall lead to better performance and a better performance shall, in turn, lead to better rewards. The higher the effort-performance-reward linkages, higher shall the attractiveness of the process to the employee and he shall be motivate to perform better and better. This is confirmed by theory (Expectancy Theory) and Research (Scholars and Practitioners). Receiving a promotion will be more rewarding to persons who did not expect than to those who did. Similarly, failure to receive a promotion might be less frustrating to those who did not expect it than those who did. Failure to provide commensurate reward (vis-a-via performance) will frustrate the employees and shall result in deterioration of performance thereby failing the performance appraisal.

Longenecker (1989) argues that accuracy in performance appraisal is impossible to achieve, since people play social and political games, and they protect their own interests. "No savvy manager..." says Longenecker, "... is going to use the appraisal process to shoot himself or herself in the foot."

Essentials of A Good Performance Appraisal System

There are ten basic steps to develop and implement an effective performance appraisal system. The emphasis should be on developing a strategy tailored to help the organisation perform well which is not too complex for the benefits it delivers.

The ten steps to an effective performance appraisal are:

1. Developing business plans:

Business planning must take account of what can realistically be delivered within the resources available in the organisation and consider the human resource development implications. The organisation's plans and priorities that have been established, needs to be translated into team and individual performance plans. This is a highly skilled task that is critical for the performance appraisal process to work well. It is important that managers are given appropriate support to carry this out effectively.

2. Establishing what aspects of performance need to be measured:

The performance indicators being used must be clearly communicated to employees along with other measures being used to define performance. The focus should be on measuring what matters and trying to keep those measures to a reasonable number.

3. Setting up systems to monitor and evaluate:

Systems need to be set up to ensure that performance can be monitored and evaluated throughout the year to ensure that it is improving continually. It is therefore, essential that the performance appraisal support the organisational development and human resource development strategies, so that it helps rather than hinders progress.

4. Defining the general performance expectations of employees:

This may be done through a combination of approaches such as the use of competences, policies and procedures. Line managers should be given specific responsibilities for managing performance. Effective ways of doing this are making it an explicit part of their job role and incorporating how to manage performance into management training and development programmes. In return there should be clear and consistent expectations of what is expected of employees while they are working for the organisation.

5. Agreeing on specific performance objectives:

Agreeing individual performance and employee development needs is normally carried out using a combined performance appraisal and development process. This approach provides the framework for helping managers to translate business plans into individual plans and objectives and agree how these will be met. Individual plans and objectives are most effective when both manager and employee agree them. Objectives should be Specific, Measurable, Agreed, Realistic and Time bound [SMART].

6. Developing an internal communications system:

It is normally accepted that to be effective, messages need to be communicated in a range of different ways that really target those employees whom the managers are trying to reach. There are wide range of different approaches that can be adopted to ensure employees are kept in contact with key performance issues e.g. HR briefings, meetings, lunch time seminars, use of the intranet, mini articles or stories in Employee magazines, posters, bulletin boards, email alerts, line management/supervision meetings.

Conducting regular employee surveys and running a suggestion scheme are also important ways of ensuring that employees have opportunities to feedback on a wide range of issues that will impact directly or indirectly on organisational performance.

7. Ensuring the performance appraisal system is in place, is well understood and working effectively:

A performance appraisal system is traditionally used to set objectives, identify support needs and measure progress against objectives. For it to work effectively, it needs to be clearly understood by both managers and employees. This means ensuring that managers have access to guidance and training to ensure that they manage performance effectively throughout the year and employees at all levels within the organisation have the necessary support, guidance or training to enable them to actively engage in the performance appraisal process.

The performance appraisal system should also be regularly reviewed to ensure that it is achieving its stated objectives.

8. Supporting employees to help them perform well:

Effective induction processes for new employees are extremely important in setting the right expectations for performance on both sides. If this early stage is managed well it may be possible to intervene to prevent or minimize individual capability issues later on through personal development or redeployment programmes. Feedback from this process may also highlight problems with job design or recruitment processes, which then need to be rectified.

Responsibility for meeting human resource development needs may be addressed within the work group may be fed back to HRD function for action. Whatever the approach, the organisation needs an overview of its capability and how it plans to address any gaps that will hamper the achievement of its objectives.

Developing employee capacity to deliver organisation's mission and objectives is likely to be achieved in a variety of ways. All employees, even those who have been in the same post for some time, should be encouraged to consider how they are performing and what else they could learn or do differently to deliver better results. In some cases these needs will be adequately met through attending training courses but there are many other possibilities, such as job shadowing, mentoring, e-learning, and working on projects or reading manuals. Wherever possible, the employee should be given the opportunity to obtain the most suitable option.

Performance needs to be actively managed and monitored throughout the year. An essential part of this dialogue is the giving and receiving of feedback. For this to work effectively the organisational climate must encourage the sharing of both success and failure. Without this, employees will be reluctant to comply and the quality of the feedback may be lacking. As well as managers, employees at all levels in the organisation may also need support, guidance or training to enable them to actively engage in the performance appraisal process.

9. Seeking performance improvement:

There will be circumstances where performance does not meet the required standard. At organisational level, this will mean identifying what are the barriers to effective performance and putting in place a plan to deliver improvement. At team and individual level, the principles will be the same, but it may be more difficult to manage. as individual sensitivities and complexities may be at the forefront.

Having in place a clear process for dealing with inadequate performance is important. However, it is essential that the process does not take over from the desired outcome, which is to seek performance improvement. Identifying the reason for inadequate performance is the first step. From this, the organisation can determine further action, which may involve disciplinary procedures, additional training or support, monitoring and review mechanisms, redeployment, changing job roles or in some cases dismissal. It is also important that learning from these actions is taken on board, for example to improve future performance appraisal system or selection methods.

Formal capability or disciplinary proceedings take much time, effort and resources, which could otherwise be targeted at more positive interventions, such as recognizing good performance. If performance appraisal is embedded into day-to-day management practice it is likely that inadequate performance will be managed and improved before it gets to this stage; that's why following the performance management cycle on an ongoing basis is so important.

10. Recognizing and rewarding good performance:

This is the part that many organisations forget; instead they take good performance for granted and focus on those who have not met the standard. However, to retain motivation and continuously improve, it is essential that good performance is recognized and where appropriate, rewarded. Recognition and reward will mean different things to different people; for some financial reward in the form of pay rises or bonuses may be important, whereas for others recognition that their contribution has made a difference will be enough.

When determining what will be the most appropriate reward the organisation will need to understand what motivates their workforce and how they can meet this need. Pay systems and processes will be important, but it will also be necessary to identify other reward mechanisms such as opportunities for development and career progression.

Recognizing performance is also about sharing success stories across the organisation and highlighting how good performance helps the organisation as a whole. This may also help with sharing good practice and learning about what works.

Types of Performance Appraisal

There two types of performance appraisal as discussed below.

1. The Evaluative Performance Appraisal

This type of appraisal focuses on administration of rewards and punishment to employees by evaluating of their performance. If performance has been found to or meet exceed standards, then employee receives pay raises and promotion and if his performance has been found to below standards then receives either pay raises or very low pay rises. The steps of an evaluative performance appraisal are depicted in figure 6.23.

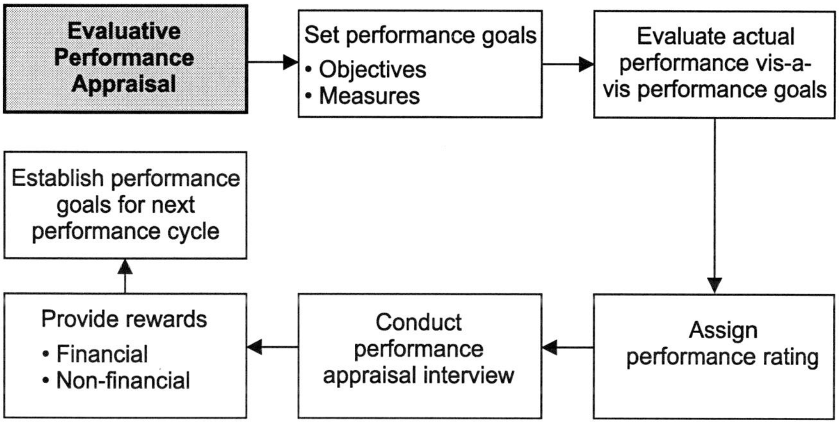

Fig. 6.23 : Steps of Evaluative Performance Appraisal

2. The Developmental Performance Appraisal

This type of appraisal focuses on determination of development plans employees. If performance has been found to meet or exceed standards, then employee receives further impetus to develop himself for higher responsibilities. For employees with performance problem, specific training, learning and development plans are prepared and conducted so as to improve his on the job performance and effectiveness. The steps of developmental performance appraisal are depicted in figure 6.24.

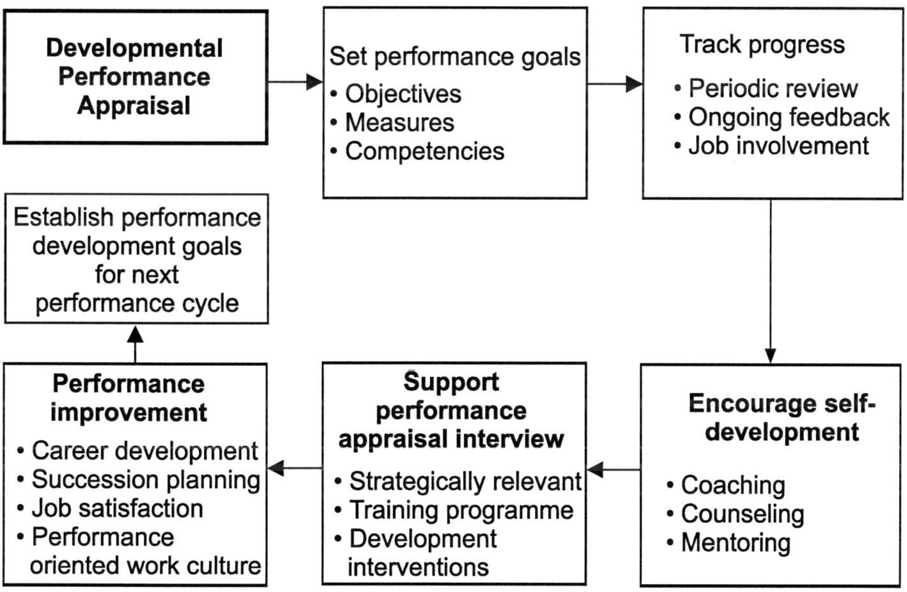

Fig. 6.24 : Steps of Development Performance Appraisal

In reality, a combination of above two appraisals is used. This is because administration of rewards and development of employees are complimentary to each and go hand in hand. Although such combination of reward administration and employee development approaches leads to several problems.

Benefits of Performance Appraisal

The benefits of performance appraisal are numerous. A good performance appraisal helps both employees as well as the organisation to increase their performance level and enhance competitive index continually. It is depicted in figure 6.25.

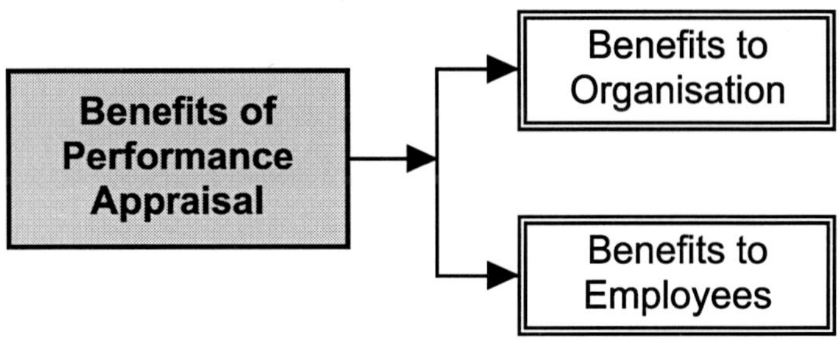

Fig. 6.25 : Benefits of Performance Appraisal

Major benefits Includes :

1. Benefits to the Organisation:

Despite imperfect measurement techniques, individual differences in performance can make a difference to organisational performance. Documentation of performance appraisal and feedback may be needed for legal defense. Appraisal provides a rational basis for constructing a bonus or merit system. Appraisal dimensions and standards can help to implement strategic goals and clarify performance expectations. Providing individual feedback is an integral part of the performance appraisal process.

Despite the traditional focus on the individual, appraisal criteria can include teamwork and the teams can be the focus of the appraisal.

2. Benefits to Employees:

Performance appraisal is as important for good performers as for weak ones. Performance feedback is needed and desired for bringing about improvement in performance, which requires assessment. Fairness requires that difference in performance levels across employees be measured and have an effect on outcomes.

Assessment and recognition of performance levels can motivate employees to improve their performance.

To conclude, performance appraisals are more effective as it if:

- Fosters commitment;
- Indicates promotability and developmental needs; and
- Moves the appraisal away from looking at the past and focuses on the future.

People IQ, a leader in performance management consulting have conducted a study which surveyed over 48, 000 employees, managers and CEOs across 126 organisations, shows that performance appraisal systems still have a long way to go. A snapshot of the results show that:

- A mere 13% of the respondents felt that their organisation's performance appraisal was useful.
- 88% says company's performance appraisal negatively impacted their opinion of HR.
- 18% agreed that their current performance appraisal system differentiated between high and low performers.
- 16% believed that performance appraisal process was user friendly.

Performance Appraisal in Future Organisations

The approach to Performance Appraisal system in organisations of the future is depicted in figure 6.26.

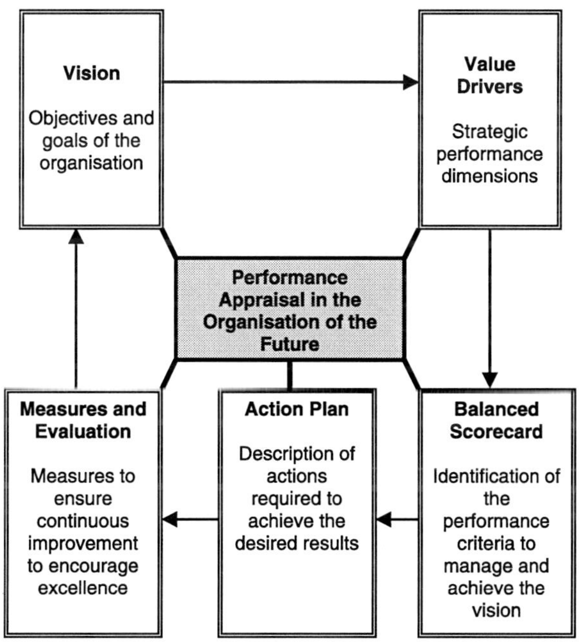

Fig. 6.26 : Suggested Framework of Performance Appraisal in Future Organization

Potential Appraisal

Potential Appraisal is fundamentally concerned with career enhancement possibilities of employees. Potential Appraisal is used for developmental planning and placement decisions because a progressive organisation has to create new roles and responsibilities as a result of its growth imperatives. Now, to perform new roles and responsibilities requires continuous identification and development of existing employees.

To conclude our discussion, we may say that performance appraisal leverages employee and organisational commitment to produce desirable result for all the stakeholders of the organisation. It can be summed up through Einstein's Theory:

$$E = mc^2$$

Where E = Employee effort

m = Mission of the organisation

c = Compensation received as reward

c = Contentment gained.

Hence, we may conclude that performance appraisal is a strategic management tool to bring about organisational excellence. Simply putting, organisational excellence refers to doing superior things with simple means. A model of organisation excellence is depicted in figure 6.27.

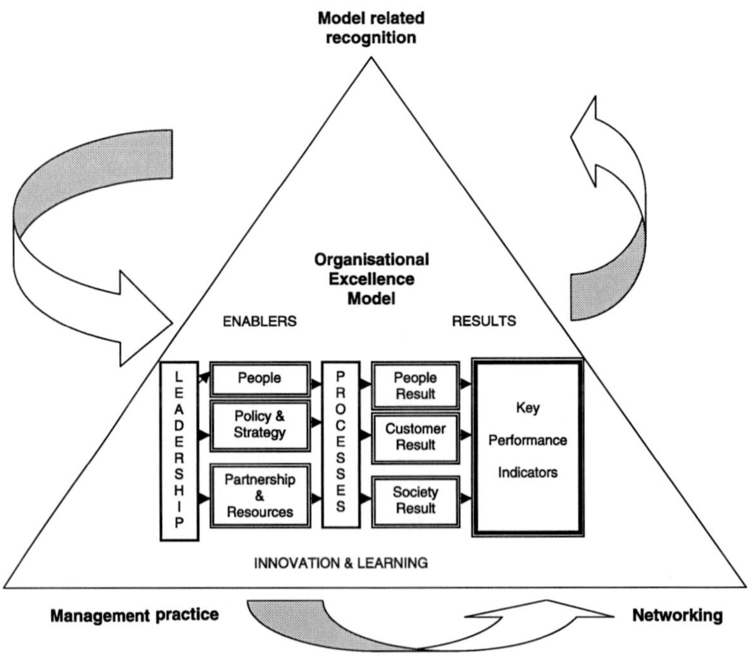

Fig. 6.27 : Organisational Excellence Model

Review and Discussion Questions

Question 1: Define and explain the concept of performance appraisal.

Question 2: What are the newer trends of performance appraisal?

Question 3: How to structure an effective appraisal interview?

Question 4: Develop a sample performance appraisal form for managerial and non-managerial cadres of a manufacturing firm.

Question 5: By which of the several appraisal methods would you want to be evaluated if you were an employee or manager. Why?

Question 6: What is performance appraisal and list down its objectives?

Question 7: Describe forced choice method of appraisal. What are its advantages and disadvantages?

Question 8: What are the uses of performance appraisal?

Question 9: Design a performance appraisal system for a manufacturing organisation.

Question 10: Explain the process of performance appraisal.

Question 11: What are the different methods of performance appraisal?

Question 12: What are the reasons of failure of performance appraisal?

Question 13: Discuss the essentials of a good performance appraisal system.

Question 14: Write short notes on:

(*i*) Performance appraisal model
(*ii*) Purpose of performance appraisal
(*iii*) Rater (or Rating) errors.

Exhibit: 6 – A

Case Situation

- *Before attempting this section please read Chapter - 14 on Case Study.*
- *Please read the following case situations and answer the questions.*

Q 1. You have started a small Company with 15 employees. You are over worked, so you want to develop one performance appraisal form you can use for all employees. Design and develop the most appropriate form with details on the chosen methodology (select one) with justification.

Q 2. You have been promoted from Production Supervisor to Assistant Manager-Production. You have been advised to find your suitable replacement. Devise your plan of action.

Q 3. A director of accounts department always has trouble with his people after performance appraisals. They quit, call in sick for a week, or sabotage operations. During a conversation with Mr. Sunil Bahri, the Vice President of human resources, the director complained about the performance evaluation process, 'I have a bunch of babies working for me. They all expect me to tell them what good performance is. Part of their job is figuring out what they are supposed to do'. What should be the best response of Mr. Sunil Bahri

Exhibit: 6 – B

Case Study

- *Before attempting this section please read Chapter - 14 on Case Study.*
- *Please read the following case study and answer all the subsequent questions.*

Introduction to the organisation:

The case study involves a female blind transcriptionist who works for a worldwide insurance firm, The XYZ group, in the claims department of one large branch office of approximately 130 employees. The transcriptionist, Reena Gupta, is a five-year employee with the firm and primarily type copy from audiotapes that are dictated by the claims adjusters with the use of specialized hardware and software. Reena has been blind since birth and this is the first long-term employment she has ever held. She is a support staff member of the operations department but her responsibilities are within the claims department.

Brief Description of the Problem:

Reena's immediate supervisor, Anil Sadana, is an operations supervisor and he is responsible for her performance evaluations and productivity. Anil reports to Kiran Chopra, who is the operations department manager. Both Anil and Kiran are fairly new to the branch office and have been instructed by the human resource development manager and the new Claims Manager that Reena's performance is well below company quality and quantity standards.

Prior to Anil and Kiran arrival to the branch office, the branch officer met with all department managers to discuss plans for improving quality in the office. XYZ's senior management had state to focus on individual performance and quality and wanted efforts increased in this area across the board. A directive came down to all branch offices to "fix the people problems as soon as possible."

As part of this focus on quality, each department manager was asked to rate his or her employees on a scale of: Needs No Attention, Needs Attention or Needs Immediate Attention. The department managers were asked to rank employees and come with a list of problem people. Reena was one of the people needing immediate attention. This was based upon the feedback from the claims department through various conversations with the manager and the claim adjusters. One of Kiran's initial goals as new manager was to set up a plan in dealing with Reena's performance issue.

It was Anil's task to bring Reena's performance up to company standards. However, prior to Anil's arrival in the branch office, Reena's performance evaluations had always been average. It was apparent that no formalized quality/quantity standards existed for Reena and previous supervisory management failed to approach the issue because of its sensitivity. Therefore, Reena was not aware of her low performance levels.

The case study outlines the events, which took place when Anil and Kiran attempted to define Reena's work standards and began to deal with her low performance.

The initial meeting:

The first meeting with Reena was timed to coincide with per annual performance appraisal (which measures quantity and quality as the primary factors in a merit increase). Anil and Kiran made a decision in agreement with the Humans Resource Development Manager and the Claims Manager that Reena's performance appraisal would be the starting point for dealing with her problem of quantity and quality. Basically, she was not typing enough of the statements to keep up with the workflow, and the statements were filled with errors.

One of the first problems that they encountered was that there were no formalized quality/quantity criteria for the transcriptionists within the claims department. Another operations transcriptioist within the claims department, Anita D'souza, was a superior performer and her performance level represented what would be considered the 'ideal' transcriptionist. However, using Anita's performance ability as the criteria was not a fair measurement. The previous supervisors to proof read Reena's work had utilized Anita.

Anita usually compared all of Reena's copy against the recordings and spent one or two hours a day going over the errors with Reena. This had always been a drain on departmental efficiency because Anita (an above average performer) was spending considerable amount of time correcting Reena's errors. Anita was delegated the task of computing Reena's error ratio for the performance appraisal which, against current standards, turned out to be significantly lower.

The Performance Improvement Plan:

Prior to Reena's performance appraisal, Anil and Kiran drew up some more performance criteria for Reena in the areas of quality and quantity. Anil and Kiran recognized that they could not immediately evaluate Reena with the new criteria or drop her average performance rating down to below average rating without prior performance plans. Therefore, it was decided that the current performance appraisal would reflect the major areas needing improvement and that Reena would be placed on a performance improvement plan in the forthcoming year. The performance improvement plan (PIP) was to measure Reena's quantity and quality based upon the established criteria. Each month, Reena was to receive an evaluation of her previous month's quality/quantity in the form of a written statement and summary of errors. Anita was put in-charge of computing the error ratios and producing a monthly report for Anil. Anita expressed an interest in helping and did not indicate to Anil that the monthly monitoring would be a problem for her.

Because Reena's error ratio had been initially calculated at such a high number, Anil and Kiran also decided to develop a timeline for Reena where her error ratio was to gradually decrease over several months until acceptable ratios are achieved. At the initial meeting, all of this information was provided to Reena and she was completely baffled by the claims of her bad performance. Reena's immediate reaction was that Anil and Kiran were ganging up and she repeated, "But my performance has never been poor in the last five years. "Reena felt she was being unfairly singled out from all of the other typists in the department.

The Post-Appraisal Reaction:

Soon after Reena was given her performance appraisal and the performance improvement plan was discussed, her attitude changed to a very defensive posture. It was apparent that Reena was concerned about the likelihood of her future employment given the attention to her performance. Reena spent her time discussing her problem with Anita and felt that a conspiracy was unfolding in XYZ to rid of her. Anil and Kiran were sensitive to these concerns and tried to resource Reena that her job was not in jeopardy and that the performance improvement plan was merely to improve her performance over the long haul. At one such meeting, the following conversation took place between Anil and Reena

"Reena, although this is a serious problem, I know that we can work together to figure out the best way to accomplish your goals, "Anil said.

Reena replied, "But I don't understand what exactly the problem is with my performance. I have always been told that I didn't have any problems."

Anil responded, "As you know, there is a real emphasis upon the quality and quantity with the company because the company wants to avoid cutbacks as we enter the soft market. I understand that your previous supervisor never talked to you about this, but now we must examine the issue and correct it."

In addition to the frequent meetings to comfort Reena, the Human Resource Development Manager was available to her for any additional reassurance. However, Reena did not initiate a single meeting with anyone.

From her initial meeting, Anil noticed that Reena did not want to accept any responsibility for her low performance level. For example, Reena remained convinced that her performance was acceptable by referencing her previous performance appraisals. She would say, "I've always been rated good. Why am I suddenly getting all the attention?'

Additionally, Reena began to blame the various claims adjusters for not dictating properly, therefore making her job more difficult. Anil and Kiran decided to not only measure the number of errors in Reena's work and her production level, but also to specifically address the types of errors in Reena's work and her production level, but also to specifically address the types of errors occurring in Reena's work. For example, were Reena's errors primarily misspelled words (which could be edited against the system's spell check) or more seriously, was Reens leaving out entire sentences and phrases?

Due to the important content of the claims adjusters recorded statements, the transcriptions must be entirely accurate and verbatim. The majority of the recorded statements were used for permanent files and evidence in claims disputes. To put it simply, the documents produced from these audiotapes were legal documents that could very easily determine the outcome of a claim settlement.

Anita was assigned to maintain all errors and produce a monthly report, which outlined those types of errors occurring in Reena's typing. Although it was an arduous task for Anita, Anil and Kiran knew that this information would be critical to Reena's continued performance improvement plan. Anil and Kiran were instructed by Human Resource Development Manager to document everything related to Reena's situation. One of Reena's additional concerns was that her equipment was not sufficient for her to perform well. Anil and Kiran contacted the vendor that sold the equipment to the company and asked that a consultant visit the office to determine if there were problems with the equipment. The vendor sent a blind transcriptionist (employed at another organization) who spent several hours with Reena to examine her concerns. The consultant indicated that there should be, some minor improvements to the system but otherwise, the system was sufficient. The consultant also offered additional training/assistance if it was needed. Reena was still not be satisfied with the visit from the consultant. The consultant's visit was also documented in Reena's file.

***The Monthly Performance Evaluations*:**

At Reena's subsequent performance evaluations, her quantity and quality levels actually began to decrease even more. Part of this was possible due to the frustration and stress felt by the continual pressure, but Anil and Kiran continued to emphasize to Reena that improvement needed to be seen in her performance. "The established time frames must be met, otherwise, we will need to begin a serious effort of performance improvement which in the worst case scenario, may result in termination," they told her.

At the monthly meetings, Reena was provided with all of the data about her performance and the meetings were fully documented and signed by all parties involved. Reena continued to blame her performance on others and the system and did not seem to take it seriously. Again, Anil and Kiran agreed to consider other potential problems, including Reena's earphones (which she claimed were distorted) and several of the claims adjusters' dictation abilities. The tapes in question were reviewed by Anil and Anita and nothing out of the ordinary were found. Were deficiencies were noted these were immediately addressed with the Claims manager. Also, Reena's earphones were replaced with new ones and she was asked to utilize her Braille dictionary when in doubt of certain spellings.

Ongoing Efforts:

Anita's involvement with Reena increased over the next few months. Reena would ask more questions and have Anita review tapes where she thought the audio was unclear. It was apparent that Reena's anxiety level continued to rise in her behaviour toward the situation but she did not discuss this with Anil, Kiran or the Human Resource Development Manager. The only individual who learned of Reena's anxieties was Anita and she tried to remain neutral to Reena's situation. Anita began to feel trapped in the middle if this issue and met with Anil to discuss her involvement in the problem.

As the monthly appraisals continued, Anil and Kiran documented Reena's lack of progress and met frequently to discuss the goals with her. However, Reena's performance levels continued to drop each month. Every consideration was given to Reena, including supplying her with improved software and having the company doctor's check her hearing.

A Year Later:

A year passed with all the efforts being made to improve Reena's performance and Reena still had not met the goals. At this point, a more formalized procedure (progressive discipline) was set in place where Reena was given specific goals to reach each month. The pressure continued to grow and Reena continued to assert that the problem was not with her abilities. During monthly meetings, Reena occasionally made various comments about how unfair the process was to her, but usually she remained quiet. She was usually silent at the performance meetings with Anil.

Because Reena's performance was not improving, Anil asked Kiran to sit in some of the performance meetings with Reena. He told Kiran he just didn't understand why Reena was not saying a word in the meetings.

Finally, after several levels of progressive discipline, Reena was terminated from the company on the basis of her inability to meet the job and the company standards of performance. The performance improvement plan had taken almost twelve months before Reena was dismissed. Prior to the initial performance appraisal, which set the performance improvement plan into place, Reena's work had been carefully scrutinized for about six months. All in all, the entire process took almost two years. During the later stages of her performance improvement plan, Reena filed a discrimination lawsuit against the company, and against Anil and Kiran. The lawsuit was based upon allegations of harassment and unfair treatment because of Reena's disability. One of the primary complaints made against the company was that Reena was unfairly evaluated on her performance in comparison with her peers. Also, the complaint stated that she was receiving undue scrutiny based upon her previous acceptable performance evaluations. Therefore, the lawsuit claimed that Anil and Kiran had acted negligently in their duties and intentionally singled Reena out based on her disability.

The following are just a few of the major modifications, which were made to support Reena's job:

Specialized hardware/software to assist Reena in her transcription typing including editing capabilities.

Customized performance standards, which gave more room for error based upon Reena's disability. In other words, Reena was not held to the same standards of the other typists who did not have disabilities.

Adequate time frames to turn performance levels around.

Adequate counseling/coaching in the performance issue.

Outside consultants/specialists hired to assist Reena in problem areas.

Considering the above criteria, a decision was made to terminate Reena because she was just unable and unwilling to improve her performance standards to an acceptable level over a period of time.

Questions:

1) Given the fact that Reena's performance has always been average upto the point that Anil and Kiran joined the department; do you feel it was unfair to begin a close scrutiny of Reena's work? If so, how would you have handled the situation?

2) Do you feel that Reena was unfairly signed out from the other workers because she was blind? Keep in mind that the same scrutiny was not being given to the other typists at the time.

3) What other resources/solutions might have been considered to assist Reena in her performance improvement?
4) Do you feel this performance improvement plan was given more/less severity due to the sensitive nature of Reena's disability?
5) What other approaches would you suggest for this situation?
6) What role should the Human Resource Manager have in this situation?
7) What type of concerns/fears would management have, when facing a situation such as this one?

Annexure

SAMPLE PERFORMANCE APPRAISAL FORMS

1. KRA Based Performance Appraisal Form
2. Trait Based Confidential Type of Performance Appraisal Form (for managerial cadre)
3. Trait Based Confidential Type of Performance Appraisal Form (for Non-managerial cadre)

PERFORMANCE APPRAISAL FORM

Form Identification No. :

Appraisal Year :

NAME OF APPRAISEE WITH EMP. CODE NO :	AGE :
FATHER'S NAME:	GROSS SALARY: (EXCLUDING INCENTIVE)
DESIGNATION :	QUALIFICATION:
POSITION REPORTS TO:	DATE OF LAST PROMOTION:
DATE OF JOINING :	SIGNATURE OF APPRAISEE:
LOCATION :	MAXIMUM INCENTIVE AMOUNT: RS. (PER QUARTER)

ROLE DESCRIPTION OF APPRAISEE	
1. Purpose of the Job/Role:	
2. Major Responsibilities & Accountabilities:	
3. Competencies Required:	
(A) Critical	
a) Knowledge:	
b) Skill:	
c) Behaviours:	
(B) Preferred:	
a) Knowledge:	
b) Skill:	
c) Behaviours:	

CHECK POINT FOR ASSESSMENT (REFERENCE TABLE)

ATTRIBUTE	CHECK POINT FOR ASSESSMENT	CRITERIA FOR ASSESSMENT			
		RATING	SCORE SCALE : 1 – 100	ASSESSED PERFORMANCE	INCENTIVE PAYABLE
ACHIEVEMENT OF KRAs	WHAT % OF THE DEFINED TARGETS ACHIEVED ?	OUTSTANDING	60-100	60% & ABOVE	100%
		EXCELLENT	50-59	50% TO 59 %	80%
		GOOD	40-49	40% TO 49 %	65%
		SATISFACTORY	35-39	35% TO 39 %	50%
		POOR	BELOW 35	BELOW 35%	NIL

Form Identification No. :

1. PERFORMANCE RESOURCING:

FROM	TO	APPRAISAL CYCLE	RESOURCES REQUIRED
01.04.200	30.06.200	1st Quarter	
01.07.200	30.09.200	2nd Quarter	
01.10.200	31.12.200	3rd Quarter	
01.01.200	31.03.200	4th Quarter	

APPRAISEE'S SIGNATURE DATE(S):	SUPERVISOR'S SIGNATURE DATE(S):	FUNCTIONAL HEAD'S SIGNATURE DATE(S):

Form Identification No. : | | | | | |

2. KEY RESULT AREAS (KRAs) FOR 1ST APPRAISAL CYCLE : FROM ________ TO ________

TO BE FILLED IN BY APPRAISEE & SUPERVISOR JOINTLY AND REVIEWED BY FUNCTIONAL HEAD

S.NO	KEY RESULT OBJECTIVES (PERFORMANCE TARGET)	MEASUREMENT CRITERIA	*WEIGHTAGE (MAX. 100 POINTS)	TIME LINE	RESULT ACHIEVED (ACCOMPLISHMENT)	FACILITATING or INHIBITING FACTORS	ACTION PLANS (Development actions, Support requirements)	RATING (SCORE ASSIGNED) (SCALE ON WEIGHTAGE :1-100)	
								SELF	SUPERVISOR

APPRAISEE'S SIGNATURE SIGNATURE **SUPERVISOR'S SIGNATURE** **FUNCTIONAL HEAD'S**

DATE(S): DATE(S): DATE(S):

* TOTAL WEIGHTAGE OF ALL KRA's SHALL NOT EXCEED 100 POINTS FOR EACH QUARTER

Form Identification No. : □□□□□

3.

APPROVAL OF DIRECTOR ON 1ST APPRAISAL WITH COMMENTS
SIGNATURE DATE:

4. ***This section should be completed & reported back to Functional Head within 30 days of close of 1st Appraisal Cycle.***

MONITORING OF PERFORMANCE PLANNING, ANALYSIS AND DEVELOPMENT SYSTEM ON 1ST APPRAISAL							
Monitoring Method	**Dimensions Monitored**					**Comments & Signature**	
	Performance Planning	**Performance Analysis**	**Performance Review & Counseling**	**Development Need**	**Review & Follow Up**	**Self**	**Supervisor**

Form Identification No. : | | | | | |

5. KEY RESULT AREAS (KRAs) FOR 2nd APPRAISAL CYCLE : FROM ________ TO ________

TO BE FILLED IN BY APPRAISEE & SUPERVISOR JOINTLY AND REVIEWED BY FUNCTIONAL HEAD

S.NO	KEY RESULT OBJECTIVES (PERFORMANCE TARGET)	MEASUREMENT CRITERIA	*WEIGHTAGE (MAX. 100 POINTS)	TIME LINE	RESULT ACHIEVED (ACCOMPLISHMENT)	FACILITATING or INHIBITING FACTORS	ACTION PLANS (Development actions, Support requirements)	RATING (SCORE ASSIGNED) (SCALE ON WEIGHTAGE :1-100)	
								SELF	SUPERVISOR

APPRAISEE'S SIGNATURE **SUPERVISOR'S SIGNATURE** **FUNCTIONAL HEAD'S SIGNATURE**

DATE(S): DATE(S): DATE(S):

* TOTAL WEIGHTAGE OF ALL KRA's SHALL NOT EXCEED 100 POINTS FOR EACH QUARTER

Form Identification No. : ☐☐☐☐☐

6.

APPROVAL OF DIRECTOR ON 2nd APPRAISAL WITH COMMENTS
SIGNATURE DATE :

7. This section should be completed & reported back to Functional Head within 30 days of close of 2nd Appraisal Cycle.

MONITORING OF PERFORMANCE PLANNING, ANALYSIS AND DEVELOPMENT SYSTEM ON 2nd APPRAISAL							
Monitoring Method	Dimensions Monitored					Comments & Signature	
	Performance Planning	Performance Analysis	Performance Review & Counseling	Development Need	Review & Follow Up	Self	Supervisor

Form Identification No. : ☐☐☐☐☐

8. KEY RESULT AREAS (KRAs) FOR 3rd APPRAISAL CYCLE : FROM ________ TO ________

TO BE FILLED IN BY APPRAISEE & SUPERVISOR JOINTLY AND REVIEWED BY FUNCTIONAL HEAD

S.NO	KEY RESULT OBJECTIVES (PERFORMANCE TARGET)	MEASUREMENT CRITERIA	*WEIGHTAGE (MAX. 100 POINTS)	TIME LINE	RESULT ACHIEVED (ACCOMPLISHMENT)	FACILITATING or INHIBITING FACTORS	ACTION PLANS (Development actions, Support requirements)	RATING (SCORE ASSIGNED) (SCALE ON WEIGHTAGE :1-100)	
								SELF	SUPERVISOR

APPRAISEE'S SIGNATURE SIGNATURE DATE(S):	SUPERVISOR'S SIGNATURE DATE(S):	FUNCTIONAL HEAD'S DATE(S):

* TOTAL WEIGHTAGE OF ALL KRA's SHALL NOT EXCEED 100 POINTS FOR EACH QUARTER

Form Identification No. : | | | | | |

9.

APPROVAL OF DIRECTOR ON 3rd APPRAISAL WITH COMMENTS
SIGNATURE DATE :

10. ***This section should be completed & reported back to Functional Head within 30 days of close of 3rd Appraisal Cycle.***

MONITORING OF PERFORMANCE PLANNING, ANALYSIS AND DEVELOPMENT SYSTEM ON 3rd APPRAISAL

Monitoring Method	Dimensions Monitored					Comments & Signature	
	Performance Planning	Performance Analysis	Performance Review & Counseling	Development Need	Review & Follow Up	Self	Supervisor

Form Identification No. : ☐☐☐☐☐

11. KEY RESULT AREAS (KRAs) FOR 4th APPRAISAL CYCLE : FROM ________ TO ________

TO BE FILLED IN BY APPRAISEE & SUPERVISOR JOINTLY AND REVIEWED BY FUNCTIONAL HEAD

S.NO	KEY RESULT OBJECTIVES (PERFORMANCE TARGET)	MEASUREMENT CRITERIA	*WEIGHTAGE (MAX. 100 POINTS)	TIME LINE	RESULT ACHIEVED (ACCOMPLISHMENT)	FACILITATING or INHIBITING FACTORS	ACTION PLANS (Development actions, Support requirements)	RATING (SCORE ASSIGNED) (SCALE ON WEIGHTAGE :1-100)	
								SELF	SUPERVISOR

APPRAISEE'S SIGNATURE
SIGNATURE
DATE(S):

SUPERVISOR'S SIGNATURE
DATE(S):

FUNCTIONAL HEAD'S
DATE(S):

* TOTAL WEIGHTAGE OF ALL KRA's SHALL NOT EXCEED 100 POINTS FOR EACH QUARTER

Form Identification No. : | | | | | |

12.

APPROVAL OF DIRECTOR ON 4th APPRAISAL WITH COMMENTS
SIGNATURE DATE :

13 *This section should be completed & reported back to Functional Head within 30 days of close of 4th Appraisal Cycle.*

MONITORING OF PERFORMANCE PLANNING, ANALYSIS AND DEVELOPMENT SYSTEM ON 4th APPRAISAL							
Monitoring Method	**Dimensions Monitored**					**Comments & Signature**	
	Performance Planning	**Performance Analysis**	**Performance Review & Counseling**	**Development Need**	**Review & Follow Up**	**Self**	**Supervisor**

Form Identification No. : ☐☐☐☐☐

14.

LIST OF SIGNIFICANT ACHIEVEMENTS BEYOND OBJECTIVES (Please be specific. In case of no such achievements, nil is to be mentioned against relevant period)				
APPRAISAL PERIOD		APPRAISEE'S SIGNATURE	SUPERVISOR'S SIGNATURE	FUNCTIONAL HEAD'S SIGNATURE
1ST APPRAISAL				
2ND APPRAISAL				
3RD APPRAISAL				
4TH APPRAISAL				

Form Identification No. : ☐☐☐☐☐

15. RATING/SCORE ON SCALE 1- 100

PERFORMANCE				BEHAVIOURAL & MANAGEMENT												TOTAL SCORE	SUPERVISOR'S SIGNATURE
APPRAISAL PERIOD	ATTRIBUTE			KEY MANAGEMENT AREAS						KEY COMPETENCE AREAS							
	ACHIEVEMENTS OF KRAs	QUALITY OF WORK	WORK ATTITUDE	PRODUCTIVITY	PROBLEM SOLVING	MEETING COMMITMEN TS	COST COUNSCIOUS NESS	COMMUNI CATION	ATTENTIVENESS	PLANNING & ORGANISING	LEADERSHIP	GOAL SETTING	JOB KNOWLEDGE & SKILLS	CREATIVITY	INTER PERSONAL RELATION		
1ST APPRAISAL																	
2ND APPRAISAL																	
3RD APPRAISAL																	
4TH APPRAISAL																	

Form Identification No. : ☐☐☐☐☐

16. TRAINING & DEVELOPMENT NEEDS:

APPRAISAL PERIOD	APPRAISEE'S IDENTIFIED NEED	APPRAISEE'S PLANNED ACTION	SUPERVISOR'S PLANNED ACTION
1ST APPRAISAL			
2ND APPRAISAL			
3RD APPRAISAL			
4TH APPRAISAL			

APPRAISEE'S SIGNATURE
DATE:

SUPERVISOR'S SIGNATURE
DATE :

FUNCTIONAL HEAD'S SIGNATURE
DATE:

Form Identification No. : ☐☐☐☐☐

17. PERFORMANCE ASSESSMENT PERIOD: FROM : ______________ TO : ______________ .

☐ Please complete this section at the end of 4th quarter of Performance Cycle for recommending Annual Increment and Internal Mobility (Promotion, Transfer, reassignments, etc) based on exhibited Performance & Composite Score of Four Performance Cycles/Quarters.

ANNUAL INCREMENT RECOMMENDED BY SUPERVISOR		
OVERALL PERFORMANCE SCORE ASSIGNED	**REVISION PROPOSED**	
	AMOUNT (IN RS)	**INTERNAL MOBILITY**

18. POTENTIAL ASSESSMENT PERIOD : FROM : ______________ TO : ______________

☐ Please tick in the relevant box :

1. Low Potential – Low Performance ☐
2. High Potential – Low Performance ☐
3. Low Potential – High Performance ☐
4. High Potential – High Performance ☐

SUPERVISOR'S SIGNATURE **FUNCTIONAL HEAD** **SIGNATURE OF COMPETENT AUTHORITY**

MANAGERIAL PERFORMANCE APPRAISAL FORM

PERSONAL DATA

Name : .... Age : ....

Qualifications : Academic : .... Technical : ....

Exam Passed / Degree	College / University	Year	Subjects	Division / Marks

Present Position : .... Present Grade : ....

Department : .... Present Gross : ....

Duration in present position : .... Present Basic : ....

Position joined at : .... Date of Joining : ....

Type of Appraisal: Confirmation / Probation / Annual Appraisal Due date of appraisal : ....

PART – A
SELF APPRAISAL
(*To be filled by Executive in his/her own writing*)

01. What parts of your present job interest you

a) The most

___

___

___

b) The least

___

___

___

___

02. Which parts of your job deserve to be given more care and attention than the Rest ?

03. What are you major contributions in your area of work during the reporting period?

04. Do you feel that your job utilizes your total abilities? If not, then mention your potential traits and abilities, which you ought to put into action.

05. In your opinion, what are you major strengths?

06. Would you like to share any of your major weaknesses which you noticed this year?

07. What efforts do you propose to overcome the above weaknesses?

08. In your opinion, which are the areas in which you still need to add more professional knowledge?

09. In your opinions which are the inputs which you need to strengthen your potential?

10. How would you rate your performance in the past one year on a ten point scale (Where 10 stands for Outstanding and 1 stands for Undesirable Performance).

1 2 3 4 5 6 7 8 9 10

(Please encircle the appropriate digit.)

Signature of the appraisee

PART – B
PERFORMANCE REVIEW

(To be filled by the immediate superior)

Kindly put a ✓ mark in the appropriate box.

Ratings

OUTSTANDING
VERY GOOD
GOOD
SATISFACTORY

PERFORMANCE CHARACTERSTICS	A	B	C	D
01. Professional Knowledge				
02. Planning and Organising ability				
03. Controlling ability				
04. Delegation				
05. Initiative				
06. Judgment and decision-making ability				
07. Communication skills				
08. Development of sub-ordinates				
09. Problem-solving				
10. Ability to motivate				
11. Team building skills				
12. Versatility in skills				
13. Capacity to achieve results				
14. Conflict-handling				
PERSONALITY CHARACTERSTICS				
01. Interest in the present job				
02. Perseverance finishing what he/she starts				
03. Loyalty/sincerity				

03. Loyalty/sincerity				
04. Punctuality				
05. Dependability/sense of responsibility				
06. Leadership				
07. Adaptability / flexibility				
08. Tact and Co-operation				
09. Self-reliance, stands on own for making decisions				
10. Drive and determination				
11. Creativity				
12. Optimism				
13. Ambition				
14. Integrity				
15. Originality				

OVERALL ASSESSMENT

Kindly put a ✓ mark in the appropriate box.

OUTSTANDING ☐

Ranks very highly in the qualities of intelligence, ability, character, drive and initiative, extraordinary performance, excellent knowledge of all phases of his/her work.

VERY GOOD ☐

Has good knowledge of every aspects of job, responsible dependable and trustworthy, performance much beyond normal requirements.

GOOD ☐

Has acceptable knowledge of the job and related work; meets standard requirements or work; takes of extra work when requested; has the potential to perform much better.

SATISFACTORY ☐

Has not gained adequate comprehension of his/her job requirements: makes frequent mistakes; hard worker but is a plodder; requires counseling, guidance and specific training; performance needs improvement.

In case the observation of the immediate superior is below satisfactory, then kindly tick the following:-

POOR ☐

Slipshod and haphazard executive; makes no effect to improve; totally irresponsible and undependable; performance highly unsatisfactory; misfit in the present position; wasteful in his/her work; knowledge of job is inadequate.

01. ATTAINMENT OF GOALS

Major Job Goals
Comments on attainment

---

02. Major job goals for the next appraisal period.

---

03. Indicate the individual's readiness for increased responsibility.

No Likely to be effective	Too early to assess	Upto 1 Year from now	1-2 years	2-3 years	Beyond 3 years

Is the individual being recommended for elevation/promotion? Yes ☐ No ☐

Grade Elevation to: **Grade** .... Promotion to: **Designation**
....

JUSTIFICATION

---

04. Training needs identified

---

05. Comments of immediate superior and recommendations

____

____

____

____

06. Comments of Department Head and recommendations

____

____

____

____

Immediate Superior	**Departmental Head**	**Head – HR**	**Director**

Action by the HR Department: Increment letter issued on ___________

Next review due on ______________

Increment details:

HR Department

NON - MANAGERIAL PERFORMANCE APPRAISAL

(FOR STAFF MEMBERS/WORKERS)

Name :........................ Age :..............................

Father's Name :.............................. Employee Code No............................

Qualification : Academic .... Technical : ....

Present Position :................................Present Grade : ....

Department :................................Present Pay : ....

Duration in present position: .... Reported to : ....

Position Joined : ....Date of Joining : ....

Type of Appraisal : ....Due Date : ....

PERFORMANCE REVIEW

S.No.	CHARACTERSTICS	A	B	C	D	E
01.	Job Knowledge					
02.	Ability to complete in time all work assigned					
03.	Proficiency in utilization of materials					
04.	Upkeep of tools / machinery /workplace					
05.	Tidiness in doing the work					
06.	Quality of work / Work attitude					
07.	Capacity to achieve results					
08.	Versatility in skills					
09.	Health / Hygiene					
10.	Interest in the present job					
11.	Punctuality					
12.	Initiative					
13.	Loyalty / Sincerity					
14.	Dependability / sense of responsibility					
15.	Self – discipline					

16.	Self – confidence					
17.	Self Development					
18.	Team adaptability					
19.	Leadership					
20.	Ability to learn higher skills					

A. Outstanding **B. Very Good** **C. Good**

D. Satisfactory **E. Poor**

OVERALL ASSESSMENT (Please Tick ✓)

Excellent	A	
Very Good	B	
Good	C	
Satisfactory	D	
Poor	E	

Is he/she suitable for your department: Yes/No

If not, suggest which department/ area he/she is best suited for

____

a) Major strengths of the appraisee

____

____

b) Major weaknesses of the appraisee

____

____

Suggest Training / development programmes for the appraisee

____

____

____

Leave availed during the year

a) Casual Leave .... Days
b) Sick Leave .... Days
c) Earned Leave .... Days
d) Leave without Pay .... Days

Counseling provided by the immediate superior and reaction of the appraisee

____

____

____

Comments of Departmental Head with recommendations

____

____

____

Immediate Superior **Section Incharge** **Head - HR**

REVIEWING AUTHORITY: ______________________________

____

Functional Head **HR Head**

ORDER OF THE SANCTIONING AUTHORITY WITH REMARKS, IF ANY:

Above appraisal is approved for

A) Promotion as :...........................

B) Total Increment of Rs. :...........................

C) Promotion / Increment

DIRECTOR

letter issued on :...........................

D) Next review due on :...........................

HR DEPTT.

CHAPTER

7 Employee Coaching, Counseling and Mentoring

Chapter Synopsis

In the organisation context, coaching, counseling and mentoring plays a pivotal role in ensuring higher performance and job satisfaction of the employees which is essential for ensuring sustained competitive advantage of the organisation. Broadly speaking, coaching is concerned with developing an employee in his job or role in order to enhance his productive contributions. Counseling is a tool used by managers to help the empolyees to cope with various individual, job, organisational and environmental challenges which could otherwise impair employee's performance and productivity. Finally, mentoring is a borad concept and is essentially focused on developing leadership competencies in the employee as well as to enable him to grow and develop to his fullest potential. A combination of these three fundamental HRD teachniques helps in ensuring individual and organisational development, effectiveness and success on a long-term basis.

This chapter explains these concepts and crucial skills for Managers, Supervisors and HRD Personnel needed to:

- Assess their own strengths and weaknesses in each area.
- Apply their counseling, coaching, and mentoring skills to teams as well as individuals.
- Use these techniques to improve their employees' performance on the job.

This Chapter contains:

Employee Counseling: Concept and definitions of employee counseling, objectives of employee counseling, Employee counseling skills, Theoretical approaches to counseling, Techniques/types of employee counseling, Counseling process, Measures of effective employee counseling, and Ethical dimension of counseling.

Employee Coaching: Concept and definitions of employee coaching, Objectives of employee coaching, Types of employee coaching, Employee coaching process, Effective coaching techniques, Elements of effective employee coaching, and Principles of employee coaching.

Mentoring: Concept and definitions of mentoring, Characteristics of mentoring, Characteristics of successful mentoring, Correct matching of mentor and mentee, Principles of mentoring, Dynamics of mentoring, Qualities of a good mentor and mentee/Role and responsibilities of mentor and mentee, Importance of mentoring, Role of a mentor, Types of mentoring, Functions of mentoring, Mentoring process, Benefits of mentoring – to mentor/mentee and organisation, Myths of mentoring, Mentoring life cycle, Elements of successful mentoring, Importance of coaching and mentoring, and The difference between coaching and mentoring.

Review & discussion questions, Case situation and Case study.

Employee Coaching, Counseling and Mentoring

Employee Coaching

Today organisations need the very best skills, efforts, and performance of its employees to fulfill its mission, and operate with the assumption that employees take their work seriously and conduct themselves with pride and self-respect. Organisations believe that their employees will rarely lapse from excellent work or adhere to established rules and regulations. Employees will quickly correct any lapse in their work or violations of policies, if these problems are brought to their attention in a professional, cooperative manner that assumes they want to improve. The first step in any effort to improve employee's job performance is coaching. Coaching is part of the day-to-day interaction between a manager and an individual employee who works in his work area, or HRD professional and line organisation staff members. Coaching often provides positive feedback about employee contributions. At the same time, regular counseling brings performance issues to an employee's attention when they are small, and assists the employee to address and correct them.

Managers help employees in achieving objectives on a daily basis. Coaching is a behavioural control technique used by the manager to give on-going guidance and instruction, to follow day-to-day progress, and to give feedback. It is the informal, day-to-day ongoing instructing of employees.

The basic objective of organisations is to achieve satisfaction of customer in order to grow and develop. Coaching believes in employees taking responsibility for their own behaviour; is supportive and helpful, yet follows the rules consistently. The manager plays the role of a coach when he brings out the best in employees. The employees are like great athletes when they work together well.

When teams in an organisation are effectively coached, employees are able to achieve their individual goals and those that benefit the team as a whole. Effective managers are coaches who help guide, support, and motivate employees. They provide necessary training when needed and recognition when earned. In the coaching process, the manager clarifies expectations and does whatever is necessary to assist employees in performing their best.

Many people are more highly motivated to participate in sports than they are in their jobs. There are many reasons why sports are preferred over work. Goals are more clearly defined. The rules of the game don't change. Performance is measured and clearly attached to a reward. Everyone knows the score. Feedback is more frequent, personal, and accurate. Therefore, for effective coaching, performance targets must clearly planned and defined, must involve the employees in target setting and performance must be objectively appraised so that fair and equitable reward can be administered.

Coaching is the ability to improve the job performance of employees. It involves teaching, the passing on of knowledge and continous support. Coaching is active, instead of passive, and is involved with guiding performance. Managers, who emphasize formal training and day-to-day coaching, reap the benefits of competence, high performance, commitment, and cooperative behaviour.

Organisations in order to improve their effectiveness rely increasingly on teams. The functions of management - planning, organizing, directing, and controlling - are used to supervise high performance teams. In planning, effective teams have clear, accepted goals. Managers ensure that employees understand what it is they are to achieve. In organizing, managers must clarify the extent of authority to be exercised by the team. Self-managed teams are empowered to make decisions. Other forms of teams may have different authority boundaries. Structurally, objectives are set; roles identified, and work processes created. In directing, managers accept leadership roles. In controlling, managers and team members determine how the team's performance will be evaluated and how will they be rewarded.

Definitions:

A few noteworthy definitions of Coaching are as follows:

1. "Coaching is a process that enables learning and development to occur and thus performance to improve. To be a successful a coach requires knowledge and understanding of process as well as the variety of styles, skills and techniques that are appropriate to the context in which the coaching takes place".

(Eric Parsloe: 1999)

2. "Coaching is a directive process conducted by a manager to train and orient an employee to the realities of the workplace and to help the employee remove barriers

to optimum work performance".

(Marianne Minor : 2004)

Objectives of Employee Coaching

The main objectives of coaching are:

1. To provide a culturally sensitive and non-judgmental service in a way that is responsive to the needs of the employees and recognizes their individuality;
2. To assist employees in the development of skills (creative, personal, social, spiritual), which will enable them to achieve their full potential;
3. To explore variety of methods for supporting employees in relation in effective performance of work;
4. To continue monitoring and improving the individual's effectiveness on the job;
5. To support and encourage employees to regularly update their knowledge and skills through continuous professional development, attendance at training events and networking with their counterparts in other organisations; and
6. To provide opportunity to employees to explore their situation in life, for example, to explore their attitudes, wishes, values, strengths, impediments, culture and social circumstances.

Managers may use a variety of coaching approaches as needed to address the specific nature of each problem in a professionally and constructive manner. The goal is to identify and resolve problems as early as possible through timely and effective partnership with employees. The relationship between a coach (manager) and an employee (learner) is depicted in figure 7.1 for clarity:

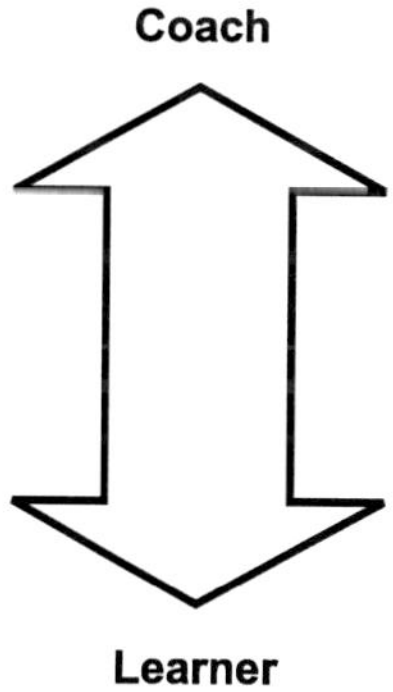

Fig. 7.1 : Relationship Between Coach & Learner

Types of Employee Coaching

Coaching is given to employees for addressing a number of professional developmental issues such as career development, performance improvement, skill and competencies development, and improving personal effectiveness. The detailed discussion is given below:

1. Performance Coaching:

Many employees will seek coaching for performance enhancement rather than the rectification of a performance issue. Coaching has been shown to be highly successful intervention in such cases. When an organisation pays premium for development of its human resources, performance is usually the key payback they are looking for. Even if an executive or manager receives support in balancing work and home life, it will be with the aim of increasing their effectiveness and productivity at work and not for more altruistic reasons.

Coaching derives its theoretical underpinnings and models from business and general management approaches.

2. Skills Coaching:

A skill coaching has some commonalities with one-to-one training. Skills coaching combine a holistic approach to personal development with the ability to focus on the core skills and competencies employees need to perform their role. Skills coaching should be must be provided by highly experienced and competent personnel.

Job roles are changing at an ever-increasing rate. Traditional training programmes are often too inflexible or generic to deal with these fast changing business requirements. In these instances one-to-one skills coaching allows a flexible, adaptive 'just-in-time' approach to skills and competencies development. It is also possible to apply skills coaching in 'live' environments rather than taking people away from the job into a 'classroom' where it is less easy to simulate the job environment.

Skills coaching programmes are tailored specifically to the individual, their knowledge, experience, maturity and ambitions and are generally focused on achieving a number of objectives for both the individual and the organisation. These objectives often include the individual being able to perform specific, well-defined tasks whilst taking into account the personal and career development needs of the individual.

One-to-one skills training is not the same as the 'on the job training'. What differentiates it is that like any good personal or professional development intervention it is based on an assessment of need in relation to the job-role, delivered in a structured (but highly flexible) manner, and generates measurable learning and performance outcomes. This form of skills training is likely to focus purely on the skills required to perform the job function even though it may adopt a facilitative coaching approach instead of a 'telling' or directive style.

3. Personal Coaching:

Personal or 'life coaching' is growing significantly in the industry today. Personal coaches may work face-to-face but email and telephone based relationships are also very common. These coaches operate in highly supportive roles to those who wish to make some form of significant change happen within their lives.

Coaches offer a supportive and motivating environment to explore what the employee's want in life and how they might achieve their aspirations and fulfill their needs. By assisting in committing to action and by being a sounding board to their experiences, coaching allows the individual the personal space and support they need to grow and develop. The coach's key role is often is assisting in maintaining the motivation and commitment needed to achieve their goals.

In many cases personal coaching is differentiated from business coaching purely by the context and the focus of the programme. Business coaching is always conducted within the constraints placed on the individual or group by the organisational context. Personal coaching on the other hand is taken entirely from the individual's perspective.

Employee Coaching Process

The steps of employee coaching are discussed below (figure 7.2):

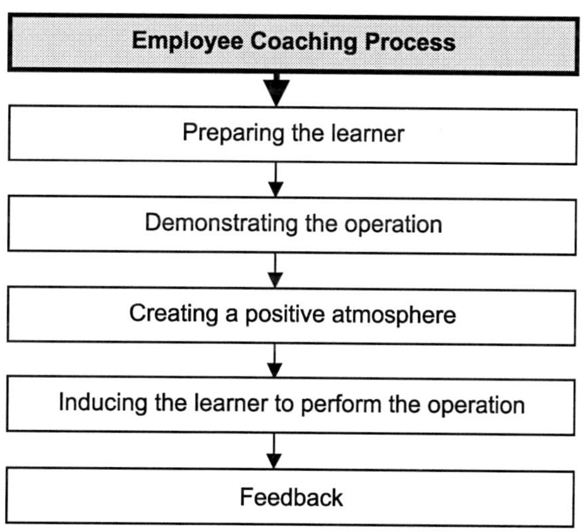

Fig. 7.2 : Process of Employee Coaching

1. Preparing the learner:

Barriers to effective coaching include the learner's fear of change or of appearing incompetent. The learner might be defensive. The manager can help the learner to relax by empathizing with him. Then, he can find out what the learner already knows. This way, the manager/coach can proceed from the familiar to the unfamiliar.

2. Demonstrating the operation:

Manager should explain to the learner exactly what is being done during a demonstration, moving from the simple to the complex. He must allow the learner the opportunity to ask questions. Explaining the relationship between what the learner is doing and the overall operation is vital for the success of employee coaching.

3. Creating a positive atmosphere:

Manager should be patient with the learner and give positive reinforcement to the learner. This will help in creating conducive environment for learning.

4. Inducing learner to perform the operation:

Manager should encourage and facilitate the active participation of the learner. Active participation is essential for instilling long-term learning.

5. Follow up:

Evaluate learning is crucial to the success of the overall coaching. Manager should check up on the learner's progress to demonstrate his availability to answer questions and to discover any new problems.

Effective Coaching Techniques

Effective coaching is key to organisational excellence through developing employee capabilities and potentialities. Effective coaching techniques involve:

1. Creating a coaching context:

The purpose of undertaking coaching must be identified. This will help the coach to define his purpose in the coaching role. Based on coaching role, parameters for improvement are to be set.

2. Actively listening to the learner:

Coach must limit interruptions from others and from himself to facilitate proper coaching. He must understand issues and/or problems and reflect back to the learner/ employee what he has heard.

3. Asking Questions:

Coach must view the goal of the interaction as helping the learner/employee to find answers that works best for him. He should not give advice but should ask questions that explore assumptions.

4. Giving useful feedback:

Coach should encourage the employee to identify his difficulties to overcome. Coach can give his input in order to help clarify what needs to be done.

Elements of Effective Employee Coaching

The goal of coaching is to work with the employee to solve performance/job related problems and improve the work of the employee, the team, and the department. There are six main steps in effective employee coaching:

1. Showing confidence in the employee's ability and willingness to solve the problem and helping him in solving the problem;
2. Describing the performance problem. Focus should be on the problem or behaviour that needs improvement, not the person. Asking for the employee's view of the situation helps a lot;
3. Determining if issues exist that limits the employee's ability to perform the task or accomplish the objective. Four common barriers are time, training, tools, and temperament. Determining how to remove these barriers and addressing these actions to the overall plan is crucial for success of employee coaching;
4. Discussing potential solutions to the problem or improvement actions to take. Asking the employee for ideas on how to correct the problem or preventing it from happening again;
5. Agreeing on a written action plan that lists what the employee, the manager, and possibly, the HRD professional, will do in order to correct the problem or improve the situation; and
6. Setting a date and time for follow-up. Critical feedback path is needed so the manager knows how the employee is progressing on the plan. Offering positive encouragement and exhibiting confidence in the employee's competence ensures that the needed improvements are made.

Managers are responsible for communicating performance and conduct standards to employees, for guiding, training and developing their employees, and for providing opportunities to correct performance or behavior deficiencies. Employees are responsible for understanding managers' performance and conduct expectations and for actively participating in coaching efforts.

Principles of Employee Coaching

For effective employee coaching, certain principles are to be followed. These principles are:

1. Principle of Communication:

For effective employee coaching, the communication between coach (Manager) and learner (employee) should be strengthened. Coaching is an art and science of effective communication. It is the fundamental basis of employee coaching. Coaching is meant to help the employee in problem identification and resolution. Active listening on the part of the manager is essential.

2. Principles of Specific Objectives:

Coaching is given to employees with certain pre-determined objectives. Therefore, specific objectives must be set before embarking upon employee coaching. Such objectives could be to improve performance, develop skills and competencies and improve personal effectiveness. Coaching must help the employee/s to attain the required objectives.

3. Principle of Motivation:

Coaching should motivate employee/s to build commitment to action plan to solve his problem/improve deficiency. Unless an employee is committed to the determined course of action for improvement, coaching will not be effective. Manager must use reinforcement techniques to shape appropriate behaviour in the employee by involving the employee in problem solving process.

4. Principle of Self-esteem:

Coaching should maintain and increase the employee's self-esteem in order to come to the desired level of expectations. While coaching, manager should not hurt the self-worth of the employee and should concentrate on the problem being faced by the employee with the purpose of solving it. Coach's focus should be on behaviour, not personality.

5. Principle of Support:

Coaching is a process of providing support to an employee to face and surmount the challenges posed by certain problems. Supporting employees to improve performance, skills and competencies etc. results in supporting the organisation's mission and objectives in the long term.

Hence, employee coaching consists of ongoing, sometimes spontaneous meetings between managers and their employees to discuss the employee's overall career goal and development.

Employee Counseling

During the past decade there has been an increasing acceptance in industry of the importance of providing counseling to employees with personal problems. Personal problems of employees can adversely affect job performance and organisational effectiveness. If there is employee counseling available in the early stage, it can prevent these problems from worsening. In doing so, the management can lay the foundation on which humanistic high- productivity policies can be built. It parallels the devotion of management to issues concerned with productivity and industrial relations.

Employee counseling is a process, which is initiated by the counselor or the manager to assist the employee to gain knowledge, understanding and insights on a performance concern. This could relate to the counselee's attitude, motivation or interpersonal skills. Essentially the counseling is to provide timely professional and confidential aid for employees whose personal problems might otherwise lead to work impairment, absenteeism, reduce productivity and cause accidents and conflicts in the workplace, or even turnover.

One of the most important aspects of the manager/HRD functionary's role is to provide advice and counseling to employees. Those who make themselves accessible to employees will find they are in great demand to provide information and to help in finding solutions to problems.

A point to remember is that counseling should not be meddlesome, and the extreme, of playing psychiatrist, should be avoided. But neither should counseling be reserved only for an employee who is having problems; counseling should also be given for their achievements and outstanding performance. Counseling of an employee who is doing a good job reinforces his job performance and ensures continued good work. Counseling also provides an opportunity to point out ways that an employee might improve an already good job performance.

Counseling the employee who is doing a good job is relatively easy, but a different type of counseling is required for an employee whose performance does not meet set standards.

Definitions:

A few noteworthy definitions of Counseling are as follows:

1. "Counseling is a principled relationship characterized by the application of one or

more psychological theories and a recognized set of communication skills, modified by experience, intuition and other interpersonal factors, to clients' intimate concerns, problems or aspirations. It predominates ethos is one of facilitation rather than of advice-giving or coercion. It may be of very brief or long duration, take place in an organisational or private practice setting and may or may not overlap with practical, medical and other matters of personal welfare. It is both a distinctive activity undertaken by people agreeing to occupy the roles of counselor and client... and an emerging profession... It is a service sought by people in distress or in some degree of confusion who wish to discuss and resolve these in a relationship which is more disciplined and confidential than friendship, and perhaps less stigmatizing than helping relationships offered in traditional medical or psychiatric settings".

(Feltham and Dryden: 1993)

2. "Counseling is a process through which one person helps another by purposeful conversation in an understanding atmosphere. It seeks to establish a helping relationship in which the one counseled can express their thoughts and feelings in such a way as to clarify their own situation, come to terms with some new experience, see their difficulty more objectively, and so face their problem with less anxiety and tension. Its basic purpose is to assist the individual to make their own decision from among the choices available to them".

(British Association for Counselling: 1989)

3. "Counseling is the discussion of an emotional problem with an employee with general objectives of decreasing it".

(Keith Davis)

4. "Counseling is a supportive process conducted by a manager to help an employee define and work through personal problems or organisational changes that affect job performance".

(Marianne Minor:2004)

Objectives of Employee Counseling:

Counseling provides employees with the knowledge and skills necessary to deal effectively with a variety of problems, both personal and professional, ranging from normal supervisory/employee conflicts to difficult conduct and performance issues. Counseling helps to handle these problems with tact, diplomacy, and knowledge of the regulations covering employee performance and conduct.

The main objectives of counseling are:

1. To solve various employee problems;

2. To provide help for adjustment or improvement through a planned and systematic approach;
3. To help in conflict resolution;
4. To improve communication and interpersonal skills for an open interactive organisational culture;
5. To prrovide empathetic yet effective problem solving - interests before solutions; and
6. To provide effective feedback.

Employee Counseling Skills

One of the most difficult human resource development skills is to acquire employee counseling skills, which are relevant to the successful operation of the organisation, and the benefits that accrue when an organisation uses effective employee counseling methods.

Counseling skills will, not only help the employees to cope personally with stressful and traumatic situations, but also counseling skills will aid in the day-to-day problems of human interface. In this way the employees will become more effective and also be able to realise their potential.

Employee counseling skills covers the following broad areas:

1. Communication skills:

Counseling skills requires the traditional communication skills of a line manager. Employee counseling styles and skills appropriate for different situations varies widely and may come in conflict with a manager's power base. Problems of acceptance within the organisation, ethics involved, and the prospect of conflicting loyalties between the individual and organisation are to be considered at the time of counseling.

2. Skills for managing feelings:

The counselor needs to identify feelings and develop confidence to self-disclosure during employee counseling sessions. He has to also learn the skill of looking behind the statements to see and appreciate the underlying feelings being expressed. These are prerequisites to dealing with the intimacy that is vital to successful counseling. Identification with, and an ability to project, one's own personality into the situation can help, in certain circumstances, establish some control, give comfort and ensure a trusting relationship. However, relationships are fragile and the employee will constantly be seeking evidence of counselor's integrity and assurance, and this can be partially enhanced with affirming behaviour.

3. Problem clarification skill:

The objective of counseling is to help employees to solve their problems. Therefore, first need is to be clarified, alternatives have to be specified, their implications need to be explored and the consequences fully understood before the changes needed, to accomplish chosen alternatives, can be implemented.

4. Motivational skill:

The employee's motivation to change or come to terms with his behaviour is a major factor in counseling skills. The counselor should use a participative management style to encourage the employee's sense of problem ownership. Only then will the employee be motivated and committed to the change/action required. A monitoring process helps to access the progress made by the employee. This can best be observed if goals can be set, and agreements reached.

Conditions for Employee Counseling

Managers use controls to help employees achieve objectives. An employee's problem performance is often related to non-job factors. Yet, personal problems generally get worse, not better without professional help. The manager is in the best position to spot and handle problems when they arise. He can use counseling to provide relief for the troubled employee. Counseling is a behavioural control technique used by the managers to solve employee problems. As a counselor, the manager is a helper, discusses the employee's personal problems that are affecting his or her job performance, aiming to resolve them. Employee counseling is guiding the employee's behaviour.

An employee should be counseled when he has personal problems that affect job performance. Managers should recognize early signs. Signs of a troubled employee include:

- Sudden change of behaviour;
- Preoccupation;
- Irritability;
- Increased accidents;
- Increased fatigue;
- Excessive drinking;
- Reduced production/productivity;
- More wastage;
- Difficulty in absorbing training; and
- Drug abuse.

In the role of the counselor, the manager listens, limits, and refers. The manager uses active listening and reflective listening skills. By listening the manager helps the employee to feel valued and understood. The employee is encouraged to talk and explore and to understand more about how he feels and why. The employee can consider options and examine alternatives and may be able to choose a solution to his problems. The manager can help the employee develop clear objectives; to form specific action plans and to do, with support what needs to be done. The manager helps employees to help themselves. In counseling, the manager limits comments to the employee's job performance, since the manager is not an expert in the problem area. The manager refers or gives information to the employee. Informing mainly passes along data and information.

Counseling techniques range from directive to non-directive, depending on the situation. Non-directive counseling reflects what is said and felt. For example, a manager using the non-directive approach would say, "You feel frustrated because you don't meet boss's approval." Directive counseling tells and advises. For example, a manager using the directive approach would say, "I want you to concentrate on your work and not worry about what the other employees do." Cooperative (or Interactive or participative) counseling combines them both.

Functions of Employee Counseling

Manager as counselor should set aside their own value system in order to empathize with the employee as counclee during counseling. The things the counselor may view as unimportant may be of paramount importance to the counselee. We tend to view the world through our own values, and this can present problems when we are confronted with values that are at odds with our own. If an employee thinks that something is causing him a problem, then it is a problem for him, regardless of how insignificant the manager might believe the problem to be.

The objective of counseling is to give employees support in dealing with problems so that they regain the ability to work effectively in the organisation. Counseling effectiveness is achieved through performance of one or more of the following counseling functions - advice, reassurance, release of emotional tension, clarified thinking, and reorientation as discussed below:

1. Advice:

Counseling is not only an advice-giving activity, but in reality it is one of several functions that counselors perform. The giving of advice requires that a counselor make judgments about a counselee's problems and lay out a course of action. Herein lies the difficulty, because understanding another person's complicated emotions is almost impossible.

Advice giving may foster a relationship in which the counselee feels inferior and emotionally dependent on the counselor. In spite of its ills, advice giving occurs in routine counseling sessions because employees expect it and counselors tend to provide it.

2. Reassurance:

Counseling can provide members with reassurance, which is a way of giving them courage to face a problem or confidence that they are pursuing a suitable course of action. Reassurance can be a valuable, though sometimes temporary, cure for an employee's emotional upheavals. Sometimes just the act of talking with someone about a problem can bring about a sense of relief that will allow the employee to function effectively.

3. Release of Emotional Tension:

Employees tend to get emotional release from their frustrations and other problems whenever they have an opportunity to tell someone about them. Counseling history consistently shows that as persons begin to explain their problems to a sympathetic listener, their tension begin to subside. They become more relaxed and tend to become more coherent and rational. The release of tensions does not necessarily mean that the solution to the problem has been found, but it does help remove mental blocks in the way of finding solution.

4. Clarified Thinking:

Clarified thinking tends to be a normal result of emotional release. The fact is that not all clarified thinking takes place while the counselor and counselee are talking. All or part of it may take place later as a result of developments during the counseling relationship. The net result of clarified thinking is that an employee is encouraged to accept responsibility for problems and to be more realistic in solving them.

5. Reorientation:

Reorientation is more than mere emotional release or clear thinking about a problem. It involves a change in the employee's emotional self through a change in basic goals and aspirations. Very often it requires a revision of the employee's level of aspiration to bring it more in line with actual attainment. It causes people to recognize and accept their own limitations. The counselor's job is to recognize those in need of reorientation before their need becomes severe, so that they can be referred to professional help.

Theoretical Approaches to Counseling

Counselor's work from a variety of theoretical approaches with counselees i.e. employees. These therapies range from the type of psychoanalysis, originally practiced by Sigmund Freud and later developed into other forms of analytic psychotherapy by his pupils, through humanistic psychotherapy (based on personal growth and self development) to the behavioural therapies used for dealing with specific phobias and anxieties.

The following are the commonly used theoretical approaches with brief descriptions of their meanings:

1. Adlerian Therapy:

This is sometimes called individual psychology and uses the personality theory and system of counseling originated by Alfred Adler. Rather than psychoanalysis, Adler placed greater emphasis on infantile experiences of power and powerlessness and the goal-orientation of human behaviour. He created the terms "inferiority complex" and "superiority complex".

2. Behavioural Therapy:

This therapy is based on the belief that behaviour is learnt in response to past experience and can be unlearnt, or reconditioned, without analysing the past to find the reason for the behaviour. It works well for compulsive and obsessive behaviour, fears, phobias and addictions. The techniques that may be used are: self-monitoring, stimulus control, coping skills and dealing with relapse.

3. Brief Therapy:

This uses the cognitive behavioural approach with a small, planned number of sessions and possibly a single follow-up session after some time has elapsed.

4. Cognitive Analytical Therapy:

This combines cognitive therapy and psychotherapy and encourages counselee's to draw on their own resources to develop the skills to change destructive patterns of behaviour. Negative ways of thinking are explored and treatment is structured and directive involving diary keeping, progress charts, etc.

5. Cognitive Behavioural Therapy:

This combines cognitive and behavioural techniques. Counselee's are taught ways to change thoughts and expectations and relaxation techniques are used. It has been effective for stress-related ailments, phobias, obsessions, eating disorders and (at the same time as drug treatment) major depression.

6. Cognitive Therapy:

Uses the power of the mind to influence behaviour. It is based on the theory that previous experiences can adversely affect self-perception and condition attitude, emotions and ability to deal with certain situations. It works by helping the counselee to identify, question and change self-denigrating thoughts, thus altering habitual responses and behaviour. It can help pessimistic or depressed people to view things from a more optimistic perspective.

7. Eclectic counseling:

An eclectic counselor will select what is applicable to the counselee from a range of theories, methods and practices. Justification is based on the theory that there is no proof that any one theoretical approach works better than all others for a specific problem.

8. Existential Counseling:

Existentialists believe that life has no essential (given) meaning: any meaning has to be found or created. Existential counseling involves making sense of life through a personal worldview and includes a willingness to face one's life and life problems.

9. Gestalt Therapy:

The name is derived from the German for "organized whole". Developed by Fritz Perls, it is based on his belief that the human response to experiences is summed up in a person's thoughts, feelings and actions. The counselee gains self-awareness by analysing behaviour and body language and giving expression to repressed feelings.

10. Humanistic Psychotherapy:

This embraces techniques coming from the "personal growth movement" and encourages people to explore their feelings and take responsibility for their thoughts and actions. Emphasis is on self-development and achieving highest potential rather than dysfunctional behaviour. "Client-centred" or "non-directive" approach is often used and the therapy can be described as "holistic". The counselee's creative instincts may be used to explore and resolve personal issues.

11. Integrative Counseling:

This is when several distinct models of counseling and psychotherapy are used together in a converging way rather than in separate pieces.

12. Neuro-Linguistic Programming (NLP):

Neuro-Linguistic Programming is described as 'the psychology of excellence' and sees a world of excellence where people can be facilitated in creating their own choice and flexibility. Presuppositions are used as the basic operating principles, some examples being 'Human Behaviour is purposeful', 'we either already have all the resources we need or we can create them', 'Modeling successful performance leads to excellence. If one person can do it is possible to model it and teach it to others'. In Neuro-linguistic programming, modeling means finding out how someone does something. The core of NLP is the process of replicating excellence with a goal of 'excellence for all'.

13. Person-Centred Counseling:

Devised by Carl Rogers and also called "client-centred" or "Rogerian" counseling, this is based on the assumption that an individual (counselee), seeking help in the resolution of a problem he is experiencing, can enter into a relationship with another individual (counsellor) who is sufficiently accepting and permissive to allow the counselee to freely express emotions and feelings. This will enable the counselee to come to terms with negative feelings, which may have caused emotional problems, and develop inner resources. The objective is for the counselee to become able to perceive himself as a person, with the power and freedom to change, rather than as an object.

14. Primal Therapy:

This is based on the theory that suppressed birth or infancy traumas can resurface as neuroses. The therapy takes the counselee back to the "primal scene" where trauma can be re-experienced as an emotional cleansing.

15. Psychoanalysis:

This is based on the work of Sigmund Freud, who believed that the unacceptable thoughts of early childhood are banished to the unconscious mind but continue to influence thoughts, emotions and behaviour. "Repressed" feelings can surface later as conflicts, depression, etc or through dreams or creative activities. The analyst seeks to interpret and make acceptable to the counselee's conscious mind, troublesome feelings and relationships from the past. "Transference" onto the analyst, of feelings about figures in the client's life, is encouraged. This type of therapy is often used by clients suffering high levels of stress and can be a lengthy and intensive process.

16. Psychodynamic Psychotherapy/Counseling:

This approach stresses the importance of the unconscious and past experience in determining current behaviour. The counselee is encouraged to talk about childhood relationships with parents and other significant people and the therapist focuses on the client/therapist relationship (the dynamics) and in particular on the transference. Transference is when the counselee projects onto the therapist feelings experienced in previous significant relationships. The psychodynamic approach is derived from Psychoanalysis but usually provides a quicker solution to emotional problems.

17. Psychosynthesis:

Sometimes described as "psychology of the soul", Psychosynthesis aims to integrate or "synthesize" the level of consciousness, at which thoughts and emotions are experienced, with a higher, spiritual level of consciousness. Painting, movement and other techniques can be used to recognize and value different facets of the personality. Psychosynthesis is useful for people seeking a new, more spiritually oriented vision of themselves.

18. Re-birthing:

In this approach, emotional or physical traumas during birth are said to create feelings of separation or fear in later life. Breathing techniques are used to release tension whilst the counselee re-experiences traumatic emotions. A skilled practitioner is essential.

19. Solution-focused Brief Therapy:

This promotes positive change rather than dwelling on past problems. Counselee is encouraged to focus positively on what he does well and to set goals and work out how to achieve them. As little as 3 or 4 sessions may be beneficial.

20. Systemic Therapies:

These are the therapies, which have, as their aim, a change in the transactional pattern of counselees. It can be used as the generic term for family therapy and marital/ family therapy.

21. Transactional Analysis:

Devised by Eric Bernie, this is based on the belief that everyone has a child, adult and parents self within him, and within each social interaction, one self predominates. By recognising these roles, a counselee can choose which one to adopt and so change behaviour. This form of therapy has produced the term "inner child", used to describe unfulfilled needs from childhood.

22. Transpersonal Therapy:

This describes any form of counseling or therapy, which places emphasis on spirituality, human potential or heightened consciousness. It includes psychosynthesis.

23. Narrative Therapy:

This therapy sees counselees as experts in their own lives. It views problems as separate from them and assumes that counselee has many skills, competencies, beliefs and values that will help them to reduce the influence of the problem in their lives.

There are number of different approaches to counseling, however each is not usually used in isolation. In practice, a combination of styles will often be used.

Techniques/Types of Employee Counseling

Employee counseling should be looked upon in terms of the amount of direction that the counselor gives to the counselee. This direction ranges from full direction (directive counseling) to no direction (nondirective counseling). The details are as under:

1. Directive Counseling:

Directive counseling is the process of listening to an employee's problem, deciding with the employee what should be done, and then encouraging and motivating him to do it. This type of counseling accomplishes the function of advice; but it may also reassure; give emotional release; and, to a minor extent, clarify thinking. Most people likes to give advice, counselors included and it is easy to do. But is it effective? Does the counselor really understand the employee's problem? Does the counselor have the technical knowledge of human behavior and the judgment to make the "right" decision? If the decision is all right, will the employee follow it? The answer to these questions is often no, and that is why advice giving is sometimes and unwise act in counseling. Although advice giving is of questionable value, some of the other functions achieved by directive counseling are worthwhile. If the counselor is a good listener, then the employee should experience some emotional release. As the result of the emotional release, ideas that the counselor imparts, the employee may also clarify thinking. Both advice and reassurance may be worthwhile if they give the employee more courage to take a workable course of action that the employee supports.

2. Non-directive Counseling:

Attributed to Carl Rogers, this technique was designed to allow the individual in emotional turmoil to talk out problems and resolve difficulties with a minimum of direction being provided by the counselor. Rogers believed that everyone has the motivation and ability to change in order to become a better, more "self-actualized" person.

Nondirective or employee-centered counseling is the process of skillfully listening to a counselee, encouraging him to explain bothersome problems, and helping him to understand those problems and determine course of action. Non-directive counseling emphasizes the importance of getting the individual to share his problems. The individual may need to unload and air his problems, and it is important that the counselor affirms the worth of the employee by listening. This type of counseling focuses on the employee, rather than on the counselor as a judge and advisor; hence, it is "employee-centered." The unique advantage of nondirective counseling is its ability to cause the employee's reorientation. It stresses changing the person, instead of dealing only with the immediate problem in the usual manner of directive counseling. The counselor attempts to ask discerning questions, restate ideas, clarify feelings, and attempts to understand why these feelings exist. Trained counselors treat each counselee as a social and organisational equal. They primarily listen and try to help their counselee discover and follow improved courses of action. They especially "listen between the lines" to learn the full meaning of their counselee's feelings. They look for assumptions underlying the counselee's statements and for the events the counselee may, at first, have avoided talking about. A person's feelings can be likened to an iceberg. The counselor will usually only see the revealed feelings and emotions. Underlying these surface indications is the true problem that the employee is almost always initially reluctant to reveal.

There are four stages of non-directive counseling:

(*a*) *Involving:* for building relationship, rapport, empathy, and trust. A clear expectation of the process is given to the counselee/employee. Attention is being paid to non-verbal behaviour and careful questioning.

(*b*) *Exploration:* for clarifying perceptions and attempts to discuss problem in concrete terms.

(c) *Resolving:* for setting goals and working out ways in which to achieve them. Counselee is encouraged to consider a number of different solutions with non-judgmental suggestions on the various suggestions from the counselor.

(*d*) *Concluding:* for final action plan, as agreed.

Strategies to use Non-Directive Counseling:

1. Arrange for a time and place, which will provide privacy for discussion;
2. If the employee does not open the session, leading statements or questions to focus him on the topic of concern should be raised;
3. Manager should listen to the employee in an interested, non-punitive, accepting

manner without making judgments;

4. Manager should respond when appropriate, using one of the recommended techniques; and
5. After the concerns have been thoroughly voiced by the employee, focus should be placed him on finding a solution for the problem that is best for him.

3. Interactive Counseling:

Interactive counseling combines the best of directive and non-directive counseling techniques. It involves problem solving through open and interactive process. Employee is encouraged to discuss fully his problem and possible best solution. The counselor gives some suggestive solutions to the employee's problems and helps the employee with decision making as far as choosing the most appropriate solution is concerned. Here, the counselor plays a vital role. He must see that the employee gives possible solution to his problem on one hand and on the other hand he must ensure that the employee takes the right recourse to solution of his problem. Thus, interactive (or cooperative or participative) counseling falls in between directive and non-directive counseling techniques.

Counseling Process

Counseling should be an initial verbal discussion between the counselor and employee to inform the employee of a problem at the earliest possible opportunity. A counselor can be line manager. or HRD Manager. The intent of counseling is to prevent a problem from becoming more serious or prolonged.

The counseling should take place in a private setting, and be based on specific facts. It should express confidence in the employee's ability to improve and indicate the counselor's willingness to assist. Informal counseling is not a form of corrective action; however, it can be referenced at a later date if corrective action is taken. This discussion can take place during periodic performance evaluations or as a stand-alone counseling.

The steps of counseling process are as discussed below (see figure 7.3):

1. Identifying the problem:

Employees should know that the organisation is concerned with work performance. The line manager/supervisor must maintain work standards by being consistent in dealing with troubled employees. He must explain in very specific terms what the employee needs to do in order to perform up to the organisation's expectations without any unnecessary preaching. Issues must relate to job performance.

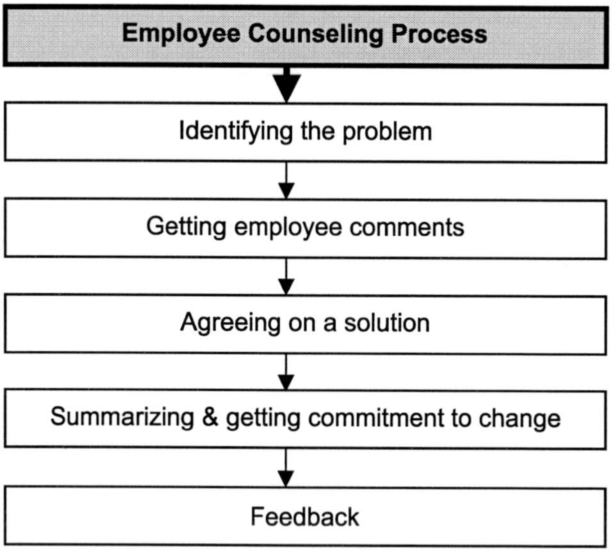

Fig. 7.3 : Process of Employee Counseling

Counselor or employee must first identify the problem(s). Examples might include poor work product, strained working relationships, attendance deficiencies, missed deadlines, etc. The problem can be defined as the "gap" between the manager's expectations and the employee's performance.

2. Getting employee comments on the changed behaviour and the reason for it:

Employee and counselor assess and clarify scope of problem. Problems can stem from skill deficiencies, lack of clear communication, behavioural styles, personal criss, procedural or structural obstacles or some combination of these and other factors. However, counselor must confine any negative comments or diagnosis to the employee's job performance. He should listen and protect confidentiality.

3. Agreeing on a solution:

Counselor establishes clear performance or conduct expectations with the employee for correcting the problem and works with employee to identify appropriate measures to correct the problem. Employee needs to know what will be viewed as successful resolution of the problem and what support and/or resources may be available to help meet expectations.

Counselor should emphasize confidentiality. However, he should not be swayed or misled by emotional please, sympathy tactics, or "hard-luck" stories. It should be explained that going for help does not exclude the employee from standard organisation procedures and that it does not open the door for special privileges.

4. Summarizing and getting a commitment to change:

Seek commitment from the employee to meet work standards and to get help, if necessary, with the problem. Employee accepts responsibility for correcting the problem and takes appropriate action. Examples might include obtaining training for skill problems, making transportation or family arrangements for attendance problems, receiving guidance to understand and stop offensive behaviour, etc.

5. Feedback:

Once the problem is resolved and a productive relationship is established, follow up is needed to ascertain the progress made and/or improvement sustained. Counselor and employees communicate regularly regarding progress. This step usually includes discussions and written documentation that describes progress toward agreed upon improvements.

Measures of Effective Counseling

Employee counseling seeks to provide effective means of dealing with problems in the workplace. Therefore, counseling must be designed to meet specific goals that have been identified as important to the well-being of the organisation and its employees. Planning a programme and evaluating its effectiveness go hand in hand. At the planning stage, goals and objectives are set; at the evaluating stage, the success of the programme in meeting its stated objectives is measured.

Counseling programmes of various types have implied goals that tend to be common across organisations. Samples of these indicators that might be used to assess the impact of the employee counseling programmes are:

- Improved performance attributable to removal of personal problems;
- The extent to which under-utilisation of employee skills are alleviated;
- Increased productivity;
- Reduction in absenteeism;
- Reduction of accidents both on and off the job; and
- Improved employee satisfaction obtained by self-reports or peer reports.

Ethical Dimension of Counseling

Counseling involves helping people to adjust to or deal with personal problems by enabling them to discover for themselves the solution to the problems while receiving attention from a counselor.

The following principles are expressions of core values in action. They form the foundation for ethical practice.

Managers as counselors shall:

1. Act with care and respect for individual employee and cultural differences and the diversity of human experience;
2. Avoid doing harm in all their professional work;
3. Respect the confidence with which they are entrusted;
4. Promote the safety and well-being of individual employees, their families, communities, and society at large;
5. Seek to increase the range of choices and opportunities for employees (counselee);
6. Be honest and trustworthy in all their professional relationships;
7. Practice within the scope of job performance of the employees; and
8. Treat colleagues and other professionals with respect.

Mentoring

The word 'Mentor' comes from ancient Greek mythology where Odysseus, King of Ithaca, asks Mentor to act as his son's guardian while he is away at the battle of Troy. Mentor acted as role model, teacher, adviser, counselor and guide for the son and prepared him for his leadership roles in the future.

Mentoring is a dynamic and reciprocal relationship in a work environment between an advanced career incumbent (mentor) and a beginner (mentee) aimed at promoting the career development of both.

Thus, mentor is someone who develops another person through tutoring, coaching, and guidance.

The concept of mentoring has undergone rapid changes from a classical view to a modern view as discussed below.

Classical Concept of Mentoring includes:

1. Knowledge transfer.
2. Wise counsel.
3. Practical know-how.

4. Intellectual capital.
5. Advice.
6. Guidance.

Modern Concept of Mentoring

Equipping mentee is not enough. Today mentees also need to be empowered:

1. Make creative contributions.
2. Utilize unique diversity.
3. Fulfill dreams & passions.
4. Pursue goals and initiative.

Definitions:

A few noteworthy definitions of Mentoring are as follows:

1. "An experienced person going out of his/her way to help a mentee set important goals and develop the skills to reach them".

(Dave Rigali: 2005)

2. "A one-to-one helping relationship or nurturing process".

(Jacobi: 1991)

3. "Guiding of a novice in professional development and the journeying together toward professional excellence".

(Christensen: 1991)

4. "Mentoring involves primarily listening with empathy, sharing experience (usually mutually), professional friendship, developing insight through reflection, being a sounding board, encouraging".

(David Clutterbuck)

5. "Mentoring is linking an experienced person (mentor) with a less experienced person (mentoree) to help their personal and professional growth".

(Vickie L. Nadolski)

6. "Mentoring is an off-line help by one person to another in making significant transitions in knowledge, work or thinking".

(D. Clutterbuck and D. Megginson: 1999)

Mentoring is a voluntary, collaborative and mutually beneficial partnership between a *mentee* (who is looking to enhance his knowledge, skills and experience) and a *mentor* (who possesses this knowledge, skills, and experience).

On analytical study of the above definitions, we may conclude that:

- Mentoring is a partnership. It is not the relationship between an employee and his manager. Even though there is an inequality in the skills, knowledge and experience of the partners, the partnership itself is equal. Both parties agree to the relationship and both parties are responsible for its success.
- Partnership is voluntary. The fact that both participants show willingness to form the partnership facilitates in its success.
- Partnership is collaborative. The mentor and the mentee have to work together to determine what objectives the partnership aims to achieve and how it will achieve those objectives.
- Partnership is mutually beneficial. Mentoring works because both parties gain from the relationship. The mentee gains knowledge, skills and/or experience. But, just as important, the mentor gains personal and professional satisfaction from being able to share valuable skills, knowledge and experience.

Thus, mentoring is a dynamic, two-way process between mentor and mentee, in which the specific purpose is to facilitate development, change or transition. Through this process mentees are encouraged to reflect on their own experiences, reach their own conclusions, explore future options and define their own directions, whilst recognising the constraints in which they are working.

Characteristics of Mentoring

The major characteristics of mentoring are:

1. Mentoring requires a high degree of mutual trust between the mentor and mentee;
2. Mentor and mentee have confidence and each other and maintain confidentiality in the issues and matters, which comes to the knowledge of mentee during the course of mentoring;
3. Effective communication is key to success of mentoring programme;
4. Availability of mentor to help the mentee is necessary for the success of mentoring;
5. Mentoring should have predictability; otherwise it will become an uncertain event;

6. Mentor and mentee must have high level of mutual respect. Without the elements of respect mentoring is doomed;
7. Self-esteem and confidence is necessary for effective mentoring; and
8. Mentoring is essentially a systematic process of partnership building.

Pre-requisites of Successful Mentoring:

The pre-requites of successful mentoring are as under:

1. Obtaining commitment based on sound business principles;
2. Clearly identifying the need of the mentoring in general and that of mentee in particular;
3. Mentoring programmes must be based on solid business reasons.
4. Benefits should be highlighted clearly;
5. Get buy-in from senior management is essential to starting, nurturing and sustaining mentoring in an organisation;
6. Obtaining visible support and involvement from top management is a pre-requisite of mentoring;
7. Proper identification of mentors is crucial factor;
8. Determination of who will participate as mentors has significant impact on mentoring programme quality and result;
9. Encouraging management strongly to establish mentoring programme for organisational success is a key attribute of HRD managers;
10. Good mentors are commitment to growth, has ability to listen, exhibit trustworthiness and asses objectivity;
11. Advertisement of the opportunity for mentoring helps in getting potential mentors and screening good mentors; and
12. Informing employees of potential benefits of mentoring contributes to its success.

Correct Matching of Mentors and Mentees

Mentoring being a process of relationship management depends primarily on alignment of personal attributes of mentors and mentees. Therefore, a correct matching of mentors and mentees is of utmost importance and contributes significantly to the success of any mentoring programme.

Matching of mentors and mentees involves:

1. Personalities of mentors and mentees must be compatible so as to avoid potential personality clashes;
2. There should be a high probability that mentors and mentees would work together and that the relationship will be productive; and
3. Voluntary participation and self -initiated pairing of mentors and mentees must be encouraged.

From the above discussions, we may conclude the relationship between mentors and mentees as depicted in figure 7.4.

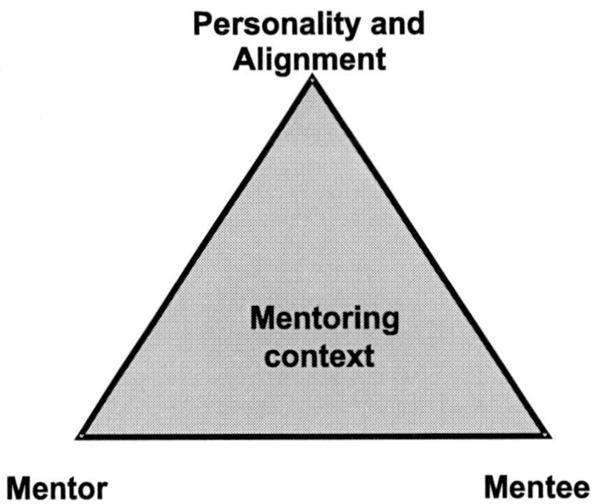

Fig. 7.4 : Relationship between Manager, Mentor & Mentee

Principles of Mentoring

The effectiveness of a mentoring relationship is based upon the following principles:

1. Reciprocal Exchange:

Each participant is responsible for the success of the relationship. Therefore, it is highly desirable for both to discuss and clarify their respective roles and their associated responsibilities.

2. Mutual Trust and Respect:

Since it is a relationship of assistance and learning, confidentiality is essential and must be respected; without it, the relationship could be superficial and unsuccessful.

3. Mutually Beneficial:

One of the main motivating factors in a mentoring relationship entails benefit to both mentors and mentees.. Mentoring allows for personal, professional, and organisational development. However, it should be noted that involvement in a mentoring relationship does not guarantee, and may not lead to a promotion.

4. Dynamic in Nature:

Mentoring describes the relationship. As the organisational needs and situations continuously change, so do the mentoring relationships. Mentoring is dynamic and the content of the relationship (i.e. intensity, subjects for discussion, objectives and so forth) changes. Therefore, relationships are created gradually to adjust over time.

5. Open and Effective Communication:

Open and effective communication is vital. Everyone in the organisation, whether they participate in the mentoring programme or not, needs to know what the mentoring programme involves, how it works, and why it is being implemented.

6. Confidentiality:

Mentoring facilitates trust in the partnership. It supports open communication and sharing of experiences and personal goals.

Dynamics of Mentoring

Mentoring is a key function and provides psychological support to a mentee. It serves as a career enhancement tool. It places heavy responsibility on mentors as well on mentees. The key dynamics of mentoring is described below:

Mentor should be:

(*a*) People oriented:

A mentor should be genuinely interested in people and must have the desire to help others to develop and grow. The outcome of the relationship is based upon the goals set by the mentees and their commitment to their own growth and development.

(*b*) Goal-oriented:

In order to have a successful and effective mentoring relationship the mentees must know what they aim to take away from the mentoring relationship. Whether this is clearly defined at the start of the relationship or developed with the mentor, a clear goal is essential for making the most out of the mentoring opportunity.

(*c*) Open to new ideas:

A mentee should be willing to learn and open to new ideas and perspectives from his mentor. A mentee must be enthusiastic and motivated to learning new skills.

(*d*) Shares personal goals:

Willing to share self-assessment of developmental needs and personal goals through personal experiences.

(*e*) Receptive to feedback:

A mentee must be open and receptive to constructive criticism from the mentor in order to benefit from their viewpoint and experience.

Qualities of a Good Mentor and Mentee/Role and Responsibilities of Mentor and Mentee

A good mentor should be:

1. An effective communicator:

An effective communicator is one who is an active and empathetic listener. A mentor should be able to effectively express how things "really work" in the organisation.

2. Open-minded:

To encourage free exchange of new ideas and methods, a good mentor is willing to learn from the mentee too.

3. Shares personal experience and knowledge:

The mentor must have a clear understanding of own skills and wisdom and shortcomings. A willingness to share personal experiences helps the mentor to lead by example and develop a relationship based on trust.

4. Offer feedback and support:

A mentor should be able to offer objective feedback and constructive criticism to support the mentee in solving his own dilemmas.

5. Committed to the development of people and the organisation:

Anyone who has the experience and desire to encourage and nurture less-experienced employees is a good candidate as a mentor.

6. Knowledge of the organisational mission and structure:

Mentors must be well aware of the mission, objectives and structure of the organisation to provide proper direction and guidance to the mentoring programme.

7. Good listener:

A good mentor must be an active listener. Listening is the heart of the interactive communication between the mentors and mentees.

8. Excellent communication skills:

Communication skills of the mentors are crucial for the success of mentoring. A good mentor must have excellent communication skills in order to explain, understand and guide the mentees.

9. Build and maintain professional networks and relationships:

Mentors must maintain good relationship and professional network to provide appropriate resources and information to the mentees.

10. Willingness to share failures and successes:

Mentors must have the willingness and courage to accept accountability for the success as well as failure of the mentoring programme.

11. Willingness to spend time for mentoring:

Mentors must have good time management skills so that they have appropriate time for the learning, development, monitoring and feedback activities of the mentees.

12. Demonstrates honesty and integrity:

A high degree of honesty and integrity is essential for the success of mentoring relationship.

13. Secure in position:

Mentors must have credibility within the organisation so that peer/colleagues and all others in the organisation respect them. A mentor should suppor a mentee's efforts in developing strengths and abilities, without viewing these accomplishments as threat.

14. Good motivator:

A mentor needs to be able to motivate mentees through encouraging feedback and challenging work assignments. He needs to stretch the mentee's potential, setting new limits for what mentee can do.

15. Achiever:

Mentors should be achievers – who sets career goals, continually evaluates goals, and strives to reach them. A good mentor is usually one who takes on more responsibility than is required, volunteers for more activities, and tends to climb the proverbial career ladder at a faster pace. A mentor attempts to inspire a mentee with the same drive for achievement.

A Good Mentee should be:

A successful mentoring relationship not only depends on the characteristics of the mentor, but also on the characteristics of the mentee. Mentee are self-motivated individuals who are committed to life long learning.

1. Eagerness to learn:

A mentee must be passionate about learning, active listening and sharing information. A mentee should seek educational and/or training opportunities whenever possible to broaden his capabilities. A mentee must strive to evaluate his level of technical skills and professional expertise to gain greater mastery of the job.

2. Patient:

He must be willing to invest time, efforts and energy into the mentoring relationship. A mentee must persevere through the difficulties that arise during the learning process. A mentee should be realistic enough to know that career advancement does not happen overnight. He must be conscientious about managing his responsibilities and completing given assignments and projects.

3. Risk taker:

A mentee must be willing to face challenges of uncertainty. He must move beyond tasks he has mastered and accept new and more challenging experiences. Task changes are never easy. A mentee must realize to grow professionally; it is necessary to assess oneself, to acquire needed skills, to develop new skills, and to make contact with others.

4. Positive attitude:

A bright and optimistic attitude can help a mentee succeed. He should not be afraid to fail. He must have the survival skills and ways to effective interaction with others.

5. Good communication:

Mentee must have good oratory, written, verbal and non-verbal communication skills.

6. High maturity:

Mentee must demonstrate potential for growth by being receptive to feedback given by the mentor. He must demonstrate his honesty, integrity and overall commitment to the success of the mentoring programme.

Importance of Mentoring

The importance of mentoring is as under:

1. Recruitment:

Good mentoring programmes helps in attracting best professionals/talents to the organisation from outside. Also, mentoring helps in identifying suitable candidates from internal sources of recruitment.

2. Employee development:

Mentoring facilitates in the development of employees to share responsibilities for higher positions. It is a process of succession planning and makes available a reliable number of employees to assume key positions in the organisation.

3. Employee retention:

Mentoring aids in retention of talented employees by taking care of their potential growth prospects in the organisation and increasing their readiness to assume higher responsibilities. Mentoring contributes to job satisfaction of employees and increases their commitment to the mission and objectives of the organisation.

4. Leadership development:

Mentoring is one of the critical tolls of leadership development. Mentees/employees can be trained by mentors various leadership skills necessary to occupy key positions within the organisation.

Role of a Mentor

The role of a mentor is crucial to the effectiveness of mentoring programme. A mentor plays various roles as mentioned below (see figure 7.5):

1. Advisor:

A mentor is an advisor to the mentee for his learning, development and growth. He provides him necessary advice to facilitate his effective learning and adaptability through motivation, encouraging feedback and challenging work assignments.

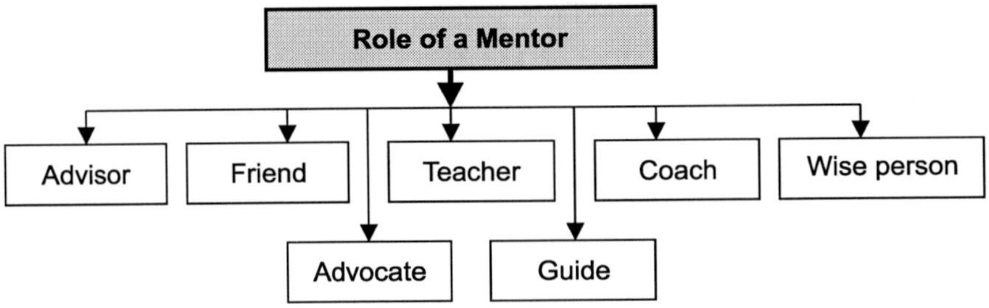

Fig. 7.5 : Role of Mentors

2. Friend:

A mentor acts as a friend to the mentee to help him to learn and develop as per the objectives of the mentoring programme. A friendly attitude on the part of the mentor aids in the development and growth of the menetee.

3. Teacher:

A mentor is a teacher to a mentee. A mentor must thoroughly understand skills and competencies required by the mentee's position and goals and be able to provide him necessary knowledge, skills and competencies to assume higher responsibilities. He transforms his useful experiences into learning concepts for ease of grasping of the mentee.

4. Coach:

A mentor acts as a coach to the mentee to help him in career development and improving his skills, competencies and performance by a process of ongoing feedback and monitoring his progress from time to time.

5. Wise person:

Experience means – past efforts and failures. A mentor has more experience and maturity and can foresee efforts required and pitfalls to be avoided thereby enriching the learning and development of mentees.

6. Advocate:

A mentor advocates for the training and development of mentee, keeping in views his needs and aspirations.

7. Guide:

A mentor acts as a guide to the mentee for solving his difficulties and problems and providing the proper direction to achieve the goals of mentoring.

Types of Mentoring

Mentoring is a partnership between two people sharing experiences and expertise to help with personal and professional growth. Through different mentoring programmes, mentors have the opportunity to share their knowledge, experience, and insight into how to get things done, give feedback to the organisation, and to develop trust through increased communication. Mentors have the opportunity to see the impact of their efforts on the professional and personal growth of their mentees. Mentees also have the opportunity to increase their organisational awareness and to reach their full potential.

Types of mentoring are discussed below (see figure 7.6) :

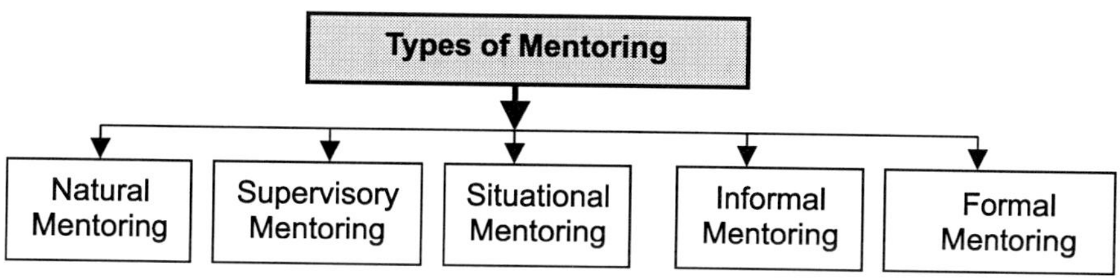

Fig. 7.6 : Types of Mentoring

1. Natural Mentoring

Natural mentoring occurs all the time and always has been there. It happens when one person (usually senior) reaches out to another, and a career-helping relationship develops. This type of mentoring most often occurs between people who have a lot in common. This is because we are usually more comfortable with those who are most like ourselves.

2. Supervisory Mentoring:

In the work place this type of mentoring is very important. All supervisors should mentor their subordinates. Supervisory mentors share valuable information about the organisation and provide meaningful work and developmental learning opportunities. They expose employees/mentees to the values of the organisation and they help employee's position themselves with the skills necessary for success.

However, this type of mentoring does have drawbacks: the manager may not be an expert on thc subject matter, the manager may be heavily tasked and not able to spend an ample amount of time with the employee, and comfort levels are compromised because employees do not want the person who is evaluating their work to see his or her weaknesses.

3. Situational Mentoring:

Situational mentoring is the right help at the right time. It is those connections that help to solve a problem or uncover hidden talent. Situational mentoring is usually short-lived and happens for a specific purpose. An example would be when one employee helps another with a new office computer system, or when someone goes on an "informational interview" with someone who is in a career they are considering.

4. Informal Mentoring:

Informal mentoring is a type of mentoring connection most employees can relate to and have previously experienced. It is an informal mentoring relationship built on mutual trust, respect and the sharing of ideas and experiences.

5. Formal Mentoring:

Formal mentoring is comprehensive and includes a facilitated matching process involving formal training and clear goals for measuring success. Formal facilitated mentoring programmes are structured programmes in which an organisation matches mentors with mentees. They may target one special segment of the organisation whose career development may be lagging behind that of others (for example, women) to help that group advance further. They may assign mentors to mentees and monitor the progress of the mentoring connection. Formal mentoring is very attractive to most organisations because it involves employees, not only in their own growth and development, but also in the growth and development of the organisation.

Successful formal mentoring is characterized by:

- Mentees have an opportunity to capitalize on the wisdom of a mentor's experience to hone their personal and professional capabilities for increasing individual and organisational effectiveness; abd

- Both mentees and mentors receive required formal training prior to entering into the mentoring partnership. This helps to forge a dyadic relationship between the two.

Formal *Vs.* Informal Mentoring

I. Formal Mentoring:

1. More challenging.
2. Requires training of mentors.
3. Encourages participation.
4. Experienced employees know what is expected.
5. The organisation can support and reward mentors.
6. Time for mentoring is protected.

II. Informal Mentoring:

1. Easier to do but less effective.
2. Little or no training needed.
3. Less experienced employees often don't ask for help.
4. Experienced employees often don't help for many reasons (e.g., don't want to be critical).
5. Time may not be available.

Functions of Mentoring

The key functions of mentoring include:

1. To provide direct assistance to the mentees;
2. To provide emotional and psychological support to mentees;
3. To act as a role model to the mentee;
4. To give advice and guidance to mentees;
5. To act as a coach to mentees; and
6. To develop and refine mentees understanding of content and ability to teach content to a particular audience.

Mentoring Process

For efficient and effective mentoring, when a process is required a mentee faces a challenging situation: personal transformation, complex problem, opportunity and dilemma. The process of mentoring is depicted in figure 7.7.

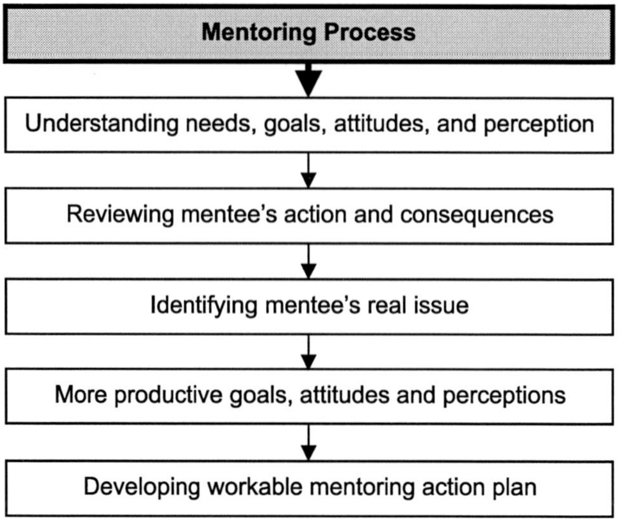

Fig. 7.7 : Mentoring Process

The steps of mentoring process are as under:

1. Understanding needs, goals, attitudes, and perceptions:

Mentoring involves the understanding of needs, goals, attitudes and perceptions of the mentee so as to align it effectively with the objectives of the mentoring programme. An effective alignment results in success of the mentoring programme and helps organisation to achieve its mission and objectives.

2. Reviewing mentee's actions and consequences:

Mentoring requires mentor and mentee to participate in mid point progress and end of programme review. The reviews provide mentor and mentee an opportunity to benchmark progress, uncover problems and recommend improvements or adjustments to the mentoring programme.

3. Identifying mentee's real issue:

Mentees complete a behavioural assessment tool known as 360 multi-rater assessment tool. Feedback provides mentees an opportunity to target developmental needs and develop effective mentoring action plan. Mentees can, based on 360 feedback, uncover real issues and solve them with the help and guidasnce of the mentor.

4. More productive goals, attitudes and perceptions:

Mentor provides mentee with developmental assignments to strive for productive goals, develop positive attitude and have proper perception about himself, his mentor and the organisation.

5. Expanding mentee's thinking to consider new options:

Mentee is encouraged to be innovative in his approach towards problem solving, developmental assignments and networking opportunities in order to develop relationships, gain exposure, and increase visibility.

6. Developing workable mentoring action plan:

Mentees design and define a mentoring action plan (MAP) with the assistance from his mentor. The mentoring action plan is based on a joint assessment of the mentee's developmental needs. This action plan includes some of the following activities:

- *Developmental assignments*: to identify and complete mastering of a new skill or competency. It may include a variety of activities such as writing an article, giving a briefing, taking a course on line or reading a book and then discussing it with the mentor.
- *Networking opportunities*: to help develop appropriate relationship and resources.

A mentoring action plan involves the following steps:

1st: Agreeing on goal.

2nd: Brainstorm:

- Ideas
- Resources
- Activities

3rd: Sequencing action steps.

4th: Carrying out steps.

5th: Achieving goal:

- Debrief
- Hone reflective thinking skills

This requires some preparation on the part of the mentee. It includes:

Step 1: Select one challenging competency.

Step 2: Identify type of challenge:

(*a*) Personal Transformation
(*b*) Dilemma

(*c*) Important Opportunity
(*d*) Complex Problem

Step 3: Write down the Competency

- Key point __________
- Key point ___________

Step 4: Request specific mentoring behaviours a mentee needs.

Benefits of Mentoring

Mentoring provides immense benefits to the mentor, the mentee and the organisation as discussed below:

I. Benefits of Mentoring to the Mentor and Mentee:

Major benefits of mentoring accruing to mentors and mentees are:

1. Specific skills, knowledge and experience:

This can be almost anything a mentee care to name: technical skills, communication skills, and supervisory skills.

2. Access to other viewpoints and advice:

Better understanding of viewpoints of employees, organisation and the customers on a broader perspective.

3. Greater confidence:

Knowing there is a way to get questions answered, knowing there is someone to ask increases confidence.

4. Job satisfaction and higher motivation:

A person being mentored feels supported and this translates into higher motivation in the workplace and greater job satisfaction.

5. Broaden professional network:

The more relationships that are formed through mentoring, the closer participants will feel to others in the department.

6. Personal satisfaction:

People want to feel valued for their skills, their knowledge and their experience. Given the opportunity to share them with a person who actively wants them is immensely rewarding.

7. Expansion of views:

Through the mentee, the mentor can learn about new and different styles of thinking, knowledge and perspectives.

8. Job satisfaction:

A common problem for longer-term employees is a loss of job satisfaction. The employee becomes stale, the everyday routines mechanical. Mentoring can rejuvenate mentors to their own sense and drive for job satisfaction.

9. Higher motivation:

Employees who experience personal and job satisfaction are more motivated. This translates directly into increased productivity, greater creativity and higher performance.

10. Personal skills development:

Mentoring passes on the legacy of the programme. Working with a mentor can cultivate and enhance management, leadership, and interpersonal skills. It also provides opportunities for professional recognition, information gathering, platform for sharing and gaining experience, knowledge and skills, professional development, job satisfaction, and career development to the mentor as well as the mentee.

The benefits of mentoring can be compared between mentor and the mentee as mentioned below:

Mentor:

1. Opportunity to share experiences, knowledge and skills;
2. Increased professional development;
3. Professional recognition; and
4. Increased job satisfaction;

Mentee

1. Opportunity to gain experience, learn new skills and knowledge;
2. Increased professional development;
3. Career development; and
4. Increased job satisfaction.

II. Benefits of mentoring to the Organisation:

Major benefits of mentoring accruing to organisations are:

1. Help new employees learn our culture and inner workings faster:

A mentoring program that pairs new employees with experienced employees can decrease the time needed to orient and train new employees. New employees become productive members of the department faster.

2. Help newly promoted employee understands and fulfill their new responsibilities faster:

Pairing a person who has just been promoted into a new position with a person who knows that role, helps the newcomer understand the role and provides the confidence he needs to perform well.

3. Increase communication and strengthen employee bonds:

An organisation that uses mentoring can expect a greater cohesion and sense of teamwork among its employees.

4. Knowledge base is shared and built on:

An organisation survives and thrives on the accumulated knowledge and experience of its employees. Mentoring programmes ensure that wealth is shared and passed on, and reduces the impact on the organisation when employees leave. Further as employees are given the opportunity to develop and learn, they are more prepared to accept and assimilate to organisational changes.

5. Mentoring develops future leaders:

The skills learned on both sides of the mentoring partnership are skills all leaders need - open communication, understanding and sharing. Some of the major aspects are:

- Gain greater insight;
- Continue personal learning, performance improvement, and talent development;
- Receive candid information, advice, and guidance;
- Get honest appraisal of skills, knowledge and abilities;
- Help to establish and achieve specific goals and objectives;
- Expand professional contacts;

- Increased recruitment/retention of employees;
- Increased productivity;
- Increased morale; and
- Captures knowledge and develops the future workforce.

Myths of Mentoring

There are many confusing myths about mentoring that often inhibit people from participating in and benefiting from a mentoring programme. Some are:

1. Mentors are the only benefactors in a mentoring relationship:

Everyone benefits from a mentoring relationship. The focus may be around the individual needs of the mentee but the mentor and the organisation also derives important benefits from a successful mentoring relationship.

2. Mentors can only be senior managers or individuals soon exiting the department:

Although these groups are ideal candidates to act as effective mentors, many groups in the department can share experience and expertise. There is also the misconception that mentors must be older or more senior in the organisation in order to have something useful to share. Consider a mentoring relationship that has a mentee who is looking to improve their information management skills. This could be a mentee who may be 10 -15 years senior to an ideal mentor who could be a younger, highly trained subject-matter expert.

3. Participation is reserved for only those who want to advance upward in the organisation:

Any employee who wants to improve upon his personal, professional and organisational development will benefit from a mentoring relationship. Consider an excutive who is seeking a mentor who can provide some insight into how to balance home and work life. Mentors can also provide insight into another sector of the organisation in which the associate has not yet had any experience but has interest in. More importantly, participation in a mentoring relationship in no way guarantees advancement in the organisation.

Mentoring Life Cycle

Since mentoring relationships have a definite beginning and ending, it is import that participants incorporate this in their expectations of the mentoring relationship as discussed below.

1. Initial meeting:

At the initial meeting, a relationship has not yet formed. Participants (mentor and mentee/s) introduce themselves to each other and establish a level of comfort in their communications styles.

2. Commitment:

Each participant will be required to make an effort to support the mentoring relationship. Although neither party is completely responsible for the success of the relationship, both must commit to spending the required time in the relationship based on the needs identified mutually by the mentee and the mentor at the start of the relationship.

3. The mentoring relationship:

A mentoring relationship is based on trust and learning will only occur through time. Scheduled meetings/activities will facilitate communications in the relationship which will in turn clarify roles and expectations.

4. Time:

After a training session, to equip a mentee with the tools to ensure the success of mentoring relationship, regular meetings with mentor will have to be scheduled. Whether it be once a month, more or less frequent, the time spent in a mentoring relationship will be clearly defined by participants in the relationship based on their agreed objectives.

5. Flexibility:

Participants must be willing to remain open-minded and flexible while participating in a mentoring relationship.

The duration of the relationship is entirely dependent upon the participants. A mentoring relationship may be reassessed at any time to determine if the relationship is still mutually beneficial to both participants. A mentoring relationship may be terminated at any time.

6. Termination:

Since there will come a time when the mentoring relationship is no longer mutually beneficial, participants should be prepared that it will eventually end. Even though the relationship ends, it does not end one participants association with the other person. The end of one mentoring relationship serves as a starting point for the next.

Over time, through several mentoring relationships, an employee will create a support network of colleagues.

Mentoring participants need to be open to all forms of communication since travel is not always an option to support face-to-face mentoring every month. The relationship may also cross age, gender, race or ethnic boundaries - participants must be open-minded and learn from the diversity of others in the organisation.

Elements of Successful Mentoring

The essential elements of a successful mentoring are:

1. May be formal or informal;
2. Requires a culture that fosters trust;
3. Acknowledges the personal commitment required and rewards the effort; and
4. Requires leaders to serve as role models.

To sum up, a mentoring programme is about:

1. Building relationships:

Mentoring is the human infrastructure of the organisation, and it's as important as the organisational chart or the physical infrastructure.

2. Building and securing knowledge capital:

Beyond physical wealth, an organisation's real capital is knowledge and that resides with employees.

3. Motivating employees:

With effective mentoring relationships that benefit mentors, mentees, and the over-all organisation.

Importance of Coaching and Mentoring

Organisational development, changes brought about by mergers and acquisitions as well as the need to provide key employees with support through a change of role or career are often catalysts, which inspire organisations to seek coaching or mentoring.

At one time coaching and mentoring were reserved for senior managers and top management personnel, now it is available to all as a professional or personal development tool. Coaching and mentoring are also closely linked with organisational change initiatives in order to help employees to accept and adapt to changes in a manner consistent with their personal values and goals.

Coaching and mentoring, both of which focus on the individual, can enhance morale, motivation and productivity and reduce employee turnover as individuals feel valued and connected with both organisational changes. This role may be provided by internal coaches or mentors and, increasingly, by professional coaching agencies.

Coaching and mentoring programmes generally prove to be popular amongst employees as coaching achieves a balance between fulfilling organisational goals and objectives whilst taking into account the personal development needs of individual employees. It is a two-way relationship with both the organisation and the employee gaining significant benefits.

There is also an increasing trend for individuals to take greater responsibility for their personal and professional development and even those who are employed in large organisations are no longer relying on employers to provide them with all or their career development needs. There has been an increase in the number of individuals contracting coaches and mentors on a private basis. Some are looking for a career change, but many are also seeking to maximise their potential with an existing employer or achieve greater balance with their work and home lives.

The Similarities and Differences between Coaching and Mentoring

As can be seen above, there are many similarities and some differences between coaching and mentoring! Mentoring, particularly in its traditional sense, enables an individual to follow in the path of an older and wiser colleague who can pass on knowledge, experience and open doors to otherwise out-of-reach opportunities. Coaching on the other hand is not generally performed on the basis that the coach has direct experience of their employee's formal job role unless the coaching is specific and skills focused.

Both coaching and mentoring are processes that enable both individual and organisations to achieve their full potential. Similarities include:

1. Facilitates the exploration of needs, motivations, desires, skills and thought processes to assist the individual in making real, lasting change;
2. Uses questioning techniques to facilitate employee's own thought processes in order to identify solutions and actions rather than taking a wholly directive approach;
3. Supports the employee in setting appropriate goals and methods of assessing progress in relation to these goals;
4. Observes, listens and ask questions to understand the employee's situation;

5. Creatively applies tools and techniques, which may include one-to-one training, facilitating, counseling and networking;
6. Encourages a commitment to action and the development of lasting personal growth and change;
7. Maintains unconditional positive regard for the employee, which means that the coach is at all times supportive and non-judgmental of the employee, their views, lifestyle and aspirations;
8. Ensures that employees develop personal competencies and do not develop unhealthy dependencies on the coaching or mentoring relationship;
9. Evaluates the outcomes of the process, using objective measures wherever possible to ensure the relationship is successful and the employee is achieving their personal goals; and
10. Encourages employees to continually improve competencies and to develop new developmental alliances where necessary to achieve their goals.

Differences include:

Coaching is the support for technical, skills-related learning and growth, which is provided by another person who uses observation, data collection and descriptive, nonjudgmental reporting on specific requested behaviors and techniques.

Mentoring is the all-inclusive description of everything done to support mentee orientation and professional development. Coaching is one of the sets of strategies, which mentors must learn and effectively use to increase their mentee's skills and success.

Joyce and Showers acknowledge that no one will take the risks of growing in front of another person unless they first have a relationship of mutual trust with that person.

Mentoring provides that relationship within which effective coaching can lead to risk-taking and growth.

Review and Discussion Questions

Question 1: Define and explain the nature and scope of employee coaching.

Question 2: Explain and discuss the different types of employee coaching. Give examples from your field of specialisation to support your answer.

Question 3: Discuss employee-coaching process. What techniques should be employed by the coach to ensure the effectiveness of employee coaching?

Question 4: State the principles of employee coaching. Also discuss the essential elements of effective employee coaching.

Question 5: Define and explain the concept of employee counselling. Why is employee counselling important to human resource development function?

Question 6: Under what conditions should counselling is given to an employee? What are the skills required to provide successful counselling?

Question 7: Enlist and explain the different techniques of employee counselling.

Question 8: Explain the process of employee counselling. What measures should be taken to ensure effectiveness of employee counselling?

Question 9: Define the nature and concept of employee mentoring. How can mentoring programmes contribute to individual and organisational effectiveness?

Question 10: Discuss the principles, importance, dynamics and qualities of participations of mentoring. Also explain the mentoring process with suitable examples.

Question 11: What do you understand by mentoring life cycle?

Question 12: Differentiate between employee coaching and mentoring.

Question 13: Write short notes on:

- (*i*) Ethical dimension of counselling
- (*ii*) Elements of successful mentoring
- (*iii*) Theoretical approaches to counselling

Exhibit: 7 – A

Case Situation

- *Before attempting this section please read Chapter - 14 on Case Study.*
- *Please read the following case situations and answer the questions.*

Q 1. Your immediate subordinate's performance is not up to the mark. What would you do now?

Q 2. You are working in HRD function in an expanding automobile company. It has been reported to you that your sales manager has not been performing well in spite of counseling, reprimand and warnings given to him by GM-Marketing. GM-Marketing wants to sack him. What would be your HRD action plan?

Q 3. You are a HRD Consultant. Recently a CEO of a merged banking company approaches you to help him in building motivation and morale of his employees. The merged organisation's employees are reeling heavily under FUD – fear, uncertainty and distrust, as informed by the CEO. What would be your action plan?

Exhibit: 7 – B

Case Study

- *Before attempting this section please read Chapter - 14 on Case Study.*
- *Please read the following case study and answer all the subsequent questions.*

Introduction to the organisation:

PANTAD Pharmaceuticals is a fast growing and profit making pharmaceutical company. It has been growing @ 12% per annum and is one of the fastest growing organisations in its class with sales turnover of 350 crores. The organisational is a traditional one striving to become a professionally managed organisation. It has instituted various HRD programme to boost morale, productivity and commitment of its employees. The organisation has recently implemented a KRA based appraisal system.

Brief Description of the Problem:

Manoj Kumar had a management position in this organisation. He was 36, had been successful and popular throughout his career and was happily married. He felt trapped in his job, but could not find any way out. He felt depressed, was sleeping badly and reported that his thinking was becoming increasingly muddled. He felt he was spending too much time at work, and felt guilty about putting work ahead of his family. He had started to use drinking and gambling as coping mechanisms. When he completed a set of standardised measures of stress, anxiety and depression at the beginning of counseling, his scores indicated a level of distress usually associated with individuals receiving inpatient treatment for severe mental health problems. Over the course of 16 sessions of psychodynamic counseling. Mathew developed a much fuller understanding of how some of the themes in his own life (for example, his sense of never having been wanted as a child) were linked to his relation ships both at work and at home. He became better able to express his needs and emotions, and found ways of delegating and receiving support at work. He reported and enhanced sense of satisfaction and commitment at work, and an improvement in his relationship with his wife.

Counseling had not transformed Manoj Kumar, or the highly pressurized environment in which he worked, but it had allowed him to stand back from what has happening, look at himself and how he related to others, and find ways of restoring a degree of balance to his life.

Questions:

1. What is the major reason of problems of Mr. Manoj Kumar?
2. How was Mr. Manoj Kumar's problem resolved?
3. How could have you, HRD Manager of the organisation helped him? Briefly outline your action plan.

CHAPTER

8 Employee Empowerment

Chapter Synopsis

To be successful in today's business environment, organisations need the knowledge, ideas, energy, and creativity of every employee. The best way to accomplish this is by transforming into an organisation of leaders - an organization in which employees at every level take the initiative and act as though the business where their own. Employee empowerment can transform a workforce and create a competitive advantage.

This chapter explains these concepts and strategies to empower employees for value creation.

This Chapter contains:

Concept of employee empowerment, Definitions of employee empowerment, Objectives of employee empowerment, Pre-requisites of employee empowerment, Types of employee empowerment, Empowerment continuum, Self-directed teams, Empowerment process, Benefits of employee empowerment, Ways to employee empowerment, Strategies for employee empowerment, Limitations of employee empowerment, Review & discussion questions, Case situation and Case study.

Employee Empowerment

Employee Empowerment

Power is not a weapon that is used by design or indiscriminately to achieve the desired results. Power is a tool to pass on to those who work on organisation's behalf. The overall performance of the organisation is dependent on the power of the people who are collectively building the future of the organisation. "To empower," means to enable, to allow or to permit, and can be conceived as both self-initiated and initiated by others. Empowerment is the process of enabling employees to set their own work-related goals, make decisions and solve problems within their spheres of responsibility and authority. An important part of empowerment is the definition of spheres of responsibility and authority by management.

Empowerment allows people, individually and in groups, to use their talents and knowledge to make decisions that affect their work. Employees are held accountable for the results produced by others, whose formal role gives them the right to command but who lack informal influence, access to resources, outside status, sponsorship, or mobility prospects, are rendered powerless in the organisation. This has resulted in the evolution of the concept of employee empowerment.

Human resources are an organisation's most under utilized resource. In this knowledge economy, intrapreneurship is needed throughout the ranks of the organisation. *Intrapreneur* is an energetic, enthusiastic, imaginative and inventive person who has ideas for creating new products or services and takes direct responsibility for turning an idea into a profitable finished product or complete service with the assistance and resources offered by his organisation. Flat hierarchical structures and multi skilled workforce characterize new knowledge-based organisations. Managers assume more leadership and coaching tasks and work hard to provide employees with resources and work cultures they need to accomplish the objectives and mission of the organisation. A critical feature of successful organisations is that they are invested with a significant degree of employee empowerment or decision making authority.

Empowerment is not a programme, it is a culture change. Empowerment is the process of enabling or authorizing an individual to think, behave, take action, and control work and decision-making in autonomous ways. It is the state of feeling self-empowered to take control of one's own destiny.

When thinking about empowerment in human relations terms, it shall be prudent to avoid thinking of it as something that one individual does for another. This is one of the problems organisations have experienced with the concept of empowerment. Employees think that "someone," usually the manager, has to bestow empowerment on the people who report to him. Consequently, the reporting staff members "wait" for the bestowing of empowerment, and the manager asks why people won't act in empowered ways. This led to a general unhappiness, mostly undeserved, with the concept of employee empowerment in many organisations.

The organisation has the responsibility to create a work environment, which helps foster the ability and desire of employees to act in empowered ways. The work organisation has the responsibility to remove barriers that limit the ability of employees to act in empowered ways. Empowerment as part of HRD approach tends to be unitarist but if extended to giving employees real power over a broader range of issues could be pluralist (tends to be limited in application/scope).

Counflicting Positions of Employee Empowerment

According to Doughty (2004), four conflicting positions on employee empowerment that exists are as follows:

- Employee empowerment represent a cunning strategy by an insidious management to gull workers not only into acqiescing in their own oppression but also into coming up with clever new methods of intensifying that oppression;
- Employee empowerment exemplify a tradition of noble proletarian struggle for recognition, respect and rightful sharing of power in the workplace;
- Employee empowerment is an important step in the evolution of organisational psychology which has the potential of building hugely more flexible and efficient corporate entities; and
- Employee empowerment constitute the most recent stage in the development of humane and democratic social arrangements in which the worth of the individual is recognized not only in increased job satisfaction but also in self-actualization

and the acquisition of attitues and skills necessary to be an exemplary citizen in a participative society.

Bibliography:

Doughty, Howard A., "Employee Empowerment: Democracy or Delusion?", *The Innovation Journal, Vol. 9, No. 1, 2004, Pp. 1-24.*

Employee empowerment has become necessary due to the following reasons:

1. Time to respond is much shorter today;
2. First line employees must make many decisions;
3. There is great-untapped potential;
4. Employees feel much more control over their lives; and
5. Empowered people do not feel like victims.

Definitions

A few noteworthy definitions of Employee Empowerment are as follows:

1."Empowerment is the process coming to feel and behave as if one is in power (autonomy and control) and to feel as if he/she owned the firm".

(Richard Kathnelson: 2004)

2. "Empowerment is the process of sharing power with employees".

(Thomas S. Bateman and Scott A. Snell: 2003)

3. "Employee Empowerment predominantly about encouraging front-line staff to solve customer problems on the spot, without constant recourse to management approval".

(Goldsmith et al: 1997)

4. "Employee Empowerment refers to management strategies for sharing decision-making power."

(Bowen and Lawler: 1992)

5. "Empowerment is giving subordinates the resources, both psychological and technical, to discover the varieties of Power they themselves have and/or accumulated, therefore which they can use on another's behalf".

(E. Neilsen: 1986)

From an analytical study of the above definitions, we may conclude that:

Empowerment is a process of risk taking and personal growth. It is the creation of work environment, which allows each individual to work to his highest capacity. An empowered workplace provides employees with freedom to take initiative, to create, to solve problems, and to assume the responsibility of completing the task with success, accountability and satisfaction. This is because employee empowerment gives employees the authority to decide and act on their own initiatives, so that the added responsibility and authority is moved to the lowest level possible in the organisation. It allows the employee to assume both managerial and operational responsibilities.

Employee empowerment changes the manager's mindset and leaves them with more time to engage in broad based thinking, visioning, and nurturing. This intelligent and productive division of responsibilities between visionary leaders, focusing on emerging opportunities, and empowered employees, running the business on day-to-day basis provides for a well-managed organisation with strong growth potential.

Employee Empowerment can be done by:

- Encouraging sharing of resource and information;
- Seeking advice from employees;
- Facilitating employees to try their ideas of their own;
- Encouraging employees to examine their values and belief systems concerning authority and behaviour; and
- Improving the communication skills of employees.

*Luthans (*1992) suggests the following ways in which management can empower employees. Management can:

- Express confidence in employees' abilities;
- Hold high expectations concerning their performance;
- Allow employees to participate in the decision-making process;
- Allow employees freedom and autonomy in how they perform their jobs;
- Set inspirational or managerial goals for employees; and
- Use position power in a prudent and positive way and limit the use of coercive power.

Empowerment results in:

- Enhances beliefs of employees that they are influential contributors to the organisational success;

- Employees perceive meaning in work;
- Employees feel competent;
- Employees derive a sense of self-determination; and
- Employees believe they have an impact on important decisions.

An empowering environment is characterized by:

- Provides information required to perform at one's best Knowledge available about how to use the information;
- Employees have the power to make decisions; and
- Employees receive rewards for contributions.

Objectives of Employee Empowerment

Human resources are often an organisation's most underutilized resource. In the new knowledge economy, intrapreneurship and initiative is needed throughout the ranks of the organisation. Involvement in an organisation is no longer a one-way street. In today's business environment a manager must work towards engaging organisation forcefully enough to achieve its objectives. Flat hierarchical structures and multi-skilled workforce characterize new knowledge-based organisations. Managers assume more leadership and coaching tasks and work hard to provide employees with resources and working conditions they need to accomplish the goals they've agreed to. In brief, managers work for their employees, and not the reverse.

Empowerment is the oil that lubricates the exercise of learning. Talented and empowered human resources are becoming the prime ingredient of organisational success. A critical feature of successful organisations especially in knowledge-based organisations, is that they are invested with a significant degree of empowerment, or decision-making authority.

Pre-requisites for Employee Empowerment

Employee empowerment provides people the responsibility and authority to make decisions. Empowerment frequently results in greater commitment and cooperation; creative ideas and solutions; and greater ownership from employees. Creating an empowered workforce is a great way to increase organisational effectiveness and success. Empowerment works when employees are given the necessary resources, proper training and effectively managed. Then only they will be able to successfully perform and make effective decisions.

Employee empowerment requires the following pre-requisites:

1. Involvement:

Employees feel more committed to the organisation when they are involved in the decision making process.

2. Quick decision-making:

Employees sometimes need on the spot decisions for the benefit of the organisation. Employees who work say in customer service need to be able to quickly respond to customer's needs and problems without having to constantly go up the chain of command.

3. Solving complex problems:

Employees directly involved with a problem can better determine the optimal solution. For example, a work group can figure out how to re-engineer its work processes far better than employees/managers that do not directly work on the process/project.

Types of Empowerment

The types of employee empowerment are depicted in figure 8.1.

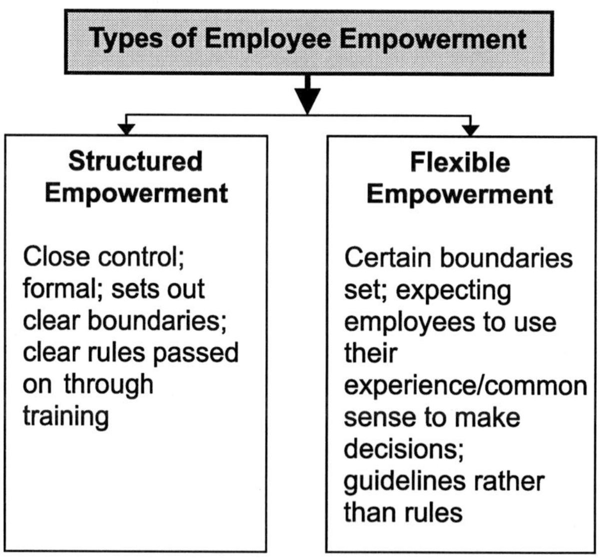

Fig. 8.1 : Types of Employee Empowerment

Empowerment Continuum

Employee empowerment efforts have gained widespread attention for their ability to make organisations more efficient and productive. A skill is an ability to translate knowledge into action that results in a desired performance. There are three categories of skill viz. - technical skill, human skill and conceptual skill.

By giving 'power', it gives responsibility to employees without extra reward and organisations get a cost saving from de-layering management. The empowerment continuum is depicted in figure 8.2.

Increasing reliance on employee's contribution and increasing acceptance of responsibility by employee is hallmark of empowerment.

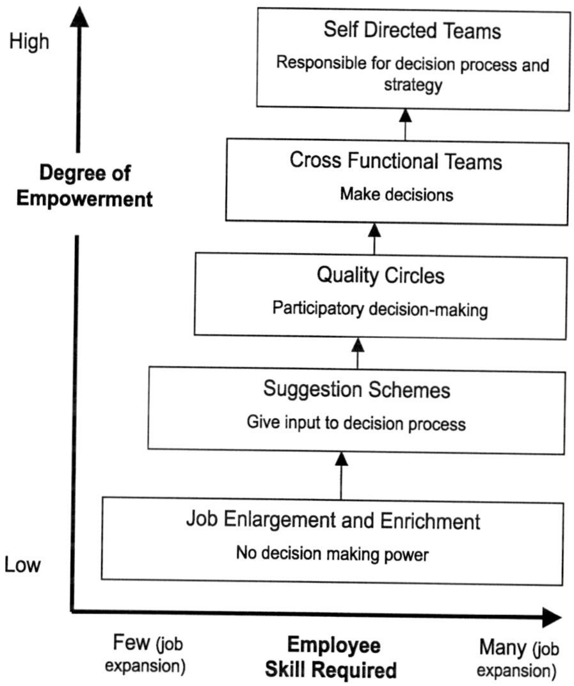

Fig. 8.2 : Empowerment Continuum

Self-Directed Teams

An organisation is bound together by these beliefs and values; by people that are committed to one another and to their common goals. As they say, TEAM stands for "Together Everyone Achieves More", a self directed team is a group of empowered individuals working together for a common goal and may be organized for short-term or long-term objectives. Self-managing teams are empowered to make the decisions needed to manage themselves on a daily basis.

Teams make decisions on:

- Scheduling work.
- Allocating tasks.
- Training in job skills.
- Evaluating performance.
- Selecting new team members.
- Controlling quality of work.

Reasons for effectiveness of self-directed team are:

- Provide employee empowerment;
- Provide core job characteristics; and
- Meet psychological needs (e.g., belonging).

Self-directed teams offer the following benefits:

- Improvement in business processes due to teamwork;
- Employees tend to know their tasks better and therefore are more suited to improve processes under their control;
- Fewer supervision is required;
- High quality work output;
- Increased job satisfaction; and
- Employees are more responsive to problem solving.

Empowerment Process

Employee empowerment is a two-sided coin. For employees to be empowered the management leadership must want and believe that employee empowerment makes good business sense and employees must act. It may be noted that employee empowerment does not mean that management no longer has the responsibility to lead the organisation and is not responsible for performance. If anything the opposite is true. Stronger leadership and accountability is demanded in an organisation that seeks to empower employees. This starts with the executive leadership through all management levels and includes front line supervisors. It is only when the entire organisation is willing to work as a team that the real benefits of employee empowerment are realized.

For an organisation to practice and foster employee empowerment the management must trust and communicate with employees. Open interactive communication is one of the strongest signs of employee empowerment. Honest and repeated communication about strategic plan, key performance indicators, financial performance, down to daily decision making.

If an organisation has not been actively cultivating employee empowerment, it may take considerable time and effort before employees start to respond. Often the first efforts and communications are met with employee derision and mockery. Those who are only interested in trying the latest management fad will give up when met with this response. A good rule of thumb for communications to employees is to enumerate what management considers adequate and then multiple by a factor of ten. When considering employee understanding and acceptance of decisions consider how long it takes for the management team to discuss and then make a decision. Allow several multiples of this time for employees to think about the issue.

For management wanting employee empowerment, the evidence will not come across the board with wide spread acceptance. A small number will accept the invitation to become more involved, say 3-5 per cent. The rest will be watching every move to see what happens. Every communication, decision and action by management will be viewed as either supporting a move to employee empowerment or not. Probably nothing demonstrates the commitment or lack of commitment to employee empowerment more than promotions and selection for leadership positions. Employees know those that attempt to "shine up while dumping down".

For an organisation to enjoy the returns from employee empowerment the leadership must diligently work to create the work environment where it is obvious to that entire employee empowerment is desired, wanted and cultivated. Management's responsibility is to create the environment for employee empowerment.

When organisational leadership has started to take actions to encourage employee empowerment, it is then up to the employees to decide if they wish to take advantage of the opportunity or not. It is not unusual for only a small minority to accept the challenge initially. Also it is very likely that some fraction will never respond. It is the large middle group that must be convinced to practice employee empowerment.

Most organisations have exactly the level of employee empowerment the management wants. This is demonstrated by the amount of communications, level of training provided to employees, opportunities for personal growth, the solicitation and implementation of ideas, the recognition and reward system, promotion and advancement criteria, and uncountable little signals from management that demonstrate whether employees are valued or not.

Part of employee empowerment is the recognition by management that often people who most know of pressing needs for improvement are those who have to work in the process.

The steps of employee empowerment process are depicted in figure 8.3.

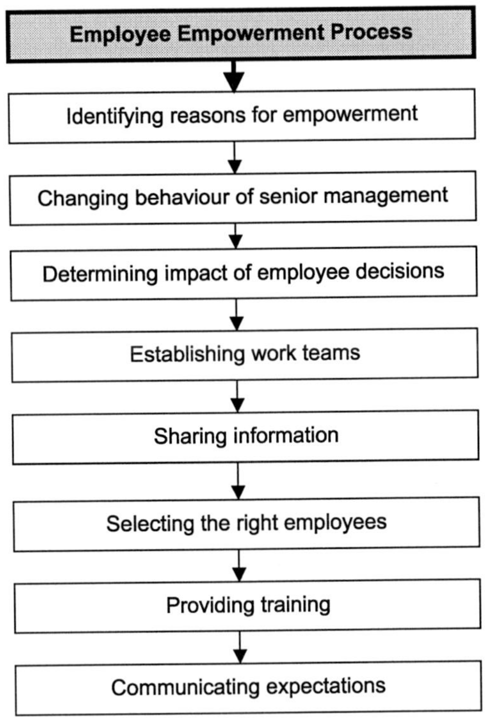

Fig. 8.3 : Employee Empowerment Process

1. Identifying reasons for empowerment:

The first step is for managers to decide why they want employees to have more decision-making authority. Is it to improve customer service, reduce cycle time, or boost product quality? It must be in commensuration with the strategic goals, mission and objectives of the organisation.

Organisations have to find out what the market needs and what can it do to meet those needs. When managers can clearly articulate the business reasons for empowering employees, then employees can begin to see what is expected of them and allows them to use their skills effectively.

Managers also must explain to employees what empowerment "looks" like. Because the level of empowerment is different at every organisation, managers need to provide concrete examples of what the employees' new level of authority will include. Will it include the ability to resolve customer complaints or determine work and vacation schedules? Or will empowerment be limited to problem solving within the employee's own work team and handling operational issues? It has to be specific. This essentially calls for coaching of employees on empowerment.

2. Changing behaviour of senior management:

The biggest challenge managers have to overcome in creating an empowered work environment is learning to let go. Empowering employee's to work directly with customers helps in meeting the customers' needs more quickly. But the transition would not be easy. By giving employees more responsibility senior management will have more time to do other things to do such as visioning. Senior management should establish the boundaries, and then move aside. This will facilitate employees to put forth their best ideas within those boundaries.

3. Determining impact of employee decisions:

One of the best ways for managers and employees to understand how their behaviour must change is by methodically determining what kinds of decisions managers are willing to hand over.

Managers typically don't want to give up any power. But by assessing the kinds of decisions that are made on a daily basis, managers and employees can begin to see where it would make sense to have employees more directly involved. Trusting employees is crucial to the success of empowerment programmes. When empowered employees are working together and trust is present, employees are able to make the necessary decisions and correct any mistakes/problems they encounter. It takes time for employees not only to learn how to make good decisions, but also to trust that managers will abide by the decisions they make.

4. Establishing work teams:

Virtually every successful empowerment effort involves to some extent the use of teams. For employees to have input on their jobs they must understand how their jobs impact other employees and the business as a whole. The best way for them to understand this is by actually working more closely with other people. Additionally, groups of employees working together will usually come up with better ideas and decisions than any individual working alone. Because teams are such an important part of the empowerment process, organisations need to redesign the organisation so that teamwork occurs more naturally. Organisations that are serious about empowerment are redesigning the organisational structure so that teams of employees understand and can have an impact on the entire business process.

5. Sharing information:

For employees to make better decisions for the organisation they need better information about the organisation. Empowered employees should have access to information that helps them understand how their job or their team contributes to the organisation as a whole — such as cost to make a product, average cycle time, customer complaints, scrap and rework costs, and annual sales goals.

The more employees understand 'the why' of what they are doing, the more they will give in return. But information sharing works two ways — it's also imperative to have employees present their own suggestions to managers as well as evaluate managers.

6. Selecting the right employees

Employees who do best in an empowered, team-based environment are those who possess initiative and the ability to get along with other people. Instead of hiring people based solely on technical abilities and hoping they can adapt to the culture, organisations should make a concerted effort to get the right people at the outset.

7. Providing training:

Few employees are naturally good at teaming activities. Courses on decision-making, problem solving, conflict management, and effective meetings are imperative for organisations' intent on employee empowerment. Training is an important strategy of empowerment effort that includes programmes on leadership, total quality management, diversity, safety, and problem solving as well as programmes to boost technical skills.

8. Communicating expectations:

Every employee may not understand exactly what empowerment means in terms of his individual job duties. Instead, communicating expectations through the employee's performance management plan can prove highly beneficial. Managers must define specific targets for employees each year including targets related to education and work performance. When people have goals they tend to work toward them.

One of the strongest signs from employees is when they take the lead to advance their skills and knowledge with education and training either provided by the organisation or out side the organisation.

Management has the obligation to create the environment that fosters employee empowerment, employees have the duty to accept the opportunity and demonstrate they are willing and capable.

Robert E. Quinn and Gretchen M. Spreitzer (1997) through their research found the characteristics of empowered employees as depicted in figure 8.4.

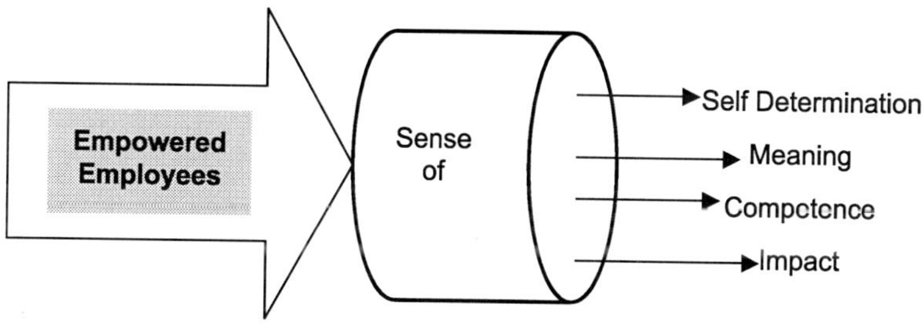

Fig. 8.4 : Characteristics of Empowered Employees

1. Empowered employees have a sense of self-determination. They are free to choose how to do their work and are not micromanaged;
2. Empowered employees have a sense of meaning. They feel that their work is important to them and they care about what they are doing;
3. Empowered employees have a sense of competence. They are confident about their ability to do their work well as they know they can perform well; and
4. Empowered employees have a sense of impact. They believe that they can have influence on their work unit and others would listen to their ideas.

Benefits of Employee Empowerment

The major benefits of employee empowerment are as under:

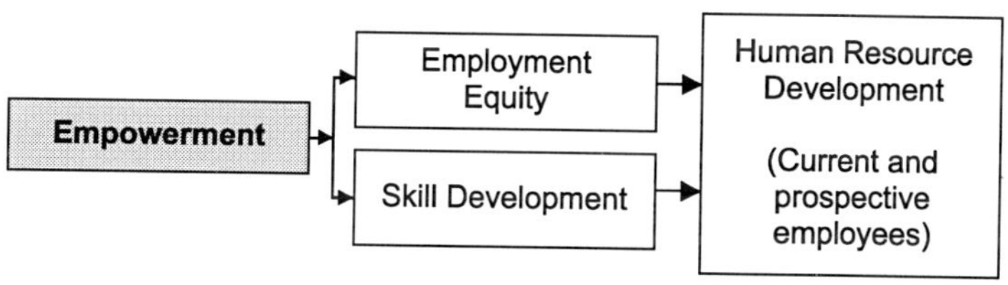

Fig. 8.5 : Empowerment for HRD

1. Having an employee empowerment effort will help an organisation by improving individual self-esteem, self-efficacy, and other desired behaviours. The investment in the workforce will yield direct and indirect cost savings for the organisation–as well as improved morale of employees.
2. Employee empowerment helps in getting individuals to be more self-reliant. However, the critical difference is the ability of this process to enable employees to take control of their responsibilities, better utilizes existing resources and makes wiser decisions. This process will invigorate entire organisation as depicted in figure 8.5.

Ways to Empower Employees

Employee empowerment can be brought about by many ways as discussed below (see figure 8.6).

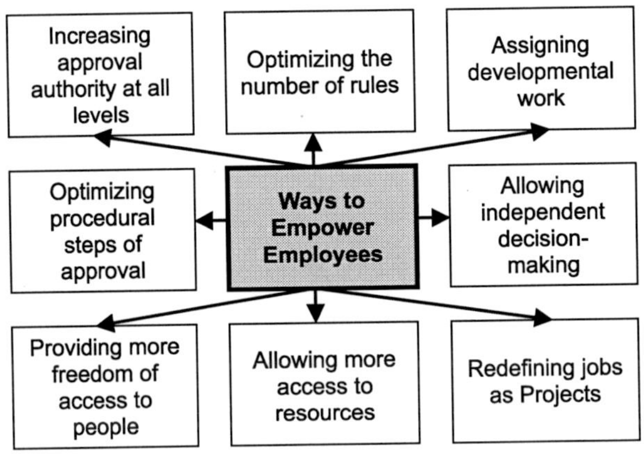

Fig. 8.6 : Empowerment Ways

1. Increasing approval authority at all levels:

The decision-making authority should be delegated to the grass root level. Employees at the lowest levels (e.g. workers) are closest to the business processes – whether manufacturing operations or customer interface. They are the people who need the decision making power more than anyone does. By giving approval authority to them organisational effectiveness through increased productivity, cost saving and customer excelleration can be achieved.

2. Optimizing the rules:

Organisations must have optimum number of rules. Neither too many nor too little. It is a difficult balancing act but by doing so an organisation can create agility and enhance its responsiveness. It must be remembered that rules should facilitate decision-making and should not hinder decision-making process. Optimum number of rules helps employees to quickly and judiciously make decisions.

3. Assigning developmental work:

Organisation needs to assign development works/projects to hone the decision-making skills and competence of employees. A competent employee can take better and useful decision.

4. Allowing independent decision-making:

Allowing employees to take decision of their own builds confidence. A confident employee will do greater justice to empowerment.

5. Redefining jobs as projects:

Jobs must be seen as dynamic concept. Each job in an organisation must be viewed as an independent project, which must give the management a fair return on investment. When jobs are treated as projects, employees tend to take more interest and responsibility for favourable outcome.

6. Allowing more access to resources:

Employees need various kinds of resources – physical, intellectual, informational and technological resources to make appropriate decisions. Therefore, organisation must provide access to resources to all employees so that they can choose the best decision to achieve the mission and objectives of the organisation.

7. Providing more freedom of access to people:

Employees must have the freedom to access the information and other resources. Restricting will only harm empowerment. Unless employees have the required freedom to access resources, they will not be able to take judicious decisions.

8. Optimizing procedural steps of approval:

Large chain of steps of approval only hinders competitiveness of an organisation. In today's business environment, success of organisations is measured by the speed and accuracy of the decision they make. A faster decision adds to higher degree of responsiveness of the employee, which is followed by greater customer satisfaction – internal or external.

Strategies for Employee Empowerment

The following strategies can be adopted by organisation to empower their employees:

- Encouraging employee empowerment for decision making in concert with organisational objectives, so as to develop spirit of ownership amongst them. Empowerment is achieved by involving people in the development of their own solutions to specific issues. This is done by expecting teams to not just propose ways forward or to hope that someone else will do something; but to actually solve the problem in their part of the organisation, according to the constraints within which they work and the resources they have;

- Maintaining a co-operative management style with employees, and customers. Empowerment is about winning both the hearts and minds of people so that they can take the opportunities made available to them for expanded responsibility. For example, at the management level, this could be achieved by sharing the vision and corporate values throughout the organisation;
- An organisation that is empowered has a flat structure with the minimum number of management layers. A multi-layered structure embellished in a non-empowered environment hinders decision-making from reaching as far down the organisation as it should;
- Not all organisational problems can be solved by one person. The sheer rate of change and turbulence implies that as fresh problems and challenges appear, individuals are likely to group together in flexible teams without barriers of hierarchy or status, to solve the problems within the framework of the organisation's values and objectives. Communicating and monitoring performance standards and celebrating those occasions when innovative decision has been made; and
- Developing employee skills and succession opportunities through the skills and competencies improvement process.

Limitations of Employee Empowerment

Employee empowerment can be a major problem for an organisation, if employees are given large increases in responsibility without preparation. Successfully instituting even a lesser degree of empowerment requires preparation beyond incentives, a management speech or memo. The followings points are note worthy in this regard:

1. **Matters Too Little:**

   Employees have been conditioned to care about little more than their own development and potential. Sometimes they can see as far as the walls of their own department. Their knowledge of the rest of the organisation is so limited that when asked to see the 'big picture', employees in many organisations don't even have the information necessary – a basic understanding of the organisation, customer, and market.

2. **Mind Your Own Business:**

   Recognizing this, some organisations break their operation into profit centers, which can be more easily understood. This can help in some respects and hurt in others. Synergy and economy of scale is often lost in the process. It may be better to begin a long-term effort to provide business basics and a gradually expand every employee's perspective.

3. Reasonable Goals, Realistic Plans:

It is reasonable to expect that empowered employees will manage the processes in their work area and provide sound input to senior management on broader business issues. Eventually, joint responsibilities between employees in various parts of the organisation can be understood and happen with minimal supervision. But first the organisation must make several investments in employees such as:

- ***Supervisory Training*** - to update skills of critical 'first line' of management;
- ***Business Training*** - to increasing employee knowledge and help them to understand why they should focus upon;
- ***Cross-Functional Interaction*** - so employees can understand the challenges across their organisation; and
- ***Improvement Teams*** - to have the people with the most knowledge make decisions, thus building respect and the ability to make decisions.

Review and Discussion Questions

Question 1: Define and explain the concept and scope of employee empowerment.

Question 2: What are the major objectives, pre-requisites and benefits of employee empowerment?

Question 3: Explain the employee empowerment process.

Question 4: Enlist the ways and strategies to increase employee empowerment.

Question 5: Critically examine the present scenario of employee empowerment in the Indian Industries. Give suitable examples to justify your answer.

Question 6: In your view how can HRD professionals contribute to make their organisation an empowered one?

Question 7: Write short notes on:

i) Employee empowerment
ii) Self-directed teams
iii) Empowerment continuum
iv) Limitation of employee empowerment

Exhibit: 8 – A

Case Situation

- *Before attempting this section please read Chapter - 14 on Case Study.*
- *Please read the following case situations and answer the questions.*

Q 1. Kuldeep empowered himself to discuss the career objectives he wished to pursue with his Manager. He told his Manager, frankly, that if the opportunities were not available in his current company, he would move on to another company. What advice would you give Kuldeep as Manager-HRD?

Q 2. The manager of the Human Resources department added weeks to the process of hiring new employees by requiring his supposedly "empowered" staff members to obtain his signature on every document related to the hiring of a new employee. What would do if you had been the manager of Human Resources department?

Exhibit: 8 – b

Case Study

- *Before attempting this section please read Chapter - 14 on Case Study.*
- *Please read the following case study and answer all the subsequent questions.*

Introduction to the organisation:

Dez's Store was established 10 years ago, and is engaged in large-scale retail business (electronics superstore) of FMCG goods such as colour televisions, VCD, DVD, washing machines, microwave ovens, etc. The Company is profit making and employs around 80 personnel.

Brief Description of the Problem:

Om Prakash bought a 29' Colour Television from an electronics superstore. Kulvinder the sales person advises him, and he goes home with the CTV.

When Om Prakash arrives home, we find that the CTV has a big scratch across the side.

Om Prakash returns to the store and tells Kulvinder of his problem, and agrees that for a partial refund he will accept the scratched CTV.

Kulvinder says this is a fair arrangement, but he needs to check with his Line Manager if this is ok.

Kulvinder comes back 5 minutes later with his Manager, who asks Om Prakash to explain the problem again. Om Prakash go through the details of the purchase and the problem, and the manager agrees to the solution, but needs authorisation from the Store Manager.

The Store Manager comes back after 5 minutes with Kulvinder and asks Om Prakash to explain the situation again. He again goes through the details of the problem, and the Store Manager agrees to a partial refund. However first he needs to get an authorisation number from Head Office.

After 5 minutes on the phone the Store Manager comes back and agrees to process the refund. Finally the problem has been solved, but at what cost?

To sort the problem the store has paid for:

- Kulvinder's time.
- His manager's time.
- The store manager's time.

The head office's time.

Not only that, but in the process of waiting and repeating himself, Om Prakash may have (as most people would) decided not to bother shopping with their store again.

If Kulvinder was given the power to do his job properly, the company would have saved the employee's time costs, as well as kept a customer.

The answer in this case would be for Kulvinder to know, and be able to enforce the company policy. (E.g.: Maximum 10% discount or replacing the product). Instead, Om Prakash became a victim of un-empowerment disease, or "Run and check" syndrome.

Questions:

1. What is the major problem in this case? What HRD instrument would you apply here?
2. What would have been the case if Kulvinder were sufficiently empowered?
3. What would have been the case if line manager or store manager were sufficiently empowered?

CHAPTER

9 Quality of Work Life

Chapter Synopsis

Globalisation coupled with dynamics of business have considerably changed trends in employment and have brought chaos and turbulence to organisations and individual employees alike. It is the time to reorganise the workplace around the idea of meaningful work - work that offers personal development, a social purpose, a decent standard of living, and a sense of economic security. Quality of work life can lay the groundwork for better lives for employees and increased organisational performance.

This chapter explains these concepts in order to strike a balance between organisational and personal lives of employees for greater job satisfaction and productivity.

This Chapter contains:

Nature and concept of quality of work life, Definitions of quality of work life, Objectives of quality of work life, Importance of quality of work life, Increasing quality of work life, Ways to increase quality of work life, Determinants/categories of quality of work life, Review & discussion questions, Case situation and Case study.

Quality of Work Life

Quality of Work Life

Louis Davis introduced the term 'Quality of Work Life (QWL)' in 1972 in an attempt to establish that performance is linked to involvement and satisfaction of employees at workplaces. Quality of work life is the overall quality of human experience in the work place. It measures the way participants in a system respond to the socio-technical aspects of that system.

Quality in work is important for individuals, and also for growth, employment and a sustainable and competitive economy. Therefore, organisations must create a working life for employees that is sustainable in the long run and that creates more and better jobs. Everybody must also have the possibility to remain in work for a longer time than today. Working conditions must permit this, and this involves paying attention not only to the work environment, but also to competence development/life-long learning, equality, and influence.

Quality of work life seeks to provide programmes, services and guidance on practices that encourage a positive, constructive and productive work experience. Flexibility must be combined with security, influence, mobility, safety and learning at work. The employees must be able to influence their own work and working time, work organisation and work content. Psychosocial work environment problems, like stress and burnout, are growing, while many traditional work environment problems remain. Prevention must be better. The cost of ill health is enormous and costs heavily the society, organisations and individuals.

The problem for the organisations is not always lack of resources or will, but finding the right tools and methods. Quality in work must be seen as profitable for all in the long run.

In the future it will be necessary to motivate organisations to take more responsibility concerning quality of work life, of employees.

Definitions:

A few noteworthy definitions of Quality of Work Life are as follows:

1. "Quality of work life refers to programmes designed to create a workplace that enhances employee well-being".

(Thomas S. Bateman and Scott A. Snell: 2003)

2. "Quality of work life emphasizes improving the human dimension of work. HR should try to improve QWL by Introducing participative problem solving, Restructuring work, Introducing innovative reward systems, and improving the work environment.

(Wheelen and Hunger: 2000)

3. "Quality of work life is the way participants in a system respond to sociotechnical aspects of that system. This is an important measure or aspect of an organisation's ability to perform."

(Sink: 1985)

4. "Quality of work life is a process by which an organisation responds to the employee needs for developing mechanisms to allow them to share fully in making the decisions that design their lives at work".

(R.E. Walton: 1973)

From an analytical study of the above definitions, we may conclude that:

Quality of work life is a process by which all members of the organisation, through appropriate channels of communication, have some say about the design of their jobs in particular and work environment in general.

Quality of work life efforts assume that employees will add to an organisation's success if they feel that their contributions are meaningful and important. Rather than using specific short-term programmes, effective organisations secure employee involvement through improved communication, ongoing survey feedback processes, suggestion systems, team building, and quality circles. Organisations differ drastically in their attention to quality of work life.

We may now jot down the meaning of quality of work life as mentioned in the following box.

Quality of Work Life

- Perceptions of the value of work
- Challenge/interest
- Achievement
- Freedom and autonomy
- Workload
- Quality of work relationships

To create a proper quality of work life, there has to be balance between organisation leadership, organisation structure and individual employee as shown in figure 9.1.

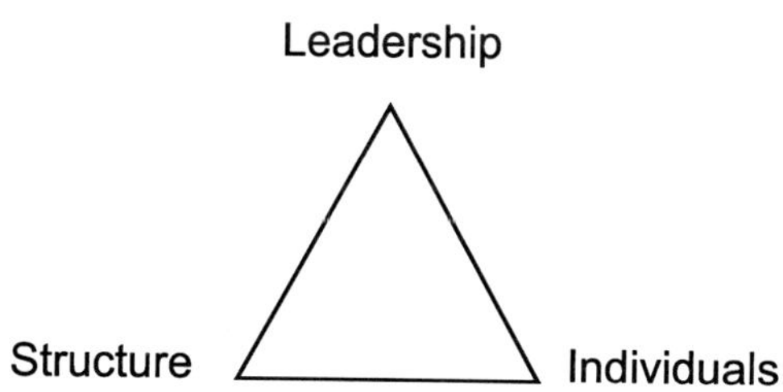

Fig. 9.1 : Organizational Balance for QWL

Quality of work life plays a critical role in the success of an organisation as depicted in figure 9.2.

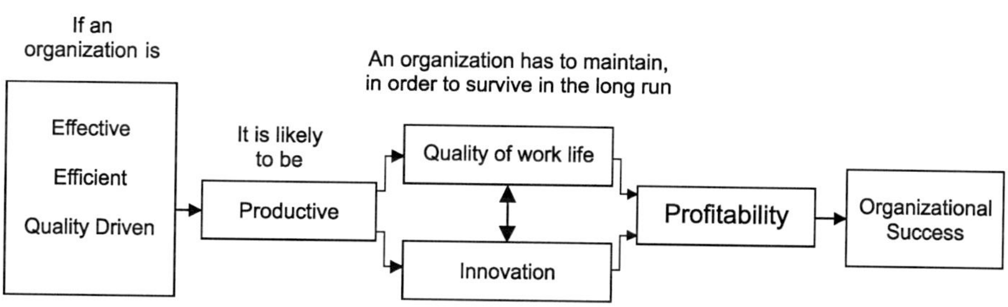

Fig. 9.2 : Organizational Success Through QWL

Studies show that low job satisfaction and low quality of work life is associated with:

1. Physical and emotional problems:

Various physical and emotional problems such as low life-satisfaction, ulcers, heart disease, fatigue, shortened life span, mental health problems; low sense of well-being, etc. contributes to low quality of work life.

2. Employee problems:

Various problems of employees such as grievance, turnover, destructive rumors and gossip, lateness, taking long breaks, etc. contributes to low quality of work life.

3. Production problems:

Various problem of production system such as faulty products, equipment/facility, sabotage, theft, etc. contributes to low quality of work life.

Objectives of Quality of Work Life

The main objectives are:

1. To attract and retain talents;
2. To prevent high levels of employee stress and burnout;
3. To facilitate effective integration of work and personal life;
4. To foster greater job satisfaction, engagement and retention of employees, especially key personnel and best professionals;
5. To increase quality and productivity through higher job satisfaction; and
6. To balance personal/family and work related demands on an individual employee for maintaining optimum levels of personal effectiveness.

Importance of Quality of Work Life

Despite many changes in family formation and a growing trend of individualization, the family remains a cornerstone of modern societies. Organisational decision-making should be a part of the work. Increasingly employees themselves now do that portion of a job that, formerly, managers did. This way work becomes more rewarding since people's jobs have a greater component of growth and learning. Organisations seeking competitive advantage through human resources require that they don't want employees who can follow rules; they want people who will make up their own rules.

Consensus theorists believe that, as far as the organisation of work is concerned, there is no fundamental conflict of interest between managers and employees. This implies that boosting performance and improving the quality of working life are two sides of the same coin. In the ideal-centered studies, this assumption is easily found. However, the restrictive use of human labour discards an important potential for productivity. All-round tasks do not involve any dangers, only opportunities; qualifications and professional autonomy are forces of production that need to be used more intensively. Today widespread and deep learning is essential as an informated

Need for quality of work life programmes

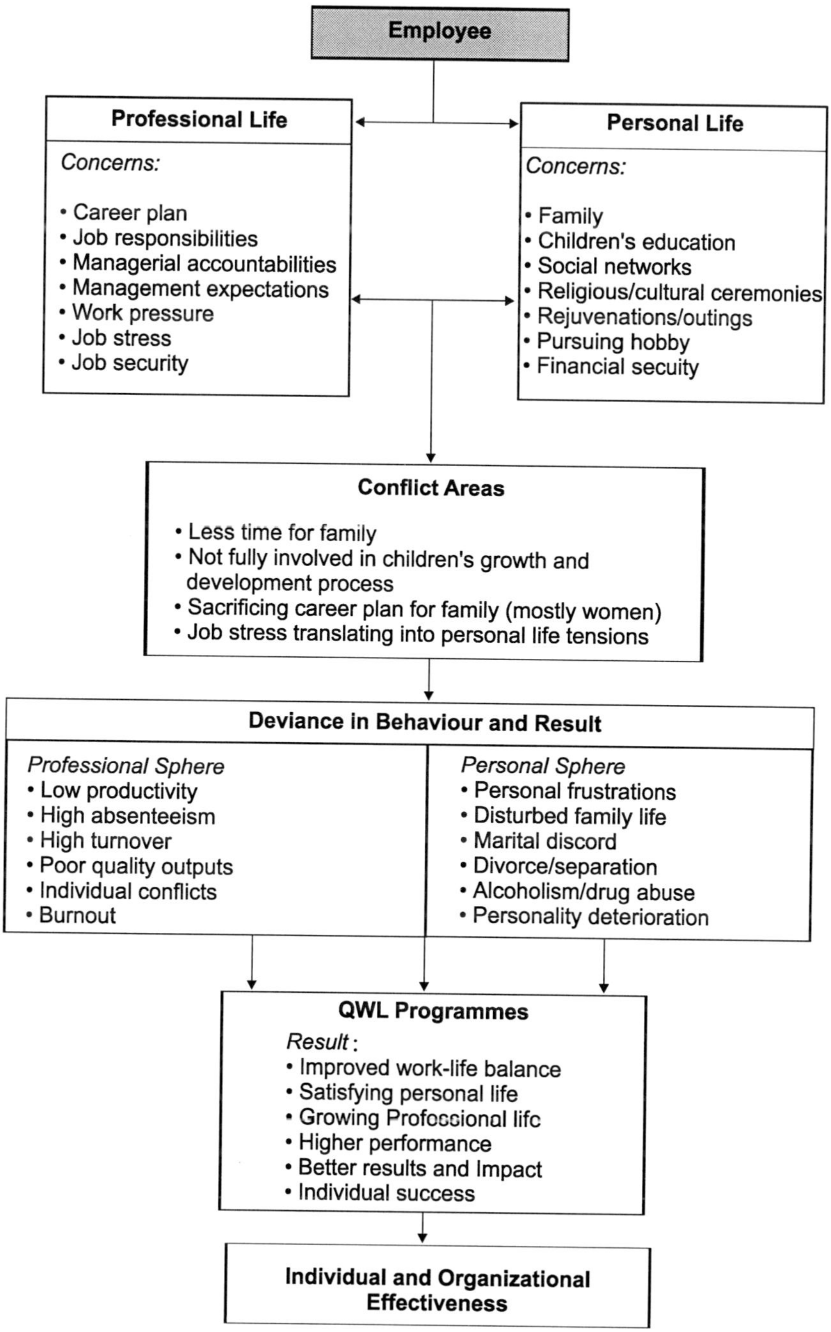

Fig. 9.3 : Need for QWL

organisation is structured to promote the possibility of useful learning among all members and thus presupposes relations of equality. *Dankbaar : (1997)* observes that in recent years, Socio-technical Systems Design also started to see performance and quality of working life as two sides of the same coin.

Thus, if quality of life at work could be improved, it would benefit and reward the individual employee and the organisation, its customers and society as a whole.

Measuring Return of Work-Life Balance Programmes

Deloitte and Touche have been measuring the saving of flexible working arrangements for over 10 years. This is done by applying the standard replacement multiplier to the average annual salary of workers who would have left had flexible work schedules not been an available option. The firm then multiplied those figures by the number of respondents to an internal survey who said they would have quit the firm for that reason. The savings were $41.5 million dollars.

Source : Levinson (1996)

Bibliography :

Levinson, H., "When Executives Burn Out", Harvard Business Review on work and life balance, Vol. 74, No. 4, July-August 1996, Pp. 153-161.

Increasing Quality of Work Life

To build and sustain quality of work life in an organisation, it is important to design motivating jobs for high internal employee motivation, high growth satisfaction and high job satisfaction. The reasons for effective job design with respect to quality of work life is as mentioned below:

→ Well designed jobs produce three critical psychological states:

- Meaningfulness - believe that work is important.
- Responsibility - feel personally responsible for how the work turns out
- Knowledge of results - know how well the job was performed.

→ Psychological states produced by five core job dimensions:

- Skill variety - different job activities involving several skills
- Task identity - completion of a whole, identifiable piece of work
- Task significance - important impact on the lives of others

- Autonomy - independence and discretion in making decisions
- Feedback - information about job performance

→ Effective job enrichment increases all five-core dimensions:

- Effectiveness of a job enrichment program depends on a person's growth need strength.
- Growth need strength - degree to which individuals want personal and psychological development.

However, while designing jobs, the following principles must be followed as mentioned in the box:

Job Design Principles

- **Core Job Characteristics:**
- Task Variety – some, not too much
- Skill Variety – use different levels
- Feedback – communicate employees immediately as they reach their targets
- Task Identity – clearly define job objectives
- Task autonomy – Employees should have some control over their work environment

- **Critical Psychological States:**
- Meaningfulness of work – opportunities for creativity, innovation and self-development
- Responsibility for work outcomes – Empowerment
- Knowledge of results – predefined job objectives

Ways to Increase Quality of Work Life

Quality of work life is key to integrating human resources into the organisation for achieving higher productivity, job satisfaction, higher morale and commitment.

Quality of work life can be increased as depicted in figure 9.4.

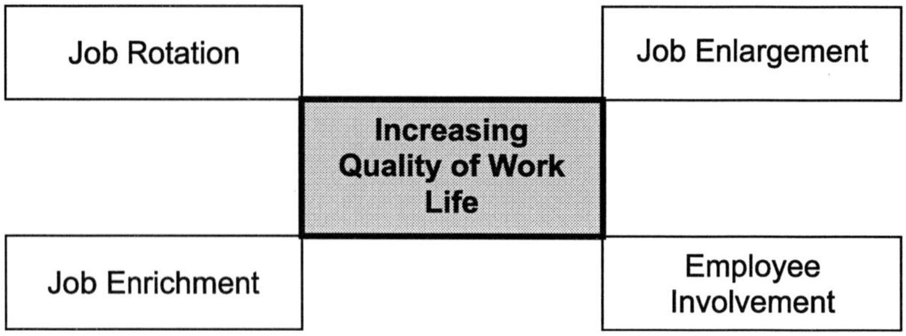

Fig. 9.4 : Increasing QWL

Increasing Quality of Work Life involves:

1. Job Rotation:

Job rotation is the movement between different jobs. One day a person may be working in one part of the organisation and the next day they may work in a different part. This prevents the employees gething bored as with job rotation they are doing different jobs all the time and learning new skills. This fosters cross training and multi skilling so they are able to carry out many different jobs. Multi skilling benefits the employer as if they are short of staff in one area, they can move people across.

Job rotation can benefit both employees and organisations. Employees learn new skills and face less boredom from performing similar tasks over and over. Greater variety and a wide range of tasks makes work more interesting and challenging. Job rotation benefits organisations by boosting innovation by enabling employees to apply knowledge of one task to others. Moreover, exposing employees to other types of jobs within the organisation promotes a better understanding of what others in the organisation do and how each job contributes to the whole. Finally, a multi-skilled workforce can more readily adapt to changing markets.

Consider LG Electronics India Ltd. In the past five years, close to half the Korean electronics major's 2,800 employees have switched functions within the organisation at least twice.

However, job rotation is to be practiced cautiously from an organisational perspective. If a performer is burned out, the better strategy is to deal with that problem by increasing positive reinforcement for day-to-day work. Otherwise the employee will not only exhibit the same behaviour problems in other positions, but also bring those behaviours back to the old job when they return to it.

2. Job Enlargement:

Job enlargement is doing different tasks and not just the same thing all the time. It may involve taking on more duties and adding variety to an employee's job. Horizontal loading is often used which is giving people more jobs to do that require the same level of skill. Job enlargement (sometimes also referred to as "horizontal loading") involves the addition of extra or similar tasks to a job.

In job enlargement, the job itself remains essentially unchanged. However, by widening the range of tasks that need to be performed, the employee experiences less repetition and monotony that is common on production lines, which rely upon the division of labour.

With job enlargement, the employee rarely needs to acquire new skills to carry out the additional task, and the motivational benefits of job enrichment are not usually experienced.

One important negative aspect of job enlargement is that sometimes employees view it as a requirement to carry out more work for the same amount of pay.

3. Job Enrichment:

Job enrichment aims to create greater opportunities for individual achievement and recognition by expanding the task to increase not only variety but also responsibility and accountability. This can also include greater employee autonomy, increased task identity and greater direct contact with other employees performing various other tasks. This increases the motivation of the employees and contributes significantly in increasing productivity and employee retention.

4. Employee Involvement:

Employee involvement is creating an environment in which people have an impact on decisions and actions that affect their jobs. The effective involvement of employees as partners in organisation's decision-making processes is a key element in developing capacity for continuing improvement. It ensures that employees understand how what they do contributes to the organisation's achievement of objectives, and that their actions affect how the organisation is perceived internally and externally.

Enhanced employment involvement is seeking the views of employees (as individuals or through representative bodies) before decisions are taken and taking them into account when reaching a decision.

There is no one template for successful employee involvement. Each organisation needs to find a solution, which suits its own culture. Effective employee involvement develops high performance workplace. Employee involvement increases ownership and commitment, retains best employees, and fosters an environment in which people choose to be motivated and contributing.

How to involve employees in decision making and continuous improvement activities is the strategic aspect of involvement and can include such methods as suggestion system, manufacturing cells, work teams, continuous improvement meetings, Kaizen (continuous improvement) events, corrective action processes, and periodic discussions with the managers.

Intrinsic to most employee involvement processes is training in team effectiveness, communication, and problem solving; the development of reward and recognition systems, and frequently, the sharing of gains made through employee involvement efforts.

Employee involvement is not the goal nor is it a tool, as practiced in many organisations. Rather, it is a management and leadership philosophy about how people are most enabled to contribute to continuous improvement and the ongoing success of their work organisation.

Clutterbuck defines 'balance' as "a state where an individual manages real or potential conflict between different demands on his time and energy in a way that satisfies his or her needs for well-being and self-fulfilment. Therefore, achieving work-life balance can arguably be boiled down to:

- Being aware of different demands on employee's time and energy;
- Having the ability to make choices in the allocation of time and energy;
- Knowing what values an employee wishes to apply to choices; and
- Making (conscious) choices.

Determinants/Categories of Quality of Work Life

Improving quality of work life is central to organisations seeking to stay competitive. There are various categories of tools and techniques of human resource development subsystems to improve quality of work life. Some of the major determinants/categories are discussed below (see figure 9.5).

1. Fair and Equitable Compensation:

Organisations have to ensure suitable assessment and determination of job worth for the purpose of compensation through a comprehensive job evaluation system. A comprehensive job evaluation system ensures fairness and equity in compensation for jobs of similar skills, competencies, efforts, responsibilities and working conditions so that the differences in relative value among jobs are consistent and accurate. Such a practice helps to motivate, seek commitment, effectively engage and strategically retain employees, especially the key personnel and best professionals.

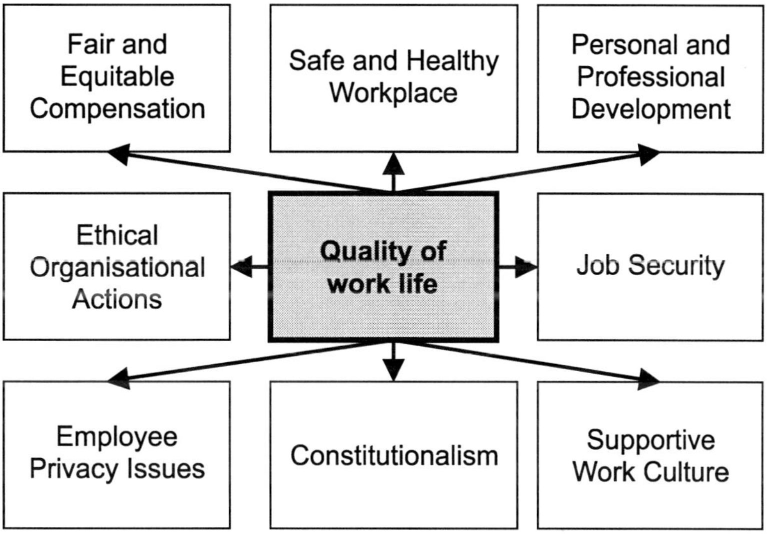

Fig. 9.5 : Determinants of QWL

2. Safe and Healthy Workplace:

Nearly all deaths, illnesses and injuries can be prevented. Workplace injuries and deaths are not really "accidents" because they normally have well-known causes that can be controlled. Eliminating or controlling dangerous working conditions will prevent "accidents." It assumes that employees have full control over how work is done. The challenge is to change the working conditions that caused the incident rather than blaming the victim.

Building a safe and healthy workplace means getting people involved. Getting employees involved with health and safety issues is a good way to increase participation in the management of an organisation, after all safety and healthy at workplace concerns all employees, shareholders and government. It is also a good way to solve problems.

Workplace safety is a good issue in which to involve members because:

- Health and safety affects all employees;
- Health and safety concerns can move employees to take action; and
- Health and safety issues can be won.

A safe and healthy workplace improves employee morale and productivity—all by creating a "safety culture."

3. Personal and Professional Development:

Personal and professional development is more than skills training and involves various integrated techniques, theories and behavioural concepts. Optimising individual performance through progressive personal and professional development significantly improves business performance.

The personal and professional development enables individuals to achieve critical personal changes and professional agility, specifically to:

- Updating personal identity, attitude, values and beliefs; and
- Increasing congruency and satisfaction.

Personal and professional development tends to achieve results because:

- It creates balance in the system (the person as a whole);
- It is realistic (and is perceived by the person as being achievable and relevant);
- It reduces stress; and
- It increases personal control.

Many situations benefit from the improvements arising from effective personal and professional development, for example:

- Within a organisational environment - producing better organisational performance and effectiveness;
- To improve self-awareness;
- To improve personal communication with others;
- To improve personal relationships with others; and
- Reducing and resolving conflict and stress.

4. Job Security:

Job security is pre-requisite of having a motivated, satisfied, committed and productive workforce. Although in today's business and employment scenario, job security is fast disappearing. Organisations now emphasize 'employability'. However, it is still a very compelling reason for effective employee performance and devotion to his job and eventually the organisation.

5. Supportive Work Culture:

The influence of the work environment on the health and wellness of employees is profound. First there is the physical look, feel, smell, and sounds of the workplace. In a supportive environment, employees feel that the organisation they work for provides them with encouragement, opportunity, and rewards for healthy lifestyles. And the spirit that results is highly contagious. Employees who feel cared are naturally more loyal and productive.

A supportive work culture involves the followings:

- Availability of friendly facilities such as vending machines with healthy food choices, Cafeteria, Noise levels are safe and conducive to concentration, Work station furniture conforms to ergometric standards, Lockers and showers are available for employees who work out before work or during breaks, Stairs are clean and well lit, convenient and pleasant to use, etc;
- Practice of proactive policies such as emergency procedures are developed, known, and practiced, flexible work schedules allow employees to exercise, attend children's school conferences, non-smoking policy is enforced, excessive overtime is discouraged, membership at fitness facility is partially reimbursed, shift workers are scheduled to allow adequate rest, employee assistance programme available to help employees with depression, family problems, etc; and
- Consistent recognition and rewards for success such as attention, praise, and rewards are given for wellness achievements, managers model and support healthy behaviour, etc.

6. Constitutionalism:

'Constitutionalism' means that the organisational framework must be stable, so as to provide an enduring set of expectations regarding the behaviour of the organisation. Constitutionalism comes from political philosophy and in the organisational context takes the position that an organisation, in order to be legitimate, must have legal limits on its powers. Thus, the organisation's authority ends up depending upon actually staying within those limits. An organisation, which goes beyond its limits, loses its authority and legitimacy. An organisation using its power and authority judiciously and justifiably fosters greater employee commitment, loyalty and ethical behaviour.

7. Employee Privacy Issues:

Organisations want to ensure that their employees are doing a good job, but employees don't want their every sneeze or trip to the water cooler logged. That's the essential conflict of workplace monitoring. New technologies make it possible for organisations to monitor many aspects of their employees' jobs, especially on telephones (to monitor calls with clients or customers for reasons of quality control), computer terminals (to see what is on the screen or stored in the employees' computer terminals and hard disks and/or to monitor Internet usage such as web-surfing and electronic mail), through electronic (to review contents of e-mail) and voice mail, and when employees are using the Internet. Such monitoring is virtually unregulated. Therefore, unless organisation policy specifically states otherwise (and even this is not assured), the organisation may listen, watch and read most of workplace communications. It is the interest of the organisation to declare its policy on employee privacy issues beforehand and strictly adhere to it. This will help in forging a dyadic relationship between the organisation and its human resources.

Unfortunately there is no explicit law on privacy issues in India.

8. Ethical Organisational Behaviour:

'Ethics' is the process of thinking that involves the values and principles that underscore our choices and commitments in decisions, actions and conduct' (*Nancarrow*). Actions are dictated by values. Identifying organisational values - both proclaimed and actual - will assist an organisation to ensure that all its actions are commensurate with these values, and enable it to put in place a robust structure to support the operationalisation of the values. Many ethical problems for multinationals and companies trading far from their home base arise because of differing value systems. Ethics emphasizes setting boundaries around what is acceptable and what is unacceptable in workplace decisions and behaviour. Being ethical involves fulfilling individual responsibilities and involves responsibly serving the customer and public interest.

Hence, the role and relevance of quality of work life can be summed up in the words of *Mary P. Malone,* "Employees will treat customers only as well as they are treated and not any better."

Review and Discussion Questions

Question 1: Define and explain the concept and scope of Quality of Work Life.

Question 2: What are the major objectives and benefits of Quality of Work Life?

Question 3: How can Quality of Work Life be increased?

Question 4: Enlist the ways/strategies to increase Quality of Work Life.

Question 5: Define the concept of Quality of Work Life. What are the determinants of Quality of Work Life?

Question 6: Critically examine the present scenario of Quality of Work Life in the Indian Industries. Give suitable examples to justify your answer.

Question 7: Formulate a Research Design for carrying out research in improving Quality of Work Life in a manufacturing company. Also state clearly the objectives and possible hypothesis of your research study.

Question 8: Write short notes on:

i) Quality of Work Life
ii) Job Rotation
iii) Job Enrichment
iv) Job Enlargement

Exhibit: 9 – A

Case Situation

•*Before attempting this section please read Chapter - 14 on Case Study.*

•*Please read the following case situations and answer the questions.*

Q 1. You are working as HRD Manager in a chemical company. One of your best performing employee puts in his paper citing personal reasons. You called him to your office and discussed the reasons of seeking a change. During the discussion, it comes to your knowledge that employees is leaving your company for the following reasons only:

- Long working hours. At times 18 hours a day.
- Hectic production schedule due to improper production planning.
- Routine and monotonous job content.

What action would you take now?

Q 2. You conducted a productivity analysis of marketing staff in your company. The results reveal that productivity levels are going down, primarily due to high stress levels induced by increasing targets to achieve sales targets, less time available to staff to spend time with their family/relatives, and fear of failure. How would you improve this situation?

Exhibit: 9 – B

Case Study

- *Before attempting this section please read Chapter - 14 on Case Study.*
- *Please read the following case study and answer all the subsequent questions.*

Introduction to the organisation:

Tandra Fashions Ltd. (TFL) was established 35 years ago, to serve a specialised niche in garment industry. The Company was profit making until a few years ago.

For the last three years, the company is not doing well. It has missed many orders from buyers; its market share has been consistently sliding down, cost per unit is steadily rising, etc.

Brief Description of the Problem:

The management called a meeting of all senior/key personnel of the organisation to solve this problem. It was decided to constitute a Management Committee under the chairperson of Head-HR for the said purpose.

The committee found that the major problems were:

- Lack of job satisfaction of the employees.
- Employee 'burnout' is increasing due to high job pressures.
- Lack of proper and adequate working conditions.
- Ambiguity in organizational policies, rules and regulation concerning employees.
- Lack of incentives higher and better production.

The committee discussed the matter with top management and it was decided to initiate the following HRD strategies:

- Planned job rotation, job enrichment and job enlargement was embarked on, especially for assembly line workers.
- Increasing job clarity through setting up of key result objectives.

- Workplace to be suitably modified in terms of ventilation, cooling/heating, lighting, walking/moving passages, material stacking, etc.
- HRD function to formulate and communicate HRD policies, rules and regulations to all employees, keeping in view a participative spirit.
- Productivity linked incentive systems are to be devised and implemented.

Questions:

1. What is the link between falling business of the organisation and satisfaction and participation of employees at the workplace in this case?

2. What are the major problems with Tandra Fashions Ltd.? How best can they be solved? What HRD instrument/ mechanism would you apply here?

3. How has leadership affected change process in this Company?

CHAPTER

10 Managing Quality & Productivity Through Human Resources

Chapter Synopsis

All strategies for improving quality and productivity in an organisation involve essentially its human resources. It's the employees who bring value to the organisation through their commitment, motivation and unrelenting drive to achieve success of their organisations. Therefore, human resource development is the prime instrument to make quality and productivity improvement programmes a grand success.

This chapter explains these concepts in order to highlight the role of human resources in managing quality and productivity.

This Chapter contains:

Managing Quality: Concept of quality, Definitions of quality, Importance/Benefits of quality, Role of human resources in managing quality, QC Circle – Concept, Constitution and Process.

Managing Productivity: Concept of productivity, Meaning of productivity, Role of human resources in improving productivity and The Link between Quality and Productivity.

Review & discussion questions, Case situation and Case study.

Managing Quality and Productivity through Human Resources

Managing Quality

Without properly mobilizing human resource it is futile to fit quality tools to their working. The challenge is not in adopting a tool, but more in whether people in the organisation use the tool. Organisation's quality endeavour will not be fruitful unless employees are not practicing the various tools they have been trained for.

Organisations implementing quality systems should not be obsessed with improving their operational processes - product quality, reduced inventory; reduce downtime and improved set-up time. But effort should be made to modify the existing management processes in the organisation:

Information flow

Delegation of responsibility

Authority

Team-based functioning

Performance-based compensation

Quality movement cannot succeed unless employees are involved in the various businesses processes in an organisation. The best way to ensure commitment is to empower employees, to involve them in making decisions of the day-to-day functioning of the organisation.

Definitions:

A few noteworthy definitions of Quality are as follows:

1. "Quality is conformance to requirements or specifications".

(Crosby: 1979)

2. "Quality is fitness for use".

(Juran: 1974)

3. "Quality is the loss that a product costs to society after being shipped other than any losses by its intrinsic functions".

(Taguchi)

From an analytical study of the above definitions, we may conclude that:

Quality is the totality of features and characteristics of a product or service that bear on its ability to satisfy stated or implied needs.

Importance/Benefits of Quality

There are many benefits of quality as enumerated below:

1. Quality lowers cost and increases productivity by reducing wastage, reworking, products returned due to poor quality cost of re-dispatch, etc;
2. Quality increases market share by satisfying customers through supply of quality products and services;
3. Quality improves organisation's reputation by providing quality products and services. This helps the organisation to secure more business and consequently more profits;
4. Quality improves employee's morale by providing job satisfaction gained from doing an error free and perfect job; and
5. Quality increases benefits for employees by;

- Lowering cost and increasing productivity.
- Increasing the market share for the organisation.
- Improving organisation's reputation.
- Giving job satisfaction.

Role of Human Resources in Managing Quality

Quality is the most important reasons, which can persuade a customer to buy a product or avail services. Quality has been and will always remain a conscious and deliberate effort on the part of organisations intending to stay competitive. In order to build Quality into the products, organisations need to realign from "Quality Control" system to "Quality Management" system. The workforce needs to be Lean Thinker i.e. to "Learn to See the Wastes Everywhere" and constantly strive to improve by focusing on driving out waste in all it's forms. The goal is to establish processes that allow people to execute them flawlessly everyday. Technique involves identification and elimination of non-value adding activities in the organisation and strive to be more productive. This involves everyone – both Managers and Workers with the following broad objectives: -

–Improvement/change for the better

–Ongoing/continuity

The first stage is to review current work standards, to check the current performance and then estimate how and how much performance can still be improved.

One of the most important measures of Quality is TRUST – of internal and external customers. The active participation of all personnel is the basis for continuous improvement in the organisation. This refers to Team Concept. Team Management is a HR and Management Technique.

Quality Management is a management approach for competitive success. It is for management of change. It shall be more successful if a great degree of management support exists, communication and teamwork between managers and employees is excellent, effective supervision, effective correction action procedures and follow up of quality problems.

It is basically a down stream management technique and it operates at lower management levels but relies heavily on senior management support and direction to develop the necessary culture that challenges worker to be creative in finding solutions to workplace problems without the need for hard cash. It enables incremental improvements.

Quality management system entails:

1. Formulate Vision of the organisation related to customer expectation i.e. understanding & quantifying customer expectations;
2. Define the strategic direction of the organisation;
3. Set measures for the strategic objectives of the organisation;
4. Collect data continually on the measures set and analyse;
5. Identify the opportunities for improvement and covert them to success;
6. Set up a management control action of continuous reviews on the improvements made;

7. Ownership; and

8. Empowerment.

Managing quality is basically managing human processes because no quality system will be effective without fundamental change in attitude of human resources and management. It involves:

- Knowledge.
- Creativity.
- Leadership.
- Learning.
- Motivation.
- Self-Management.
- Teamwork.
- Job security.
- Change Management.
- Job satisfaction.

Human resources have a major role to play in quality management in an organisation and they stand benefited in the long run with the success of an organisation's quality movement.

Given below are some key roles:

1. To achieve quality everywhere:

Quality does not mean product or service quality only, but it is broad concept and includes housekeeping, discipline, interpersonal relations, behaviour and customer service also.

2. To achieve excellence:

Employees should always look for excellence in their work and never settle for anything less than that.

3. To be improvement oriented:

Quality is a way of life, which is a continuous process. Employees should always be have improvement goals in their minds and should seek every opportunity to improve their work and processes. This will help sharpen the skills and competencies of the employees and inculcate a deep conviction towards quality.

4. To be well informed:

To achieve quality in work, employees must know their jobs well and be familiar with the products and services of the organisation. They should continually seek information from appropriate sources to know more about products and services, which will enhance their contributions to quality improvement.

5. To learn on life long basis:

Learning process in a human being never ends. Therefore, employees, irrespective of their age, skill, background, qualification, etc. should come out freely to learn new things and increase their competence.

6. To achieve customer excelleration:

Employees should serve their internal and external customers with respect, enthusiasm and honesty. This is critical because only customer satisfaction will keep an organisation in business and employees can play a pivotal role in it.

7. To take pride in work:

Whatever an employee does in an organisation, he should take pride in his work. All jobs in the organisation are important because every work is interdependent and failure at one stage will result in failure of the entire work process.

8. To participate actively:

Employees must participate actively in the organisation's quality improvement programme by giving constructive suggestions about improvement in the environment and jobs.

The evidence of the correlation between successful quality programmes and competitive advantage is growing. Research during the last decade has proved that the stock prices of total quality companies in the US have grown by almost 17 per cent compared to a CAGR of 10.5 per cent for the stock market during the same period. Quality management tools and techniques, properly implemented, have the power to create sustainable competitive advantage.

Therefore, having a dedicated and pool of talented people can build superior quality of products and services built in which in turn generate customer satisfaction and loyalty. This in turn generates high profits and growth and in turn generates owner satisfaction.

QC Circle

A Quality Control Circle is a small group of employees who meet regularly to solve problems in their work area.

QC circle mainly handles the following kind of problems:

- Reducing defect ratio.
- Reducing customer complaints.
- Improve customer service.
- Reduce wastage of material.
- Reduce wear and tear of tools.
- Reduce lead-time.
- Increase daily output.
- Reduce inventory levels.
- Improve safety.
- Reduce absenteeism.
- Improve housekeeping.

QC circle includes a **Steering committee,** which is made up of senior management staff to provide leadership i.e. to direct, support, encourage, guide, evaluate and reward the QC circle programme of the organisation, **Circle leader,** each circle has a leader who is also the member of the circle to provides training, supervision and facilitate the inter-acts of the circle, **Circle members** who are usually employees from the same work area so that they share a common understanding and knowledge of problem and **Facilitator** is not a member of the circle and is a link between the circle and the organisation. He trains, coaches and advises members and helps them through difficulties.

A QC circle process involves the following steps (see figure 10.1):

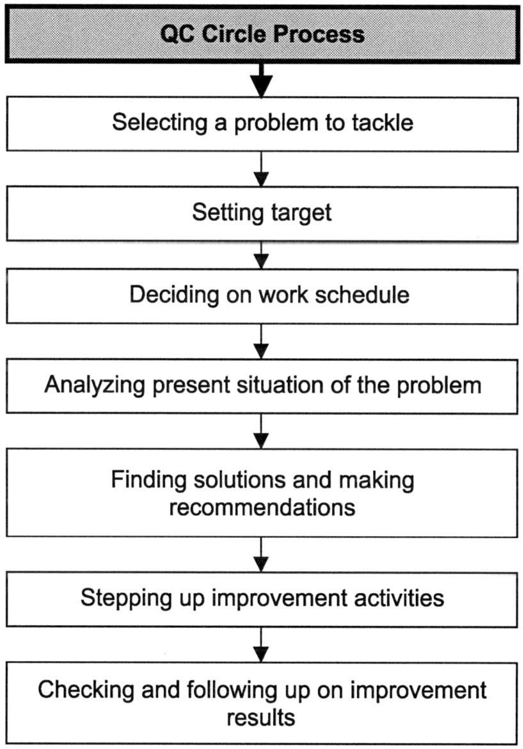

Fig. 10.1 : QC Circle Process

1. Selecting a problem to tackle:

The problem is to be identified in order to tackle it in the QC circle. This requires having a deep understanding of the problem in question.

2. Setting target:

Once a problem has been identified, the level of results expected is to be decided. It is important to set a target so that the objective to be achieved is clear to all.

3. Deciding on work schedule:

For problem solving to be carried out, it is important that everyone must think and put in their effort. The basis for good teamwork is an appropriate allocation of the workload with everyone sharing a common goal – problem solving.

4. Analyzing the present situation of the problem:

To get a focal point, all possible sources should be tapped to collect relevant information and data. QC tools such as pareto chart, check sheet, flowchart, fish bone diagram (cause and effect diagram), histogram, scatter, control chart, can then be used as weapon to thoroughly analyze the data.

5. Finding solutions and making recommendations:

Once the situation has been analyzed and all data are ready, various alternative solutions can be found through brainstorming and the best solution must be chosen.

6. Stepping up the improvement activity:

Using the ideas which are accepted, plans for implementation is drawn out and executed positively. However, before doing that permission of the required authority (e.g. Manager) should be obtained.

7. Checking and following up on the improvement results:

It is essential to check the improvement results and maintain the process to ensure success of QC circle.

Managing Productivity

One of the major objectives of human resource development is to enhance the productivity of the organisation. Productivity is defined as ratio between output and input. Productivity is a dependent on competence, motivation and empowerment. Mathematically, it can be shown as:

Productivity = f (C, M, E)

Where, f = function of
C = Competence
M = Motivation
E = Empowerment

Competence is the ability of human resources to perform effectively a given job and it depends on motivation, knowledge, skill and attitude of the jobholder, which can be continuously enhanced by training and development by the organisation. Motivation depends on enabling factors provided by the organisation such as coaching, mentoring, career management and feedback. Environment of the organisation is key to effective functioning of its personnel and is dependent on level of trust between superiors and subordinates, empowerment, leadership skills and human resource philosophy of the organisation. The inter-linkage of productivity with HRD is depicted in figure 10.2.

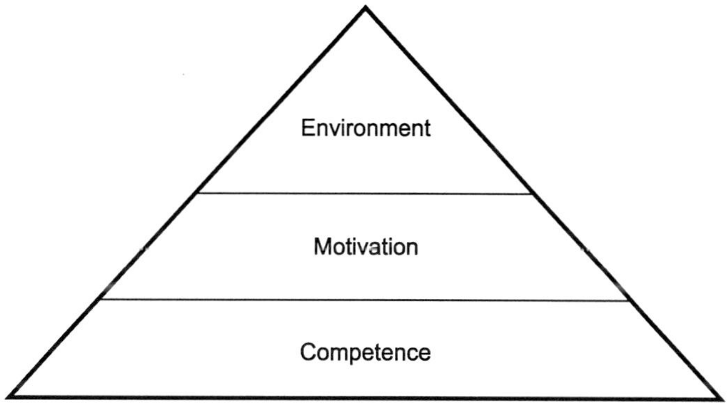

Fig. 10.2 : Relationship between Productivity & HRD

Before embarking on productivity improvement programmes, it is important to identify causes of low productivity. Common causes of low productivity are:

- Low employee motivation due to lower salaries, lack of recognition, monotonous jobs and lack of career development;
- Dissatisfied customers;
- Waste of resources such as material, time, labour, and finance;
- Careless wage negotiations;
- Poor conflict and grievance management; and
- Ineffective communications.

Role of Human Resources in Improving Productivity

Human resource development plays a vital role in improving productivity in the organisation. No method will be successful unless human resource development plays a key role. For this, organisation has to create appropriate environment and strategies for development of human resources and only then the employees can contribute to improving productivity. Human resource development function plays the role of facilitator and intervenes through training and development programmes. Productivity programme should be implemented in a systematic and step-by-step manner with a time frame in mind.

Given below are some key roles:

1. To put team efforts:

Teams can generate better results, as mind of many is superior to the mind of one.

2. To develop competitive spirit:

Employees always look forward to new challenges and like competing with others. Creating competition among various groups and announcing rewards for best performing group can greatly enhance productivity.

3. To institute suggestion schemes:

A suggestion scheme encourages employees to offer ideas relating to their work areas or other areas, which will help the organisation to reduce cost.

4. To improve communication:

Communication with employees plays a vital role in improving productivity. Therefore, a proper communication channel provides no scope for rumor-mongers to take undue advantage of the situation.

5. Morning assemblies:

Employee's loyalty increases through various morning assemblies which includes exercises, company song, reciting company objectives, short talk and daily announcements, if any.

6. Training and development:

Training and development programme of an organisation should be well planned and generally covers:

(*a*) *Orientation:*

Upon recruitment, new employees should undergo through a structured orientation programme to provide information on the organisation, knowledge of rules and regulations, socialization with other employees and job requirements.

(*b*) *Product knowledge training:*

Employees must be informed about the organisation's products and services. This will keep the employees updated and they will feel proud of being involved.

(*c*) *Customer service training:*

To compliment product knowledge, employees must also be informed and trained on the importance of customer service as each employee is serving the customer in one way or the other.

(d) Personal development:

Employees should be sent to courses for personal development related to their work, which will foster development of their competencies, skills and teamwork.

The Link between Quality and Productivity

1. Effective quality improvement can be instrumental in increasing productivity and reducing cost.
2. The cost of achieving quality improvements and increased productivity is often negligible.

The impact of increased quality on organisational performance is depicted in figure 10.3.

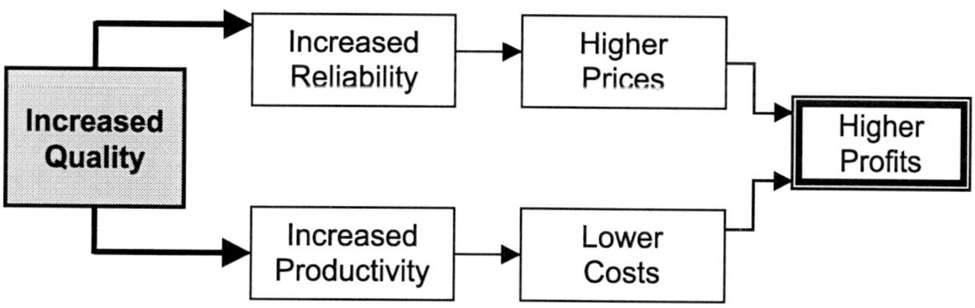

Fig. 10.3 : Relationship between Quality & Profits

The purpose of HRD is to improve organisational performance through increased productivity and quality.

Role of HRD Manager shall be managing individual expectations and experience in the workforce as team role preferences are influenced by the immediate organisational task environment.

Review and Discussion Questions

Question 1: Define and explain the concept quality.

Question 2: What are the benefits of quality management?

Question 3: What is the role of human resource in improving quality in an organisation?

Question 4: What is QC Circle? What is the process of QC Circle?

Question 5: Discuss the concept of Productivity. What is the role of human resource in improving productivity?

Question 6: Write short notes on:

i) Link between quality and productivity
ii) QC Circle

Exhibit: 10 – A

Case Situation

- *Before attempting this section please read Chapter - 14 on Case Study.*
- *Please read the following case situations and answer the questions.*

Q 1. Design a productivity improvement programme for a manufacturing company. Outline:

- Objectives of your study
- Methods you would use to study the existing productivity standard
- Recommendations you would like to make

Q 2. Design a QC Circle programme for a TV assembly unit.

Exhibit: 10 – B

Case Study

- *Before attempting this section please read Chapter - 14 on Case Study.*
- *Please read the following case study and answer all the subsequent questions.*

Introduction to the organization:

Partho Autoplast Pvt. Ltd. (PAPL) was established 10 years ago, to manufacture and market automobile plastic ancillaries to auto majors. The Company is a profit making and has been growing steadily. The company is major OEM suppliers to large auto companies and has won a few national awards for its unfailing commitment to quality.

PAPL has successful/effective quality control circles. Many innovative and cost saving ideas have been reaped from it which has improved not only the quality but productivity of the company.

The MD of the company started TQM journey some years back with focus on long-term transition to excellence.

Brief Description of the Problem:

The MD threw the huge challenge to his team to win the Deming award. He evolved a TQM model for his employees. He indoctrinated amongst his employees through training and quality circles. The company has built total quality in the product using cross-functional team. The TQM experiment has atleast four implications for successful implementation – relation to strategy, customer awareness, integration and flexibility.

Questions:

1. Why did the MD initiated TQM programme?
2. How was TQM instituted in the hearts and minds of the employees?
3. What programmes the company had prior to TQM to manage and improve quality?

CHAPTER

11 HRD Audit and Human Resource Accounting

Chapter Synopsis

Human resource development is a key factor in business success and improved organisational performance. Therefore, it is of utmost importance to organisations to evaluate the adequacy and appropriateness of their present HRD systems, structures, styles, cultures and competencies. Human resource development is an investment for improving the match between costs and revenues, therefore it is crucial for organisations to identify, quantify and account the value of human resources in order to get an optimum economic return on human capital investment.

This chapter explains these concepts in order to make HRD more business driven.

This Chapter contains:

HRD Audit: Concept of HRD audit, Definition of HRD audit, Objectives and purposes of HRD audit, Methodology of HRD audit, Role of HRD audit, Structure of HRD audit report, Concept of HRD scorecard, and Importance/ benefits of HRD audit.

HR Accounting: Concept of HR accounting, Definitions of HR accounting, Need of HR accounting, Objectives of HR accounting, Methods of HR accounting, Uses of HR accounting, Recent scenario of HR accounting, and Limitations of HR accounting.

Review & discussion questions, Case situation and Case study.

HRD Audit and Human Resource Accounting

HRD Audit

In the last two decades a large number of organisations have established human resources development departments, introduced new systems of human resource development, made structural changes in terms of differentiating the human resource development function and integrating it with HR function. A good number of CEOs saw a hope in human resource development for most of their problems, issues and challenges. In spite of substantial investments, there is a widespread feeling that human resource development has not lived up to the expectations of either the top management or the line managers. There are also examples of organisations where human resource development has taken a driver's seat and has given a lot of benefits. In today's competitive world, employees are the only reliable source of sustained competitive advantage. To get the best out of employees, there should be a good alignment of the human resource development function, its strategies, structure, systems, and styles with business and its goals. It should be aligned both with the short-term goals and long-term strategies. Also, the skills and styles of human resource development staff, the line managers and the top management should be synergistic with the human resource development goals and strategies.

HRD audit is a comprehensive evaluation of the current human resource development strategies, structure, systems, styles and skills in the context of the short and long-term business plans of an organisation. HRD audit attempts to find out the future HRD needs of the organisation after assessing the current human resource development activities and inputs available. *Dr. T. V. Rao* with his colleague *Dr. Udai Pareek* pioneered in India, a methodology for auditing human resource development function and implemented the same in a good number of Indian organisations successfully.

HRD audit starts with an understanding of the future business plans and corporate strategies. While HRD audit can be done even in organisations that lack well formulated future plans and strategies, it is most effective as a tool when the organisation already has such long-term plans. The HRD audit starts with the following objectives:

1. To analyse the long-term plans of the organisation;
2. To examine the current skills and competencies of the employees vis-à-vis the long term plans of the organisation;
3. To assess the available instruments and mechanisms of human resource development system in relation to their maturity and effectiveness; and
4. To examine the capabilities of human resource development staff to handle the pressing and future human resource development needs of the organisation.

These objectives form subsequently the basis of HRD audit strategies and methodology. The HRD audit normally attempts to assess the existing skills and the competency gaps in order to achieve the long-term business goals and short-term results of the organisation. The competencies may deal with technical managerial people and conceptual aspects. They may cover knowledge base, attitudes, values, skills and competencies.

Definition:

A few noteworthy definition of HRD Audit is as follows:

"HRD Audit is a comprehensive evaluation of human resource development encompassing strategies, systems, practices, structures, competencies, styles and culture and their appropriateness to achieve the short and long term business goals of the organisation".

(Dr. T.V. Rao)

Objectives and Purposes of HRD Audit

The major objectives are:

1. Organisational Growth – expansion, diversification and entering into a fast growth phase;
2. Professional Endowment – for promoting more professionalism and professional management;
3. Benchmarking – for improving human resource development practices;
4. Coping with Dissatisfaction – with any component; and
5. Leadership Change.

Methodology of HRD Audit

HRD audit is a tool to measure the maturity level of human resource development system of an organisation and starts with an evaluation of human resource development strategies. This is based on four metrics such as HRD competencies of the employees, human resource development systems maturity, HRD culture and linkage of human resource development to business strategy of the organisation.

HRD Audit starts with a close examination of the following organisational issues:

1. Examination of long term and short term plans and vision to assess competency requirements;
2. Identification of broad competency requirements for future business goals and objectives;
3. Examination of the existing human resource development strategies, systems and practices and assess their appropriateness to have the required competencies; and
4. Examination of the adequacies and inadequacies of human resource development structure, staff and their competencies, line managers and their attitudes, top management and their support, unions and their role in competence building for future.

HRD audit requires the use of a number of methods, which can be used in combination for desired results. In order to validate HRD audit, following methods are adopted:

1. Interview Method:

Top management and senior management (Line managers and HRD personnel) of the organisation are interviewed by the HRD auditor to solicit information, thinking and perspectives on the future growth plans and goals of the organisation. It involves understanding of the organisational culture, working style and work planning system of the organisation. Also, the readiness of human resource development strategies to pursue future organisational goals is also analyzed.

Such interviews are generally structured and must be intelligently drafted to seek relevant information and insight.

Now, the employees of the organisation are to be interviewed on same line, but the modus operandi will vary. Given large number of employees and constraints of time and resources, auditor uses sampling tools to interview representative employees about their perceptions on organisation's vision, mission, values, culture, strengths and areas of improvement, various opportunities, SWOT analysis of human resource development function and their activities, future prospects and their role in achieving the goals of the organisation. This is essentially a vision making exercise where the employees have a free hand to air their views and concerns.

2. Questionnaire Method:

Auditor designs, develops, and administers a questionnaire to asses various dimensions of human resource development including the competency of human resource development staff, line manager's styles, and implementation of various human resource development systems. It is a good practice to pilot the questionnaire before administering it to the employee to tests its validity and reliability. The questionnaire should be carefully constructed and must be in commensuration with the objectives of the HRD audit. The questionnaire should be given to a representative sample of the employees and its size should be as large as time, cost and resources permit for greater reliability of the data.

3. Observation Method:

HRD auditor should observe the employees in their natural environment such as at workplace, canteen, training centers, residential colony, etc. to assess the extent to which a human resource development conducive and supportive environment exists in the organisation.

4. Analysis of Records and Secondary Data Method:

Various secondary sources of the human resource development data such as training and development programmes conducted, frequency of the programmes, their duration, number of participation, evaluation and feedback of training, manner of assessment of training needs of employees and their business relevance, learning programmes and cultures to support learning, profile of human resources – biographical and professional credibility, etc. can provide the much needed insight into the organisation's human resource development assets and liabilities.

5. Workshop Method:

Large scale interactive process can be utilized to asses human resource development systems such as performance appraisal, potential appraisal, counseling, coaching and mentoring programmes, etc. a large number of employees is gathered in a single room and divided into small groups to conduct SWOT analysis on different dimensions of human resource development. Each group is then required to make a presentation on their theme and a representative presents it before all the groups for discussions and suggestions.

6. Task Forces Method:

A task force can be constituted to identify, evaluate and recommend a appropriate solution to the identified human resource development issues, problems, strategies and concerns. HRD auditor can work on this for further development and insight.

Role of HRD Audit

HRD Audit plays a pivotal role in proving business of an organisation as mentioned below:

1. Cost Effective – HRD audit is cost effective;
2. Provide Insight – it can give many insights into an organisation's affairs;
3. Promotes Strategic Leverages – it could get the top management to think in terms of strategic and long-term business plans;
4. Modify Style – changes in the style of top management;
5. Role Clarity – of human resource development department ;
6. Improves human resource development systems ;
7. Developing Competencies – increased focus on human resources and human competencies;
8. Effective Recruitment – better recruitment policies and more professional staff
9. Effective Training – more planning and more cost effective training; and
10. Enhancing Accountability – strengthening accountabilities through appraisal systems.

Many of the leading Indian Companies have done HRD Audit such as A.V. Birla Group, L&T, Crompton Greaves, Gujarat Gas, Apollo Tyres, Godrej Soaps, Wokhardt Hospitals, etc.

Structure of HRD Audit Report

HRD audit report is to be prepared by the auditor on the conclusion of HRD audit for appropriate consideration of the top management and senior managerial personnel. It should be brief, to the point and written in a generalist style. An outline of the report is given below:

1. Introduction:

This chapter deals with a brief introduction of the organisation and its characteristics, objectives and purpose of the HRD audit, various tools and methods employed, description of the human resource development systems framework, and future plans of the organisation.

2. Current status of HRD function:

This chapter deals with structure and staffing of human resource development function, its objectives and skills, various human resource development instruments and mechanisms employed, strengths, weaknesses, opportunities and threats of human resource development function.

3. General observation:

This chapter deals with general strengths, weaknesses and opportunities of the organisation in relation to its present competencies, future potential and competitors and various factors affecting the organisation's human resource development culture, competence and commitment building activities.

4. HRD systems:

This chapter describes the findings and recommendation of the audit pertaining to human resource planning, staffing, career planning and development, and succession management practices of the organisation and strategies for improvement, performance practices and improvement strategies for the organisation. It encompasses setting of performance objectives, evaluation, and development of employee's performance. Also, the practices pertaining to the feedback of performance evaluation are included. Approaches to needs identification of training and development programmes, their strategic relevance, application to workplace, methods of evaluation, organisational development initiatives, healthy culture and development-oriented climate

5. Recommendations and suggestions:

This chapter provides the various conclusions and recommended suggestions for improvement of human resource development policies, programmes, practices and strategies for the organisation based on the audit findings.

HRD Scorecard

The HRD scorecard assigns a four letter rating for each organisation on the extent of maturity level of human resource development in it. The letters represent the four critical dimensions of human resource development that contribute to business performance or organisational performance (for non-profit organisations). These four dimensions include:

- HRD systems maturity;
- HRD competencies in the organisation;
- HRD styles, culture and values; and
- Business linkages with HRD.

The human resource development systems maturity assesses the extent to which various human resources development subsystems and tools are well designed and are being implemented.

-First the systems should be appropriate and relevant to business goals or organisational goals.

-Second they should focus on as well as balance between current and future needs of the corporation.

-Third the human resource development strategies and systems should flow from the corporate strategies.

-Fourth the systems should be well designed and should have a structural maturity.

-Fifth they should be implemented well. The employees should be taking them seriously and follow meticulously what has been envisaged in each system. The overheads of implementation should be low. That is the monitoring requirements should be less arising out of the employees taking them seriously.

-Sixth the subsystems should be well integrated and should have internal synergy.

-Seventh they should be adequate and should take care of the HRD requirements of the organisation.

The following subsystems are assessed on the above criteria and depending upon the extent to which they meet the requirements a score is assigned.

- Human resource planning and recruitment.
- Performance appraisal system.
- Feedback and coaching mechanisms.
- Training, career development and succession planning.
- Job-rotation.
- OD Interventions.
- HR Information systems.

- Worker development methods and systems.
- Potential appraisal and development.
- Other subsystems, if any.

Each of them is assessed on a ten point rating scale where a score of 10 represents an extremely high level of maturity, 5 represents a moderate level of maturity and 1 represents an extremely low level of maturity. This dimension indicates the extent to which human resource development competencies are well developed in the organisation. The competencies include knowledge, attitudes, values and skills. The nature of competencies required for each category of employees are listed and assessed on the basis of the HRD audit.

Importance/Benefits of HRD Audit

HRD audit is cost-effective and can give many insights into an organisation's affairs. HRD audit can lead to several benefits as enlisted below:

1. Fostering strategic business plans:

The HRD audit begins with such strategic plans, but wherever it is non-existent, HRD audit compels top management to think about such plans. Since the employees cannot participate in an HRD audit without some sharing of these plans, the audit forces the top management to share their plans, which increases employee involvement and commitment to the achievement of the strategic business objectives of the organisation.

2. Clarity of role of HRD function:

HRD audit draws the attention of employees at various levels to the important role of the human resource development department, current as well as the future. Enhanced role clarity of human resource development function increases understanding of line managers about their human resource development role and increases their managerial and strategic support to the function. This helps in making human resource development activities more aligned to the business priorities of the organisation.

3. Organisational competency analysis:

HRD audit identifies the strengths and weaknesses in the some of the management systems existing in the organisation. It also points out to the absence of systems that can enhance human productivity and utilization of the existing competency base, which may have an effect on the work procedures, delegation of powers, clarification of roles and responsibilities, developing or streamlining of financial and accounting procedures and systems, strengthening the information systems, and sharing of information.

4. HRD systems analysis:

An HRD audit points out to the competence base required. It sets the stage and gives direction for the competency requirements of employees at various levels and thus provides a base for recruitment policies and procedures, retention strategies, talent management programmes, leadership development, performance appraisal, induction training, job-rotation, career planning and promotion policies, mentoring, communication, and training, etc. The HRD audit has helped most of the organisations in taking stock of the effectiveness of their human resource development systems and in designing or re-designing the human resource development systems.

5. Changes in the styles of top management:

One of the objectives of human resource development is to create a learning organisation. A learning culture can be created only if the top managers of the organisations exhibit a human resource development style of management. Such a style requires an empowering attitude, participative style of management, and an ability to convert and use mistakes, conflicts and problems as learning opportunities.

6. ROI analysis:

An HRD audit examines the return on investment (ROI) on various human resource development programmes and strategies such as training by looking into process of identifying training needs and utilization of training inputs and learning for organisation growth and development. As direct investments are made in training, any cost-benefit analysis draws the attention of the top management and HRD managers to review the training function with relative ease.

7. Increased focus on human resources and human competencies:

One of the results of an HRD audit is to focus on new knowledge, attitudes and skills required by the employees in the organisation. Comments are made about the technical, managerial, human and conceptual competencies of the staff at various levels. This differentiation has been found to help organisations identify and focus sharply on the competency requirements and gaps. The audit establishes a system of role clarity and fixing of accountabilities. This can take place through separate role clarity exercises or through the development of an appropriate performance appraisal system. In any case the attention of the organisation gets focused on developing the competency base of the organisation. More sensitivity is developed to the missing aspects of competencies.

8. Strengthening performance improvement mechanisms:

An HRD audit can give significant inputs about the existing state of the accountabilities of employees. This gets assessed through performance appraisals as well as through the work culture and other cultural dimensions. A number of organisations have introduced systems of performance planning, sharing of expectations and documenting the accountabilities of employees.

Human Resource Accounting

Until recently, the "value" of an organisation as measured within traditional balance sheets, e.g. buildings, production plant, etc., was viewed as a sufficient reflection of the organisation's assets. However, with the growing emergence of the knowledge economy, this traditional valuation has been called into question due to the recognition that human capital is an increasingly important part of an organisation's total value. Human resources are one of the most important features of many businesses - especially in an economy where there is an increasing shift towards service-based industries. Human resources account for a large proportion of many businesses' costs and it is the people that invariably drive a business. Accounting of these resources therefore is an integral part of business success.

This has led to two important questions:

- How to assess the value of human capital in addition to an organisation's tangible assets; and
- How to improve the development of human capital in organisation. The emergence of methods for accounting human resources aimed at measuring, developing and managing the human capital in an organisation, can thus be said to reflect the need for improving measuring and accounting practices as well as human resource development.

Hermansson (1964) was the first to attempt to include figures on human capital in the balance sheet, which became known as human resource accounting. Human resource accounting (HRA) as an approach defined as "the process of identifying, measuring and communicating information about human resources in order to facilitate effective management within an organisation". It is an extension of the accounting principles of matching costs and revenues and of organizing data to communicate relevant information in financial terms.

The accounting of human resources can be seen as just as much a question of philosophy or technique. This is one of the reasons behind the variety of approaches and is further underlined by the broad range of purposes for which accounting human resources can be used, e.g. as an information tool for internal and/or external use (employees, customers, investors, etc.), and as a decision-making tool for human resource development.

The emergence of methods for accounting human resources (methods aimed at measuring, developing and/or managing the human capital in an organisation) can thus be said to reflect the need to improve measuring and accounting practices and human resource development.

Definitions:

A few noteworthy definitions of HR Accounting are as follows:

1. "Human Resource Accounting can be defined as the process of identifying, qualifying, accounting and forecasting the value of human resources in order to facilitate effective human resource management".

(John Bratton and Jeffrey Gold: 2003)

2. "Human Resource Accounting is the process of identifying and measuring data about human resources and communicating this information of interested parties".

(American Accounting Association: 1973)

3. "Human Resource Accounting is the process of developing financial assessments for people within organisation and society and the monitoring of these assessments through time. It deals with investments in people and with economic results of those investments".

(R. Lee Brummet, Eric G. Flamhoitz and William C. Pyle: 1969)

4. "It is an extension of the accounting principles of matching costs and revenues and of organizing data to communicate other information in financial terms. It involves measuring the costs incurred by business firms and other organisations when they recruit, select, train and develop human assets. It also involves measuring the economic value of people to organisations".

(Hermansson: 1964)

From an analytical study of the above definitions, we may conclude that:

Human resource accounting is a process to state the value of human resources in the language of accounting and to represent this value in an organisation's financial statement. It is about measuring the value of human resources in organisations, which can include figure and non-figure reporting on such issues as costs and benefits of training, staff turnover, absenteeism, the value of the knowledge in employees, etc.

However, providing adequate and valid information on human resources in statistical terms and within traditional balance sheets has proved extremely difficult. Consequently, new approaches introduce financial as well as non-financial information in human resource accounting. There are still immense problems to overcome before a coherent and reliable measuring technique is established. Part of the dilemma originates from basic questions such as:

- Is human resource accounting only for internal use in organisations?
- Should human resource accounting have a standard format for comparability purposes?
- Should human resource accounting be included in traditional financial statements?
- Is it possible to obtain data on human resources, which are reliable and comparable across organisations?
- Will the costs of gathering and processing this information exceed the benefits of doing so?
- How to establish a coherent terminology?
- How to link reporting on human resources with improved human resource development?

Need of Human Resource Accounting

The need for developing human resource accounting methods is:

1. Inadequacy of traditional balance sheets in providing sufficient information on organisation's performance;
2. Measuring problems deriving from the valuation of human resources;
3. Redistribution of social responsibilities between the public and private sectors.;
4. Security versus flexibility in employment;
5. Improved human resource management; and
6. Formal learning versus in-firm competency acquirement.

The focus on human resource accounting in organisations has lead to a growing interest by stakeholders who have started to identify and formulate their positions. The main stakeholders, such as the organisations, investors, employees, trade unions and governments, are therefore gradually becoming aware of the potential of human resource accounting albeit from different perspectives. Governments in many countries, notably in the Scandinavian countries, and the European Commission have identified public sector interests in human resource accounting. This ranges from a desire to support further improvement of enterprise competitiveness to an interest in diminishing the public sector funding of vocational education and training and, more generally, the implementation of lifelong learning.

Objectives of Human Resource Accounting

The main objectives of human resource accounting are:

1. To support human resource development:

HRA is not only about putting figures on human capital; it is also about supporting human resource development. Human resources play the most important part in the development of an organisation. Human resource accounting helps to measure the value of employees, which helps management, take the vital decisions related to human resources in order to increase productivity. It requires the measurement of the performances of an organisation and the optimum use of the resources under its direct and indirect control. The human resource accounting valuation is important for decision making in order to achieve the organisational objectives and to improve the output.

Increasing pressure will encourage or force organisations to report on human capital and to enlarge the perspective from serving mainly the interests of investors to include the interests of other stakeholders, notably government, trade unions and employees. This process is being further reinforced as stakeholders come to realize the potential of human resource accounting not only as an accounting system but also as a means of establishing new structures across interests and policies.

2. To increase employee participation in HRD policy formulation:

The main stakeholders, which includes government, trade unions, investors, organisations and employees, are increasingly formulating policies on human resource accounting in order to influence the design of human resource accounting. Consequently, there will be a gradual transformation in the tendency to see human resource accounting as either a management tool or an information system, and so as primarily a matter for manager and investors. However, the search for a standard human resource account has led to focus on accounting problems and the design of individual accounts in organisations, and it has generally failed to link the rise of human resource accounting to the processes of change in the HR market and in society in general. The models being developed for individual organisations tend to be more pragmatic and oriented towards specific organisation-based objectives of the organisation, perspectives which are generally focused less on technicalities and more on human resource development than is generally acknowledged.

3. To standardize measurement of HR worth:

Since most effort has been devoted to the measurement aspects of human resource accounting or model building, there is no consensus, neither among researchers nor among organisations about the exact content of human resource accounting exactly. Furthermore, since human resource accounting is considered to be primarily a management tool or an accounting technique, there is a tendency to overlook the different and potentially conflicting interests surrounding human resource accounting. Therefore, it is essential to set up a standard human resource account to achieve the organisation's mission and objectives.

Methods of Human Resource Accounting

Human resource accounting aims at depicting the human resources potential in monetary terms while casting the organisation's financial statements. With the emergence of the knowledge economy, recognition of human capital as an important part of the organisations total value has gained importance. Organisations, trying to reflect the 'value' of "its people" are using different approaches.

The methods to value and account for human resources can be classified into the following categories:

I. Methods based on *costs* (which include costs incurred by an organisation to recruit, hire, train and develop human resources)

II. Methods based on *economic value of human resources and the capitalization of organisation's earnings.*

I. Methods based on cost:

1. Historical cost method:

Under this method, the cost of acquisition i.e. selection, hiring, training costs of employees are capitalized and written off over the expected useful life of the employees. In case, the employee leaves the organisation before the anticipated period of service, then the unamortised portion of costs remaining in the organisation's books is written off against the profit and loss account in that year. If the period of service exceeds the anticipated time, then amortisation of costs is rescheduled.

2. Replacement cost method:

Under this method, the human resources are valued at their replacement cost i.e. the monetary implications of replacing existing employees. Replacement costs could be positional i.e. replacing an employee for particular positions or personal i.e. replacing specific talent or ability of particular persons.

3. Competitive bidding method:

This approach suggests competitive bidding for scarce employees in an organisation i.e. opportunity cost of employees linked to scarcity. The approach proposes the capitalizing of additional earning potential of each human resource within the organisation.

4. Standard cost method:

Under this method, standard costs of recruiting, hiring, training, and developing per grade of employees are determined annually. The total standard cost for all employees of the organisation is the value of human resources.

II. Methods based on value:

1. Jaggi and Lau method:

This method estimates the worth of human resources on a group-basis, as human resource group's account for productivity and performance in organisations.

2. Economic value method:

Under this method, the net present value of incremental cash flows attributed to human resources is taken as the asset value.

Human resource accounting provides quantitative information about the value of human assets, which helps the top management to take decisions regarding the adequacy of human resources. Based on these insights, further steps for recruitment and selection of human resources are taken. Outside the organisation, quantitative data on the most valuable asset has an impact on the decisions of the investors, clients, and potential staff of the organisation. When proper valuation and accounting of the human resources is not done then the management may not be able to recognize the negative effects of certain programmes, which are aimed at improving profits in the short run. If not recognized on time, these programmes could lead to fall in productivity levels, high turnover rate and low morale of existing employees.

Uses of Human Resource Accounting

Human Resource Accounting is basically an information system that informs management what changes are occurring over time to the human resources of the business. Human resource accounting also involves accounting for investment in people and their replacement costs, and also the economic value of people in an organisation. According to *Gröjer and Johansson*, the major uses of human resource accounting are:

1. As a **political tool,** used to demonstrate mismanagement of human resources, and therefore to argue more strongly for more investment/better management.
2. As a **pedagogical instrument** for analyzing and structuring, and thus better understanding of human resources problems from an applied perspective, and thus being better able to balance applied values against other values.
3. As a **decision-making** aid to ensure that decisions on human resources are more rational from the management point of view.

However, providing adequate and valid information on human capital in figures and within traditional balance sheets has proved extremely difficult; consequently, new approaches such as social accounting and human resource auditing take into account the fact that human capital and tangible assets are different in nature by introducing broader perspectives into human resource accounting. Human capital is the knowledge that individuals acquire during their lives and use to produce goods, services or ideas in market or non-market circumstances. Further, human resource accounting encompasses three elements: a) identification and measurement of human capital in figures, b) identification and measurement of human capital, including non-figure terms, and c) provision of information internally and/or externally on human capital.

Recent Scenario of Human Resource Accounting

Human Resource Accounting may be considered as a very controversial subject in management science. Even though the very origin of the debate on human capital in economic and social sciences may be considered as quite remote and besides such field of studies has been observed through different perspectives on a managerial point of view, today human resource accounting is mostly seen as a scarcely fertile subject. Apparently human resource accounting advocates have perhaps too much focused their field of research on accounting problems, particularly on those related to the allocation of human capital costs in the balance sheet. It is possible to maintain that today the field of research on human capital could be broadened to the wider context concerning the control of discretionary costs and, more particularly, of those referred to the building and development of decisional or managerial capabilities of people who act at different hierarchical levels within an organisation. Decisional or managerial capabilities may be considered as the ability of people to make choices and/or actions that may better acquire, co-ordinate and deploy human, information, technical, financial and other intangible resources. They are the levers through which resources may be converted into strategic assets that according to a credited doctrine are the main determinants of the competitive advantage of an organisation.

Therefore, organisations may improve its capabilities through the coordination of design policies concerning human and information resources, and particularly:

1. Human resources management and development systems;
2. Organisational structure and macro-procedures;
3. Accounting and non-accounting information systems; and
4. Management and strategic control systems.

A growing resort to human resource accounting conceptual framework, together with the support of clan through market and joint responsibility control mechanisms could allow to evaluate performance of techno structure units, not only referring to input measures, but also and especially to process or output or even to impact (on overall organisation's performance) parameters. Even though there is a growing tendency, particularly in large organisations, to pay more attention in coordinating human and information resources management and development activities and in assessing productivity of the related costs, it is quite difficult (especially with respect to human resources costs) to introduce market related or joint responsibility control mechanisms. However, such solutions may be considered, particularly for those firms whose critical success factors are closely related to the availability of intangible strategic assets - and also of decisional or managerial capabilities - as a "milestone" to which it is possible to converge.

It is true that worldwide, knowledge has become the key determinant for economic and business success, but Indian organisations lacks focus on 'Return on Investment' (ROI), with very few concrete steps being taken to track 'Return on Knowledge'. The current accounting system is not able to provide the actual value of employee capabilities and knowledge. This indirectly affects future investments of an organisation, as each year the cost on human resource development increases. Experts point out that the information generated by human resource accounting systems can be put to use for taking a variety of managerial decisions like recruitment planning, turnover analysis, personnel advancement analysis and capital budgeting, which can help organisations save a lot of trouble in the future.

Organisations can actually find out how much they can earn from an individual, as the intellectual assets of an organisation are often worth three or four times the tangible book value. Human capital also provides expert services such as consulting, financial planning and assurance services, which are valuable, and very much in demand.

Realizing this, many organisation world-over are making human resource accounting as a necessary element on their balance sheets. One of the best examples is of the

Denmark Government. The Danish Ministry of Business and Industry has issued a directive that with effect from the trading year 2005, all companies registered in Denmark will be required to include in their annual reports information on customers, processes and human capital. A minimum of five measures for each is required, and comparison with the previous two years must be shown. Figures for investment in intellectual capital must be shown and compared with the previous two years. A narrative should accompany each set of figures. Information for investors about intellectual capital, both current and future, should occupy at least one third of the report. Where relevant, information must also be provided regarding care for the environment.

In India, there are very few companies like BHEL, Infosys and Reliance Industries, which have implemented HRA and some are working on it. Infosys, which started showing human resource as an asset in its balance sheet, has been reaping high market valuations. NIIT has been following a similar method called Economic Value Addition (EVA), which also helps in assessing the real value that an employee can fetch for the organisation.

Once organisations realize the actual benefit and take it as a growth process, it will only help them in increasing their shareholders' value. When an organisation is able to assess an individual's worth, it helps in increasing its own worth.

Human resource accounting can be tracked through two methods—cost-based analysis and value-based analysis. The cost-based approach focuses on the cost parameters, which may relate to historical cost, replacement cost, or opportunity cost. The value-based approach suggests that the value of human resources depends upon their capacity to generate revenue. This approach can be further sub-divided into two broad categories: non-monetary and monetary.

The disposition of resources can also be examined by allocating relative human asset values to different job grades. HRA also helps in examining expenditure on human resources and in re-appraisal of expenditure on services and training. It can also serve as a key factor in case of mergers and takeover decisions, where the human asset value becomes a relevant factor. Another very significant role, which human resource accounting can help in creating, is goodwill for an organisation. It can project itself in having best practices with superior policies in place, which may help the organisation to attract more investments.

While human resource accounting as a concept has been present in India for more than a decade, with BHEL taking a lead, it is only now that the awareness is being translated into application. However, in terms of awareness and acceptance, the level is still low as many organisations take little initiative to make the numbers public to shareholders, despite having the data.

Another major deterrent is the lack of an industry standard. This means that every organisation has to evolve its own standard, which can become a tedious process, considering that most of them are still involved in improving their business. Industry bodies like Nasscom can help set a standard.

Another aspect working against the acceptance of human resource accounting is the need for extensive research that it entails. Many organisations do not want to go into the intricacies of finding the value of their human resources because most big organisations (with a large manpower) can afford to dwell into such best practices, it is not an economically viable option for small and medium sized organisations.

However, it's ultimately the people who deliver results. Realizing the benefits, which it can provide, the responsibility lies on the organisations, as to how much importance can they or do they give to their human resources.

In India, The Companies' Act, 1956 does not explicitly provide for disclosure on human assets in the financial statements of the companies. But sensing the benefits derived from valuing and reporting the human assets, many companies have voluntarily disclosed all relevant information in their books.

Limitations of Human Resource Accounting

Besides numerous benefits, human resource accounting method has the following limitations as enumerated below:

1. Human resource as expense:

Human resource accounting has contributed to the view of human resources being an expense to be minimized and cut when necessary. Human resources today occupies a central/pivotal position in the organisation because of their ability to provide sustained competitive advantage to an organisation through their talents, knowledge, adaptive capacity and leadership skills. Without human resources, an organisation has no value. Human resources are assets and not liabilities. They have capacity to bring enormous value to an organisation they are part of. Research has indicated that these intangible assets constitute about 60% of worth of an organisation.

2. Underrating of intellectual capital:

Human resource accounting underrates the value of human resources in terms of intellectual capital. Intellectual Capital is the combinations of patents, processes, management skills, and technologies, information about customers and suppliers and experience. People, knowledge and technology are the determining factors for an organisation's success because knowledge is more powerful and valuable than natural resources. In an economy based on knowledge, intellectual capital – the untapped, unmapped knowledge of organisations has become an organisation's greatest competitive weapon. It is found in the talent of the people who work there, the loyalty of the customers it serves and learns from, the value of its brands (including employer brand) and intellectual properties, the collective knowledge embodied in its cultures, systems, management techniques, and history. Thus, intellectual capital is the only differentiator between success and failure.

People therefore have a value, which is greater than the cost of their employment.

Review and Discussion Questions

Question 1: Define and explain the concept HRD audit. Why is HRD audit necessary?

Question 2: Explain the methodology of HRD audit.

Question 3: What is the role of HRD audit in an organisation? Is it beneficial for the employees also?

Question 4: Briefly describe the structure of a HRD audit report.

Question 5: What are the benefits of HRD audit?

Question 6: Define and explain the concept of human resource accounting.

Question 7: What are the objectives of a HR accounting? Explain the different methods of HR accounting.

Question 8: Examine the recent scenario of human resource accounting in India. What are the reasons of slow progress of HR accounting in India?

Question 9: Write short notes on:

i) HRD scorecard
ii) Methods of HR Accounting
iii) Limitation/shortcomings of HR Accounting

Exhibit: 11 – A

Case Situation

• *Before attempting this section please read Chapter - 14 on Case Study.*

• *Please read the following case situations and answer the questions.*

Q 1. You have recently started your practice as HRD consultant. The CEO of a manufacturing company has offered you an opportunity to conduct HRD audit in his company. Enlist the procedure you would adopt.

Q 2. Design a human resource accounting system for a software company. Outline:

- Objectives of your study.
- The method/s you would use.
- Recommendations you would like to give.

Exhibit: 11 – B

Case Study

- *Before attempting this section please read Chapter - 14 on Case Study.*
- *Please read the following case study and answer all the subsequent questions.*

Introduction to the organisation:

Pharmaco (India) Pvt. Ltd. was established 100 years ago, to serve a specialized niche in the pharmaceutical industry. The Company is a profit making and has been growing exponentially. The company has introduced HRD system some time back.

The MD of the company wanted to examine the effectiveness of the HRD system; he has been pivotal in initiating. He had difference of opinion with other board members who considered it to be waste of time. He hired the services of a professional HRD audit firm to help him out.

Brief Description of the Problem:

Tarun, a secretary in MD's office has been talking to his friend Arun, who works in as secretary with the GM-Operations:

Tarun: I have heard that our MD has engaged some consultant to interview employees for a very fat fee. As I had told you last time that he (MD) is having serious differences with our Chairman on aspects concerning the running of the organisation, so there could be a vertical split in the organization. I guess this interview is important.

Arun: What for? I feel that MD wants to pick 'the best' employees through this interview and leave others in lurch.

Tarun: Yes, this could be very true. But if we could impress the consultant then we would be rewarded well in terms of promotion, fat salary, great career and we will have a great time. Otherwise what else is HRD?

Gradually all other employees came to know of it through grape wine.

10 days hence ……..

The date for interaction between the consultant/s was decided for 25/02/2005. The Manager-HRD hurriedly issued an IOM containing the selected names of employees from different departments who have to ensemble at 9:30 a.m. on tomorrow morning through e-mail informing that the company has been in the business for the last 100 years and has achieved various landmarks and milestones. It briefly described the profile of the consultant and that it will be group discussion, with each group will consist 25 members for sharing unique strengths and opportunities for improvement in the organisation in general and HRD activities in particular. It also assured that employees are free to air their views with an assurance that their names will not be quoted. All employees, including Tarun and Arun got confused as they could not get the opportunity to clarify about the discussions/interview. Hence, they decided to freely express their views and passed on some highly critical remarks against the organisation, HRD function and leadership, particularly that of MD, hoping that:

- They will be highly rewarded for their honest opinions and views.
- They form part of his key team members.

Two months later ……..

Tarun and Arun were sacked. Their bosses informed that their performance has not been up to the mark and that they have not improved in spite of opportunities accorded to them.

It was later discovered that the MD had overheard the statement and uttering of each and every participant through a hidden camera and microphone.

Questions:

1. What went wrong for Tarun and Arun?
2. Were the attitude of Tarun and Arun about HRD correct and valid? Why?
3. What is the genesis of this case study? Summarize in 10 lines.
4. What suggestions would you like to give to the MD of the Company?
5. Was the role of HRD Manager appreciable? What would you do if you had been in his place?

CHAPTER

12 Strategic Human Resource Development

Chapter Synopsis

Human Resource Development is playing an increasingly strategic role in developing learning and development processes in order to enhance the contribution of 'knowledge workers' to the strategic development of an organisation. The links between corporate strategy and human resource development is necessary to establish the strategic relationship between HRD and improving performance in the organisational context.

To facilitate this requires an in-depth knowledge of Strategic Human Resource Development.

This chapter explains these concepts and strategies to meet the strategic goals of the organisation.

This Chapter contains:

Concept of strategic human resource development, Why study strategic human resource development, Definitions of strategic human resource development, Business strategy and human resource development, Characteristics of strategic human resource development, Objectives of strategic human resource development, Strategic human resource development system, Strategic human resource development process, Review & discussion questions, case situation and case study.

Strategic Human Resource Development

Changing business conditions and changes in organisational structures have compelled human resource development function to increasingly alter their perspectives on its role and function. For organisational effectiveness, human resource development must become a strategic tool for achieving business goals and objectives and its present and future needs and justify itself as a value added function.

Given that organisations have restructured and downsized, competitiveness demands up-to-date skills and competencies and a diverse workforce, which can work well in teams. The free market belief in 'buying-in' skill has proven inadequate, even in times of high unemployment. Human resource development requires managers to be proactive, focusing on employees as investments for the organisation. One of the great strategic contributions of human resource development lies in the planning of skill availability in advance of need. Human resource development programmes involve more than training and may be focused on competence, gender and role. They require constant accurate assessment, counseling and personal challenge. Human resource development also involves socialisation of employees to fit the cultural requirements of the organisation.

The changing nature of work and the political, economic, social and technological pressures upon organisations are forcing them to develop and communicate new corporate strategies; upwardly to develop new human resource development strategies and policies, to empower employees at all levels and to determine the most effective and efficient work processes; to build teams with the capacity to learn and become self managed; and to develop individuals and encourage management development.

Due to relentless change in market expectations and demands for new products and services, knowledge based organisations has emerged replacing capital and labour intensive organisations, in which personal and organisational learning is central to the future growth and development of an organisation. In the knowledge based organisations, information, knowledge and learning are central to organisations operating in a more sophisticated marketplace and with employees whose needs and aspirations are more demanding than hitherto.

Thus, strategic human resource development has emerged as a result of two pressures. First, the new climate of disorganized capitalism and second, from the internal developments and debates within organisational development. This general direction seeks to replace overt control oriented cultures with organisational cultures characterized by creativity and learning.

The word 'strategy' in strategic human resource development incorporates organisational development, human resource development and strategic management. In a limited sense, strategic human resource development is the contribution of human resource development to strategic management with a distinctive focus on strategic change management of the organisations. It is based on the supposition that development of human resources must be treated by organisations as a deliberate business process rather an accident. There is ample research experience to support that human resource development is linked to business strategy and firm performance and it derives competitive advantage. 'Business Strategy' has been defined by *Hit, Ireland and Hoskisson* (2004) as 'an integrated and coordinated set of commitments and actions the firm uses to gain a competitive advantage by exploring core competencies in specific product markets'. Business strategy focuses on improving the competitive position of an organisation's products or services within the specific industry or market segment that the organisation serves. A central tenet of strategic human resource development is the promotion of humanistic values. Conflicts arise between humanistic objectives and organisational needs resulting in value dilemmas and value conflicts.

Managing change today is fundamentally concerned with organisational design in order to anticipate customer's needs. Organisational design involves integrating human operations, organisational structure and systems for the deliver of products and services in an effective and economic manner as well as differentiates the product or service from that provided by the competitors (see figure 12.1).

Fig. 12.1 : Interlinkage of Organization's Vision & Mission with HR Strategy

Why Study Strategic Human Resource Development?

Strategic human resource development has assumed importance owing to emergence of a new business environment and a new human environment and the need to assimilate them for organisational excellence and success as depicted in figure 12.2.

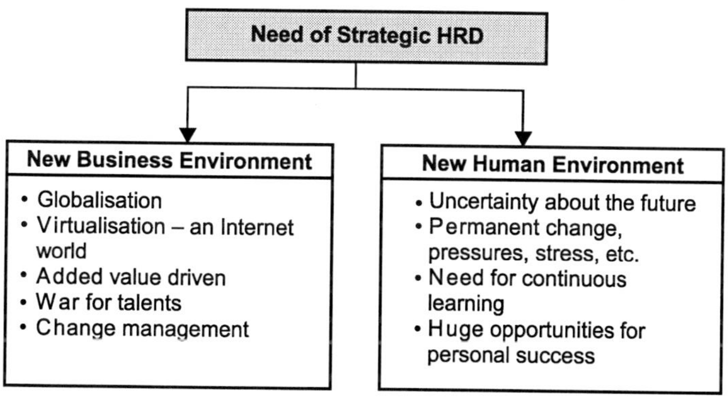

Fig. 12.2 : Need of Strategic HRD

Definitions:

A few noteworthy definitons fo Strategic Human Resource Development are as follows:

1. "Strategic Human Resource Development focuses on the development of personal skills and learning in order to achieve personal and organisational transformation".

(Jim Grieves: 2003)

2. "Strategic Human Resource Development may be defined as human resources and development functions, policies and practices that emanate from the strategic activities of an organisation with an impact on its achievement".

3. "Strategic Human Resource Development may be defined as ensuring that human resource development policies are congruent with and in support of the organisation's strategy, structure and control".

Thus, Strategic Human Resource Development is to link the practice of human resource development to enhancing organisational strategy and developing performance capability through learning specifically creating a focus on strategic learning and developing performance throughout the organisation.

Strategic human resource development possesses the following salient features:

1. Linkage to organisational strategy (vertical alignment);
2. Aligned with HR policies and practices (horizontal alignment);
3. Holistic – more than just training;
4. Interventions at all levels – individual, team and organisation; and
5. Proactive – creating the learning climate.

Strategic human resource development is about gaining competitive advantage through human resources as in figure 12.3.

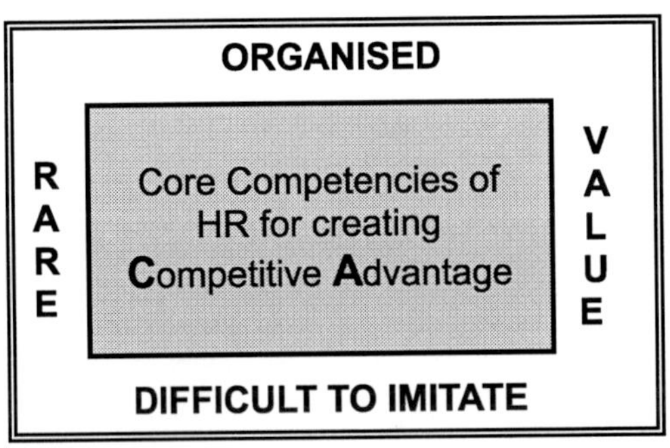

Fig. 12.3 : Competitive Advantage through Strategic HRD

Strategic human resource development views the main activities of the organisation – the human processes – to be prior to the task itself because organisations are viewed as pluralistic rather than unitarist. This means that in order to redefine the task, it is essential to redefine the human processes.

Strategic human resource development sees its role as the development of human resources and organisations. Thus, learning (rather than training) has become the central characteristic of change and accordingly individual and organisational learning has become vital for strategic human resource development.

Strategic human resource development requires six conditions as mentioned below:

1. Alignment with organisational objectives;
2. Top management support;
3. Involvement of line managers;
4. Quality of programmes design and delivery;
5. Motivation of trainees; and
6. Integration with human resource management policy.

The Strategic orientation of human resource development is clear from the *Michael Armstrong's* (1992) observation:

"Resourcing is about providing the skills base needed by the organisation. Human resource development is about enhancing and widening these skills by training, by helping people to grow within the organisation, and by enabling them to make better use of their skills and abilities".

Learning and possessing knowledge of something is one thing but applying the learning is yet another; thus learning has limited value unless it is put into practice.

There is a persistent need to develop an organisation in which learning and the desire to learn are second nature to all employees. Since competitive advantage lies in the talents of employees, then it is necessary to create circumstances in which those talents can blossom.

Organisations need to develop learning activities, which have a clear business focus.

A strategic human resource development assists in achieving purpose of an organisation and pursuing its objectives as an organisation - an organisation that must demonstrate its value to its stakeholders, and ensure that the above values and principles are adhered to. Human resource development cannot achieve the principles by itself or in isolation from other human resource practices and policies - it is one of the foundations that an organisation is built upon and not the only foundation. It must support organisation's corporate and operational plans, be consistent with the human resources plan and become an integral part of organisation's business environment. This requires a commitment from all employees for it to be effective, a commitment to identify areas requiring development and a commitment to action in order to address these identified needs as depicted in figure 12.4.

Fig. 12.4 : Linkage of Organisational Strategy to HRD Tactics

Strategic human resource development promotes a more enlightened, ethical and skills focused change management that puts human resources back to where they belong – at the top of the change management agenda. Since strategic human resource development focuses on humanistic values, but given increased global competition wherein down sizing is commonplace, there is significant pressure on strategic human resource development to focus less on humanistic values and more on activities which have a direct impact on the organisation's bottom line. This has resulted in a tendency to concentrate on radical change strategies.

Strategic human resource development is concerned with processes, which lead to tasks. This is in contrast to many programmed approaches, which are task focused. This means that strategic human resource development's role is that of a dynamic process of modifying patterned behaviour consisting of four styles:

- An initiative;
- Requires change to critical organisational processes;
- Influences individual behaviours; and
- Impacts organisational outcomes.

Business Strategy and Human Resource Development

The close relationship between an organisation's business strategy and human resource development strategy is crucial for business success and sustainability of the organisation. Human resources development strategy entails developing a match between certain strategic or organisational conditions and certain specified aspects of human resource processes and skills. Human resource development strategy, being part of the organisational systems and processes should be consistent with its strategy. This is because HRD policies and practices influence employee behaviour, which in turn impacts the outcomes. Therefore, it must vary systematically with the business strategy of the organisation.

Organisations are increasingly realizing that the success of their long term planning and strategic approaches rests on motivation, commitment, flexibility, involvement and competencies of their human resources to remain competitive in a constantly changing environment. Therefore, business strategy should give direction to HR activities, and issues, internal and external, for better fitment into business planning process.

The above discussion is depicted in figure 12.5.

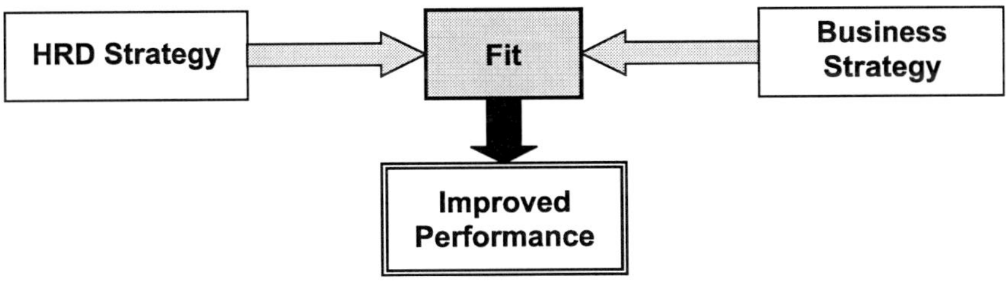

Fig. 12.5 : Fitment of HRD Strategy-Business Strategy

In the absence of such linkages, the organisational performance and effectiveness may be adversely affected. The linking of strategic human resource development strategy to business strategy of an organisation is depicted in figure 12.6.

Designing a strategic human resource development process involves the following

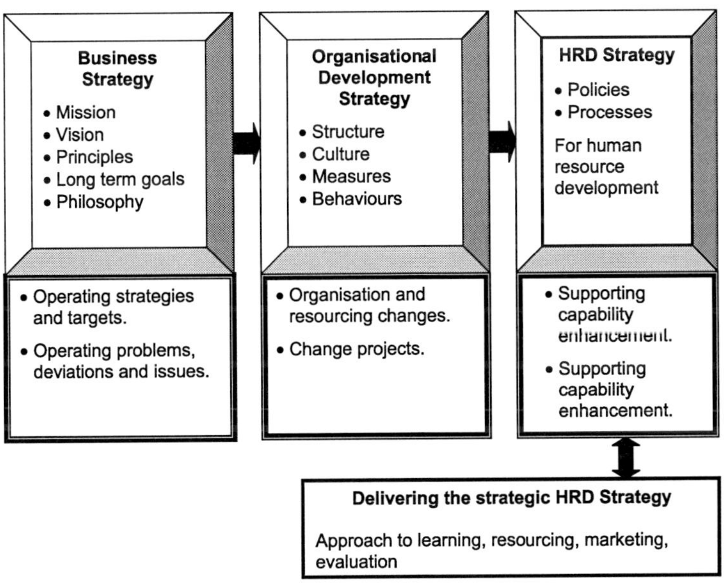

Fig. 12.6 : Interlinkage of Business Strategy & Strategic HRD Strategy

steps as shown in figure 12.7.

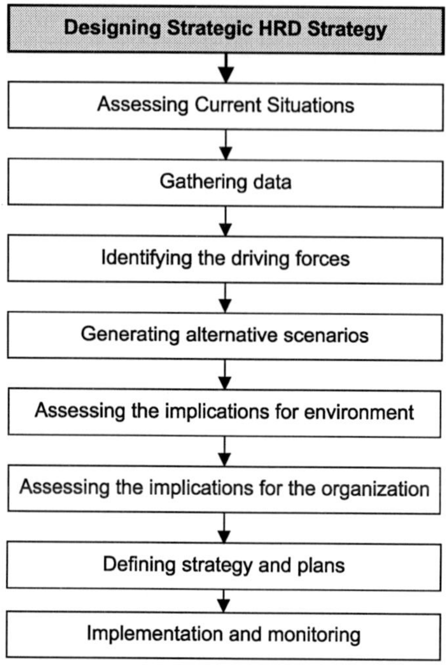

Fig. 12.7 : Steps of Designing Strategic HRD

Characteristics of Strategic Human Resource Development

The four major characteristics of strategic human resource development are:

1. Focus on organisation's business strategy:

Strategic human resource development considers the development of human resources as a strategic advantage. Internal developments from individuals and teams influence greatly the achievement of objectives of the organisation than external market trends. The strategic level of the organisation can no longer act as an all seeing central planner because threats will emerge which have to be dealt with incrementally in ways not originally foreseen by the strategy.

2. Devolved responsibility of line managers:

Line managers are required to facilitate change by developing individuals and teams. This requires the development of key skills and competencies and ability to be driven by values and ethical responsibility. They must stimulate and develop creativity in their employees either as mentors or as change agents to facilitate a proactive incremental adjustment of the organisation to its environment.

3. Transition from training to learning:

Learning results in greater impact on work performance, productivity and commitment of employees being a self-assuming responsibility, which comes naturally to human beings. Learning allows employees to challenge conventional ideas and replace them with creative alternatives borne out of their intellect and imagination. Strategic human resource development seeks to reposition human resource development quite differently from a confused and mundane existence in the depths of training programmes.

4. Work based organisational learning:

In an entirely stable world, learning would not be needed much. However, in a changing world, learning at individual and organisational levels is essential and inspired mainly by change. Continuous development of business processes is essential for sustaining in global economy, which would, requires culture of creativity. Work based learning fosters intuition with a mental image of a future state amongst the employees.

Objectives of Strategic Human Resource Development

The main objectives of strategic human resource development are:

1. To achieve strategic thrust for integration of business with human resource development strategies with capacity for knowledge creation.
2. To facilitate culture change and build knowledge based productive learning culture;
3. To promote high quality and lifelong workplace learning processes that will enhance the value of social and human capital;
4. To help develop managerial and leadership capability that will aid process of strategizing, organizing and human resource development especially in newer organisational forms; and
5. To promote skills and competencies development for greater productivity and sustainable employability.

Strategic Human Resource Development System

Strategic human resource development system consists of comprehensive and integrated set of arrangements of strategic practices and strategic enablers as discussed below:

1. Strategic Practices:

Practices refer to a holistic framework entailing developmental initiatives such as learning, performance management, career planning and development, quality of work life and employee empowerment. It may be emphasized that these development initiatives must be closely linked with business strategy of the organisation based on core organisational values and ethics. These are essential to sustain the success of strategic human resource development programmes in an organisation.

2. Strategic Enablers:

Enablers refer to those factors, which either facilitate or inhibit implementation of strategic human resource development programmes. They enable an organisation to compete in a knowledge based market environment. These factors could be philosophy of top management, union-management relations, employee relation scenario and managerial attitude. These factors are essential for building positive relations at workplaces in order to increase teamwork, collaboration and employee ownership for enhanced organisational performance and success.

Thus, strategic human resource development system results in change in employee behaviour as depicted in figure 12.8.

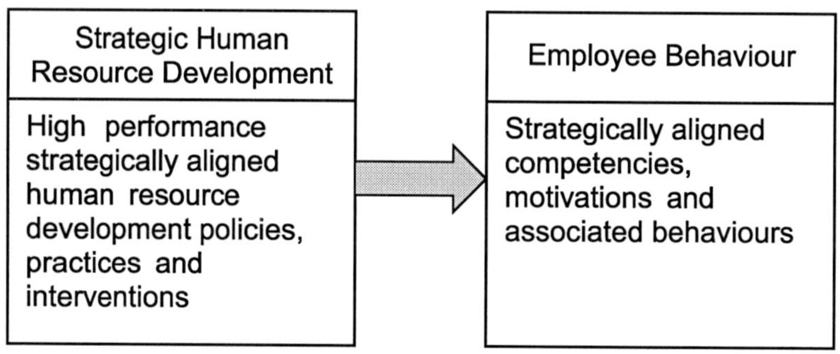

Fig. 12.8 : Impact of Strategic HRD on Employee Behaviour

Strategic Human Resource Development Process

Strategic human resource development is concerned with aligning human resource development strategy with an organisation's business strategy for business success and sustainability of the organisation. Human resources development strategy entails developing a match between certain strategic or organisational conditions and certain specified aspects of human resource processes and skills. As the business strategy of the organisation varies to adjust with changed conditions, so must the human resource development strategy. Human resource development programmes, policies and practices must have strong linkage to the business strategy for the long-term success of an organisation. It is increasingly realized by organisations today that embarking human resource development on generic patterns and models is not likely to bring the desired results in a highly complex and competitive market. All human resource development programmes and strategies must be formulated as per the requirements of the business strategy of the organisation. Therefore, organisations have strategic learning development programmes, strategic career planning and development programmes, strategic performance appraisal programmes, strategic pay programmes, etc. in order to effectively contribute to the bottom line of the organisation through customer excelleration.

The process of strategic human resource development is depicted in figure 12.9:

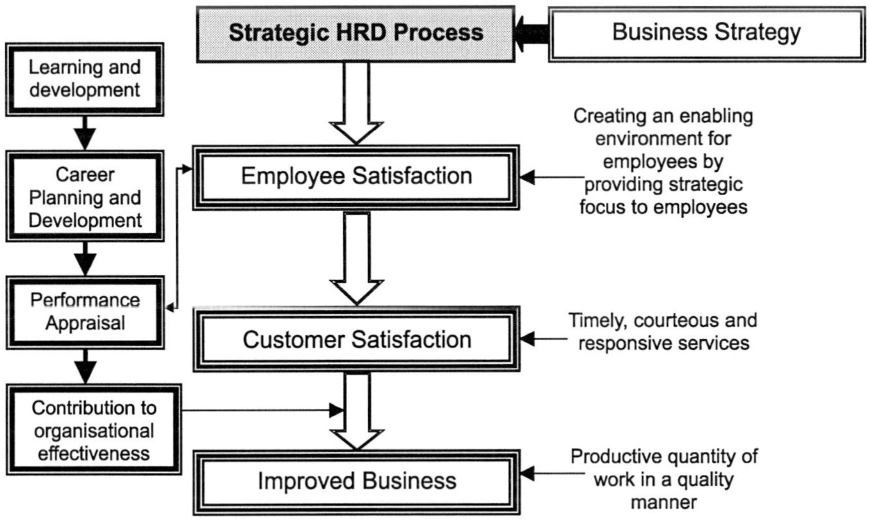

Fig. 12.9 : Strategic HRD Process

Human resource development programmes and strategies shall be developed based on the business models of the organisation. Various key human resource development mechanisms and instruments such as learning and development, career planning and development, and performance appraisal must satisfy the needs strategic imperatives of the organisation. This implies that those training, learning and management development programmes will be taken up in the organisation which contributes to their competencies development and which will help the organisation to stay competitive. Strategic human resource development will help to define and connect critical competencies to organisation's strategic business and process drivers. Identification of the values, behaviours and goals that support an organisation's strategic mission and promote its business success will be the core issues. Employees and managers should be educated to understand business strategies and goals of the organisation so as to help them focus on strategic matters of the organisation. This requires focusing on goals, values and imperatives of the organisation and the customers. A variety of methodologies, including focus groups, interviews, observation and survey research to analyze the knowledge, skills, abilities and behaviours required for success at the job, job family, team and organisational levels could be employed. Competency models can be used to build a comprehensive "roadmap" for recruiting, learning, training and development, career planning and development, and performance appraisal.

Learning, training and development will focus on linkages to both critical business objectives and individual development needs. A variety of systems, from modular-based programmes to outdoor learning can be employed. A meticulous blending of skills and competencies is essential with a focus on results—empowering employees to make choices and take action.

Similarly, career planning and development will be linked to growth attained by the organisation and also the opportunities for career enhancement shall be governed by scope for making high impact on strategic business planning and objectives of the organisation. Those employees who prove their worth and value creation in business development of the organisation will have opportunities for career advancement. Individual employee roles must be supportive of the organisational and job goals.

Also, performance appraisal of employees shall be viewed by organisations in terms of specific and significant contribution of the employees in innovation, creativity and productivity in attaining competitive advantage for the organisation. Based on business strategy of the organisation, ethical behaviours will determine the factors and/or objectives that should appear on every employee's appraisal on organisation wide basis. Strategic performance appraisal and development system measures and rewards the strategic competencies critical to the success of the organisation. The goal is to design a process that employees will actually value and use—because it's tied to the real work that gets done, not to "ivory tower" ideals. Performance appraisal systems will be based on solid research, rather than the latest management fad. This will necessitate use of a variety of systems, including 360-degree or multi-rater feedback, business scorecard and computer-based performance appraisal.

Strategic human resource development instruments and mechanisms, as discussed above, will increase the employee satisfaction as employees are focused on their priorities and critical success factors. Positive customer experiences can only happen when processes and employees (with passion) work in harmony. A satisfied employee will deal better with the customers and help in increasing customer satisfaction because of the harmony between employee's roles and organisation's strategic goals. The productivity, and quality goes up and customers stand delighted. This will result in improved business performance of the organisation.

Thus, strategic human resource development supports the business strategy of the organisation in enhancing its competitiveness.

Hence, we may conclude that strategic human resource development is a strategic developmental tool to bolster competitive advantage of an organisation.

Essential Characteristics of Effective Strategic Human Resource Development

The characteristics of an effective strategic human resource development programme entails the following organisational practicer:

- Intergration into a human resource strategy, which in turn is aligned with an organisational or corporate strategy;
- Competency based HRD derived from structural, systemic, technological and work re-organisation needs; this in contrast to menu offerings by centralized training departments in large organisations;
- Partnership between HRD specialists and line managers in developing employee competencies required to achieve organisational peroformance goals;
- Creating an organisational culture of contiuous learing and transfer of learning between units;
- Measuring and evaluating the effectiveness of HRD practices on individual, team and organisation;
- Adding peroformance areas for specific development initiatives, which potentially enhance competitive advantage such as customer excelleration, product innovation, creative problem solving, leadership and team development; and
- Business and work process integration which involves learining to work collaboratively acreoos traditional functional disciplines in multifunctional/ disciplinary teams, which requires both new interactive skills and organisation redesign.

Review and Discussion Questions

Question 1: Define and explain the concept and scope of Strategic Human Resource Development.

Question 2: What are the major objectives of Strategic Human Resource development?

Question 3: What is the link between business strategy and human resource development?

Question 4: Explain the process of Strategic Human Resource Development.

Question 5: What do you understand by Strategic Human Resource Development system? Why is Strategic Human Resource Development important in contemporary business scenario?

Question 6: Critically examine the present scenario of Strategic Human Resource Development in the Indian Industries. Give suitable examples to justify your answer.

Exhibit: 12 – A

Case Situation

- *Before attempting this section please read Chapter - 14 on Case Study.*
- *Please read the following case situation and answer the question.*

Q 1. You are working as Manager-HRD in an upcoming fast food chain. Major business strategy of the organisation includes: open more new outlets across the country, improve speed of delivery, improve customer care/services, provide values added services, etc. To spear head the growth plans, develop the following HRD systems based on stated business strategy of the organization:

a) Strategic performance appraisal system
b) Strategic career development plans
c) Strategic training and development programmes

Exhibit: 12 – B

Case Study

• *Before attempting this section please read Chapter - 14 on Case Study.*

• *Please read the following case study and answer all the subsequent questions.*

Introduction to the organisation:

Gearbox (India) Ltd. was established 20 years ago, to manufacture gearbox components for diesel engines. It employs around 250 people, having a head office, which employs a wide range of personnel who are generally well educated and enthusiastic about their work, and a factory, which employs semi-skilled local people who are generally disinterested in the products of the Company and who have an instrumental attitude to work, seeing salary as the only reward.

Brief Description of the Problem:

The performance of the Company has not been good and the records revealed the following facts:

- Wastage within the factory was costing the Company approximately Rs. 100, 000 a month.
- There was wide spread differences in individual work standards
- Processes were non-standardised resulting in repeated problems
- Management made all decisions and cascaded the results down to employees

The top management became concerned about the performance of the factory and they hired Mr. Tanmoy Deb, an OD consultant to study the problem and suggest specific changes to relationships and tasks with the following objectives:

- To review and improve communication systems.
- To restructure the organisation and to review teamwork and quality practices.
- To review leadership issues across all levels.

Mr. Tanmoy Deb carried out discussions, interviews and surveys and made the following observations:

- 'Them' and 'us' attitude was widely prevalent between head office and factory personnel
- Production personnel showed little accountability towards quality of work
- Production personnel lacked technical skills
- Factory employees felt alienated from sharing the Company's success
- Production systems were adhoc and defective because of frequent variations in standards set
- Many times raw material was found to be of inferior quality
- Rigidly defined job descriptions

Questions:

1. What is the linkage between productivity and human processes?
2. What in your view are the central human resources issues involved in this case?
3. What strategy should Mr. Tanmoy Deb develop and implement for improving the present system?

CHAPTER

13 Concluding Remarks on Human Resource Development

Chapter Synopsis

This chapter concludes the entire discussion of the conceptual framework, tools, techniques and strategies of Human Resource Development. The essence lies in nurturing and building organisational excellence through development of human resources.

It may be emphasised that human resources are not just the strategic assets of an organisation, but they are the actually the most valuable assets of the customers of the organisation.

Human Resource Development is the true Engine of the new economy as it is capable of bringing enormous value to an organisation.

Concluding Remarks on Human Resource Development

Human resource development is an evolutionary system and its paradigm is changing as depicted in figure 13.1.

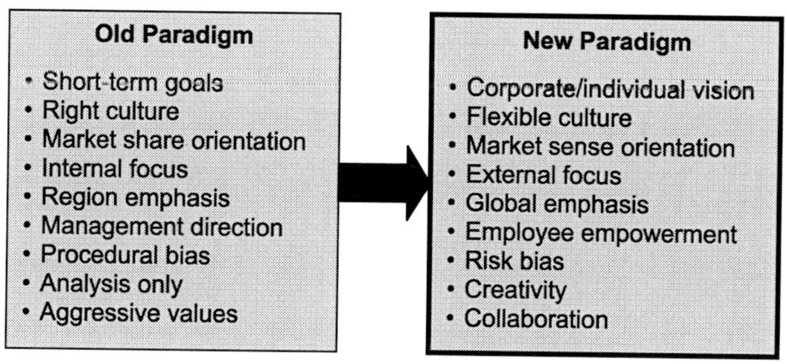

Fig. 13.1 : Changing Paradigms of HRD

The relationship between management and its human resources is like partners in a family. Its important for the organisation to choose the right man for the right job otherwise it will be like *'Marry in haste; Repent at leisure'*.

Human resource development programmes needs the commitment of top management to grow and develop. Human resource development will be effective if healthy atmosphere in day-to-day organisation administration exists so as to facilitate a development-oriented environment for the employees. It is a prime responsibility of the management of the organisation. Therefore, while administering the organisation, management must ensure, among other things, the followings:

- Just and fair treatment;
- Transparency in all processes and systems, especially people oriented;
- Open interactive communication;
- Performance based reward management and growth opportunities;
- Financial, humanitarian and administrative support in times of hardship of people;

- Establishing 'dyadic' relationship across different levels;
- Participative decision-making process; and
- Sharing profit and organisational success.

If the top management satisfies the above needs of their human resources, so that equal opportunity and guarantee and scope of security for their life is there, in reciprocity much satisfied human resources will willingly put all their energies, commitment, devotion and loyalty thereby making human resource development programmes successful. This will ensure the improvement of the organisation.

Human resource development is instrumental to people management, driven by market-oriented activities that affect the business as a whole. In India, management practices on human resource development subsystems have remained more or less traditional. The following table depicts clearly the differences between Indian human resource development practices against international practices:

HRD PRACTICES		
Practice	**Indian**	**International**
Approach towards Employees	Policy generally projects employees as a factor of Production Employees generally Treated on the basis Of paternalism or patronage	Policy exists in that it is often divorced from closeness between employees and management
Training	No planned training No follow up on need identification More funds for managerial Training but far less or none For worker training or skill Upgradation	Planned training High level orientation and retraining
Performance Appraisal	Policy exists Does not work No faith in formal System Selectively used in Career progression	Policy exists Plays major role in career planning and development
Employee Empowerment	Does not exist	Widely practiced by organisations

After having an elaborate discussion on the concept of human resource development and its components, Human Resource Development can be defined as:

"Human Resource Development is the process of ensuring that the skills, knowledge, abilities and performance of the workforce meet current and future organisational and individual needs through developing, implementing and evaluating activities and programmes addressing employee training and development, change and performance management and the unique needs of particular employee groups".

Thus, human resource development is a process to:

- Analyze.
- Propose.
- Create.
- Implement.
- Assess.

Human resource development function often has a clear picture about its strategy, but it still has not made a noticeable impact on organisational outcome due to:

- An unclear role for human resource development department.
- Lack of measurable targets for human resource development.
- The existence of new processes, which is often concerned with long term processes.
- "Newness" of the human resource development activities.

HRD Benefit - Forecasting Model

The basic human resource development benefit-forecasting model uses three components to determine financial value: the performance value to result from the human resource development program, the cost of the HRD program, and the benefit resulting from the human resource development programme (*Swanson and Gradous:* 1988). Performance value is the dollar value of the performance units resulting from a human resource development programme. Benefit is calculated by multiplying the total number of units expected to result from the programme by the dollar-value amount of one unit. Cost is an item of outlay that is incurred in the operation of human resource development programmes; it may include such items as direct and indirect costs, fixed and variable costs, and amortization. Human resource development cost is any expenditure that the organisation chooses to attribute to an human resource development programme.

This approach is useful in that it contributes useful metrics for concepts like performance unit, performance value, and benefit. It is not a post hoc method of evaluation, but it does not seem to suffer much from this condition. Forecasting benefits can yield a realistically derived monetary value expected from a human resource development programme. From the numbers on a forecasting worksheet, other measures such as expected ROI and payback time could be calculated. The projected numbers can then be compared to the actual numbers. This kind of comparison can make forecasting efforts much more accurate and believable.

Managing HRD Function Effectively

HRD professionals (practicing and/or prospective) should have strategies for running HRD function/department effectively. Some of the major success strategies for effective management of HRD function are given below:

- Building a partnership with the organisation by assessing what its business priorities are and how a HRD function can contribute to meeting them, and agree on mutual expectations to gain management's sponsorship and support of human resource development;
- Creating a vision and a realistic plan based on sound needs analysis, to ensure that HRD programmes will address business-focused HRD needs and help enhance credibility;
- Being creative in finding internal and external resources to design and deliver programmes and services so that HRD has an impact far beyond the direct staff power of HRD function;
- Marketing human resource development programmes so that employees understand how HRD function supports the organisation and how they are expected to participate in HRD activities to ensure that the organisation gets the most out of any HRD effort;
- Managing time wisely helps to stick to HRD Programme priorities and avoids getting bogged down in insignificant activities or projects;
- Budget should be managed carefully by knowing what HRD costs and what the return on investment of HRD will be;
- Developing HRD staff and network so that professional growth takes place and staying on top of changes in the organisation, the business world, and the professional community; and
- Tracking HRD effectiveness and making adjustments to keep pace with changing demands of the organisation and making sure that HRD programmmes are meeting its needs.

It must be clearly borne in mind by the HRD professionals that an organisation will invest in human resource development if the marginal return on investment is greater than the marginal cost of capital invested for human resource development. Therefore, economic aspects needs to taken into active consideration while introducing human resource development programmes and strategies.

HRD Scenario in Indian Organisation: Its Problems and Prospects

The Company is a large organisation and is into insurance business.

The Company introduced the system of work plan and review for all the class-I officers of the organisation at all levels in all its offices. Through the instrument of WPR, an attempt was made to integrate the individual growth and the organisational growth through a process of role scanning, job survey, SWOT analysis and periodic review of result areas and monitoring of performances as per work plan drawn up by each individual officer for a particular financial year. Emphasis was laid on the task of discussion, review, counseling and mid-course correction in the activities of the individual officer for realization of his performance targets. From 1989 onward through intensive workshops, interface and comprehensive programme, these WPR instrument was internalized with the organisation. The individual officer observed lot of clarity in understanding the role and making realistic job survey. A systematic line of critical thinking on the concerns of the department and organisation emerged as a result of intensive work planning and reviewing.

Central Office, also guided to re-structure of functioning of different Departments at the Central Office and Zonal Office level with the help of desk system where each department was divided into several distinct desks with fixed accountability and responsibility. The desk system brought about lot of clarity and accountability among the officers of the organisation at the Central Office and Zonal office level. Red tapeism, delay in decision-taking, procrastination and other tactics in the organisational behaviour of the organisation were removed or reduced to a substantial degree through the desk control system. The prescribed role element and the discretionary role element in the decision maker's work area become clearer by successful utilization of the desk control mechanism. Overlapping functions were avoided, duplication was reduced and with the help of service bureau for data control, data monitoring, data building, and each desk had to perform a distinct role with support from each section under the desk. This has developed a new working culture in the organisation in the organisation in the early part of the 1990s.

From 1993 onward, Central Office evolved a comprehensive programme of OD/HRD awareness for all the branches as a whole through a medium of well-articulated

Action Plan. Here, the focus was on making the organisation customer friendly and market friendly. To be brief the interests of customers have been kept at the central focus. To develop a prompt, error free and expeditious service for our ever-growing Policy Holder's segment in this age of competition has become the main goal before the organisation today. If the loyalty of the policyholders is eroded and they are not satisfied with the standard and levels of service, then in the very near future, it is most likely that some customers will switch over their loyalty and patronage from the organisation to other organisations, given the liberalization and privatization of insurance sector. For any organisation with a marketing and servicing goal such a scenario will be the most difficult and undesirable. Therefore, the Central Office developed a comprehensive OD/HRD Action Plan covering all the Branches and including all the classes of employees I, II, III and IV attached to the branches. They have also made this awareness programme mandatory for all the Officers and HGAs of the Divisional Office, so that, the Divisional Office can give proper support service to the branches to make their servicing effective and fault free. All the important Divisions have been covered in phase-I & phase-II in all the Zones of the organisation. The Action Plans have been prepared by around 1200 Branches in the entire Country and on the basis of the Action Plan it has been attempted to develop a new working culture based on the principle of co-ordination, co-operation and collaboration among all sections of employees, with the idea that the branch office will function as a fully equipped working team and their main aim will be to serve the customers equally, promptly and accurately. The branch management committee's role in understanding the concerned problems and issues of the branches have been highlighted and the co-operation from each level has been sorted out to make the branches modern performers in the field of insurance sales and servicing.

The entire organisation need for facing the change and entire HRD thrust will be determined by comprehensive modern and effective system of training to be imparted to the Assistants, HGAs and different levels of Officers in the organisation, both in the marketing side as well as in the administrative side.

Another important and significant decision has been taken by the organisation to upgrade its servicing standard by technical up-gradation, by introducing over a period of time in a phased and progressive manner the front-end application in branches, indicating that the Cash, NB, Sales, PS work will be controlled, monitored and regulated through machines. This was contemplated in order to reduce response time and also in order to generate speed in our working of different desks of branches. This has also been envisaged that through front-end which will ultimately be developed to a Local Area Net-working System (LAN) definitely, the organisation will be in a position to satisfy the customers who are having high levels of expectations and who want that organisation should use modern technology to satisfy their demands and needs. The entire programme for 2,000 plus Branches in the organisation was implemented in a phased manner through a process of trial and experimentation and reviewing the results achieved and arranging for mid-course correction and co-ordination at different levels.

The entire organisation need for facing the change and entire HRD thrust will be determined by comprehensive modern and effective system of training to be imparted to Assistants, HGAs and different levels of Officers in the organisation, both in the marketing side as well as in the administrative side.

This also involved a wide networking of training for large number of agents on a selective and time budgeted basis. Without adequate efforts, total sincerity and massive involvement in the training field, the organisation can not develop appropriate strategy to face the changes and challenges of modern competitive world. 180 degree turn in the organisation is possible only if the operating departments, the supervisors and executives of the organisation supported by the massive co-operation of all classes of employees and agents, work in close co-operation with the training establishments. The different instruments of HRD have to be integrated through proper implementation of organisational objectives for the raising of the standard of output and productivity of each employee and bringing about a new change in the organisation so that it can serve its objectives and successfully implement the goals of the organisation.

HRD cannot be conceived in isolation; it is the imperative need for the individual's growth, organisational growth and making the organisation prepared to face any new challenges, which may emerge from the external and internal environment. HRD has been assigned a major role in changing the work approach and work ethics of the employees and officers but even in a small Organisation in our Country, the need for Human Resource Development, the need for training updation and bringing about innovative strategy have been felt comprehensively.

This is a continuous process. Magical results should not be expected. This is also painstaking and has to pass through lot of organisational constraints and difficulties. The internal Policy of the Government, the internal outlook, the outlook of the Government towards employees in the PSUs and other Semi Government concerns, the overall IR climate, the social, political, cultural network in the country, the fulfillment of legitimate aspirations of employees of different cadres and different organisations - all these are variable factors for a new instrument of Human Resource Development. New interventions, new innovative practices and lot of creative designs have to be thought of in making HRD design and HRD strategy successful; there cannot be a set pattern of HRD implementation for all organisations. The organisation's potential, existing state of affairs and existing industrial relation climate also have to be specially considered to bring about effective change in the organisation, through HRD Interventions.

To sum up, there is huge scope in making HRD really effective, result-oriented and achievement-oriented. Potentiality of every human individual in the organisation is immense and people will have to change their perception about the job, work systems and work approach on a continuous basis. Because the market is in the midst of, massive and radical changes in the present world, the customers' expectations and demands are also changing very fast. So, by upgrading capability and by utilizing optimum level of skill through training and orientation, a vibrant and customer-friendly organisation can be developed. Problems before HRD practitioners are many. Social problems, organisational problems, psychological problems relating to mental blocks and prejudices, problems from the trade unions, problems relating to lack of commitment from the top management and middle level management - these are all passing phases in the developing scenario of an organisation. The constraints before HRD implementation have to be faced in a radical manner through process of Organisational diagnosis. Once the problems are sorted out and solved, new prospects emerge before the organisation. HRD helps the power of rational judgment to understand the problems; it also helps to build up new initiative and vision to solve the problems in the organisation concerning people, product, system and technology. Therefore, HRD is the most important challenge before all organisations in the 21st Century.

Thus, to conclude HRD function needs to focus on:

1. Managers should fulfill a key role in changing HRD practices but it has been found that it is sometimes difficult to get them to fulfill this active role, either because of their workload, lack of affinity with HRD tasks or a lack of skills in this field.

   Therefore in the short term, it is necessary to find strategies to involve managers in HRD, by changing their views on learning and increasing their motivation to support learning. In the long run, consideration should be given to incorporating HRD skills in all management training programmes.

2. HRD functions should be more precisely defined and recognized by top management as a major part of the global development strategy of the organisations and seen as an investment rather than a cost.

3. Professional associations from different organisations and countries should organise events where HRD professionals can reach a common terminology, exchange

ideas and collectively try to solve difficult challenges.

4. There is a need to change the view that learning is just a classroom, teacher-based activity.
5. Organisations should seek cooperation with (higher) institutions for vocational education and with universities in order to assist in the creation of an infrastructure for lifelong learning.
6. Administrations and governmental agencies should set the example in adopting a clear learning organisation approach and more sophisticated human resources development policies.
7. Since competence development is seen as a key element of implementing the concept of the learning organisation, further research is needed to develop valid and useful competence profiles; better understanding of the facilitating and inhibiting factors in competence assessment and development; and in coping strategies of organisations that try to overcome problems in implementing competence systems.

Many commentators still take the view that HRD should be subject to tight quantitative justification that HRD needs to demonstrate that their activities add value to the organisation, which is their paymaster. However, this view falls short of believing that value is the only issue in developing a learning organisation through a HRD function. Yet there remains a broad body of support that does lean towards this view. Swanson and Arnold (1997) consider that HRD in an organisational context has no meaning unless the connection is made to performance and their needs to be a systematic method of linking business goals with the learning process.

However, there remains a danger that the HRD function, however defined, becomes over indulgent, becoming the end rather than the means to add some value to the sponsoring organisation. It is this fear, which when added to high-level managerial naivety of modern HRD approaches, has seen many a HRD organisation becoming the first casualty of any downsizing.

HRD into the 21st century will see a gradual shift from an emphasis on training to Human performance Improvement (HPI). *Rothwell* defines 'Human performance Improvement' as a systematic process of discovering and analyzing important human performance gaps, planning for future improvements in human performance, designing and developing cost-effective and ethically justifiable interventions to close performance gaps, implementing the interventions, and evaluating the financial and non-financial results.

The main aim and objective of human resource development policies, programmes and practices is to develop a sustain competitive advance for an organisation through the last and only reliable source of competitive advantage – human resources so that the organisations is able to deliver high quality customer service through various people oriented instruments such as talent management, employer branding, diversity management, customer excelleration, organisational development and capacity building initiatives.

Thus, human resource development refers to a range of actions that can be taken by the organisation to strengthen the contributions of all employees to the success of the organisation. It essentially refers to:

- Organized learning and training activities with the objective of improving and strengthening the performance of all employees;
- The work and career development of all employees;
- Integrating the organisation's business strategy and objectives with the training and career development needs and plans of all employees; and
- Increasing productivity, annual sales turnover and profits.

Hence, human resource development is the instrument by which overall organisation's strategy and the functional components of the organisation can be integrated and implemented successfully.

CHAPTER

14 Case Study

Chapter Synopsis

A Case Study is a methodological approach in teaching in which an actual or fictitious scenario is used to engage students in active learning of concepts, facts and/or problem-solving skills. It's a story with an educational message.

Effective cases portray real people in moments of decision, faced with a need to take action and accept its consequences.

A case study:

- tells a story
- creates empathy with characters
- includes dialogue (not just narrative)
- is relevant to the reader
- serves a teaching function
- contains a dilemma to be solved
- has generality
- is short

This chapter explains these concepts and essential steps to solving case studies.

This Chapter contains:

Introduction to case study, What is case study, Why a case study, What is the structure of a case study, What is the process followed in a case study, How to analyse and solve a case study, What are the benefits of a case study approach, What is the approach of case study presented in this textbook – case situation & case study, and Critical success factors in a case study.

Case Study

Case Study

Case Study is a time tested and proven tool for management training and development. Case study is an in-depth study of a few people, events or organisations. Case study provides valuable insight into the various issues and problems in applying management techniques to solve complex business problems. Solving case study involves not only skills but art also. It's like bringing "boardroom" to "classroom". Here in this Chapter we shall proceed to briefly understand the concept of case study, its methodologies and approaches so as to enable the readers to analyse and solve various case studies incorporated in this text. This is necessary because practice without theory is blind.

What is a Case Study?

A case is a description of organisational problem or situation presented for the purpose of business decision-making.

A case presents facts, events and circumstances surrounding a particular organisational situation with a view to its effective solution. The process of reading, understanding, analyzing and providing solution to an organisational problem is known as Case Study.

Therefore, a case study is:

- Narrative about an actual business situation in all of its complexity and uncertainty.
- Focuses attention on a particular topic for the purpose of in-depth analysis.
- Involves a decision, challenge or opportunity.
- Faced by person/s in the actual business organisation.
- A snapshot taken at a given point of time.

- Students make decisions without the responsibility and authority to implement them.

Why a Case Study?

Business in today's scenario is highly competitive, complex and uncertain which requires management students (future Managers) to develop appropriate skills, expertise and analytical ability to solve business problems in the most efficient and effective manner in real life situations. Case study provides a platform to bridge the gap between 'Theory' and 'Practice' by equipping the students with skills to apply accurately relevant theories and concepts on one hand and to develop a realistic and broader outlook to business issues and processes on the other hand, at the same time.

Case study provides ample opportunities to students to hone not only their management skills but also to verify application of appropriate management tools and techniques for business success.

Thus, case study is necessary to:

- Provide context for analysis and decision-making designs in different business situation, organisations and industries.
- Allows students to step into the role decision maker.
- Help sharpen analytical skills.
- Enhance one's ability to think and reason rigorously.
- Repetitive opportunity to identify, analyse and solve issues and problems in real life.
- Provide a focal point for exchange of student's individual experiences.
- Test understanding of theoretical concepts.
- Develops self-confidence, ability to think independently and work co-operatively.
- Foster development of insights into own strengths and weaknesses.

What is the Structure of a Case Study?

The general structure of a case study is as under:

- Problem
- Causes/Issues
- Criteria
- Alternatives

- Analysis
- Select/Implement

What is the Process followed in a Case Study?

A case study generally follows a process as depicted below:

How to Analyse and Solve a Case Study?

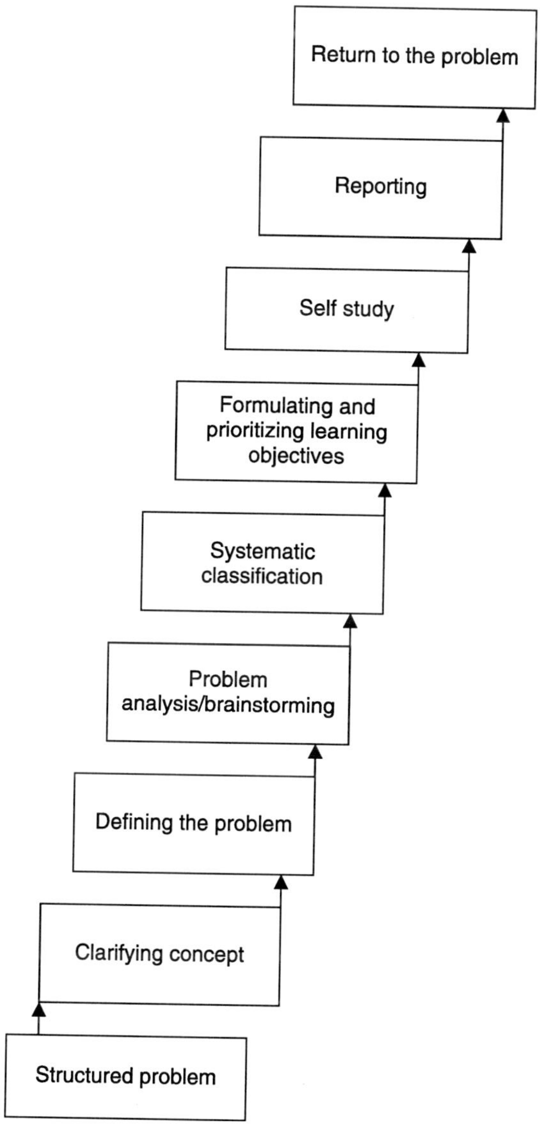

Fig. 14.1 : Steps to Analyzing Case Study

A case study can be analysed and solved by using a number of specific techniques. It must be borne in mind that there is no one best solution to a business problem as it depends on a number of factors. A good solution must be rationale, logical, case based, justifiable and justiciable. A case can be analysed from many angles, as there are various interest groups in an organisational context such as employees, union/s, management, customers, government and society. A balanced approach is therefore crucial. However, some general guidelines can be developed for correct analysis and solution of case studies as depicted below:

- ▶Read the cases study very carefully three times. The first quick reading provides the familiarity; the second reading provides the initial understanding and the third reading provides a full command of the facts, information, opinions, views, issues, etc. of the case.
- ▶Develop analytical base for solving the case based on the following approach:
  - □ Define the central issues in the case
  - □ Select the relevant areas for consideration and further examination
  - □ Explore possibilities and weigh both the qualitative and quantitative evidence carefully
  - □ Evaluate relative significance of all possibilities and rank them
  - □ Draw a final conclusion by choosing the best solution
- ▶Support final conclusion with diagnostic reasoning and evidence.
- ▶Read between the lines i.e. fill-in the gaps, if any, through inferences and assumptions with the help of available information and correlation of relevant theory.
- ▶Prepare an action plan for executing the best solution.
- ▶The solution to a case study must be written/reported in three different parts:
  - □ Summary of the problem
  - □ Brief note on the main considerations
  - □ Recommend solution with in pointed reasons and justifications.
  - □ Conclusion in one line

However, while analysing and solving a case study, following qualitative criteria must be kept in mind:

- Time
- Likely acceptance of affected parties
- Competitive advantage
- Money
- Ethics
- Legal compliance
- Corporate image
- Customer satisfaction

What are the Benefits of a Case Study Approach?

Case study approach offers numerous advantages. Followings are the major benefits of the approach:

- Increased Motivation for self directed learning.
- Fosters greater understanding of business context and relevance of methodical decision making.
- Leads to higher order thinking
- Brings about more authenticity to academic programme, including theory and concept.

What is the Approach of Case Study presented in this textbook?

Each chapter in the whole textbook contains two types of case studies as mentioned below:

1. Case Situation:

These are mini case study. These deal with a very brief and specific problem given at the end of each chapter and seek to test application of specific chapter concept. These should ideally be answered in not less than 50 words.

2. Case Study:

These are the typical and elaborate case study and included at the end of each chapter. These deal application of complete chapter concepts and should be ideally answered in not less than 200 words. The approach to solving case study has already been explained above.

Each case study is inspired from real life business problems and situations and carefully selected. But, for the sake of confidentiality policy, the name of the organisations and persons are fictitious and bears no resemblance.

Each case study has been structured on the following pattern as mentioned below:

- Introduction to the organisation
- Brief description of the problem
- Questions

Role of Teacher should be to act as a resource person and facilitate discussion, ideation, debating and participation of all students in the classroom.

Role of Student should be to apply full attention and concentrate on teachers instructions. Then, analyse the case and try to come up with best solution without any hesitation or inhibition.

Critical Success Factors in a Case Study

Some of the major critical success factors are as under:

- Class participation is a must.
- Analytical skills, judgment and conceptual understanding are built through interchange and constructive criticism.
- Active listening and being open minded.

Thus, to summarize, case study:

- Help develop rigorous analytical thinking to tackle familiar and/or unfamiliar problems.
- Identifying salient facts about organisation.
- Developing problem definition.
- Analysing problems through situational frameworks and relevant facts.
- Formulating recommendations.
- Delineating implementation strategies.

Appendices

In this section, two appendices have been added. The first appendix relates to general guidelines for preparation of dissertation/project report and presentations and the second appendix relates to the art of appearing interview.

Students have to prepare Dissertation/Project Report as part of their course curriculum. Preparing a good dissertation/project report requires understanding and applying proper methodology, style, language, format, etc. so as to avoid painful delays and even failures and consequent reworking. Presentations are now a day increasingly practiced, as these are crucial to the wholesome development of the students.

Students have to face interview as candidates after completing their management programme. Many times good students falter due to lack of interview skills. Course curriculum often does not prepare them for appearing interview artfully. Therefore, a need was felt to add this new appendix to help students prepare well for their campus and other professional interviews by proving a practical step-by-step approach to the art of appearing interview.

This section explains these concepts and approaches.

Appendix : 1

Dissertation/Project Report

Dissertation/Project Report is a methodical investigation into a subject or problem to seek answers that involve understanding and explanation. It involves written work which must demonstrate an independence of thought and an ability to take a stand on an issue he/she is dealing with, and be prepared to defend that position.

A dissertation/project report is a process and involves a number of activities, which are carried out either sequentially or simultaneously.

A dissertation/project report has a specific structure. It should conform to this structure, though; university/management institute concerned may suggest a small variation of this structure. However, the general structure includes the following main sections as discussed below.

Structure of Dissertation/Project Report:

A possible "skeleton" of dissertation/project report is:

- Recognition of and thanks to sponsors and supporters
- Executive summary
- Table of contents
- Objective and goals
- Major recommendations
- Background
  - -Environment
  - -System of the organisation where study was carried out
  - -What currently exists, the situation prior to the presented work/project
  - -Needs of the organisation where study was carried out
- Scope of the project work

- Deliverables as a result of the work/project
  - -Priority
  - -Time table
- Cost/benefit
  - -Items
  - -Timing
  - -Value
- Constraints – organisational, legal, financial, workforce, time, etc.
- Work performed and its evaluation
- References
- Appendices

In a report, a spiral approach should be adopted: starting with an executive summary, then table of contents, then the report body, then appendices with detailed and technical data. Each iteration contains more detail than its former: The body of the report expands on the (at most) one page executive summary, the chapters present issues at a high summary and general level while the appendices have the details, and "heavy" technical information is provided after the appendices.

Reports and Summaries:

1. Starting pages should have 1" margins for top, bottom, right, and left with 1.5 lines spacing.

2. Reports are constructed in a spiral approach: A very general summary of the report is given in the executive summary (or the abstract), a more detailed presentation is given in the chapters and sections of the report, and the highly technical details are given in the appendices.

3. Structure of the report: Title page, executive summary (or abstract; if the report extends beyond a few pages, put it on a separate page), table of contents, list of assumptions and available information, list of options and alternatives, analysis of each alternative, students recommendations, and references. Appendices for details should be used.

   In a lengthy report each of these sections, and each chapter of the report, should be started on a new page. However, for a short, few-pages report, the executive summary and table of contents, and the title page should be omitted.

4. The title page should include the title of the subject, a reference to the course for which the report is prepared, the date, group identification (if prepared by a team), the name(s) of the author(s) (usually in alphabetical order), thank-you or

acknowledgement statement to supporting personnel (if pertinent), and similar information.

5. With regard to table of contents - all pages including all appendices must be numbered. Each chapter (and major section), as well as each appendix, should be separately identified in table of contents. A good way to accomplish it is to use Word's Headings for each chapter and section; Word's Table of Contents then uses these headings, and their page numbers, to set up a proper table of contents for the document.

6. A short report (of 5-6 pages or less) should not have a title page or a table of contents. Similarly, in a short report starting each section or the references section on a new page should be avoided.

7. Each appendix should be treated as a "chapter": It should have its own title, and should be numbered separately (e.g., Appendix A or Appendix 3). Appendices should have explanatory text to enable the reader of the appendix to understand the information presented therein.

8. While using an abbreviation for the first time, it must be ensured that its full form is written so that the reader will recognize it as an abbreviation. For example: Information Technology (IT).

9. "Widowed titles" are best avoided – a situation where the title of a section (or the first row of a table, or the heading of a list of points) is on one page, while the following text is on the next page. To prevent that, use Word's Format -> Paragraph -> Line and Page Breaks -> Keep with Next (or Keeping Lines Together).

10. Book references: each reference should include author(s) name(s), name of the book, (usually italicized), publisher's name, place of publication, edition (if pertinent), year of publication and page number/s. For example: Deb, Tapomoy, *A Conceptual approach to: Strategic Talent Management*, Indus Publishing Company, New Delhi, 1st edition, 2005, Pp. 45-50.

11. Article references: each reference should include author(s) name(s), name of article (within double quotes), name of journal where it appeared, volume number, issue number, month and year of publication, and then page number/s. For example: Deb, Tapomoy, "The art of appearing interview", *Human Potential*, Vol. 1 Issue 4, July-August 2002, Pp. 15-18.

12. Internet and World Wide Web references should include the URL where the source is found, *e.g.*, http://www.uic.edu/~ybabad/531annc.html, and, to the extent identifiable, names of author(s), title, company/organisation, and (particularly)

date. Note that often you identified a book or an article through a web-search. In this case you must provide the whole book or article reference (as given above) in addition to the URL.

The reference list is usually ordered by the authors' last names (and not by the order of appearance in the text - in contrast to endnotes and footnotes).

13. If project report needs to be submitted in soft copy also, then it should include a single file: either a Word DOC file, or an Acrobat PDF file.

Tables and images' must fit into the width of a single page width, as it is very hard to view, for example, the left half of a table on one page and the right half on another page. If needed, reorientation should be made such as reducing the margins, decreasing the font size, and so forth. If these techniques still do not achieve the goal regarding page width, restructuring of table or "cutting" the image should be considered.

While a short and concise report is always desirable, it is worth remembering that quite often a one page cannot "do honour" to the subject of the report. Just presenting the background for the subject and the conclusions takes space, not to mention justification and discussion of the arguments and observations.

A possible "skeleton" for a report:

Thus, a dissertation/project report should something like this:

- Recognition of and thanks to sponsors and supporters
- Executive summary
- Table of contents
- List of illustrations/graphs
- Chapter: Introduction and summary
- Chapter: Objective and goals
- Chapter: Major recommendations
- Chapter: Background
  - -Environment
  - -Client/system
  - -What currently exist, the situation prior to the presented work/project
  - -Needs
- Chapter: Assumptions
- Chapter: Scope of the presented work/project
- Chapter: Requirements and constraints
- One or more chapters (one for each main delivery): Deliverables

-Description
-Which objective and requirements does it fulfill
-Characteristics
-Limitations
-Priority
-Time table (if relevant, e.g., during development – but not in a final report)

- Chapter: Cost/benefit
  -Items
  -Timing
  -Value
- Chapter: Constraints that affected (or will affect) the work/project
- Chapter: Work performed and its evaluation
- Chapter: Other considerations
- Chapter: Lessons from the project (both positive and negative)
- Chapter: Conclusions
- Chapter: Recommended future enhancements
- References
- Definition of terms used in the report (alphabetically)
- Appendices

However, while preparing the dissertation/project report, the following points are note worthy:

1. Language must be well taken care of. Supervisors do not have time, and should not be distracted into making comments on spelling errors and faulty sentence constructions.

2. It is important to adopt an acceptable mode of writing, which involves:

(*i*) Narrative form should be used so that the writing is logical and sequential throughout.

(*ii*) Data should be weaved from various sources (interviews, questionnaires, observations, statistics, etc.) into the storyline.

(*iii*) Supporting evidence should be described to back the conclusions and suggestions using the full range of data from various sources (interviews, questionnaires, observations, statistics, etc.).

(*iv*) A narrative should be developed around the evidential statements i.e. putting down table, graphs and illustrations with explanations, analysis, interpretations, and connecting one evidence after another.

Presentations:

Presentations are an important part of any business executive today. HRD professionals are making a lot of presentations before their superiors, peers, board of directors, business delegates, etc. accordingly, in educational institutes presentations are increasingly becoming popular and management students have to hone their presentation skills to make significant impact on their audiences (internal or external customers). Keeping in view that, a brief about presentation techniques is produced below to facilitate the students in their presentation endeavours.

The first phase in presentation is the introduction – *tell them what you're going to tell them.* Next comes the middle phase or main body of the presentation – *tell them.* The third, and final, phase is a summary of the main points and recommendations covered in the presentation – *tell them what you've told them.* The two commonest faults of inexperienced presenters are 'gabbling' and 'mumbling'. These can be overcome by proper practice/rehearsal.

In presentations, the following points must be considered:

1. Visual aids such as graphs and pictures are often more convincing and effective than text, numbers and figures.

2. Visual aids are there to enhance a student's presentation and talk, not to replace it. Thus, if they include text (as in transparencies) keep it short and as a reminder of the subject, with just key words and one-issue phrases. Avoid long sentences and multi-lines points.

3. Slides and transparencies are an aid to the speaker - they do not replace the speaker. Thus, they should be concise - let the speaker explain and enhance. They should be simple - complex slides distract the attention of the audience from the speaker's words. Sound effects can be distracting; do not use cash register sounds or other inappropriate sounds.

4. Transparencies should not be overloaded. It is prudent to follow the 7x7 thumb rule: No more than 7 words horizontally and no more than 7 lines vertically on a slide.

5. Transparencies should be evaluated in the eyes of someone sitting at the back of the class. Are they readable? Are the letters too small? Is the transparency too "crowded"? Are the colors such that they enhance (rather than distract) from the impact of the presentation? In particular, is the background enhancing the contents of the slides, or is it making the transparencies hard to read?

It may be worthwhile to have one person managing the slides or transparencies, while another member of the team talks. However, coordinate carefully the presentation, and let the speaker control when the slides should be changed (or lines within animated slides being revealed); often the slides, if not managed well, are either ahead or behind the speaker.

6. Do not "run through" slides. Showing a slide for a couple of seconds and then hurrying to the next slide is worse than not showing the slide at all. Give the audience time to grasp the contents of the slide.
7. What kind of handout and when it should be given to the audience must be skillfully planned and executed.
8. Professional attire tends to make presentation more effective. It does not necessarily have to be formal. If several team members appear before the audience, there should be matching of attire, if possible.
9. If several team members to present, their names should be given to the audience. a separate transparency may be used for the said purpose. However, as a rule no presenter should talk for less than 5 minutes, as then the transition between speakers tends to be disruptive.
10. An agenda of the presentation must be put on a separate slide.
11. It is worthwhile to rehearse and time presentation. A very good way to do so is to rehearse a mock presentation before mirror, and then analyze and adjust presentation accordingly.
12. Deciding strategies for managing questions is vital to effective presentation: During the presentation, after each segment of the presentation, or at the end of the presentation. Announce the selected procedure to the audience. All questions raised must be attended to.
13. Presentation should be available in a PowerPoint format, so that it can be distributed to the audience after the presentation.

As a general rule, 2-3 minutes per slide should be allocated. The audience cannot effectively digest slides shown faster, and slides shown slower should better be divided into two or more slides. The proper balance between preparation and presentation can be illustrated by the fact that a good presenter is likely to spend several hours on a presentation which may last as little as 10 minutes.

A point worth noting in presentation is that the presentation material on a particular topic must be arranged in the following order:

- Urgent and important.
- Non-urgent but important.
- Urgent but not important.
- Non-urgent and not important.

Today technology makes it very easy to create quite colourful and animated slides; but these may also distract audience from the contents to present.

In a presentation, a student (presenter) can give their audience positive strokes by:

- Smiling and showing enthusiasm.
- Looking at all the audience individually during the presentation.
- Showing a sensitive sense of humour.
- Paying them a compliment by looking smart.
- Expressing gratitude.
- Praise.
- Keeping presentation brief and to the point.
- Using visual aids.
- Welcoming questions from the audience and responding to them in an open and friendly manner.

In a presentation, especially a long one, a summary or recap at the end may be worthwhile.

Remember

As a student, your work is intended for others to see, read, understand and evaluate, and the acceptance of your work is in the eyes of the beholder. Thus, always strive to direct your work to your intended audience, and organise it in a way that will enhance your audience understanding and ease of use.

Always remember the 3Cs:

- **C**reativity – Innovation is the critical success factor.
- **C**onfidence – Believe in Yourself (Yes, You Can Do It).
- **C**ommunication – It is how you make people know about your creativity and confidence that creates opportunities.

Appendix : 2

The Art of Appearing Interview

Every student of management courses will have to appear interview to get suitable placement soon after completing their management programme. Also, as Managers they have to take interview and assist their organisation in recruiting best professionals. This can be only meticulously executed if management students know and practice the art of appearing interviews at this stage so that they can stay better equipped to face interviews and avoid failures and disappointments. A general guideline on the art of giving interview is given below:

Interview means the oral examination of a candidate to assess suitability for employment. It seeks to ascertain:

- Job knowledge.
- Attitude.
- Emotions.
- Skills.
- Aspirations.
- Fitment.

The good old days of trial and error learning is long over. In this era of global economy, cut throat competition and high awareness amongst the job seekers, appearing for an interview successfully needs meticulous preparation. Today's enlightened managers are cost conscious and give high emphasis to smart hiring, retaining and training good employees.

To give an interview successfully, let us understand the process of interview as enumerated below:

1. CV Designing:

The CV should not more than two pages for experienced candidates. However, for freshers, a single page would be good enough. CV must be neatly, legibly and attractively written (jargons to be avoided), typed (devoid of typographical errors) and laser printed, incorporating:

- Career objective.
- Name of candidate in bold and capital letters.
- Father's name.
- Date of birth.
- Contact telephone number – land line and/or mobile.
- Professional qualifications.
- Educational qualifications.
- Summary of experience – to indicate career path.
- Details of experience – from current to the first job.
- Main achievements – use of too much I should be avoided.
- Training programmes attended.
- Signature of candidate with date and place.

Candidates must write CV separately for different types of vacancies in different organisations even for similar position in order to meet the requirements of each position.

2. Interview Call:

As soon as CV of a candidate is short listed for interview, appropriate information about the interview – date, time, venue, contact person, etc. will be intimated through post, telephone, e-mail.

The candidate prior to attending interview should make the following preparation:

- Collecting information about the organisation viz. nature of business, number of unit/s, sales turnover, product profile, market share/position, etc. through internet, websites, friends, journals. Annual reports, etc.
- Sharpening competencies through rehearsals.
- Checking order and manner of presentation for self-marketing.
- Making a brief outline of self introduction – beginning with 'Thank you very much for giving me an opportunity to introduce myself .... Then personal details .... Family background ..... employment details, if any ....

1. Interview:

The objective of interview is to ensure that the right man fits the right job. The interview process consists of three phases as mentioned below:

(A) *Pre-Interview Phase:*

- Candidate must dress in formals. In winter, a suit or blazer with necktie and in summer, trouser (dark coloured) and shirt (white) with necktie must be worn. For ladies, they should wear a saree or salwar suit or western formals and avoid putting up heavy make-ups and jewellery.
- Pleasant light perfume/deodorant is recommended.
- Candidate must reach venue of interview with all essentials like updated CV, colour passport size photograph, certificates/testimonials, etc. atleast 15 minutes prior to scheduled time and announce arrival to appropriate person/s.
- Candidate should keep himself composed and should not engage in unnecessary talking/gossips with fellow aspirants.

(B) *During Interview Phase:*

There could be two or more rounds of interview and each round presents one selection hurdle.

Candidate should smartly, and confidently enter interview room with a soft and pleasant smile to reflect warmth. He should greet all interviewers.

Interviewers will be probing candidature on the following outline:

- Ambition – low, moderate and high.
- Communication and presentation skills.
- Initiative and drive.
- Technical job knowledge and aptitude.
- Stability and clarity in though process.
- Growth path.
- Relevant experience.
- Intelligence, personality, dedication, sincerity and interest.
- Reason for leaving past/present job/s.
- Work achievements.
- Authentic references.
- Qualifications – over or under.
- Distance between place of job and residence.
- Economic status – independently wealthy.
- Present and expected remuneration – capacity to pay. It is the single most restraining factor in job selections.
- Approach of presentation – analytical.

- Overall fitment in organisational culture and value systems.
- Brief information about job responsibilities, reporting pattern, working conditions, growth prospects, service bond, transferability, etc. candidate must seek these information, if untold by interviewers.

(C) Post Interview Phase:

- At the end of interview, the candidate should thank his interviewers.
- Candidate must seek feedback of interview after 2-3 days from the HR department. Good organisations have proper feedback giving mechanisms and systems.

Students/Candidates to remember:

- Not to over emphasise or exaggerate candidature.
- Not to falsify facts relating to professional or personal aspects like job profile, salary, etc.
- Not to stare at the interviewers like a snake.
- Not to make a drooping face. Keep personal problems, frustrations and failures at bay.
- Not to judge interviewers.
- Not to promise something which you know that can't deliver.
- Not to argue unnecessarily or make personal comments at interviewers or organizations.
- Not to think negatively. Instead, think Win-Win approach.

Master the formulae for success: speed, quality, credibility, innovation and value addition.

Bibliography

Academy of Human Resource Development, *Standing Committee on Ethics and Integrity*, Baton Rouge, Los Angeles, 1st Edition, May 1999

American Accounting Association, Report of the Committee on Human Resource Accounting, *Accounting Review*, Supplement to vol. XLVIII, 1973, Pp. 169

Armstrong, Michael, *A Handbook of Human Resource Management*, Kogan Page Ltd., London, 7th edition, 1998

Ahuja, Narender, *Productivity and Quality Awareness Module: A Training Resource for HR Professionals*, Proman Concepts, Bainguinim, 1st edition, 1999

Babcock, Pamela, "Find What Workers Want", *Times Ascent*, Times of India, Wednesday April 27 2005, New Delhi, Pp. 1

Bates R, Hatcher, T., Holton , E. and Chalfonsky, N., "Redefining Human Resource Development: An integration of the Learning, Performance and Spirituality of Work Perspectives", *Proceedings of the annual AHRD Conference*, Tulsa, February-March 2001.

Becker, G.S., *Human Capital*, Columbia University Press, New York, 1964

Becker, G.S., *Human Capital: A Theoretical and Empirical Analysis with Special Reference to Education*, University of Chicago Press, Chicago, 3rd edition, 1993

Bratton, John, and Gold, Jeffrey, *Human Resource Management: Theory and Practice*, Palgrave MacMillan, London, 3rd edition, 2003

Bhat, A.K., "Leadership Through Developing Global Manager: Indian Oil Corporation Ltd. Experience", *Business led HR Strategies*, AIMA/Excel Books, New Delhi, 1st edition, 1998

Bohlander, George W., and Snell, Scott, *Managing Human Resources*, South Western College Publishing, New York, 13th edition, 2004

Bateman, Thomas, and Snell, Scott, *Human Resource Management*, McGraw Hill Companies, Inc., New York, 5th edition, 2002

Brummet, R. Lee, Flamhoitz, Erl G., and Pyle, William C. (eds), *Human Resource Accounting: Development and Implementation in India*, Michlgan: Vraun and Braumfield, Inc., 1969, Pp. III

Burnham, Byron Robert, *Evaluating Human Resources, and the Organisation*, Krieger Publishing Company, Florida, 1995

"Corporate Social Responsibility: A Statement of Intent", *Human Touch*, Vol. 1, No. 6, September 2004

Deb, Tapomoy, "The Art of Giving Interviews", *Human Potential*, Vol. 1, Issue 4, July – August 2002, Pp. 15-18

Deb, Tapomoy, *A Conceptual Approach to: Strategic Talent Management*, Indus Publishing Company, New Delhi, 1st edition, 2005, Pp. 45-50

DeNisi, Angelo S. and Griffin, Ricky W., *Human Resource Management*, Houghton Mifflin Company, Boston, 2nd edition, 2004

Davis, L.E., and Chems, A.B., *The Quality of Working Life*, Free Press, New York, 1975

Garavan, T., Heraty, N., and Barnicle, B., "Human Resource Development: Current Issues, Priorities and Dilemmas", *Journal of European Industrial Training* 23 (4/5), Pp. 169-179

Grieves, Jim, *Strategic Human Resource Development*, Sage Publications, London, 2003

Giri, D.V., and Chaudhury, Anuva, "Towards A Positive Work Culture: The NALCO Experience", *Indian Journal of Industrial Relations*, Vol. 40, No. 2, October 2004

Gosky, K.L., and Belfry, "Achieving Competitive Advantage Through Employee Empowerment", *Employee Relations Today*, 18 (1991): 213-220; L.R. Rothstein, "The Empowerment Efforts that Came Undone", *Harvard Business Review*, 73 (1995): 2031

Heizer, Jay and Render, Barry, *Operations Management*, Prentice Hall, Inc., New Jersey, 7th edition, 2001

Heizer, Jay and Render Barry, *Principles of Operations Management*, Prentice Hall, Inc., New Jersey, 5th edition, 2004

Jackson, Susan E., and Schuler, Randall S., *Managing Human Resources*, South Western College Publishing, 8th edition, 2003

Jain, K.C., and Chitale, A.K., *Quality Assurance and Total Quality Management*, Khanna Publishers, New Delhi, 2nd edition, 2000

Krietner, Robert, *Foundations of Management: Basics to Best Practices*, Houghton Mifflin Company, Boston, 3rd edition, 2004

Kandula, Srinivas R., *Strategic Human Resource Development*, Prentice Hall of India Pvt. Ltd., New Delhi, 2001

Legge, Karen, *Human Resource Management: Rheotic and Reality*, McMillan, London, 2005

Labour Law Reporter, Vol. XXXVI, No. 5, May 2005, New Delhi, Pp. 142

Lynham, Susan A., Chermackad, Thomas J., and Noggle, Melissa A., "Selecting Organisation Development Theory from a HRD Perspectives", *Human Resource Development Review*, Vol. 3, No. 2, June 2004

Lussier, Robert N., *Management Fundamentals: Concepts, Application, Skill Development*, South Western college Pubslishing, New York, 2nd edition, 2002

McGolgrick, J., Stewart, J., and Watson, S., "Researching HRD" in McGoldrick J., Stewart, J. and Watson, S. (eds), *Understanding Human Resource Development: A Research Based Approach*, Routeledge, London, Pp. 1-17

McLean, G., "HRD: A Three Legged Stool, An Octopus or a Centipede", *Human Resource Development International*, Vol. 1, Issue 4, 1998, Pp. 375-377

Magginson, David, Joy-Mattews, and Banfield, Paul, *Human Resource Development*, Kogan Page Ltd., London, 1993

Mathis, Robert L., and Jackson, John H., *Human Resource Management*, South Western College Publishing, New York, 10th edition, 2003

Mohnot, S.R., "Conflict and Convergence Between Human Values and Governance", *Courseware*, 33rd IFTDO World Conference and Exhibition, New Delhi, 2004

Mentoring Program Handbook: A Guide for Human Resources Professionals at NASA, May 2003, Pp. 1-8

Nafukho, Fredrick M., Hariston, Nancy R., and Brooks, Kit, "Determining the Link Between Human Capital Theory and Human Resource Development", *Public Policy Working Paper Series*, Vol. 3, No. 2, University of Arkansas

Nelson, *Managing Human Resources*, Thomson Canada Ltd., 2004

Rao, Dr. T.V., *HRD Audit: Evaluating the Human Resource Function for Business Improvement*, Response Books, New Delhi, 1st edition, 1999

Rao, Dr. T.V., "Integrated Human Resource Development Systems", in Leonard D. Goldstein and J. William Pfeiffer, *The 1985 Annual: Developing Human Resource*, University Associates, Inc., San Diego, 1985

Raymond, T.J., "Written Analysis of Cases" in Nair, M.P. (ed): *The Case Method* at the Harvard Business School, McGraw Hill Companies, New York, 1954, Pp. 141

Schwind, Wagar and Das, *Human Resource Management*, McGraw Hill Companies, Inc., Montreal, 7th edition, 2005

Sambrook, Dr. Sally, "A Critical time for HRD?", *Working Paper*, University of Wales Bangor, Gwynedd, 2004

Sambrook, Dr. Sally, "Talking of HRD", *Human Resource Development International*, Vol. 3, No. 2, 2000, Pp. 159-178

Sambrook, Dr. Sally, "HRD as Emergent and Negotiated Evolution", *Human Resource Development Quartely*, Vol. 12, No. 2, 2001, Pp. 169-193

Swanson, R., "HRD Theory, Real or Imagined?, *Human Resource Development International*, Vol. 2, No. 1, 1999, Pp. 2-5

Schermerhorn, John R., *Management*, John Wiley and Sons, Inc., New York, 7th edition, 2002

Staff Correspondent, "What Makes People Switch Jobs", *Times of India*, Sunday 3rd April 2005

The Outsourcing Question, *Working Paper*, Development Dimensions International, Inc., McMXCVII

Ulrich, Dave, "A New Mandate for Human Resources", *Harvard Business Review*, January - February 1998.

Virmani, B.R., "Future Directions for Repositioning HRD in India", *Courseware*, 31st ISTD National Convention, 22-24th January 2001, Pp. 9-11

Young, Michael, "HRD Strategies: Some Conceptual Issues and Their Implications", *Human Resource Development International*, Vol. 4, No. 3, 2001

Index

Subject Index

Author Index